Matheus Miller's Memoir

Early Modern History: Society and Culture

General Editors: **Rab Houston**, Professor of Early Modern History, University of St Andrews, Scotland, **Edward Muir**, Professor of History, Northwestern University, Illinois, and **Bob Scribner**, sometime Professor for the History of Western Christianity, Harvard Divinity School, Cambridge, Massachusetts

This series encompasses all aspects of early modern international history from 1400 to c.1800. The editors seek fresh and adventurous monographs, especially those with a comparative and theoretical approach, from both new and established scholars.

Titles include:

Rudolf Dekker
CHILDHOOD, MEMORY AND AUTOBIOGRAPHY IN HOLLAND
From the Golden Age to Romanticism

Steve Hindle
THE STATE AND SOCIAL CHANGE IN EARLY MODERN ENGLAND, c1550–1640

Craig M. Koslofsky
THE REFORMATION OF THE DEAD
Death and Ritual in Early Modern Germany, 1450–1700

Samantha A. Meigs
THE REFORMATIONS IN IRELAND
Tradition and Confessionalism, 1400–1690

Craig Muldrew
THE ECONOMY OF OBLIGATION
The Culture of Credit and Social Relations in Early Modern England

Niall Ó Ciosáin
PRINT AND POPULAR CULTURE IN IRELAND, 1750–1850

Thomas Max Safley
MATHEUS MILLER'S MEMOIR
A Merchant's Life in the Seventeenth Century

Johan Verberckmoes
LAUGHTER, JESTBOOKS AND SOCIETY IN THE SPANISH NETHERLANDS

Early Modern History: Society and Culture
Series Standing Order ISBN 0–333–71194–7
(*outside North America only*)

You can receive future titles in this series as they are published by placing a standing order. Please contact your bookseller or, in case of difficulty, write to us at the address below with your name and address, the title of the series and the ISBN quoted above.

Customer Services Department, Macmillan Distribution Ltd
Houndmills, Basingstoke, Hampshire RG21 6XS, England

Matheus Miller's Memoir
A Merchant's Life in the Seventeenth Century

Thomas Max Safley
Associate Professor of History
University of Pennsylvania
Philadelphia

First published in Great Britain 2000 by
MACMILLAN PRESS LTD
Houndmills, Basingstoke, Hampshire RG21 6XS and London
Companies and representatives throughout the world

A catalogue record for this book is available from the British Library.

ISBN 0-333-73664-8

 First published in the United States of America 2000 by
ST. MARTIN'S PRESS, INC.,
Scholarly and Reference Division,
175 Fifth Avenue, New York, N.Y. 10010

ISBN 0-312-22646-2

Library of Congress Cataloging-in-Publication Data
Safley, Thomas Max.
Matheus Miller's memoir : a merchant's life in the seventeenth
century / Thomas Max Safley.
p. cm. — (Early modern history)
Includes bibliographical references and index.
ISBN 0-312-22646-2
1. Miller, Matheus. 2. Augsburg (Germany) Biography. 3. Augsburg
(Germany)—History—17th century. 4. Merchants—Germany—Augsburg
Biography. I. Title. II. Series.
DD901.A92S33   1999
943'.37504'092—dc21
[B]   99-15613
                                                                              CIP

© Thomas Max Safley 2000

All rights reserved. No reproduction, copy or transmission of this publication may be made without written permission.

No paragraph of this publication may be reproduced, copied or transmitted save with written permission or in accordance with the provisions of the Copyright, Designs and Patents Act 1988, or under the terms of any licence permitting limited copying issued by the Copyright Licensing Agency, 90 Tottenham Court Road, London W1P 0LP.

Any person who does any unauthorised act in relation to this publication may be liable to criminal prosecution and civil claims for damages.

The author has asserted his right to be identified as the author of this work in accordance with the Copyright, Designs and Patents Act 1988.

This book is printed on paper suitable for recycling and made from fully managed and sustained forest sources.

10   9   8   7   6   5   4   3   2   1
09   08   07   06   05   04   03   02   01   00

Printed and bound in Great Britain by
Antony Rowe Ltd, Reading and Chippenham

Contents

List of Illustrations   vi

Preface   vii

Introduction   1

1 Marriage and Patriarchy   20

2 Public Office and the Public Sphere   48

3 Sociability and Social Structure   84

4 Death and Confession   116

Conclusion   149

Notes   158

Index   219

List of Illustrations

2.1 Allegory of Commerce (Courtesy of the
     James Ford Bell Library, University of Minnesota)   64

3.1 Map of early modern Augsburg   88

Preface

I have known Matheus Miller for more than a decade. His memoir came into my hands in 1987, when I explored the City Archive of Augsburg as a fellow of the Alexander von Humboldt Foundation. Its entry in the register of the *Evangelisches Wesensarchiv*, a collection devoted to the history of the city's Lutheran community, read simply 'Miller Tagebuch'. Who or what was Miller? A document with such a title normally belonged in a private family archive or in the collections of a library. No less importantly, what was a 'Tagebuch'? Translated, the word usually meant 'diary'. Students of early modern Europe know, however, that the genre did not exist then, as it exists today. Literate individuals chronicled their daily experiences but larded their recollections with records of events in a wider world or with reflections on a world unseen. The term can also refer to a merchant's journal, that is, an account of daily transactions. In either case, the 'Miller Tagebuch' promised to be interesting.

The document was not what I expected. It was obviously no merchant's account book. Construction and size argued against its use as a permanent record of commercial activity. It was apparently an inexpensive notebook, probably purchased ready-made. Stitched into a heavy, unadorned paper cover, its pages were of rather cheap rag paper cut to a convenient size, roughly 21 × 16 centimeters, slightly larger than our own notepaper today. It contained 100 pages, some 85 of which were over-written in a tight, difficult script made even less legible by the use of numerous abbreviations.

Nor were its contents easily categorized. The title page contained a clear statement of purpose, one that reflected an autobiographical motivation.[1]

> In this little book are written down all manner of things concerning me, Matheus Miller of Augsburg. From my birth onward, so long as God gives me life and grace to continue writing, is [my life] with few words recorded to that end that my own may find it after God grants me the grace to leave them.

Accordingly, I could expect to find here the milestones of a life lived three centuries ago, signposts carefully selected to be of interest and use to the author's descendants. What followed, however, was no ordinary diary. In its structure, Matheus's memoir bore striking resemblance to philosophical discussions of the good life. A lengthy narrative of his youth, written in retrospect, preceded three discrete collections of episodes from his adult life, each devoted to a separate theme, organized chronologically but recorded simultaneously, like concurrent entries in a merchant's account. He listed family matters first, public offices second, and social connections third. In its arrangement of events in time, the memoir obscured its own point of origin. I could determine neither when Matheus had written it, whether over a period of some 40 years or at one point late in his life, nor how distant he was, chronologically and psychologically, from his youthful self. The accuracy, or better, the specificity, of detail along with the episodic character of its structure suggested events recorded periodically, but the consistency of his written voice seemed to indicate one sustained, continuous effort at writing. All factors signified an intention much more complex than that usually associated with a diary, a purpose in writing at once historical, didactic and apologetic.

It has taken me nearly ten years to reach some kind of conclusion about Matheus and his memoir. In that time, many things intervened. Other aspects of early modern Europe seized my attention. And the present made demands of its own. Yet, the mystery, as I saw it, of the man and the document might not have been solved more speedily for all that. It took time to locate other traces of Matheus's life. He was an important figure in Augsburg, a wealthy merchant and a devout Lutheran, who left surprisingly few public records of his existence. It took time to grasp his sense of family, office, friendship and faith. Matheus's own, sometimes idiosyncratic, notions were implicit in his retelling of events but never explicitly abstracted and articulated. And it took time to realize that he offered both a window on the seventeenth century and a mirror for our interpretations of it.

In that time, many friends have shared my interest and encouraged my research. Among them I must list two organizations. The Alexander von Humboldt Foundation underwrote my introduction to Augsburg and to Matheus, and the University of Pennsylvania provided time and support to pursue the acquaintance. Jerry Drew, Rolf Kiessling, Philip Kintner, Eric Olsen, Leonard Rosenband, James Saporito, Adam Shear, Amy Smith, Anthea Waleson, Lee Wandel, and Michele Zelinsky generously discussed my ideas and read the manuscript. Rab Houston, Ed Muir, and the late Bob Scribner, editors of Macmillan's Early Modern History: Society and Culture series, greatly improved the book with their questions and suggestions. Fine scholars and discerning critics all, they will find themselves at various points in my understanding of Matheus. For all their help I thank them even as I reserve to myself all responsibility for the final interpretations.

As has always been the case, my family supported my efforts to make sense of Matheus and his memoir. He became an unseen but accepted presence in our household. This book is for Michele, therefore, whose patience, humor and intelligence extended my own and made this study possible.

THOMAS MAX SAFLEY
Havertown, Pennsylvania

Introduction

In 1639 Matheus Miller came home to Augsburg. Fourteen years of age, he had spent the last three as a student at the Latin School of Johann Conrad Merck in the imperial city of Ulm. There he had studied grammar, arithmetic and music. He had progressed quickly and had reached the sixth class in a humanist curriculum that included elements of logic and Greek. It had been an encouraging start toward a scholarly or professional career that was not to be. As he wrote in a memoir, begun at least a decade later, 'My inclination and desire were more toward business, and my father was optimistic that it would serve me in time, if he were able to use me in his own firm'.[1] His decision made, Matheus left school.

Thus begin two tales. The first tells of a life considered in the seventeenth century. In his memoir, Matheus recorded the important events that marked the changes in his family, his stature and his faith over nearly 40 years. More important still, for he was no simple chronicler, he considered the meaning of these changes. His memoir was a place of ethical inquiry, where his worldly experience and his learned vocabulary merged and evolved. His career as a man of business fostered certain habits of mind first acquired in his aborted education: attention to details, evaluation of conditions, reliance on standards, maintenance of records. That his reflections took the form of a memoir had to do with Matheus's purpose in writing it. He wanted to establish and defend the propriety of his life; he wanted to write an apologia. Accordingly, the second tale relates a process of ethical justification and social vindication. Matheus offered no casuistic defense of conduct past. Rather, by recording the events of his life and exploring their causes, he sought to explicate their propriety to himself, to his readers and, quite possibly, to his God.

As a result, Matheus's memoir differs from those of other early modern merchants. It offers little or no material on the fortunes of his business or on events in the world. His purpose in writing was incompatible with that: it furthered neither economic success in the marketplace nor social legitimacy in a wider world. Rather, he turned his attention inward. He sketched occurrences in the lifecycle of his family and, in so doing, portrayed himself as a patriarch. He considered his conduct as a state official and so weighed the distinctions between private and public engagements. He described the ties that connected him to a larger social network and so revealed his understanding of friendship. Finally, he considered the nature of Providence and so challenged the notion of confession. Matheus's memoir eschews most of the predictable early modern certainties born of a society fixed hierarchically in ranks and propelled by events divinely ordained. It challenges and confounds many of the current categories of scholarship. Matheus's notions of patriarchy, the public sphere, social hierarchy and confession are individual. Thus, his memoir testifies to the singularity and idiosyncracy of each person in the face of scholarly rubrics and generalities. It is a sweatily insecure – and surprisingly modern – work.

Matheus was born about 10:00 a.m. on 14 November 1625, the first child of Michael Miller, a Lutheran merchant of Augsburg, and his wife Sibilla, the daughter of Matheus Hopfer.[2] It was not the best of times. The city had just begun to emerge from a catastrophic inflation, known among historians as the *Kipper- und Wipperzeit*, and stood poised on the brink of a no less catastrophic epidemic. Before the first decade of Matheus's life passed, his hometown lost 75 percent of its population to famine, disease and warfare. None of this found a place in the memoir.

For Matheus's immediate family, too, it was a time of struggle and loss. Years later he wrote, 'Now my beloved and honored parents had other children yearly and exercised great diligence as well as care and concern to raise us as much as possible in the fear of God and never let an opportunity to teach us escape them, which was a great expense to them, may God reward them with grace elsewhere.'[3] Augsburger tax records indicate that Michael Miller's fortunes went into steep decline after Matheus's birth. The assessment of his wealth dropped to less than half its initial value from fl. 86 kr. 15 in 1625 to fl. 36 kr. 40 in 1635.[4] As a young man with a family of his own, Matheus came to appreciate the effort and expense his parents put forth.

Yet, the Millers were not without means, both economic and social. Though diminished, Michael's estate remained comfortable according to the standards of his day. At its lowest value, calculated on the basis of his tax assessment in 1635, his total worth still lay somewhere between fl. 7,332 and fl. 14,664.[5] This placed him among the top 10 percent of the city's taxpayers.[6] He and his family lived in one of two houses owned by his father, either Annastraße 3 (D263) or Steingasse 11 (D167), both located in the Upper City (*Oberstadt*), Augsburg's most prosperous quarter.[7] Beyond Michael's wealth, his connections to other, prosperous merchant houses sheltered and supported his young family. His brothers and sometimes partners, Hans Jakob and Gabriel, were successful Augsburger merchants. His father-in-law, Matheus's grandfather and namesake, Matheus Hopfer, had been one of the 25 wealthiest men of the city, with a fortune estimated between fl. 76,000 and fl. 152,000 in 1618.[8] In 1632 it still retained a value between fl. 38,600 and fl. 77,200, sufficient to place the widow Hopfer, like her late husband, among the 25 wealthiest persons in Augsburg.[9] Moreover, Matheus's godparents represented prosperous and powerful families as well. Jakob Hoser, the Elder, stood for the Miller side; Barbara Endorfer, born Hopfer, stood for the Hopfer. The Hoser were an ancient Augsburg clan, long involved in Lutheran affairs and state politics at the highest levels.[10] Though less well placed, the Endorfer were no less noteworthy. A forebear, Stephan Endorfer, was one of the few Lutherans to support the introduction of the Gregorian calendar in 1586 and, ironically, earned a seat on the city's Secret Council for his service in a Catholic cause.[11] Thus, Matheus embodied the connection among four families who belonged to Augsburg's commercial and Lutheran elite.

With these economic and social resources, Matheus's parents were both willing and able 'to endure great expense on [Matheus's] behalf', including the costs of a humanist education.[12] From the passage emerges, indirectly as at other points, the question of parental expectations. That he was sent to Ulm may reveal nothing more than a concern for Matheus's safety. By 1636, Augsburg had endured not only inflation and disease but also a ruinous siege that ended with the surrender of the Swedish garrison to imperial and Bavarian forces. It was a good time for young Lutherans to seek their fortunes elsewhere, and the fortifications of Ulm were widely acknowledged to be impregnable.[13] Yet, training in classical languages might indicate ambition for Matheus's future as well as concern for his safety. Though no mention of specific plans was made, Matheus's parents possibly foresaw a university education for him and a career in law or theology. His rapid progress – to the sixth class within three years – suggests a talent, but apparently, given his decision to quit, not an inclination for learning. Nonetheless, when Matheus announced his desire to leave the academy and enter business, his father acceded readily, at least in Matheus' retelling. He needed exposure to the language and methods of commerce, however. To this end, his father arranged the classical education of a German merchant-in-training.[14] He sent Matheus to Italy: first a year in Verona, where he learned Italian in the house of Innocentio Tomasini; then via Venice, where he resided in the German factory, to Florence, where he entered the chancery of Georg and David Wolff. He also spent time perfecting his command of Italian by taking dictation for Antonio Gallacino and Lorentio Francesco.

Under the guidance of these men, who probably represented familial or commercial connections of the Miller family, Matheus trod a well-worn path. Italian commerce had stood godparent to German mercantile houses since the fifteenth century.[15] Certainly, Matheus learned the language of trade, to which he makes direct reference, but he acquired a broader worldview as well. As he observed the conduct of business, Matheus absorbed an economic mentality that found expression in a tendency to speculate on the future, to calculate risk, to analyze circumstance, and to develop organization. These were the essential tools of trade in early modern Europe; they left an impression as well on a memoir that had nothing to do with business.

Whatever the rigors of life as a merchant's apprentice, Matheus apparently enjoyed his stay in Italy and, as he wrote, 'would have stayed there longer'.[16] Perhaps he enjoyed it too well. Citing the cost of living and other expenses that were typical in such places, he recorded that his father cut short his stay and ordered him home via Venice. Having been in Florence no more than nine months, Matheus was in no hurry to leave. Rather than immediately submit to his father's authority, he seized the 'opportunity before going home to have a look at Pistoia, Pisa, Lucca, Livorno and Siena in good company'.[17] After this 'pleasant walking tour' of Tuscany he recalled the obedience due his father and 'took himself hastily with the post messengers to Venice and from there with Sigmund Deibold via Verona to Augsburg'. After less than two years in Italy, in 1641, Matheus Miller came home for the second time.

His delayed return constitutes the second instance in which Matheus may have disappointed or even defied the wishes of his father and, perhaps, other senior members of his clan. Yet, the memoir records neither domestic disturbance nor paternal discipline. Quite the contrary, Michael appeared unperturbed by changes of heart or itinerary and determined to further the future of his son. Matheus writes, 'Upon my arrival at home my father hoped to employ me, like other cousins, in the chancery and in business.'[18] The principals of the firm, however, who included not only his father but also his uncles, Gabriel Miller and Hans Jakob Miller, wanted Matheus placed again in the service of foreign merchants. They finally attached him to the company of the Nuremberger Balthas Schnurbein, in whose service he saw his first Frankfurt Fair in the fall of 1641. His employment signaled trouble in the family.

It was, in fact, a crisis of considerable proportion. Matheus admitted being outcast from his own family: 'I had become to some a thorn in the eye and in the good estimation of my relatives such that all their counsels inclined to keep me out of the Miller chancery, whether I immediately went to Cologne or to the next Catholic place and indentured myself for ten years had no meaning.'[19] He was to be banished from the family business and, indeed, from Augsburg, but he never names or even ponders the cause of this catastrophe. He never reveals a specific animus on the part of certain members of the family. He makes clear, however, that, although God had arranged it thus and knew best the reasons why, he was the victim of some particular vendetta, the loser in some contest of personal advantage (*privat aigennutz*).[20] The basis of early modern business organization in the family did not exclude competition, suspicion and hostility.

Under these circumstances, conflict might destroy a family's wealth as well as threaten the social order. Early modern merchants controlled hitherto unparalleled capital. In seventeenth-century Augsburg, they comprised 75 percent of its wealthiest citizens, those who paid a property tax in excess of fl100.[21] Economic power notwithstanding, they enjoyed only limited access to political authority. The Government Ordinance (*Regimentsordnung*) of 1548, also known as the Caroline Constitution, forced on the city by Emperor Charles V, permitted the merchants to elect from among their ranks only three senators to the Inner Council and two associates (*Beisitzer*) to the City Court.[22] The executive offices of *Stadtpfleger* and *Burgomaster* and membership in the Secret Council were closed to them; they filled the ranks of appointive functionaries in the city's growing administration. Consequently, merchants like Matheus, and his father and uncles, sought extra-legal, extra-political, extra-market means to assure business as usual. They protected reputation as the principal guarantor of credibility and creditworthiness. They formed partnerships to expand their resources and minimize their risks. They cultivated connections of patronage and clientage to influence policy-making and police activity. In a world that offered few alternatives, they relied on the institution of patriarchy and the exercise of paternalism to preserve their economic organizations and foster their commercial activities. For them, as Matheus came to understand, the economy was a seamless web of market forces, social relations and political maneuvers. This 'confusion' of motives explains their cold-eyed pursuit of advantage as well as their sometimes economically irrational solidarities and animosities.

In a diary, written one and one-half centuries earlier, Lucas Rem complained bitterly about the dishonest business practices of the Welsers, whose factor in Portugal and France he was, to the point that he finally demanded his release.[23] Rem had no close connection to his principals, beyond that of loyal and valuable service, but the same friction might exist between blood relatives. He also had no means of protecting himself from their animosity. Hence, he took care to conceal his opinions and emotions and to preserve their patronage and approval. Matheus did likewise.

And discretion was essential. Matheus's father, Michael, formed several businesses with his brothers. As a general rule, the lack of reliably enforceable legal instruments to regularize business relations encouraged a reliance on family members as partners.[24] Moreover, given the nature of trade in southern Germany, based as it was on raw materials and textiles traded overland to Italy, these partnerships tended to be durable. Business contracts often stipulated a two- to eight-year term, but associations lasted longer in fact, often ending only with bankruptcy.[25] Though merchants, the Millers did not conform to this rule. They reorganized frequently, and Michael's status within those concerns was not stable.

The exact scope of the Millers' business cannot be reconstructed, but at least one part of it involved the transshipment of goods between Italy and the Rhine basin. In 1628, for example, Michael and Gabriel acted as partners to arrange the delivery of gunlocks from Milan to Pisaro on behalf of Michael Glaser of Cologne.[26] The brothers apparently flourished but not all alike. While Michael's fortunes withered between 1625 and 1635, Gabriel and Hans Jakob rose to be numbered among the 80 wealthiest Augsburgers in 1632.[27] The divergence of fortunes coincided with a restructuring of the family business. A transit declaration (*Fede di sanità*) from about 1645 listed only Hans Jakob and Gabriel as partners in the delivery of 2 bales (*Ballen*) of Augsburger fustian to Marc Antonius Arigoni and his brothers in Mantua.[28] If Michael was still involved in the enterprise, he had the status of an unnamed associate only. From 1649 to 1652 the brothers reorganized their business again and made *Michael, Gabriel, and Hans Jakob Miller and Associates* one of the largest trading companies in Augsburg.[29] They continued the transshipment of a wide range of goods, including furs, pharmaceuticals and clothing, among Italy, Augsburg and the Low Countries, but specialized in trading linens and woolens to the south and silks to the north.[30] Michael's fortunes never again matched those of Gabriel and Hans Jakob, which suggests that he remained a junior partner, despite his place in the company name. For this reason, Matheus's father might have had difficulty realizing his ambition for his son.

Perhaps Matheus was simply the son of a less fortunate, and therefore less influential, partner. It seems equally possible, however, that he caused his own misfortune. His sudden determination to change careers, thus altering a future in which his entire family might have had an interest, and his unapproved detour through Italy, done in apparent defiance of his father's expressed wishes, might have convinced his uncles, the senior members of the firm, that he was untrustworthy and his actions improper. This accords closely with the structure of the memoir and its function as an apologia.

Whatever the cause, at age 16 in 1641, Matheus found himself in Frankfurt looking for a suitable position. He finally, reluctantly as it seems, accepted a situation in the company of another Nuremberger merchant, Zacharias Schoap.[31] Matheus took the job 'in order not to return to Augsburg'. Schoap agreed to hire him only because Matheus's father 'offered to pay room and board until the dear Lord provided some other situation'. The arrangement struck neither party as ideal.

Yet, it was to be a turning point for Matheus. Schoap proved a sympathetic and knowledgeable master, under whose patient instruction Matheus's real commercial education began.[32]

> I arrived at the house of Master Shoap in October 1641 and was held to business and similar matters with such diligent zeal that I can say of myself in especially grateful honor and to his fame that a flesh-and-blood father could not have done more than he did for me a stranger in that I got the opportunity to consider these matters in one way or another more earnestly and industriously after he began to entrust the business accounts to me and showed great patience in teaching me the composition of business letters and bills of exchange.

If he considered business practices earnestly and industriously for the first time in Nuremberg, then Matheus may not have used his time as well in Verona and Florence. Also, the reference to flesh-and-blood (*leiblicher*) implies criticism of his own family. His treatment at the hands of a stranger contrasts sharply with his ostracism, presumably by his uncles. Thus carefully read, the passage supports certain impressions of Matheus's experience since abandoning his studies in Ulm. Though not misspent, his youth failed to measure up to the standard of filial obedience and subservience expected in a patriarchal society. The resulting distance between himself and his family left Matheus bitter. Unable to rely on their support, he had to succeed on his own.

His training in the house of Schoap was a first step toward independence and success. In 1642, after a year in Nuremberg, 'God wondrously let a condition blossom'.[33] Matheus found employment as a commercial agent for Hans Schlumpff, a Swiss merchant. After a 14-day trial, he was sent to St Gall, where he agreed to work for $6\frac{1}{2}$ years at an annual salary of fl. 43 plus board. Matheus had misgivings about the terms because, as he noted, 'From [the agreement] one could determine exactly how long the time and how meager the solvency of my masters.' No longer an indentured servant learning his trade, he was now a salaried employee.

Whatever his doubts, Matheus claims to have gotten on well in the house of Schlumpff.[34] In the first two years, he served as secretary and cashier for the firm, thus maintaining all correspondence and accounts. He engaged in sales and accompanied his master to the annual market in Zurich, 'everything with good content on both sides'. He writes, 'I did everything as well as I could according to my youth.' He was 17 years old.

The reference to youth – an *obiter dicta* – seems out of place. At 17, Matheus was no longer a boy according to the reckoning of his time. Both Charles V and Francis I had become kings at age 15. The most influential pedagogue of the seventeenth century, Johann Amos Comenius, defined the onset of adulthood as age 25.[35] Prior to maturity, a human being experienced four growing phases of six years each: infancy, childhood, adolescence and youth. Thus, Matheus remained formally a young man, not yet fully grown or mature, during his St Gall years. His experience, however, was typical for young men of his station and age. Lucas Rem, for example, made his journey to Italy to learn the techniques of business in 1494, at the age of 13.[36] He returned from Italy to Augsburg in 1498 and immediately joined the Anton Lauginger Company as a secretary and accountant. He was 17.

That same year, he entered the Welser Company, which he served as factor, a position of great responsibility and independence, for nearly 20 years. Matheus's duties were not, therefore, unusual for his age. Nor were the expectations placed on him. The question arises why Matheus would have felt compelled to plead tenderness of years and experience unless his service was the cause of complaint and dispute. Such proved to be the case.[37]

> Soon after two years the wife of my master died whereby the household fell into greater disorder from day to day so that various disputes arose between us to the point that I saw no means to resolve the animosity that grew from day to day and continued over one and one-half years other than to write to my father for help.

Again, Matheus was unable or unwilling to recall and record the immediate problem beyond a death in the household and disorder caused by the lack of a housewife. Tensions continued for a long time but did not rise to such an extent that he was dismissed. He finally found himself driven to the extreme of quitting. This was a serious step. It involved the violation of a formal – perhaps contractual – agreement of service. It reflected negatively on the Miller name, a possibility that would be disastrous in a business world, where reputation determined credibility and creditworthiness. It required the tact and influence of a senior man of affairs, one of recognized experience and standing. Matheus had to call on his father's assistance. Doubtless disturbed, Michael responded to his son's plea and traveled in person to St Gall where, 'after much and great effort he finally secured [Matheus's] release'.[38] Such difficulties may not have been unusual in the early modern business world, but they neither reflected well on Matheus nor sat well with his censorious uncles.

The terms of release involved a six-month notice; Matheus could not leave St Gall before February 1646. In that time, as he retold it, relations with his master improved to such an extent that he was asked to stay. Yet, Matheus was now 20 years old, and, as he put it, 'My foremost intent, especially because I had a good introduction, was to marry a widow's daughter of good means in [the imperial city of] Leutkirch.'[39] He refused, therefore, to prolong his period of employment. After closing the books and settling his accounts, he parted in friendship from his patron and, with acquaintances accompanying him as far as Lindau on Lake Constance, traveled to his destination. He wrote, 'Arrived in Leutkirch, I found the opportunity not as I hoped and so had to alter my thoughts of marriage once again.'[40] So, without prospects for the future, in the spring of 1646, Matheus Miller came home to Augsburg for the third time.

Marriage had no place at this point in Matheus's life. The daughter of a wealthy widow – or, at least, her dowry – might have made an attractive inducement, but she could only consider seriously a suitor who had achieved a position. At age 20, with no business and no income, Matheus lacked the means to support a bride and had nothing to offer her family.

His actions violated the standards of behavior prescribed at that time, and contrast with those of other men of his station. In 1518, when he first married, Lucas Rem was 37 years of age, had founded his own firm one year earlier, had been a factor in the Welser Company for 19 years before that, and had been a recognized businessman in Augsburg for even longer.[41] Nonetheless, he sought and received the counsel of family and friends before he decided to take a bride. Rem wrote,

> Upon much, long, and earnest persuasion by my honorable mother, brother, and other trusted friends and good patrons, on 14 May 1518, my marriage was negotiated between Lucas Welser and Batholomeo Rem with Marz Echäin and Conrat Relinger and on 17 the same, Monday between 1:00 and 2:00 finally concluded between myself, Lucas Rem, and Miss Anna Echäinin, the legitimate daughter of Jerg Echäin and Anna Endorfer.

Caspar Koch, a merchant of Memmingen, married in 1598 at age 21.[42] A youth, like Matheus, he had been indentured to learn commerce in the house of a Nuremberger merchant. Yet, the arrangements for Koch's marriage were made by his father who called him home not only to establish his own household but also to enter the family business. In contrast to Matheus, Koch recorded his marriage settlement in painstaking detail in his own diary. His father weighed the union and outlined an agreement before consulting him. In the company of an uncle and a servant, Koch rode to Kempten, where he met members of his prospective bride's family and, under carefully arranged circumstances, spoke briefly to the young woman herself. After their conversation, he met again with members of the family, expressed his willingness to marry, and settled general terms for the marriage contract. This stage of the negotiation closed with a festive meal and an exchange of gifts between the intended bride and groom. Koch then returned to Memmingen and reported the results of his trip. His parents congratulated him and immediately planned the formal betrothal. Over the next few days, letters and gifts were exchanged. Ten days later, Koch, his parents, and a large party of relatives set out for Kempten again. Arriving there, they were met by members of the bride's family and conducted to ceremonial chambers in their business headquarters, where the marriage contract was formally read and sealed. Another festive meal followed. The formalities closed with an official betrothal conducted by a Lutheran pastor. The wedding celebration, which would last several days and would involve hundreds of guests and great expense, was set to occur several weeks later in Memmingen. Carefully contrived and conducted, these negotiations assumed the appearance of ritual and were the picture of propriety.

Because marriage among merchants joined fortunes as well as families, such unions were usually matters of cautious negotiation and formal ritual between the relatives and associates of the bride and groom. As Koch's description makes clear, they participated from the beginning, indeed long before bride and groom were actually consulted. Matheus married three times in the course of his life, and, regardless of his age, the members of his family were intimately involved in the arrangements of each. Perhaps Michael provided the introduction to the widow's daughter; perhaps he accompanied his son to Leutkirch. In this instance, however, Matheus made no mention of his father or his uncles, a significant omission in light of their possibly strained relations. Given the nature of the entry in his memoir – without reference to the bride's name, without indication of familial approval, without attention to ceremonial formalities, without mention of his own feelings – the affair appears spontaneous and surreptitious.

Matheus's memoir offers no clue to his family's reaction to his abortive attempt at marriage. As in the description of other conflicts with his uncles, he neither comments on the situation nor indicates its cause. Yet, the conjecture that his behavior led to their rejection seems consistent with the structure and language of the narrative. If, as seems probable from the evidence of the memoir, he acted on his own initiative without the advice and consent of his father and uncles, then they could not have been pleased. Indeed, it would have seemed a confirmation of an already negative opinion, formed on the basis of other, irresponsible actions. Once returned to Augsburg, he had no choice but to seek service in foreign parts because, 'no one wanted me in my uncles' chancery'.[43] His reputation made the search for a position difficult because 'no one knew why the Miller concern refused to accept [me]'. In the end, he joined the Wertemann Company, bound for Vienna.

Matheus never made the journey. Another turn of fortune set his life on a different, more stable course. His father decided to set up a business of his own and take his son as partner. As noted in the memoir: 'My beloved father, although it had often been difficult for him to begin something of his own, finally took heart and decided to sell cotton to weavers.'[44] The business flourished. It was the end of youth, illusion and adventure; it was the beginning of adulthood, reality and propriety.

What follows the narrative of his younger days falls generally into three distinct parts. Matheus recorded the growth of his family as a cycle of demographic events. He marked his rise to stature through a series of appointive public offices. He described the circle of his friends through lists of gifts and godchildren. It is an explicit selection of themes on his part, an exploration of practical virtue such as he would have learned in the classical studies of his youth. In this regard, his memoir also demonstrates a noteworthy similarity to an earlier, better known reflection on family life, Leon Battista Alberti's *I Libri della Famiglia*.

Alberti's work is neither diary nor autobiography but rather a dialogue, written in a humanist tradition and expressing a bourgeois outlook. *Della Famiglia* has been called a monument of attitudes, a treatise on what it meant to be a merchant in a Renaissance city: to experience the forces of market economy and social mobility, to suffer political upheaval and familial instability.[45] Werner Sombart took it to be the first clear articulation of a spirit of modern capitalism.[46] Alberti divided his work into four books, fictional conversations among members of his own family: Book One addresses paternal responsibility; Book Two deals with conjugal love; Book Three treats the domestic economy; Book Four considers friendship. As a whole, *Della Famiglia* moves outward through concentric circles, from emotional relations within the family to material relations among the members of the household and between household and community, to social relations with relatives, friends, neighbors and associates. Matheus organized his memoir similarly. By writing first of his family, then of his offices, and finally of his friends, he turned his attention from emotional ties, to material functions, to social relations.

For Alberti and Matheus, family solidarity and stature were not theoretical constructs. Both men drew upon their own experiences. Alberti wrote of his family and for his family. He was illegitimate, a fact he never mentioned but which may explain the harsh treatment he received at the hands of his family after his father's death.[47] Thus, his work assumes ironical tones whenever the various interlocutors insist that mutual support should characterize the family. *Della Famiglia* examines the ideal family and, by so doing, excoriates real practices. Indirect criticisms of his relatives contain reflections on himself. Alberti recognized, and supposedly conformed to, the standards of behavior advocated in his book. Arguably, Matheus intended a similar defense of himself. Excluded from the family business for reasons he also refused to examine, forced to make his way alone in the world, he reflected on his life as a means of demonstrating the truth about himself as he saw it. He had learned from the sins and mistakes of his youth. Acting upon this knowledge, he had become successful in business and life.

His adulthood as father and husband, as merchant and functionary, and as associate and friend demonstrates propriety rather than contemporary notions of honor or civility. Honor in hierarchical societies is defined by behavior appropriate to one's station, whereas propriety defines a standard of comportment consistent throughout society. Civility implicates two people in a series of social negotiations, but propriety refers ultimately to the conduct of an individual alone.[48] Thus, propriety escapes the trammels of hierarchy and makes of the individual both an agent and an object of change. It imparts to the natural order, divinely created, a degree of flexibility. The criticism of Matheus's family is, perhaps, more veiled and the irony more muted than Alberti's, but the light shed on himself is clearer. In his memoir, he offers a general model of proper comportment and a specific vindication of his life.

Though striking, the parallels of structure and argumentation between Alberti and Matheus are presumably fortuitous. Some intellectuals of the sixteenth and seventeenth centuries knew *Della Famiglia*; it was cited at least eight times in the period.[49] Yet, it is unlikely that Matheus read it. While a few, incomplete manuscripts had circulated since the final book was written around 1441, the work was not assembled and published in its entirety until the first decade of the twentieth century.[50]

That both men fastened on similar arguments for similar purposes may have more to do with their common background in the languages and literature of classical humanism.[51] Both likely read the works of Cicero and Seneca, for example, and learned the Stoic philosophy of virtue, much admired and discussed by humanists of the fifteenth and sixteenth centuries.[52] Virtue consisted in the conformance of human conduct to human reason and took the form of moral insight and self-control, of justice, temperance and courage. As such, it was internal, as opposed to goods, which were the transitory, external gifts of Fortune. The cultivation of virtue was a process, often lifelong, that required effort on the part of the individual. These notions run throughout both *Della Famiglia* and the memoir.

Arguments for the family as the basis of political life, for the household as the basis of economic activity, and for friendship as the engine of social relations may be found in the works of Aristotle.[53] In a famous passage from Book One of the *Politics*, he reasons that 'man is by nature a political animal', that men and women come together naturally to form families 'for the supply of man's everyday wants', that families coalesce into villages 'aimed at something more than daily needs', and that villages unite to form states 'for the sake of a good life'.[54] Thus, all forms of community are natural expressions of the physical and emotional needs of human beings, and from these needs all political, economic and social activities arise. Such reasoning might have inspired Alberti and Matheus to consider family, friends and the state as spheres of activity to which family members and especially the paterfamilias must attend carefully. Not only is the family the simplest social unit but, as Aristotle states in the *Nicomachean Ethics*, the emotion that binds family members together, friendship, 'is most necessary with a view to living' in that it inspires both social and economic activity, and binds communities and states together.[55] It is the basis for the exchange of services and the model for justice. The family, friends and the state were the three most important settings for the exercise of friendship, the cultivation of virtue and the achievement of a good life. Hence, in seeking to justify his life, to present it to the reader as proper, Matheus may have done nothing more than borrowed the fundamental assumptions of Aristotelian politics and ethics, and fit them to his particular purpose. His memoir offers no concrete demonstration of the filiation of ideas. He cited neither Aristotle, nor Alberti, nor the householder literature of his day that also shared these notions. Rather, his writing contains analogies and similarities that suggest Matheus's familiarity with and reliance on a common stock of ideas, a common cultural good.

Though the motive behind the memoir remains implicit, several facts support the notion that Matheus wrote to justify his later life. The turning points of the introduction, especially his spontaneous decisions regarding career or marriage and the mounting tension between himself and his uncles, indicate difficulties within the family. Such deviations from broadly accepted standards of domestic comportment and harmony may have demanded rationalization. The close parallel to Alberti and Aristotle, that is, the description of his life in terms of family, state and friends, suggest an effort to formalize it in terms of classical ideals. Rhetorical tactics of this sort are consistent with argumentation rather than exposition. Finally, the autobiographical form itself, as opposed to a chronicle, diary or account, encourages a selective rather than a comprehensive retelling of events, one that treats the life as allegory. All of these elements suggest a desire to confirm the propriety of his adult life that operated just below the surface of Matheus Miller's memoir.

To contend, however, that Matheus was nothing more than a latter-day Alberti, that he wished either to defend himself against the supposedly poor opinion of his relatives or to demonstrate that he had learned his lessons, is to over-simplify his motives and misunderstand his milieu. Vindication was his implicit motive. Other, traditional, explicit reasons shaped his writing as well.

Matheus's memoir imparts more than a life's history. It records a soul's sojourn – a pilgrim's progress – in reality rather than allegory. He states this purpose explicitly in the dedication to an anonymous reader.[56]

> Oh reader, think of me that I must die and that my days are numbered. And that I must live those days as the Lord did, must die as the Lord did, thus living and dying as the Lord did. Christian living sanctifies one and gains a holy death and eternal joy. God help us gain all three.

It echoes the fourth verse of Psalm 39.[57]

> Lord, let me know my end and the number of my days; tell me how short my life must be.

It is a cry of spiritual awareness, an admission that life is transient: 'Man, though he stands upright, is but a puff of wind, he moves like a phantom; the riches he piles up are no more than vapour, and he does not know who will enjoy them.'[58] The psalm urges the faithful to abandon the world and put their trust in God. Matheus framed the story of his life in accordance with this dictum, relying on his faith to explain the unknowable and ease the unbearable.

Spiritual confessions and meditations have a long, literary tradition that takes its inspiration from St Augustine's *Confessions*. In the sixteenth and seventeenth centuries, this form of autobiography gained considerable popularity among certain Christian sects and became a genre in its own right. English Puritans and German Pietists used spiritual diaries as a means to discipline the soul and to glorify God.[59] Accordingly, their journals were highly personal, focused on the struggle against sin and damnation. They captured worldly events chiefly as evidence of divine Providence, a chronicle of God's treatment of His children and their actions on earth. Their interest in life, except *sub specie aeternitatis*, remained secondary.

Yet, the prayer to know the number and end of one's days can serve also as a call to secular action, a summons to life lived properly. Matheus was not prepared to dismiss his life as a phantom or to discount his worldly engagements as vapor. Early ignorance and transgression had led to a more Christian life and a proper work ethic. His purpose involved the temporal as well as the eternal, that is, he intended to record certain events in his life and, by so doing, preserve them for his posterity, 'that my descendants may find it after God grants me the grace to leave'.[60] Thus, his is no spiritual diary in the strict sense. It combines secular and spiritual perspectives, material and transcendent concerns. He wished to preserve his worldly experience and knowledge for the benefit of his descendants.

Matheus shared this intention with a great many other German diarists and autobiographers of the late Middle Ages and the early modern period.[61] All believed that some aspect of their individual lives had achieved a more general interest and utility. They drew inspiration from a long and varied, semi-autobiographical tradition that included the accounts of merchants, the lives of saints, the travels of pilgrims and the correspondence of literati. Accordingly, their writings served a purpose potentially apart from God's glory, the soul's discipline or the family's convenience. They wrote to organize, preserve and perpetuate their experience. Among the earliest and most common of these writings were the *ricordanze* of Italian and German merchants, which recorded business accounts and personal affairs.[62] In its categorical organization, its chronological progression and its episodic character, Matheus's memoir resembles the merchant diaries and *ricordi* with which he must have been very familiar. The lack of formal business records notwithstanding, it reminds the reader that Matheus formed his patterns of thought in the marketplace.

Bourgeois autobiographies became more common during the fifteenth and sixteenth centuries, but they retained elements of the traditional, ordered society of ranks from which their authors sprang.[63]

In general, economic expansion, which began in the fifteenth century and was accompanied by a gradual transformation of social hierarchies and a no less gradual intensification of personal contacts, encouraged a desire for individual identity.[64] So long as social status defined personality, however, the singularity of any individual remained stunted. Not surprisingly, because they existed outside traditional social categories, merchants were among the first to breach this social convention. In keeping *ricordanze* and refining them over time, businessmen explicitly delineated private preoccupations as distinct from public affairs.[65] Despite its preoccupation with public affairs and social relations, Matheus's memoir contains confidential reflections, clearly intended for a private, domestic audience.

Traditional forms inspired late medieval and early modern diaries and autobiographies; Matheus freely borrowed from several without completely adopting any.[66] His memoir expressed profound spiritual concerns without ever meditating upon salvation. He considered the state of his eternal soul but justified his temporal behavior. He was conscious of divine Providence in his life but questioned its workings.[67] Ultimately, providential events become the setting for proper actions.[68] Matheus's memoir recorded the most important aspects of his life – his family, his offices – supplying information that might have been profitable to his heirs as indications of the need for propriety. He concentrated on his own thoughts and actions without regard for their social, political or economic contexts. He specified personal relationships rather than their material bases. Identity is not submerged in event, nor is its exploration the point.[69] Rather, the memoir serves as a crucible of experience, of events interpreted from the singular perspective of the author. Matheus sketched the marriages, births and deaths in his family, but left out their implications for his wealth. He noted the names of his various public offices and business associates but never evaluated their costs or their benefits. Although it combines elements of the *ricordanze* and the *libri di famiglia*, the memoir pointedly ignores a mercantile *ragione* that conflated the private and the public by connecting private well-being with public engagement.[70] The memoir resembles several kinds of autobiographical writings, but unlike any of them it constantly emphasizes Matheus's means rather than his ends, his behavior rather than his achievement, in this world rather than the next. In this, it captures his cognizance of a multidimensional world, a place of choice and change, of conflict and compromise. It records his experience – not just what happens to him but how he understands it – his particular interpretation of the meaningful events of his life. In this regard, the memoir assumes the form of an apologia above all else.

Insofar as it seeks to vindicate Matheus's actions, his memoir offers a selective account of his life. It differs little in this respect from other 'ego-documents', a term coined by Jacob Presser and propagated by Rudolf Dekker to describe a broad array of sources that reveal, either intentionally or unintentionally, the self-impression or ego of an individual.[71] The wide variety of autobiographical accounts, which became commonplace in the early modern period, have attracted the attention of twentieth-century historians, who have turned from the exploration of collective mentalities to confront issues of meaning, perception and value in the context of single persons.[72] At the center of this examination stand open questions of definition and interpretation. What exactly is an ego-document? Recent suggestions would extend the category to any text in which a person gives testimony concerning him- or herself, integrating with diaries and autobiographies such diverse materials as correspondences, petitions, interrogations, testimonies and testaments.[73] Matheus's memoir conforms to a narrower, more traditional interpretation of ego-documents that include only such autobiographical materials as voluntarily attempt to define the uniqueness of an individual and establish its distinctness from others. It describes its author's expectations, illuminates his values, exposes his fears, and explains his behavior. It voices, deliberately and immediately, an individual's perceptions of himself in society.

Interpretive difficulties remain, however.[74] All autobiographies are, to a greater or lesser degree, self-conscious. Rather than provide a spontaneous narration of a person's life, they refract experience and perception through the written conventions, the rules and models, of their day. Rather than offer a complete account, they include only such content as suits their authors' purposes. Whenever compared to other historical records, Matheus's memoir has proven painstakingly precise. Yet, the 'facts' presented are often incomplete, chosen apparently to convince rather than to clarify. Matheus explains himself from the perspective of the end toward which he wrote, the vindication of his life. Memory complicates the issue of interpretation. After the narrative of his youth, Matheus recorded a series of episodes that extended more or less chronologically from his first marriage in 1647 to shortly before his death in 1685. Though his voice and outlook are remarkably consistent, suggesting composition over a concentrated period of time, the questions of when or how often he wrote remain unanswered. Using the memoir as a narrative and a counterpoint to other sources of information, which provide context and fill lacunae, it is possible to examine the life thus retold.

What follows, therefore, is necessarily more a study in early modern values than a biography of an early modern merchant. Four chapters reflect the same spheres of activity that Matheus worked into his memoir. Chapter 1 examines his marriages. Matheus offers a personal interpretation of patriarchy as an exemplary rather than an authoritarian institution. Chapter 2 turns to the public offices he occupied. Matheus demonstrates the function of the public sphere not to delimit but rather to define private ethics. Chapter 3 recreates his social network, the ties that bound him to relatives and associates. Matheus provides a vision of the nuclear family at once closed and open, insusceptible and susceptible, to the demands and needs of friends and relatives. Chapter 4 considers his faith, a topic that runs throughout the entire memoir. Matheus evinces little consciousness of confession in an age of confessionalism. What emerges finally is Matheus's particular sense of the proper paterfamilias – the dutiful husband, virtuous citizen, reliable partner and devout Christian – whose qualities his uncles found lacking in Matheus's youth.

1
Marriage and Patriarchy

Matheus Miller was a family man. His memoir records the growth of his household. The narrative of his youth ends with his marriage on 30 July 1647 to Anna Maria Warmberger and the birth eight months later of a son named Michael. The child survived a week, and Matheus dutifully sketched the ceremonies and recorded the expenses of its baptism and burial.[1] At this point the form of the memoir changes abruptly, and narrative gives way to chronicle. The first entry concerns the birth, in 1650, of a second son and heir, Philip Jakob.[2] Marriage and birth mark a turning point in Matheus's consideration of his own life. Despite the simplicity of its description, that transition loomed complex in his mind. More than a simple change of circumstance, it was the foundation of a domestic kingdom, of mastery over wife, children and servants.[3] Matheus had changed. The trials of his early years had ended; he had made a new beginning. He had moved from youth and dependence to adulthood and independence. He had become a husband, father and householder; he had become, in other words, a paterfamilias. In his memoir, he offered his own notion of patriarchy as practice.

The patriarch stood at the center of early modern social thought, which assumed it to be the key to political, economic and ethical stability. A long intellectual tradition that extended from classical philosophers, such as Aristotle, to eighteenth-century cameralists, such as Christian Wolff, understood the household as a composite of three societies: the marital society of husband and wife; the parental society of parent and child; the authoritarian society of master and servant.[4] In each of these, the male figure of husband/father/master was dominant. The householder represented his household and its members to the larger community. He alone possessed the legal personality required to enter into contractual relations or to stand before the law. He alone possessed the political rights required to participate in government or exercise public office. He alone possessed considerable economic powers that seemed to be expanding at the expense of other members of the household, especially the housewife, in the early modern period.[5] With this process, the householder's social status and domestic authority may have grown as well.

Yet, patriarchal authority was neither unlimited nor undivided. The householder literature of that period captures these distinct but inseparable perspectives. In his *Hauβtafel*, the Lutheran Cyriacus Spangenberg describes the patriarch's three essential roles as a provider, educator and authoritarian.[6] He sustains and shelters his dependents; he instructs them in their various tasks; he disciplines them to appropriate behavior. Johannes Coler insists on the same roles but in different terms.[7] In the *Oeconomias*, he writes that the paterfamilias has to be pious, industrious and knowledgeable. Piety inspires discipline; industry provides sustenance; knowledge guides instruction. Despite the differing emphases on functions or qualities, the essence of patriarchy is in all places the same: the governance of self, family and society through the authority of the paterfamilias. Forces within individuals and communities, whether attributed to appetite or sin, created disorder. Thus, good governance was essential for harmony and virtue. Whatever its negative overtones to modern ears, discipline and order were prized as essential to peace as thinkers of the seventeenth century understood it. And patriarchal order was the only kind that century knew. 'The household is a monarchy in which only one rules.'[8] Loving, reasonable and moderate, at least in theory, that rule is to be received with submission, deference and gratitude. The tension between functions and emotions, between coercion and affection, between submission and antagonism, remains unmentioned and unresolved.[9] For Spangenberg, Coler and their contemporaries, the householder was charged with the inculcation and maintenance of proper social relations among persons of different age, gender and status.

Matheus portrays his household in very different terms. He offers vignettes of family life in which the omnipresent figure is he himself, the patriarch. These scenes reveal his consciousness of patriarchy as a code of personal conduct rather than a theory of social discipline.

The material aspects of his role are muted. He hardly mentions the fact that he provides for his family successfully under difficult circumstances. Discipline and instruction receive scant attention; they appear as little more than *obiter dicta* in the chronicle of his life.

Vital events absorb more of Matheus's attention, measured by the number of pages accorded to them, than any other aspect of his life. Yet, his is no simple demographic record. Connected with the lifecycle are complex transactions and associations: the transfer of property, the consolidation of kinship, the elevation of status. Matheus not only lists the fact of his son's birth and the names of the godparents but also takes care to record the expenses of the event.[10] No less important is the range of affections. Though rarely fulsome, Matheus makes his feelings clear. Marriages, births and deaths form crucial turning points in the lifecycle of the family that fundamentally alter its material circumstances and its emotional texture. As principal actor, celebrant and, in this case, recorder, the paterfamilias stands at the center of all such events. His reflections reveal something of the relationship between 'interest and emotion' not as an opposition but as a dialectic from which consciousness developed.[11] His experience, therefore, provides a perspective on patriarchy and family.

Especially in his descriptions of marriage, Matheus fixes on the emotional and ethical aspects of the paterfamilias. Through his narration, he articulates the affective bonds between himself and other members of his household. Through his comportment, he represents the proper moral content and social form of these relationships. Read transparently, the paterfamilias becomes an exemplary figure, an embodiment of propriety, and patriarchy becomes a representative institution. It reflects less the structure or function of a complex society than the stature and behavior of a single, crucial individual within it. The patriarch represents an ideal of governance and comportment. Placed in a context of material circumstances, understood here as economic processes and social relations, the patriarch Matheus is the guarantor of familial security and solidarity. Far from being a stable authoritarian figure, therefore, he must constantly reposition himself in a changing world.

That the world changed abruptly in Matheus's lifetime cannot be doubted. At the time of his birth, in 1625, Augsburg had passed through a period of tremendous creativity and productivity. The signs were evident to the travelers and observers of that day. Gilles de Faing, who accompanied Archduke Albrecht of Austria on his trip through Augsburg in 1598, said of the city that 'she is great, rich, beautiful and has expensive buildings'.[12] Duke Henry II of Rohan named it 'among the most noteworthy cities in all of Germany'.[13] The poet, Peter Lindeberg, wrote of 'buildings that seem to threaten heaven with their pinnacles and floors decorated with stylish pictures, the many men who turn all they touch to gold and venerable fathers of great age, also the walls and fountains...the copper roofs and the buildings glittering with gold'.[14] He likened the citizens to Croesus in their wealth and the women to Venus in their beauty.

And the realities seemed to support such statements. Long-distance commerce and export-oriented industries, especially fustian production and metalworking, set the pace of economic life and made Augsburg home to a flourishing community of wealthy entrepreneurs as well as to a growing stratum of impoverished laborers. Total population doubled during the sixteenth century from approximately 20,000 to 40,000 inhabitants.[15] Wealth expanded even more quickly: taxable assets rose from a minimum of fl. 2.58 million in 1498 to a maximum of fl. 16.9 million in 1554.[16] Buildings and monuments grew apace. Fortifications were expanded and improved. Mills were constructed inside and outside the walls. Arcades of shops were added to the Church of the Franciscans and the Collegiate Church of St Moritz. New monumental edifices appeared: a city customs house (1605), a city armory (1607), a city butchery (1609) and a city hall (1624). According to every standard, Augsburg was one of the great cities of the empire and of Europe.

Baroque facades concealed more than work-a-day structures, however. Augsburg's building frenzy, so often admired by visitors, occurred while its economy stagnated, several decades after the years of peak prosperity. Fiscal discipline rather than private fortunes – cheese-paring rather than money-making – made those projects possible.[17] Superficial grandeur hid profound destitution. Although wages rose for many occupational groups, rapid population growth increased demand for essential commodities with the result that 'in the entire sixteenth and early seventeenth centuries [real] wages hobbled behind [prices]'.[18] The poor were everywhere and the common ground between them and the rich eroded in the sixteenth century. Between 1498 and 1554 the middling strata of Augsburg grew only 17.3 percent while the number of have-nots grew 88 percent and the number of rich grew 94 percent.[19] Economic hardship and social tension found tongue in a poet's diatribe against the stockpiling and price-gouging of a heartless, self-serving elite: 'The merchants were so clever...that many died of want, cold, and hunger'.[20] He spoke not only of the consciousness of exploitation but also of a growing sense of deprivation, a loss of dignity, prosperity and self-sufficiency. In 1582, Hans Fugger saw Augsburg as 'a small village where once was a great city...all is in decline and all matters give evidence of worsening rather than bettering'.[21] Magnificence seemed transient, fragile and superficial.

Although he was born a generation later, Matheus inherited this worldview. How could it be otherwise? In youth he witnessed suffering and destruction; in adulthood he struggled to recover and rebuild. He often described the world as a *Jammertal*, a vale of lamentation. Yet, he told no tale of helpless suffering and passive endurance. Though written in resigned, pessimistic terms, his memoir intimated optimism. Matheus's career as merchant and magistrate testified to his interest in improvement and the world's capacity for change. As he observed and recorded his experience, Matheus redirected and animated his world. His memoir reveals the calm forbearance of a Christian stoic in the face of life and its mischances.[22] Yet, it also reveals the constant struggle of a man on the make. Stoicism did not, after all, exclude purposeful action.

And the times required action. When he established his household, in 1647, Augsburg had experienced catastrophe. Pestilence, famine and war had reduced its grandeur to a pale, unrecoverable memory. The inflation (*Kipper- und Wipperzeit*) of 1622–23, the epidemic of 1627–28 and the siege of 1634–35, decimated the population, ruined the economy, and shook the society.[23] The material dimensions of the disaster are well known. The population sank from 40,000 in 1618 to 19,960 in 1645.[24] At its nadir in 1635, Augsburg housed only 16,422 inhabitants. Approximately 2,216 dwellings stood damaged or abandoned.[25] The total wealth of the population lost over 75 percent of its value during the war years.[26] A list, compiled by the City Council, claimed fl. 9,330,248 in damages and losses to the city between 1618 and 1648.[27] The public debt rose from fl. 200,000 in 1610 to fl. 1,828,000 by 1650.[28] Large-scale commerce and banking, the most profitable sectors of Augsburg's once burgeoning economy, suffered the greatest losses: the total worth of those families in the highest tax brackets, principally merchants and bankers, declined 91 percent during the war. The leading sector of Augsburg's export industry, textile manufacturing and finishing, endured a similar decline. The number of weavers sank from 2,184 in 1618 to about 500 in 1654. Their production fell from 400,000 pieces of bleached, dyed and raw fustian in the pre-war years to 60,508 pieces in 1662.[29] Such losses compromised the economic viability of the city as a whole and complicated the fortunes of individual families. The great commercial clans, those whose wealth had been the lifeblood of the city, simply disappeared.[30] The Welser were bankrupt by 1614. The Fugger withdrew from the economic and political affairs of Augsburg with uncollectible debts worth more than fl. 2,000,000. The Rehlinger and Österreicher lost nearly everything.

Many failed, but most of the Millers thrived. Augsburg's tax books reveal that the family made its fortune at the worst of times. Matheus's father did not fare well. As noted, his estate declined from an assessed maximum value of fl. 34,500 in 1625 to an assessed minimum of fl. 7,332 in 1635.[31] While Michael's wealth decreased by half, however, that of his brothers and partners nearly doubled. Gabriel Miller rendered fl. 112 kr. 30 on property valued between fl. 22,500 and fl. 45,000; Hans Jakob Miller paid a tax of fl. 125 on a gross worth between fl. 25,000 and fl. 50,000.[32] Both men belonged to the 80 wealthiest Augsburgers of that year. In 1639, while Michael's assessment remained stable, Gabriel paid fl. 175 on an estate worth between fl. 35,000 and fl. 70,000, and Hans Jakob paid fl. 266 on property valued between fl. 53,200 and fl. 106,400.[33] Their assessments remained at those levels through the 1640s.[34] Michael's fortunes never again matched those of his brothers. That fact may have influenced Matheus's struggle to enter into business; it certainly is reflected in his memoir and influenced his family.

The crisis years were hard on families, and they left an indelible mark on the demography of Augsburg. Total population dwindled to less than half its original size, as noted.[35] The recovery proved painfully slow. Exact census data survive from 1635 and 1645 only, when the city sheltered 16,422 and 19,960 inhabitants respectively.[36] The next census occurred in 1807, when officials counted 28,534 inhabitants after the city's mediatization into the Kingdom of Bavaria.[37] Apart from these, Birth, Marriage and Death Registers provide the only reliable statistics for Augsburg's population in the period between 1501 and 1807.[38] Aggregate lists, composed and published by city officials, they show total births, marriages and deaths in the city. They provide no information regarding average age at marriage, inter-natal periodicity, family size or other demographic measures of family life. That notwithstanding, the registers are useful. They indicate, for example, that Augsburg experienced an excess of deaths over births that was greater than most other cities in the empire and that grew steadily from 2.3 percent in the second half of the seventeenth century to 31.1 percent in the second half of the eighteenth century.[39] Apart from the usual explanations of high infant mortality and low public hygiene, which all cities suffered alike, Augsburg's relatively high proportion of deaths had to do with an unusually low number of marriages and births.[40] Taken together, these factors account for the near stagnation of the population. From 19,960 in 1645, it sank to 15,186 in the 1650s before rising slowly to 17,002 in the 1660s and 19,794 in the 1670s.[41] In the last decade of Matheus's life, it fell again to 19,703.

His own family did not correspond to the Augsburg demographic regime. The Millers demonstrated neither low natality nor high mortality. Matheus made only passing references to his own brothers and sisters.[42] One brother, Michael, joined Matheus and his father in business in 1653. Two others, Thomas and Daniel, regularly received New Year's gifts. Matheus was particularly close to Thomas; he records his death in detail. He also mentioned two sisters, Elisabeth Schorer and Regina Peirlner, as godmothers to several of his own children. Thus, Matheus came from a sizeable family, of whom at least five children survived to adulthood.

The same applied to his own household. He married three times, beginning in 1647. His first wife, Anna Maria Warmberger, bore five children of whom two survived. Within a year of Anna Maria's death, in 1654, Matheus married Helena Schorer. In 20 years of married life, seven children were born. Five survived. After Helena died, in 1674, he quickly married his third and last wife, Johanna Katharina Miller. She bore one child, a daughter, who survived her father. Remarriage followed hard on the heels of death; Matheus never imagined – much less attempted to keep – a household without a housewife. Children belonged to the domestic scene as well. Childbearing began within a year of each marriage, and births followed at a regular pace, a bit less than two years apart. The only exception was the last child, Johanna Katharina, who was born four years after her father's last marriage, late in his life. Inter-natal periodicity suggests that each child was nursed by its mother at home; Matheus's memoir offers no evidence to the contrary. The resort to maternal nursing might explain the relatively low infant mortality in the Miller household; of thirteen children born, four, including one set of twins, died in infancy, one died in childhood, eight survived to adulthood. This was no small matter for Matheus. In his mind, children were both a blessing and a challenge.

Had Augsburg's population grown as the Miller family did, its recovery from crisis might have been much harder. Because a stagnant population placed fewer demands on limited resources, however, the economy regained some of its old vitality in the second half of the seventeenth century. The process was not without setbacks, such as the food shortage of 1693-95 and the siege and occupation by French and Bavarian troops in 1703-04, and the city never fully recovered its former economic stature. Yet, the accomplishments and prosperity were no less real. By 1670, Augsburg had overcome many of the direct economic effects of the mid-century crisis both through a tough-minded fiscal policy that limited interest payments, and through the renewal of trade that increased customs revenues.[43] From 1650 onward Augsburg's economy rested on three forms of enterprise: finance and banking, gold- and silver-smithing, and mill-based calico printing.[44] All of these relied fundamentally on connections to international markets. Though warfare never completely interrupted trade, as soon as the hostilities of the Thirty Years' War ground to a halt Augsburger merchants returned to Europe's major commercial fairs, provided market access to Augsburger artisans, and encouraged exchange activities. As a result, industry and banking flourished from the second half of the seventeenth century to the end of the 1700s.

Matheus participated in the early years of this recovery. Thus, he continued his family's tradition of commercial success and provided for his growing household. As is the case with his father and uncles, no record of Matheus's business survives. Yet, his dealings and their success provided the material basis for his family life, above all, the financial and social prerequisites for his marriages.

He mentions his dealings briefly in his memoir. With the help of his father, he began selling cotton to Augsburg's fustian weavers in 1646-47.[45] No other record of this business survives.

From the later period, only isolated indications exist. Between 1650 and 1651, when his father and uncles were partners, Matheus relied on his own capital and connections – and probably his family's name – to ship goods independently among Italy, Augsburg and the Low Countries.[46] For example, on 13 August 1650, he shipped one cask (*Lägel*) of Nuremberger finished goods (*Krämerei*) to Johann Philip and Nicolaus Fleischbein and Christoff Rotenhofer, merchants in Venice.[47] The firm of Fleischbein and Rotenhofer became one of Matheus's preferred trading partners; their names appear most frequently in the surviving fragments of documents, which list them as recipients of a total of fourteen casks of Nuremberger finished goods and six bales of Belgian wares (*Waren*).[48] But they were not the only ones. On 17 February 1651, Matheus declared one barrel (*Faß*) of tin and one cask of Ulmer linen sent to Christoph Weiss and Franz Christoph Ambtmann, also in Venice.[49] On 5 October 1652, he arranged for Lindauer teamsters to ship one cask of hides to Martin Riedinger in Genoa.[50] At this stage in his career, he appears to have been the quintessential opportunist, dealing in all kinds of wares, doing whatever he could to attract business and establish connections.

Eighteen months later, on 2 April 1654, Matheus reorganized his business into a partnership with his father and his brother.[51] Again, fragmentary evidence reveals only the vaguest contours, but these all hint at expansion. On 1 July 1666, son and father ordered the seizure of property belonging to two Lyonnais merchants, David Couvreur and Vincenz Hertner, in payment of debts totalling 5,000 *Cronen*.[52] They delegated execution of the order to old and trusted associates, Johann Philip and Nicolaus Fleischbein, now of Frankfurt, and Christoff Rotenhofer, still of Nuremberg. Six years later, they gave power of attorney to Philip Lidell of Amsterdam to secure payment of unspecified debts.[53] There is even evidence to suggest that the Millers helped engineer the theft of calico-printing technology from Holland and the establishment of a new and highly successful industry in Augsburg.[54] The expansion of his business apparently brought other changes in its train. Incomplete though the testimony is, it suggests that Matheus had abandoned the peripatetic life so often associated with early modern commerce, traveling constantly from one market or fair to the next, for the stable existence of a manager. After 1654, he executed all surviving transactions through third parties. In his memoir, he implies that factors and junior associates, specifically his brother, Thomas Miller, assumed this burden.[55] For Matheus's business, therefore, growth entailed not only a broader geographic range, but also a broader range of economic functions and a different way of doing business. For Matheus himself, growth entailed a narrower geographic range – it is doubtful that he ever left Augsburg again – and greater financial well-being.

Tax records indicate that Matheus's wealth grew with his business. In 1646–47, when he married and started in business, he paid fl. 15 kr. 10 in property taxes. During the 1660s, his assessment increased to fl. 30 kr. 10. By 1674, his wealth rose even faster as reflected in taxes of fl. 83 kr. 40. A year before his death, in 1684, he paid fl. 115 kr. 10.[56] Thus, his estate grew steadily from a minimum of fl. 3,034 to a maximum of fl. 46,068.

Matheus's rise was self-made to a degree unusual for merchants of seventeenth-century Germany. He never entered the established family firm but created his own business, in which his father and brother were partners. He made little use of his family's capital or connections, relying more on his own skill and experience. Success enabled him to secure the future not only of his family but of a broad circle of dependents and relations. Matheus Miller was more his own man than were many of his contemporaries.

Historical studies too often portray the family as a vector of impersonal forces. The classical, Marxist, base–superstructure dichotomy, according to which economic structure, strategy and destiny determine all else absolutely and solely, captivated early historians of the family. Studies of late medieval and early modern merchant families in Italy and Germany, for example, accept that business and family were structurally and psychologically contiguous, that the imperatives of economic life determined the size of families, the distribution of their resources, the fates of their members, and even the emotional texture of their lives.[57] In other works, such as studies of the rural family, which interpret patriarchy as a form of economic rationality, this assumption continues to hold sway.[58] Whatever lip-service is paid to personality, politics, gender or society, these factors were generally submerged by the over-arching attention to survival.

Cultural studies since the 1960s have rejected material determinism and have sought to revise its interpretive excesses.[59] A desire to decipher symbol, ceremony and meaning, and an occasional propensity to divorce them from experience and its constraints, created a new set of problems for family history. It encouraged what some scholars call the myth of the modern family.[60] According to this theory, the modern family, characterized as nuclear in its isolation from kin and affective in the ties among members, arose as a consequence of industrialization.[61] Though the myth of the modern family assumes a fundamental economic transformation, still it avoids close analysis of family structure or material conditions, the evidence of which argues strongly against it.[62] That notwithstanding, the focus of historical studies has swung from behaviors to values, from structures to mentalities.

Concerned to explore the inner world of early modern families, some historians found a ready tool in literary criticism. Its 'deconstructionist fashion has it that texts are impermanent, independent of the intentions of their authors, and interpreted meaningfully only by readers'.[63] Postmodernist histories of the family, inspired particularly by Michel Foucault, have yielded bold reformulations of the modern family.[64] These new myths describe the emotional landscape of the early modern family in terms of patriarchy and gender instead of privacy and love.[65] Such caricature makes the family a mechanism of impersonal, anonymous oppression, a passive extension of state and economy. Three problems arise from these arguments: the discipline they envision is strictly 'top down'; the families they study are impotent to resist or modify it; historical individuals and groups are without independent agency.[66] The result is no more or less convincing than earlier attempts to cast the family as the fountainhead of psychological or political liberation.

A few recent histories suggest that the analytical pendulum may be swinging toward a more convincing medium, one that accounts reasonably for the lived experience of early modern families as well as the sense they made of it without unduly ignoring or emphasizing either. To say nothing of the variety imposed on relationships by the variety of personalities, 'the existential necessity of a division of labor within the patriarchal system often compelled partnership or, better put, collegiality even against all legal constraints and traditional legitimations, which intended to limit women to a position dependent upon men and to deny them any unique authority'.[67] On the one hand, historians of capitalism have begun to take the Foucauldian concern for discipline as a historical theme and work it back into empirical, organizational and structural accounts of industrialization.[68] On the other hand, innovative studies of patriarchy seek to balance their reliance on prescriptive literature with careful reference to individual experience and perception.[69] Such studies conclude that patriarchy was, in fact, 'vulnerable', that its paradigms of male authority and female subordination did not accord well with experience, that it functioned best where a degree of flexibility obtained.[70] Both of these approaches offer the possibility of a new dialectic between social forces and individual actions.

Matheus was no pawn. His memoir served as a place to meditate on events, to explore their social, political and moral ramifications. He was a business man who refused to dwell on business. Dependent as they were on his business success, his wives and children were not the sacrificial lambs of his ambition. He was an intensely private person, who nevertheless took his place in the public life of the city. Though office and family existed in his mind in clear contradistinction, still the public sphere served to articulate a private, domestic system of ethics. He kept careful count of his friends and associates but tended to draw them from the circle of his extended family. They were not obviously instrumental in any social sense. He was an entirely orthodox

Augsburg Lutheran but no simple-minded schoolboy of the Protestant church or the early modern state. Rather, he came to his own, original terms with those prescribed standards of behavior and accepted systems of value that comprised patriarchy. Matheus presents his family as constantly shifting between the demands of society and the desires of its members, neither a mechanical response toward convention nor an unpredictable impulse toward peculiarity.

Far from overturning general theories, autobiographical accounts offer specific alternatives. They point to the individual agent within social forces. Families cannot be understood apart from their material circumstances. Matheus's memoir permits an examination of the relationship between the two; the economy of the seventeenth century helped to shape but by no means determined the life of the Miller family. Individual personalities, social relations, economic imperatives and cultural constructs played equally influential roles. The memoir exposes its author's worldview, the values and ideals that inspired him. It is a meditation on life; his musings do not inform but derive from concrete events. Matheus implicitly reminds his readers that meaning and experience are interdependent. This turns attention necessarily away from 'anonymous ... discursive practices'.[71] The memoir is a text, but one that can be understood best in the context of Matheus's life and purpose. From his pen flow notions of patriarchy and family that modify prescribed meanings. Without opening to question the validity of scientific inquiry or the utility of aggregate models, whether Marxist or Foucauldian, materialist or cultural, Matheus's memoir demonstrates the agency of the individual in the family and in history.

Though a chronicle of domestic life, Matheus's memoir lacks the rich personal detail of Hermann Weinberg's celebrated memorandum (*Gedenkbuch*); Matheus supplies no 'detailed descriptions of his physiognomy, likes and dislikes, clothing and dwelling, food and drink'.[72] It lacks as well the close conjunction of family and fortune, characteristic of less well known, but more typical, merchants' records (*ricordanze*); Matheus refused to pepper his journal with business accounts and notes.[73] He limited his telling of family life to demographic events – marriages, births, and deaths – with occasional digressions into their moral and social consequences. Yet, each had a broader significance. Birth affirmed the network of social relations of which he and his family were part. Death challenged his notions of Providence and confession. Marriage evoked his understanding of patriarchy. Of these events, marriage exposes most directly the private world of Matheus's family. In 1647 Matheus was 21 years of age and an established merchant. That summer he married Anna Maria Warmberger. The entire transaction merited a brief entry that seems laconic almost to the point of disinterest.[74]

> God the Almighty gave his blessing to it [Matheus's business] so I turned my thoughts again to marriage and sought out the maiden Anna Maria, a Warmberger by birth, whose late father was Johann Warmberger, by his second marriage namely to her still living mother Susanna, a Wild by birth, the widow of the late Elias Shröcken. Their only daughter became my favorite beloved so that nothing would keep me from winning her favor as well as the consent of my and her esteemed parents. All showed themselves willing, from which I perceive God's special blessing. The day of the wedding was set. My representative (*Werber*) was Master Hans Jakob Miller the Elder and the wedding took place on 30 July 1647, everything with the greatest peace and contentment for which the Highest be praised and thanked.

Economic conditions promised a certain material security. Matheus's business flourished; this permitted him to wed. Anna Maria's status assured social stability. Matheus took care to list her parents, all Augsburger citizens and merchants of untarnished reputation. His emotions sought fulfillment through a consensual union. Bride and parents had to agree; no marriage could occur otherwise. Although he mentioned neither church nor state, neither pastor nor magistrate, Matheus included a couple of details that suggest a concern for a legal, enforceable contract. He recorded the date of the ceremony and the name of a witness. His notice contains the essentials; it is a microcosm of the Lutheran ideal of marriage.[75]

Echoing St Paul and St Augustine, churchmen regardless of confession preferred affection to passion as the most stable emotional foundation of marriage. A thirteenth-century canonist, Berthold von Freiburg, named 'too great lust' an 'unchaste evil'.[76] In his well-known 'Little Book of Marriage' (*Ehebüchlein*, 1472), the Bamberger Canon Albrecht von Eyb warned that 'excessive love on the part of married couples is not fundamentally praiseworthy because love brings harm (*Unheil*), distracts humans from great and good thoughts and leads them to endless, depraved things'.[77] Among Lutherans who wrote frequently about marriage, the Mansfelder pastor Cyriacus Spangenberg echoed the common theme when he wrote that 'married people should avoid all heathen, Roman, Florentine, and other forms of lewdness (*Unzucht*) and should stay together (*sich zusammen halten*) in an honorable, orderly manner and also with moderation and not despise one another'.[78] 'Patience and friendship', to paraphrase St Paul, illustrated the proper nature of Christian love between husband and wife.[79] In answer to the question how a husband should demonstrate this love, Spangenberg advised that 'he should care for [his wife] as himself, should provide her sustenance and shelter, food and drink, shoes, clothing, and such necessities, protect her from all outrage and wantonness of evil people, and, above all, provide her with the Word of God and bring her to the knowledge of God and to all things that lead to holiness and salvation'.[80] An orderly community of life, embodied in mutual dependence and cooperation, would result in an emotional kinship and intimacy, most often described as friendship.

Matheus did not necessarily disagree, but his memoir reveals that he also did not explicitly share this pastoral interpretation of an orderly domestic existence. His disinterest deceives. The truth emerges briefly in the reference to his beloved, whose favor had to be won. He married for love.

As such, practical arrangements received no mention. They can be reconstructed, nonetheless. After the death of Anna Maria and before his marriage to Helena Schorer, Matheus named trustees (*Scheinpfleger*) for his two sons, Philip Jakob and Matheus the Younger.[81] This was typical in Augsburg. The children's maternal inheritance had to be secured, and guardians from both sides of the family were named to protect their interests. Chosen were Matheus's father and a relative of the late Anna Maria, Hans Jerg Rauhwolff, of whom more later.

According to the formal contract of settlement (*Abkommenbrief*), Matheus agreed to raise and support his sons until they came of age or married.[82] This included paying for their 'studies, the learning of a language or other honorable business to which they are inclined and suited' and providing a fitting settlement when they married.[83] At that time, Philip Jakob and Matheus the Younger would receive their maternal inheritance, a total of fl. 1,100 in cash and fl. 200 in personal property divided equally between them. Until that time, Matheus would retain usufruct of this property. The agreement specified certain other arrangements. Anna Maria's gold- and silverware passed to her sons. Should the debt owed her by the City of Kempten be collected, each son would receive a 25-percent share that Matheus would hold with the rest of the estate. Finally, Matheus guaranteed the agreement with all of his property and claimed right of survivorship should either son die before him.

Usually, the inheritance of children amounted to a sum equal to the property brought to the marriage by the deceased spouse. Thus, the agreement, dated 10 November 1654, hints at the original marriage contract. Anna Maria brought close to fl. 1,500 in cash and valuables as her dowry (*Heiratsgut*) and trousseau (*Fertigung*). Beyond that, the capital invested in Kempten had a face value of fl. 20,000. Anna Maria originally possessed a half-interest in it, as did her brother Hans Philip Warmberger. In 1648, one year to the day after their marriage, she and Matheus purchased the brother's share of the capital for fl. 1,400 in cash, a sum which reflected the difficulty of collecting debts owed by governments at the close of the Thirty Years' War.[84] The agreement between Matheus and his sons' guardians indicates that it proved uncollectible in fact. That notwithstanding, Anna Maria was a propertied woman. All her wealth would have passed into Matheus's hands at marriage. Moreover, he would have matched it with an equal amount of his own (*Widerlegung*). The value of the settlement established the elite status of Matheus's first marriage.[85] That it and all subsequent unions were listed in the marriage books of the *Kaufleutestube* confirmed his right to mingle in the select world of merchants and patricians.[86] According to the memoir, however, none of this made Anna Maria more attractive. Her property had no great bearing on its purpose.

Matheus's second marriage, to Helena Schorer, received greater notice in the memoir than did his first. Its description remains terse nevertheless, a chronicle of events told plainly but selected carefully. Anna Maria died on 7 June 1654. Six months later, in November, Matheus's thoughts turned again to marriage. During a walk in the country, his brother Michael, his brother's wife, and her brother, Anton Christoff Schorer the Younger, began 'to vex me that I must have a wife again'.[87] With a household, business and family to manage, Matheus needed a spouse. Indeed, his experience in St Gall, as a young commercial agent in the House of Schlumpff, had demonstrated the potentially disastrous consequences of widowerhood for household and business. Although he does not mention it, the impropriety of a young man of his position without a wife might also have compelled him to 'a change of heart' despite the fact that he 'had not yet had such thoughts'. Matheus prevaricated by asserting that 'there was no one who measured up'. But he had someone in mind, as did they. Schorer began to name one potential bride after another, but did not name his own sister. When Matheus challenged him about it, he disingenuously offered Matheus a compliment by deprecating his sister's eligibility. At that point, Anton and Matheus understood well the point 'to which we were both coming'. With these preliminaries completed, events moved swiftly. Matheus discussed the matter with certain unnamed relatives and with representatives of the Schorer family. Once the parties had agreed in principle, it was time for the prospective bride and groom to meet. Matheus met the maiden Helena Schorer 'for the first time' one day in the City Garden, where he gave her a ring as a token of his feelings. She responded by giving him a 'beautiful diamond ring on the Feast of St Matthew', a sign of her consent that also left 'not the least doubt about her beloved parents affections'. After the consent of the couple had been demonstrated, Matheus's father spoke with Helena's father and 'arranged all matters so that the wedding day could be set for 23 November 1654'.

It is a charming encounter described with obvious affection. The knowing negotiation with a man who over the years would become a steadfast friend and associate must have remained a fond memory for Matheus. And the meeting in the garden appears both chaste and romantic, a scene that gives the lie to all who maintain that such sensibilities were improbable before the advent of Enlightened individualism.[88] The memoir leaves no doubt that this marriage, which lasted 20 years, was the central relationship in Matheus's life.

Its description differs from that of his marriage to Anna Maria. Importunity and need rather than opportunity and fancy drove him to remarry. Consensuality, stability and enforceability remain present in Matheus's mind, but other concerns stand out. This marriage clearly united two individuals and two families. These were not mutually exclusive but rather inclusive and reinforcing, as Matheus's description makes clear. A deliberate ceremony that did justice to the intentions of the couple and to the interests of their families emerges from the retelling of a complex negotiation. Matheus and Anton first broached the possibility of a union between their families indirectly and abstractly. This preserved the feelings of all concerned and prevented conflict in the event that the discussion proved fruitless. Once a basis for agreement had been reached, they put the matter before a larger circle of relatives. Though initially uninvolved, perhaps to preserve her reputation, Helena had the final word in the discussion. Once she gave it, the fathers of each family came together to resolve practical matters.

Again, Matheus passes silently over all financial considerations. They found their place, doubtless, in financial records that do not survive. Here, however, he focuses attention on the affection that bound Helena and himself and the 'good will and contentment' of the families. If his marriage to Anna Maria seems to have been the love match of a younger, more impulsive man, as revealed by the terms of endearment he uses and the urgency he ascribes to his wooing, Matheus's partnership with Helena appears no less affectionate but friendlier and sturdier.

Material concerns certainly figured in Matheus's decision to remarry. The demands of a business, family and household inclined him to hear the arguments of friends and family. Yet, those calculations merited only a brief mention in his memoir. Matheus refused to record the extent of his business or the value of his estate. Nor do surviving documents permit a reconstruction of Helena's dowry. It may well have been valuable because the Schorer were well-to-do. Merchants often recorded the receipt of dowries in their diaries or journals.[89] The absence of any discussion of her wealth suggests that it may not have been central to Matheus's decision to marry.

His third and last marriage, to Johanna Catharina Miller, came late in life. At this point, practicalities dictated his thinking. Neither enthusiasm nor warmth mark the entry in his memoir.[90]

> After the death of my second beloved housewife Helena, born Schorer, I soon learned that I could not persist in the state of widowerhood because of my large household. With six children, all unmarried, young, and innocent, three servants, an expensive open house because of the chancery, and many other considerations, it would not seem good to allow matters to continue without a housekeeper.

Matheus confronted a difficult problem alone. He found comfort and guidance not in the advice of friends or relatives but in his memory of Helena. When she knew that she would not survive, she urged him to remarry quickly for the good of their children and household and even suggested a likely bride in the daughter of Baltas Miller.[91] He needed no encouragement from others; the situation seemed clear. Having taken counsel with himself, Matheus took steps on his own.[92] He admitted that 'the usual way [to marriage] should well have been longer' but 'many reasons' moved him to bring the matter to a speedy conclusion. Three months were, indeed, an abbreviated period of mourning though, interestingly, not much shorter than the five months that separated the death of his first wife from the marriage to his second. Resolved to act for the sake of his family and his affairs, as he put it, Matheus approached Baltas Miller the Elder and asked for the hand of his daughter, the maiden Johanna Catharina. After a week's time to consider Matheus's proposal, the father approved the match. The same day, Matheus spoke to Johanna in her father's house and secured her consent to wed. Although Matheus was the head of his family, since his father's death in 1665, he nonetheless placed the matter before his relatives.[93] He mentions the wife of his brother Michael, who was also Helena's sister, and his own sister. That women played a noteworthy role in Matheus's decision, as they did in many others, may have had to do with the importance of the household in Matheus's thinking. With their approval, the day was set. Matheus and Johanna Catharina wed in the house of Baltas Miller, with the permission of the authorities, on 7 May 1674.

Despite a certain constancy of form, Matheus's memoir betrays a change in tone. The romantic ardor of his younger days died with Anna Maria, and the warm affection based on friendship and experience passed with Helena. What remains is cool calculation that might lead him to love but must serve his interests. Too often understood as diametric opposites, interest and emotion are variables in the same equation. Neither is entirely absent; each shapes and influences the other. Anna Maria was Matheus's heart's desire; his business enabled him to pursue her. His own inclination, spurred by his expanding obligations, encouraged him to seek out Helena, the love of his life. At last, the burdens of family, household and business outweighed personal considerations and compelled him to marry Johanna Catharina. As a young man, so he claimed, Matheus acted on his emotions. Older, perhaps wiser, saddled with greater responsibilities, he viewed marriage in a more dispassionate – not to say passionless – way. Interest and emotion vary over the lifecycle; their weights shift with the accumulation of experience. Their meaning in specific instances depends ultimately on the individual's personality and circumstance. Though tendency to calculate, to measure costs and benefits, may be a universal human characteristic, Matheus's consideration of the factors influencing his marriages reflects rather his individuality.

In all three marriages, the process contrasts starkly with the cryptic, perhaps shamefaced, mention of his nuptial adventure in Leutkirch as a young man. At that time, Matheus lacked the means to support a household, the counsel of his family and the approval of his elders.

Successful marital negotiations assume a standard form in the memoir. Matheus resolved to marry. He discussed the matter initially with a member or members of his future bride's family. With their approval, he approached her directly. Once she gave her consent to wed, the fathers forged a specific agreement. Propriety – as distinct from honor, interest or emotion – seems to be the constant element.

In all three marriages, patriarchy showed a different face, each revealing the shifting ground between interest and emotion, between discipline and propriety. Approaching each marriage, Matheus found his authority as householder and as man – his freedom to act – constrained. At no point did marriage simply unite individuals. It joined the fates and fortunes of many. Accordingly, families had to be consulted, formalities had to be observed. As Matheus aged and his household grew, the interplay of interest and emotion became more complex. Yet, at no time was he free to act arbitrarily, neither without marriage nor, presumably, within it. Similar tensions obtained between the disciplinary and behavioral elements of patriarchy. Caught in a web of obligations and considerations, the patriarch was bound to uphold them, even against his own inclinations. He modified that discipline of which he was master. He abrogated that authority which was his to exercise. He submitted himself and his actions to scrutiny and, perhaps, censure. At each turn, he measured his behavior against that other aspect of patriarchy, the ideal conduct of a householder. The result was a resort to apologetics.

Even in the marriage of a young maiden to an older man, even in the context of rational decision-making, other factors needed to be considered. The memoir makes but brief, indirect mention of these: the urgency of the decision; the brief period of mourning; the great difference in age. They come to light in a curious wedding pamphlet.

Occasional verse was a mundane literary genre in early modern Germany. Like published funeral sermons, which often marked the deaths of prominent Germans in the seventeenth century, the *Flowery Wedding Celebration* commemorated an important social moment, the marriage of Matheus and Johanna Catharina Miller.[94] Moreover, it reflected on the moral content of the event and, hence, on the character of the persons involved. In this case, however, its purpose was not homiletic. Rather than elevate the manner of death of one Christian as a model for others, this pamphlet sought to justify the grounds for marriage between two individuals and two families. Matheus's third marriage, this time to a much younger woman so soon after the death of his wife of 20 years, was potentially a cause for scandal. The subject, therefore, was less the character of the parties than the propriety of their union. As such, it takes its place alongside Matheus's memoir as an apologia.

The contents initially obscure the purpose of the pamphlet; it begins with a series of greetings. These take the form of congratulatory poems, written in Latin or German, that belong to the genre of published occasional verse so common in Augsburg in the late seventeenth century.[95] Yet, the identity of the authors hints at the deeper intent of the publication. Most of them had reputations as occasional poets. Narziß Rauner, for example, an instructor at the Collegium St Anna, enjoyed the title of Poet Laureate in Augsburg, a claim that had little meaning in the late seventeenth century but that somehow qualified him to compose, among other things, a mediocre commemoration of the coronation of Emperor Joseph I in 1689.[96] Johannes Crophius, Friderich Keller and Adam Klosterbaur, also members of the faculty of the Collegium St Anna, were occasional poets as well. Like Rauner, Crophius wrote a poem commemorating the coronation of Joseph I.[97] Klosterbauer, an impecunious schoolteacher, wrote a sermon in verse to acknowledge the financial support that he had received from Lutheran merchant Alexius Egger.[98] Having no substantial connection to Matheus, these men might have written their contributions to the *Flowery Wedding Celebration* on commission or in the hopes of remuneration. Their presence in the collection suggests that the work was carefully planned and executed for effect.

Some of the authors appear in the memoir, though their exact relationships to Matheus remain vague. Matheus gave New Year's gifts to Rauner and Keller in the late 1660s and early 1670s.[99] The same applies to Johann Baur and Georg Philip Riß, who were Lutheran pastors, the former at the Church of the Franciscans and the latter at Matheus's own parish of Holy Cross.[100] Johann Ludwig Henisius was a City Physician of Augsburg who futilely attended Matheus's first wife in her final illness in 1654.[101] Few of the poets whose verses praise the marriage of Matheus to Johanna Catharina are among the acquaintances and associates named regularly in Matheus's memoir, the close circle of friends who might, therefore, have been expected to rejoice at the marriage.

Yet, Matheus's family is not unrepresented. Poems ascribed to three of his children by Helena, those still living at home, appear in the pamphlet. Although it is conceivable that the children actually composed these verses, they are so like the others in voice and content as to suggest that the actual authors may have been adults.

All of these poems celebrate the third marriage as a renewal of joy and prosperity after a period of sorrow and need. Again, emotions and interests were simply inseparable in the early modern conceptions of marriage and family. The metaphors and allegories allude uniformly to nature rather than to Scripture. Marriage symbolizes spring, the restoration of fertility after the barren winter of widowerhood.[102] The bride is likened to the rainbow or the sun, signaling gladness after the storms of sorrow.[103] Rauner's contribution displays, perhaps, a readier originality and wit by virtue of a play on the names of the two families. He praises the mill that produces new bounty now that the miller has his mill-wife.[104] Matheus's 'children' seize the themes of happiness and prosperity as well. Sibilla, aged 15, urges her new stepmother to 'live with my father, who will be your husband, in such a way that the sun of happiness shines again over our house'.[105] Twelve-year-old Anna Maria rejoices that 'joy and prosperity will live with us again'.[106] To these sentiments, Anton Christoff, aged 10, offers the benediction: 'Blessed be the hour and prosperous, when your foot first enters our house.'[107] These poems express more than formal felicitation. They echo Matheus's expressed concern for the continued well-being of his business and his household. They reflect his own attitude.

The issue of propriety, raised by the disparity of ages and the brevity of mourning, tacit throughout the pamphlet, is addressed most directly in the principal piece, a 'Confidential Conversation of a Good Friend with the Virgin Bride concerning her Marriage'.[108] The friend, Fililla, finds the bride, Nymfe, busy cleaning house in preparation for her marriage. A groom will take up residence, and Nymfe invites Fililla to guess his identity. Fililla asks for a hint, and Nymfe admits her intended is a widower. Had she never heard of Matheus Miller? Fililla wonders incredulously how a young maiden could come to marry a much older and twice married man, to which Nymfe replies that he asked her father for her hand. 'What should I say? No?'[109] At that point, they launch into a debate over the propriety of the planned marriage. Fililla expresses amazement that Nymfe would consent to keep so large a household, one with so many children. Nymphe responds that a bride should not avoid children but trust to God, who, 'wanting to bestow offspring on the rabbit, provided grass as well'.[110] Moreover, by caring for the children of a widower, who are orphans, she will find favor with God and everyone. Fililla then asks whether it is good to accept a man who shows that he has forgotten his last wife by remarrying quickly after her death. Nymfe points out that the entire city knew how much Matheus loved Helena. He made her his 'household goddess to whom he was as devoted as humanly possible; he cared for and waited on her day and night'.[111] Fililla insists that Matheus should have waited a year to marry were his love proper and correct, but Nymfe answers that a man must do what is necessary for his household. A widower who does not remarry risks ruin because 'men have no experience how to keep house properly'.[112] Finally, Fililla worries that the marriage will cause gossip in the city. Nymfe admits that time gives rise to all kinds of talk but maintains that one cannot attend to rumormongers. But the final, compelling reason for the marriage – the reason that Matheus remarried quickly and chose Johanna Catharina for his third bride – came from Helena herself.[113]

> N. Did she not advise him,
> The former light of his eyes?
> Believe me, she prodded her beloved,
> And not one time alone,
> That he quickly adorn his house
> With a third spouse.
>
> F. And perhaps she herself
> Gave you to him in her place.

The argument, drawn directly from the intimate reflections of the memoir, leaves little doubt that the author, who signed himself 'Secretary of the Mill', was Matheus Miller himself.

The concluding soliloquy of Adelfia reveals more of the private element within this public discussion. Having eavesdropped on their conversation, she now joins Fililla and Nymfe. To the points made in defense of the marriage, she adds nothing: 'Because [Nymfe] knew best how to answer the questions, it is not necessary that I speak here.'[114] One further observation must be made regarding Matheus's seemingly quick resolution to remarry.[115]

> He is uxorious, and cannot live without them,
> For that reason he needed a wife soon.
> Not only to keep his house,
>   which is very large and active,
> And adorn it with an able housewife,
>   who would care for him, his children, and his servants,
> But because to be alone and lonely
> Would be impossible for him.

Adelfia exposes Matheus's innermost feelings about marriage, feelings implied in his remembered conversation with Helena. Family, household and business figure in his calculation. Yet, all calculation admits a certain element of irrationality. After 20 years of marriage, Matheus will not and cannot be without feminine companionship.

It is a strange confession to make, and it is a strange document to publish. It breathes a fear of scandal and a concern for propriety. But what sort of scandal? The pamphlet emphasizes the haste of Matheus's remarriage and the youth of his bride, both of which could set tongues wagging in early modern society.[116] Certainly, the period of mourning was brief. In general, custom and law dictated a year as fitting for a widowed or divorced person to wait.[117] No slave to custom, Matheus never let more than six months pass. As he took pains to note, his circumstances forbade delay. Accordingly, his 'quick' remarriage to Helena Schorer, which involved a period of mourning only a bit longer and more acceptable than in the present case, occasioned no elaborate apology. Why should the union with Johanna Catharina do so? She was some 25 years his junior. In many places so great an age difference between spouses might have provoked rough music.[118] Cities with large merchant communities, however, witnessed such alliances more frequently and may, therefore, have tolerated them more readily, if not more willingly. Certainly, the memoir mentions no public opposition to the match. But these concerns are all tangential. Adelfia, whose name suggests wisdom and prophesy, points to the real issue, Matheus's psychological predisposition. 'He is uxorious and cannot live without her... because to be alone and lonely would be impossible for him.' Ironically, his consciousness of scandal and concern for propriety lead Matheus to make a scandalous confession. His need for female companionship, whether social or sexual, must have offered further grist for the rumor mills. Yet, the pamphlet enlists that very trait, which might have caused tensions between Matheus and his father and uncles, in the author's own defense, a testimonial to the sovereignty of the individual against social hierarchies and social institutions. That he announced his need publicly speaks to the unresolved tensions not only between patriarchy as a form of social discipline and as a code or personal conduct but also and more importantly between prescribed behavior and personal inclination. Like the memoir itself, Matheus's *Flowery Wedding Celebration* speaks a language of vulnerability, responds to an unpublished, unspoken rebuke. In many respects, such insecurity suggests a person who has risen above his station.

Matheus Miller was a parvenu. His wealth and station rose greatly as a result of his business acumen. Were he driven by obvious social ambitions, he might have attempted to promote his ascent through a series of advantageous marriages. In fact, nothing of the sort happened. The Warmberger, Schorer and Miller families were all established members of the *Kaufleuteschaft*, Augsburg's association of merchants. All enjoyed strong connections to the better strata of Augsburg society, the *Gesellschaft der Mehrer* and the patricians of the *Herrenstube*. Yet, none were distinctly superior in either economic or social terms to Matheus himself. At the time of Matheus's first marriage, his father-in-law claimed less wealth than he.[119] His second father-in-law, Anton Christoff Schorer, was better situated, but the difference was one of quantity rather than quality.[120] Baltas Miller, like the others, was an established merchant of comfortable means, but his wealth was less than that of Matheus.[121] More important than considerations of their relative wealth is the fact that Matheus viewed these men as equals and friends. His memoir refers to them affectionately, and a sense of loss marks the records of their deaths. There is none of the anxious deference and inferiority that marks the contact between social unequals.[122] Matheus's marriages and those of his children played no apparent role in an extended strategy of upward social mobility. His father and uncles were established, successful Augsburger merchants, who married within their social stratum. Matheus continued that practice. Throughout his life, the need to justify his behavior derived not from a social insecurity but rather from an ethical unease.

Matheus's conception of the proper foundation for marriage and family – hence, the proper role of a paterfamilias – changed over time in close association with his own age and experience. Somewhat over-simplified, it evolved from love to companionship to sustenance. This transition captures the malleability of patriarchy, the fact that it was understood not in static or monolithic terms but within the dynamic relationship between the individual patriarch and his household.

Like Matheus, Alberti noted the relationship between the age of a patriarch and his understanding of his function. In Book II of *Della Famiglia*, in which Alberti attempts to define the balance of interest and emotion proper to marriage and family, Battista, aged 17, advocates passion in terms that might have appealed to the young Matheus, were it not for the playful irony with which he surrounds it.[123]

> We may consider the love of husband and wife greatest of all. If pleasure generates benevolence, marriage increases an abundance of

all sorts of pleasure and delight: if intimacy increases good will, no one has so close and continued a familiarity with anyone as with his wife; if close bonds and a united will arise through the revelation and communication of your feelings and desires, there is no one to whom you have more opportunity to communicate fully and reveal your mind than to your own wife, your constant companion; if, finally, an honorable alliance leads to friendship, no relationship more entirely commands your reverence than the sacred tie of marriage.

Yet, the 'crimes' of passion, which Battista marshals in support of his argument, testify against these otherwise noble sentiments. His uncle Lionardo, a bachelor of 29 and, therefore, a somewhat paradoxical choice as spokesman for the institution, responds in more practical terms: 'Let him be minded to marry for two purposes: first to perpetuate himself in his children, and second to have a steady and constant companion all his life.'[124] This mature and reflective voice captures Matheus's attitude toward his second marriage, the one based not on passion but rather on friendship. It is that 'honorable and benevolent affection' that Lionardo sets in contrast to 'the evil of love's madness'.[125] A family elder, Giannozzo, speaking on household management in Book III, offers the final perspective. The family is an economic unit in which considerations of wealth and labor take pride of place. Never denying the importance of emotional or social factors, such as friendships, those connections that exist between neighbors and allies and may be strengthened through ties of marriage, he nonetheless insists that rational management holds the key to a family's wealth and status. The householder must 'see that the lady is watching over the children, seeing to the provisions, supervising the household, that the children are at work on their studies, that the others are trying diligently and well to do what their superiors tell them'.[126] Such calculation apparently governed Matheus's last marriage, at least as set forth in his memoir. Age and experience, Alberti seems to suggest and Matheus seems to agree, shift the balance of interest and passion in domestic matters.

To assure that economy and emotion are properly weighted, despite the variety of perspectives imposed by the circumstances of the householder, Alberti advocated the combined counsels of all family members. Lionardo puts the matter directly.[127]

> When, by the urging and counsel of their elders and of the whole
> family, young men have arrived at the point of marriage, their

mothers and other female relatives and friends, who have known the virgins of the neighborhood from earliest childhood and know the way their upbringing has formed them, should select all the well-born and well-brought up girls and present that list to the new groom-to-be. He can then choose the one who suits him best. The elders of the house and all the family shall reject no daughter-in-law unless she is tainted with the breath of scandal or bad reputation. Aside from that, let the man who will have to satisfy her satisfy himself.

In Matheus's experience, the same constraints applied to older as to younger men. In describing each of his three marriages, he carefully records the advice and consent of male and female relatives. The patriarch served the combined interests of the family. His was not arbitrary authority or unlimited power.

Matheus takes a more latitudinarian view of interest and emotion and has a more flexible understanding of patriarchy. Alberti argues for the paramount importance of a single aspect of patriarchy. As head of a large, propertied, urban family with mouths to feed and interests to serve, the patriarch must elevate the material needs of the collectivity over the emotional requirements of any individual, himself included. Without denying the necessity of this perspective – and, indeed, authority and discipline, management and control, had places in his life if not in his memoir – Matheus admitted other perspectives. For Matheus, the principal role of the householder – the proper function of a patriarch, and the proper content of patriarchy – shifted with circumstances from lover to friend to provider, each appropriate in its time. It had to be flexible. And all of these roles include a sense of partnership. On this point, practice diverged from theory. Most prescriptive literature, focused as it is on the division of labor and the articulation of competencies within a household, obscures this fact. Absent in his memoir are clearly defined, explicitly discussed notions of authority and discipline, of management and guidance. Indeed, Matheus leans on and learns from each of his wives. He shares none of Alberti's wry misogyny, his tongue-in-cheek praise of woman, or his doubt about the advisability, even the possibility, of love between husband and wife. His particular approach to marriage probably derived from a fundamental physical and psychological need, to which he makes no direct reference but places in the mouth of Adelphia: that is, the need not to be alone. Matheus particularly valued the companionship of a wife. It shaped his behavior as householder and patriarch.

What, then, is patriarchy? How ought it to be understood? Certainly, applied to society at large, it functioned as a prescriptive system of discipline. It is, as Weber attested, the most important type of domination, a system of inviolable norms, based on personal relations and legitimated by traditional usage, that assumes the authority of husband, father or elder over other members of the household.[128] At its heart, however, lay a code of honor, that is, a set of qualities, the possession of which conferred status on the patriarch.[129] Rather than organize social relations, as early modern writers on the household would have it, to say nothing of modern students of social institutions, patriarchy defined proper comportment for a specific group, in this case, male heads of households.

The actual authority of a householder derived from his exclusive control over domestic resources, his right to dispose of property and labor.[130] Important as it was, however, economic power was not regarded as a sufficient basis for social status in early modern Augsburg. Indeed, as many an impecunious patrician would have insisted, status stood apart from, often in contrast to, the pretensions of wealth. Patriarchy appealed to householders for this reason: it guided their behavior in such a way as to display honor among themselves as a group and acquire status in society as a whole. Honor found expression in a style of life, a standard of behavior expected of every individual householder that, properly observed, granted moral status in contrast to economic status. Matheus wrote his memoir to demonstrate his conformance, to defend his honor, to confirm his status.

Understood in these terms, applied in this manner, patriarchy remains a prescriptive code, a fixed system of values and norms that governed the behavior of householders. Yet, Matheus's own experience argues for a sensitivity to changing circumstance and perspective that seems to contradict the static model. In fact, honor did possess a fixed meaning, apparent to all, that corresponded to the disciplinary dictates of Alberti in one age, Spangenberg and Coler in another. Simply put, certain standards defined patriarchal honor: the piety, industry and knowledge of the householder manifested themselves in a properly governed household.[131] That such social and moral expectations existed in such fixed, recognizable form did not, however, prevent individuals from applying them quite flexibly to their own circumstances. Patriarchy was a practice. Hence, Matheus could recognize and acknowledge the differing emphases of his relationships to his different wives without fearing loss of status because he had internalized a sense of patriarchy. He understood the legitimacy of his actions. He could defend the honorableness of his third marriage, including the admission of personal need. He did not doubt that his arguments would be recognized and credited. Flexibility, the capacity to apply those conduct-guiding rules variously according to circumstance, enabled patriarchy to transcend the traditional locus of authority within the household and gave rise to paternalism in modern public life. In conjunction with economic power, to which it adds an essential, moral quality, patriarchy transcends traditional society, both justifying the status qualification of property and providing a personal component to bureaucratic authority. It is this flexibility in application, revealed by Matheus, that gives patriarchy its particular power.

2
Public Office and the Public Sphere

Matheus Miller was a public figure. Among the important events of his life he listed the offices he held, a public career that extended over the last decade of his life. It began inauspiciously however. In October 1673, Augsburg's highest Lutheran officials, the *Stadtpfleger* and *Burgomaster*, chose him to be captain of a newly formed company of militia.[1] Matheus refused, only to have his refusal denied.

Ironically, this first, unwilling step marked Matheus's rise to public prominence. It also extended his tale into a new sphere. He recalled his offices selectively and purposefully. His memoir records nothing of the great events to which he was party and nothing of the partisan politics to which he was subject. Rather, it concentrates on his moral landscape in order to establish the propriety of his motives, his decisions and his actions. Public office serves as a milestone in his journey to personal stature and as a touchstone to his understanding of good works, public office and the autonomous citizen.

Office-holding in the early modern city-state was multivalent and ambiguous. It served a number of functions and derived from these a variety of meanings. Intended to provide public services, office also established private fortunes. It permitted the amassing of wealth and power for the sake of personal gain as well as the exercise of authority and honor on behalf of the common good. Cicero, to whom early modern theorists and philosophers often turned for a discussion of public service, recognized this potential for perversion. He insisted both on a strict identification with the public interest and on the philosophical temperament of the office-holder as the best guarantors of the *res publica*.[2] Civic humanists took up this theme, praising the virtues of public service while acknowledging the vices of public servants. Leonardo Bruni, in his 'Panegyric to the City of Florence' attributed the city's glory to its magistrates, 'outstanding in virtue and authority'. That virtue notwithstanding, 'care has been taken that these upholders of the law to whom great power has been entrusted do not come to imagine that, instead of the custodianship of the citizens, a tyrannical post has been given to them.' They are 'controlled by a system of checks and balances.'[3] Bruni's contemporary and associate, Poggio Bracciolini, understood the tension between private virtue and public service. In his dialogue 'On Avarice,' he notes that 'when one is in a position of power it is very difficult (and, indeed, beyond the abilities of most rulers) always to follow reason and be moderate.'[4] To the argument that private interest is useful and necessary, the engine that drives all human endeavor and achievement, he responds that a man so driven 'will be a slave to his own private interests and mold himself to them in thought, word, and deed, attentive only to his own affairs, unmindful of public duties.'[5] Private interest was irreconcilable with public service. The humanist tradition cultivated men whose honor inhered in the disinterested exercise of authority and extolled institutions that guarded against the all-too-frequent lapse.

Alberti, too, captured the ambivalence of public life in his *Libri della Famiglia*. Yet, the poles of the argument shifted in his hands. Depending on one's perspective, office could be a thing intrinsically evil or intrinsically good. In Book III, Lionardo puts the question whether honor extends to holding office and to participating in government. Ever an advocate of the narrow interests of the family, the elder Giannozzo denounces public engagement as 'all full of pretense, vanity, and lies'.[6] Such service is a trap: 'Whether you follow popular thought in its errors or rely on the arrogance of a leader, you are disgraced as though the mistake were your own.'[7] It sets family interests at risk: 'You are obliged to ignore your own concerns in order to untangle the folly of other men.'[8] It corrodes common decency and ethics: 'You deserve to be hated if you enjoy the perversion of moral life'.[9] Giannozzo argues without exception for the avoidance of all public affairs in favor of private interests. He aims, as Lionardo rightly concludes, at 'self-sufficiency... to live with no need of anyone else, to be contented with what fortune grants us.'[10] Such sentiments might well reflect the frustrations and aspirations of political exiles, which the Alberti were at the time of this conversation. Yet, admitting the virtues of independence, Lionardo responds with a balanced, circumspect view.[11]

> Like you, I would say that a good citizen loves tranquillity, but not so much his own tranquillity as that of other good men. He rejoices

in his private leisure, but does not care less about that of his fellow citizens than about his own. He desires the unity, calm, peace, and tranquillity of his own house, but much more those of the country and of the republic. These good things, moreover, cannot be preserved if men of wealth or wisdom or nobility among the citizens seek more power than the other citizens, who are also free but less fortunate. Yet neither can these same republics be preserved if all the good men are solely content with their private leisure.

Thus, Lionardo returns to the Ciceronian ideal of public service but with an ironic twist. He identifies the interests of the Alberti family with their service to the republic. That service becomes a means to the accumulation of honor, however. And honor, as Lionardo argues in another context, 'concentrates full attention on whatever concerns us'. As regards the desired ends of all their endeavors, he and Giannozzo agree completely. By attending to our honor, 'we shall grow rich and well praised, admired, and esteemed among men.'[12] In the final analysis, public service serves private interest.

It is reasonable to assume that Matheus knew *De officiis*, implicit in the brief reference to his education, if not in the content of his memoir or in the course of his life. Cicero's writings furnished a staple in the training of young Latin scholars, and Alberti offered a cynical twist to daily discourse. Matheus was probably familiar with this humanist tradition, in all its permutations, even as it is certain that he did not completely share its estimation of office-holding.

Another tradition that would have shaped his views on public service was the Lutheran Reformation. Whereas John Calvin and his colleagues, especially Theodore Beza, wrote extensively on the office of the magistrate, Martin Luther's views are less systematic and more dispersed. He treated the injunctions of St Paul, especially Romans 13, as authoritative on questions of political conduct. These prescribed submission to the secular authorities, the range of whose powers were crucially extended.[13] Luther argued that the church was a congregation of the faithful (*congregatio fidelium*) that lacked any separate jurisdiction to regulate Christian life. All such coercive powers belonged solely to the secular authorities, who were ordained by God and whose enactments, therefore, were to be treated as acts of divine Providence. The responsibilities of godly princes and magistrates were correspondingly clear: foster religion; maintain peace; promote prosperity; prevent evil. If the authorities failed in these tasks or involved their subjects in ungodly behavior, then their subjects were relieved of any responsibility to obey or respect them. Non-obedience did not mean resistance, however. As all authority derived from God, those Christians not burdened with the responsibilities of office had no recourse but to submit. Important as they were, Lutheran political ideas had little direct influence on theories of office-holding. By arguing for expanded jurisdiction, they justified the extension of secular regulation to marriage, education and charity, social concerns that had been the traditional purview of the church. In fact, many states had already begun the process of reducing or invading ecclesiastical prerogatives and jurisdictions well before the Reformation.[14] Lutheran political philosophy might be said to have encouraged the process and, thereby, to have increased practical opportunities for office-holding. Moreover, by insisting on the divine origin of secular authority, Lutheran theorists may have provided office-holders greater legitimacy as well. Those magistrates who believed themselves to be executors and administrators of a divine political will basked in a kind of reflected glory. Accordingly, even as religious reform increased the numbers of offices, so Luther's insistence on the divine origins of secular power added luster to the office-holder's authority and prestige. Compelling as such reasoning may be, however, it remains speculative.

Despite this apparent lack of discussion, Lutheran teachings shaped Matheus's views on office. This applies to the theology of works no less than the teachings on obedience. In *The Freedom of a Christian*, Luther summarized the relationship between faith and works succinctly.[15]

> He [the Christian] ought to think: 'Although I am an unworthy and condemned man, my God has given me in Christ all the riches of righteousness and salvation without any merit on my part, out of pure, free mercy, so that from now on I need nothing except faith which believes that this is true. Why should I not therefore freely, joyfully, with all my heart, and with an eager will do all things which I know are pleasing and acceptable to such a Father who has overwhelmed me with his inestimable riches? I will therefore give myself as a Christ to my neighbor, just as Christ offered himself to me; I will do nothing in this life except what I see is necessary, profitable, and salutary to my neighbor, since through faith I have an abundance of all good things in Christ.'

Through faith alone, the soul achieves salvation. Yet, the body may revolt against faith and hinder salvation. 'Here the works begin; here a man cannot enjoy leisure; here he must indeed take care to discipline his body by fastings, watchings, labors, and other reasonable discipline and to subject it to the Spirit so that it will obey.'[16] Works do not justify the soul but rather purify the body and subjugate it to God. 'Good works do not make a good man, but a good man does good works; evil works do not make a wicked man, but a wicked man does evil works.'[17] Nor do works apply to the individual alone. Citing St Paul's letter to the Philippians, Luther identified what he called a 'rule of life' for Christians, namely that they devote all their works to the welfare of others.[18] Applied to public office, this teaching charged each burgher and magistrate to serve the community.

Matheus may have had this principle in mind when he acceded to magisterial duress and accepted his first commission. Only when the authorities 'set upon me so earnestly, and warned me not to ignore the fact that the entire Lutheran magistracy had weighed this appointment but to accommodate myself to it' did he reluctantly accept the commission.[19] Considering the particular circumstances of his appointment, as he put it, he wished 'to help promote the good work'.[20] What did he mean? For any Lutheran, raised in the expectation of salvation by faith through grace, good works existed as expressions of faith. Though extrinsic to the inner Christian, still they were understood as a result of God's saving mercy. Moreover, they remained fundamental to the outer Christian, to the Christian community. Given the historical context of the passage, good works might have referred obliquely to the common good – the need for a common defense or for Lutheran self-defense – in troubled times. Given the particularly Lutheran context of his commission, Matheus might have intended the phrase to acknowledge his Christian obligation to obey and to serve. Raised in the Lutheran Church, Matheus heard its precepts, witnessed its struggle, and, in his turn, aided its administration.

Yet, though familiar with humanistic and evangelical teachings, both of which cast the magistrate and his office in ideological terms, Matheus gives evidence of neither in the end. Unlike Alberti, he expresses none of the social needs and aspirations of his class. He pursued neither grandeur nor fame. Unlike Cicero, he articulated no abstract notion of civic virtue. He associated public service with mercantile virtues, such as productivity, regularity and honesty, rather than philosophical character. Unlike Luther, he never attributed his actions to Christian selflessness. He revealed no concern over the state of his soul. Matheus accepted public office as a result of compulsion rather than by virtue of talent or temperament.

Why, then, did he bother to write about his offices? Given the purpose of the memoir – Matheus's intention to demonstrate and defend his propriety – public service testified to his personal rectitude and expressed his private morality. For Matheus, these things remained essentially apart from his private affairs and interests. As such, they had no ideological content in the strict sense. Yet, they occupied the last years of his life and a discreet space in the memoir, crowding out other references to his family or himself. Through them he articulates an empirical, rational standard of public service and public ethics.

Modern studies of the ideology of public office and public action begin properly with Max Weber. According to his analysis, bureaucracies come into being in an effort to introduce continuity and stability into charismatic or patriarchal authority.[21] They routinize personal power and introduce rationality, understood as sets of calculable rules exercised without regard for persons.[22] They develop slowly, passing through a variety of historical stages, depending on the economic and political realities of a given society.[23] In the course of routinization, an inner circle of disciples, supporters or counselors initially receive authority, conferred by the ruling figure. This articulation of power ultimately gives rise to the state apparatus.

In Augsburg, the growth of a bureaucracy was less volitional and more confrontational. The bishop of Augsburg ruled the city as late as the thirteenth century.[24] A city privilege (*Stadtrecht*), issued by Emperor Frederick Barbarossa in 1156, granted to burghers the limited exercise of criminal justice while confirming the overall authority of the bishop.[25] No independent council of burghers (*Rat*) existed; the bishop appointed his own councillors and officials. In general, during the early period, bishop and city cooperated with few signs of tension between ruler and ruled.[26] As Augsburg grew in population during the twelfth and thirteenth centuries, however, its burghers became more self-conscious and self-assured. Over time, they successfully petitioned the Holy Roman Emperor for a series of rights and freedoms, all at the expense of the bishop's authority. By 1257, a City Council had come into being independent of the bishop and had begun wresting government and administration from his hands.[27] When the city issued its own code of law (*Stadtbuch*) in 1276, that process was complete. The bishops never forgot their ancient suzerainty, however, and nursed ambitions to restore their authority. In Matheus's day, despite a nominal independence, Augsburg had to tread softly between its imperial overlord and its powerful neighbors, not only the bishop but also the dukes of Bavaria, a fact which shaped both the structure and the function of its government.

Bureaucratization continues as the exercise of authority expands, according to Weber. Here, he emphasized the qualitative enlargement of administration – its increasing pervasiveness and invasiveness – rather than the quantitative increase of its functions.[28] The increasing demand for order and protection occasions the growth of police activities. Rising consumption, based on increased wealth and sophisticated taste, gives rise to an expansion of market regulation. Intensifying contact, in the form of new modes of transportation and communication, encourages bureaucratization in general. All of these forces, which depend upon the existence of a money-based economy and large-scale patterns of exchange, broaden the deployment of administration and quicken its pace.[29] They create the preconditions for bureaucratization; they permit the existence of the bureaucrat.

Expanding authority alone, driven by a quickening economy, does not tell the tale, however. In Augsburg, the constitution of government also determined access to public office and affected the size and scope of administration. Two revolutionary changes had direct consequences for the rise of a modern bureaucracy. The first revolution involved a popular movement.[30] In the Guild Rising of 1368, artisans forced the patrician government to declare a commune (*Zunft*), including all artisans, merchants, and patricians of the city, for the purposes of ensuring the peace and of ruling the city.[31] For elective purposes, the population was divided into seventeen craft and mercantile guilds and one patrician (*Geschlechter*) guild.[32] Each of the seventeen guilds sent representatives to the Small Council, the seat of political power in Augsburg, which in turn selected the most important administrative officers of the city: two *Burgomaster* who served as chief executive officers; four *Baumeister* who exercised supervision over buildings and finance; two *Siegler* who controlled the city seals; a *Stadtschreiber* who directed the chancellory and provided legal counsel; and six *Steuermeister* who administered the system of tax assessment and collection.[33] The second revolution resulted from an imperial decree. Following the military defeat in 1548 of the Schmalkaldic League, of which Augsburg had been a member, Emperor Charles V compelled all free imperial cities to accept new constitutions. In Augsburg the changes amounted to a closing of the government, an undoing of the constitution of 1368.[34] The seat of power remained the Small Council and, within it, the Inner or Secret Council (*Geheimer Rat*). Patricians dominated both until the dissolution of the imperial city and its mediatization into the Kingdom of

Bavaria in 1806.[35] Likewise, access to the upper echelons of the administration was limited to the scions of Augsburg's greatest families. Whereas the rising of 1368 greatly expanded the ability of commoners to enter politics or hold office, the Caroline Constitution all but completely restricted that access. By 1675, Matheus could serve the city-state only as a functionary.

According to Weber, bureaucracies are essentially, if not necessarily, modern organizations that possess characteristics distinct from every other form of administration.[36] They have fixed, jurisdictional areas, ordered by administrative laws or regulations. They are hierarchical, organized in a firm system of super- and subordination. They are managed on the basis of written documents, preserved by staffs of subalterns and secretaries. They require, on the part of officials and staff, thorough training in a field of specialization. They demand the full working capacity of these individuals. They follow general rules that are stable, exhaustive, and discursive. So described, bureaucracies are permanent structures, in which professional staffs carry out predictable functions. These bureaucrats hold office as a vocation.[37] The requirement of specialized training and the demand on working capacity make this inevitable. They receive regular, pecuniary compensation for their services and enjoy a social status and esteem distinct from both the governors and the governed. Bureaucracies create a social group, utterly dependent on money transactions, not found in traditional societies.

Relatively little is known about the bureaucratic structure in Augsburg. Piecemeal evidence suggests, however, both a gradual expansion in the pervasive and invasive qualities of the administration as well as a slow emergence of the rational and hierarchical elements of its structure. The *Zunftverfassung* of 1368 made specific reference to five high administrators, though others must have existed. By the end of the fifteenth century, the number of important offices had grown to some 40, from the *Burgomaster*, the *Baumeister*, the three *Einnehmer*, heads of the city's financial apparatus, and the other more prestigious heads, to the inspectors (*Schaumeister*) of the various guilds, to the marriage and penalty masters (*Hochzeits-* and *Bußmeister*).[38] As had been the case earlier, the majority of these offices were held by members of Augsburg's merchant association, among whom a clear hierarchy was established. By 1548, the number of offices had grown further still, but the extent of that growth is difficult to assess. According to Ingrid Bátori, office (*Amt*) referred to any function for which one or more members of the Small Council were directly responsible.[39] These could range over a broad spectrum, from the Construction Office (*Bauamt*) with its many subdivisions and hundreds of servants and employees to the alarm bell (*Sturmglocke*), to which a councillor held the key. The total number of offices can be tabulated only inexactly, therefore. Bátori insists that approximately 40 high administrative offices remained the rule in Augsburg into the eighteenth century but admits that, depending on the definition, the count could rise as high as 600.[40] And these were now reserved for members of the Small Council, the majority of whom were patricians. There were fewer opportunities for commoners to acquire that honor, of which Lionardo Alberti spoke with such feeling, to say nothing of the income, by which individuals and families 'grow rich and well praised, admired, and esteemed among men'.[41] Perhaps as a result, Matheus took a more detached, objective view of office. His limited ability to 'profit' from service to the city-state possibly encouraged him to emphasize different virtues. Excluded from political power, he engaged in political life.

Modern bureaucracies did not exist in most early modern cities, including Augsburg. Certainly, some of the fundamental elements were present. Complex administrative structures had evolved in the course of the Middle Ages. These had fixed jurisdictional areas and hierarchical patterns of authority. Functionaries, some of whom had specialized training and pursued careers within the nascent bureaucracies, notaries and jurists especially, received their appointments from superior authority and drew salaries for their service. They conducted the business of administration on the basis of written records, to which modern archives bear mute witness. Yet, these specialists and careerists remained a minority. Not vocational bureaucrats but rather 'avocational notables' conducted the routine business of the early modern city-state.[42] Unlike the professionals, supposedly, such amateur, part-time administrators were disinterested in office as such. Government and bureaucracy in Augsburg after 1548 came to be seen by the patricians who controlled them as little more than a means to provide themselves with sinecures.[43] Matheus could have had no hope of a sinecure, however. Nor could he expect advancement. Augsburg's political constitution made such opportunities impossible. He had other interests and ambitions.

Why, then, did he participate? Avocational notables accepted public office and engaged in public action out of a complex of motives. They displayed what Amitai Etzione refers to as an 'active orientation'.[44] They were self-conscious actors who used their access to power to pursue certain goals. Weber argues that all social action, including the public action of office-holding, involved four basic impulses, of which the instrumental (*Zweckrational*) is but one.[45] Ethical (*Wertrational*), emotional (affectual), and habitual (traditional) motives also influenced social actions.

Commentators on public office and public service saw things in simpler terms. Cicero clearly understood the official as a person who sought and exercised power out of ethical or moral conviction. He separated the public actions of the ideal official from all notions of that official's interest.[46] Writing from the perspective of domestic politics, Alberti emphasized the instrumental quality of office-holding. It brought honor, wealth and power to the holder and his family and was to be pursued for that reason alone. The *Libri della Famiglia* offers eloquent testimony to the role of interest in early modern politics.

Modern social and political histories, too, emphasize the interest and instrumentality of office-holding. Like Alberti, some scholars tend to understand public action as a means to some material end. Administrative histories concentrate on such practices as venality, partisanship and patronage. The sale of offices pervaded every aspect of administration to the point that it seemed the immutable essence of public life, especially in early modern France.[47] Offices served their holders as a means to advancement. The price purchased not a career but wealth, prestige and privilege. So understood, officers were ideologically driven; their pursuit of office served their ambition to 'ape their social betters'.[48] Yet, venality resists such easy characterization. Far from testifying only to a lack of social identity, it could actually foster collective awareness and a sense of partisanship.[49] Purchase gave office-holders a common stake in maintaining the market value of their investments. They emerged as an interest-block, often acting in concert to preserve their privileged position in the Old Regime.[50] Office served not only as a means to individual advancement but also as a medium for corporate action.

Even when it was not purchased, office might bolster solidarities. The power of appointing people to governmental or political positions was widely regarded as key to effective central government.[51] Royal patronage attached noble families to the service of the king; secular patronage placed ecclesiastical office in the hands of the state. And the instrumentality, which characterized office-holding, was reciprocal. For the client, offices provided access to prestige, wealth and power; for the patron, offices secured the loyalty of noble or notable individuals and families. Hence, office continues to be understood as the means to some social end, the expression of some material interest, but not the end itself. For privileged amateurs, public service and public action were instrumental but disinterested.

Most recently, Jürgen Habermas has shifted attention from the avocational notable to the autonomous burgher. By so doing, he has redefined public action and recast its motives.[52] He asks under what conditions and at what time private individuals, by which he means householders and property owners, without official duties and, so, detached from state affairs, join in a rational-critical debate of issues bearing on state authority.[53] What has become known as a bourgeois public sphere emerges when such persons form a general public, that is, when they enter into communication against public authority and its regulation.[54] Historically, that process was a long one.[55] Early capitalist commercial economies, beginning at the time of the Italian Renaissance, promoted the creation of territorial and national states, governed by aristocrats. The rise of states involved an expansion of public authority, an extension of its regulation into areas hitherto deemed private, aided by armies and bureaucracies that became sources of impersonal authority, apart from the ruler or the people.[56] Meanwhile, civil society, enriched by the same capitalist commercial activities, detached itself from the state and became more overtly bourgeois.[57] It developed unique forms of sociability that included rational-critical debate in such venues as coffeehouses, newspapers and salons. By the late seventeenth and early eighteenth century, the bourgeois public sphere had crystallized within civil society, institutionalizing state opposition and rational discourse.[58] According to Habermas, specific conditions in Germany retarded this process.[59] German aristocrats failed to associate with bourgeois intellectuals to the same degree as in France or England. German burghers failed to develop the same political self-consciousness and engagement until much later. As a result, discussion of political issues remained essentially private, that is, distinct from office and divorced from the state. The bourgeoisie confronted these issues at home and among themselves. Regardless of time or place, however, the creation of a public sphere separated public action from public service and gave it an abstract quality, not easily associated with material interests. In this regard, it breaks with the assumptions that have guided most recent social and administrative histories.

Habermas casts the bourgeois public sphere as the unique product of capitalism and absolutism, of a bourgeoisie that had grown conscious of its achievement but had been excluded from politics. Rational discourse was carried forward by private persons, interested in public affairs but without direct connection to the state. Thus, the bourgeois public sphere articulated public opinion and, so, mediated the complex relationship between state and society, the point being to supplant arbitrary rule with rational governance.[60] Insofar as its object was to alter the nature and content of policy through debate and criticism, the bourgeois public sphere offered an alternative to office, a new venue for public action.[61] The pursuit of particular advantage yielded to the search for general truth. The detached selflessness of the autonomous burgher supplanted the involved selfishness of the avocational notable.

No bourgeois public sphere, in Habermas's sense of a newly emergent, widespread practice of rational dissent, existed for Matheus. The boundaries were less clearly drawn. Like most prominent burghers, Matheus remained a figure in both worlds. As a state official, he occupied a public sphere that was still given over to private interests. By virtue of his domestic and commercial engagements, he inhabited a private sphere that was open to public scrutiny and regulation. The state had long intervened in family and business affairs; burghers had long engaged in debate critical of it. Authority remained personal and paternal; dissent focused on its morality rather than its rationality. The link between public and private was Matheus's ethical construct, the system of values, forged in his personal experience and his religious sensibility. He created his own space, in which he engaged in rational-critical discourse. Nor was this discourse necessarily private. In all probability, the sentiments and judgments that he recorded in the memoir, he rehearsed in the counting house, the public house, and the marketplace. Indeed, the boundaries between paternal and bureaucratic, between public and private, or between system and lifeworld, are difficult to map.

Confession, intrinsic to but not contiguous with state and society, figures neither in Weberian bureaucracies nor in Habermasian spheres.[62] Yet, the only network of connections and interests to which Matheus makes even oblique reference is that of the Lutheran community. Recall that the Lutheran magistracy commissions him a captain of the militia. Moreover, confession determines most of his public offices, such as his position on the Marriage Court or his administration of various charitable foundations. The eminence of religion in Augsburg provides Matheus with both a venue and a motive to reflect critically on public life.

Matheus conforms to none of the modern models perfectly. Excluded from high public office, he served extensively in the lower administration of the city-state. A part-time amateur – and a reluctant one at that – he displays none of the supposed rapacity of his kind.

Indeed, Matheus occupied an ambiguous position on the margin of Augsburg politics and society, a position from which he could note the many benefits but never fully enjoy them. It was an ideal position from which to be critical without becoming subversive. Matheus holds himself and his colleagues in office to an abstract notion of probity that utterly condemns the least hint of venality, partisanship or patronage. Though his memoir harbors the implicit recognition that office reflects standing, he never explicitly examines the advantages that might accrue to him or to his family through public service. He seems ambivalent toward birthright or connection as criteria for participation in government. He lacks 'agility and adaptability', the capacity to alter means and ends to fit shifting circumstances, that characterize Weber's professional bureaucrat. While Matheus manipulates the system in pursuit of specific ends, his ends are determined by a stable standard of ethics rather than in the momentary pursuit of advantage. This is not to say that he existed above partisanship or that he was not cognizant of his own interests. He belonged to networks of interaction and engaged in the acts of reciprocity that were integral to early modern political and social life. Yet, he does not discuss these things; they seem irrelevant to his public service, if not to his private life.

Matheus was neither inside nor outside the structures of power, a common situation in early modern city-states. Distinctions between the realm of personal relationships and communicative action and that of power and monetary relations, connected in his experience and bridged by his scruples, had no apparent meaning.[63] His recollection of public life accords imperfectly, therefore, with most scholarly categories. He offers a reminder of the complexity of human experience and perception. And he offers us an image of the bourgeoisie, neither ruthlessly exploitative nor critically detached, creating the bureaucracy it wanted through direct participation and rational reflection.

Part-time civic employment was 'the essence of the city-republic'.[64] Communes and republics relied on their citizens to constitute governments and administer states. As the purview and function of the state became broader and more complex, the titular heads of council offices required an army of subalterns and servants, many of whom were highly educated or skilled, to advise their deliberations and execute their policies. The list of their functions goes on and on: the servants and players who sustained and entertained guests in the City Hall; the masters and journeymen who built and maintained the city's structures; the agents and inspectors who regulated and taxed the city's trade; the secretaries and administrators who recorded and managed the city's business; the soldiers and guards who policed and defended the city's territory; the advocates and bailiffs who arbitrated and executed the city's laws; the midwives and teachers who delivered and educated the city's young; the carters and sweepers who cleared and cleaned the city's streets.[65] A growing number of these employees and bureaucrats were trained professionals, but many remained what they had always been, avocational notables, neither materially nor ideologically attached to their bureaucratic functions. Among these, Matheus reluctantly took his place.

His appointment to the militia marks a first step beyond the bounds of household and business. In one sense, Matheus merely took part in an age-old tradition. Since the Middle Ages, Augsburgers had numbered military duties among the fundamental responsibilities of citizenship. Each burgher was required to participate in the watch, to provide his own arms and armor, to maintain the city's fortifications, and, at need, to contribute to its defense.[66] Augsburg relied on its residents to such an extent that it made no use of professionals or mercenaries before the sixteenth century.[67] Even then, when enemies threatened, such as during the imperial siege of 1634–35 or the Franco-Bavarian siege of 1703, Augsburgers still took to the walls in their own defense. Hence, Matheus accepted duties that were integral to his social and political station. In another sense, however, he participated in a vast experiment. In the seventeenth century, private interests gradually separated from public obligations.[68] A series of personal exemptions gradually emerged whereby clergy, officials, patricians and even merchants were exempted from compulsory military service. Population loss and economic ruin made it impractical to require of citizens that they provide their own arms and armor.[69] The growing technical complexity of warfare worked to the same end. Moreover, confessional tensions made an armed citizenry positively dangerous.[70] Between 1632 and 1648, depending on the fortunes of war, the authorities forcibly disarmed either Augsburg's Catholic or its Lutheran community. After 1635, it became customary to store all armaments in the armory rather than to allow individuals to keep them at home. As they lost their weapons, the burghers gradually lost their military functions. Until 1673, the city fielded armed contingents only for representational purposes. Yet, some kind of force was necessary to guard and protect the city in times of crisis. After much deliberation in 1673, probably in response to the political uncertainties that spread across Europe following the French invasion of the United Netherlands in 1672, the city instituted a militia.[71] It was drawn from the entire city rather than according to quarter. Its organization was modern in some respects: ranks were sharply defined; command structures were rigidly hierarchical. Officers were selected according to the principle of parity; a Lutheran captain was assigned Catholic executive officers – a lieutenant and a cadet (*Fähnrich*) – and vice versa. The common soldiery, though heavily Lutheran, represented both confessions.[72] City authorities seized upon a practice that had lain dormant for a generation and revived it in a form that ignored Augsburg's internal structures and stresses. Small wonder, therefore, that Matheus viewed his commission with misgivings.

But his initial refusal is not so easily explained. Matheus displays a personal unwillingness to accede to the demands of the magistrates and writes a surprisingly detailed account of his initial exchange with them. Aware of the trust placed in him, he declines nonetheless.[73] He claims that his education and profession were mercantile rather than military, and he offers his service in any capacity more appropriate to his profession. Despite its apparent self-interest, Matheus's argument that he 'was not capable of occupying this position with the expected success because it was not [his] profession' approximates an argument for merit.[74] Perhaps the limited opportunity for advancement, a common disadvantage for those outside Augsburg's patrician elite, frustrated him as well. Whatever his reason, Matheus trod a well-worn path. Most merchants, who comprised over 90 percent of Augsburg's officer corps, tried to avoid militia service by claiming lack of means, poorness of health, or conflicts of interest.[75] They had good reason. It was a real financial burden without commensurate political or social reward. Commissioning and other ceremonial festivities involved bouts of eating and drinking at the officer's expense.[76] In return, he enjoyed no political weight in Augsburg. Nor did a commission facilitate social mobility. At best, it offered a degree of stature, an acknowledgment of service and achievement. Given these liabilities, the captaincy may have seemed a burden best avoided. Finally, it may be that Matheus simply had no ambition for public office of any sort. His interests, as reflected in his memoir, were narrower, less cosmopolitan, than those of Lionardo Alberti. The concerns of family and business took him into the community at large, but that community would never occupy the center of his life. Wealth and power would come from other engagements. He understood himself as a householder and a merchant; these occupations left room for little else.

Political office often conflicted with commercial employments. The *Allegory of Commerce*, a complex woodcut, printed in Augsburg in 1585, illustrates contemporary mercantile life.[77] Apart from certain allegorical facets – references to the characteristics of a successful merchant, the circumstances of commercial enterprise, and the imponderables of fickle fate – it displays the daily activities of a trading company. Accountants, cashiers, clerks and couriers tend the daily paperwork. Colporteurs and teamsters handle goods of all sorts. At the center of all this activity, the merchant consults the firm's master journals. The woodcut refers to the merchant's integrity and duty, his languages and experience, and his discretion and versatility, all useful administrative and political skills. It shows him as a hub around which these activities turn, lending dignity to their enterprise, setting procedures that govern their actions, and accounting for their results. Nonetheless, the *Allegory of Commerce* makes no mention, direct or otherwise, of the merchant's political obligations. Enforced political engagement compromised his many tasks in the counting house and his frequent visits to foreign marketplaces, all of which required his full time and energy. Frequent appeals for release from service by Augsburg's merchants reflected the irreconcilability of business and politics. Public service interfered with mercantile life.

For the time being, however, the city's highest Lutheran councillors and officials would hear no excuses. The city-state required the service of its citizens. They warned Matheus not to resist a legal appointment (*ordentlicher beruf*) but rather to trust in God, who would help him to do his duty properly. By appealing to their combined opinion and mature consideration, that is, to their moral authority, they required him to set aside not only his doubts but also his interests and ambitions, a thing he did reluctantly. Here, too, he suffered the same fate as his brother officers. The *Stadtpfleger* controlled all commissions and promotions. Service was not voluntary; only the very wealthy managed to buy exemptions.[78] Faced with these constraints, Matheus's sense of responsibility overcame his apprehension and bound him till the end of his life.[79]

Other appointments followed immediately. The memoir contains a chronological but incomplete listing. With few exceptions, Matheus offers no details. Some fleeting sense of his public service must be sought elsewhere.

Much of that service was devoted to the Lutheran community of Augsburg. As such, the Reformation shaped its character by promoting secular control of ecclesiastical organizations and extending government purview to church jurisdiction.[80] The Discipline Ordinance of 1537 cut

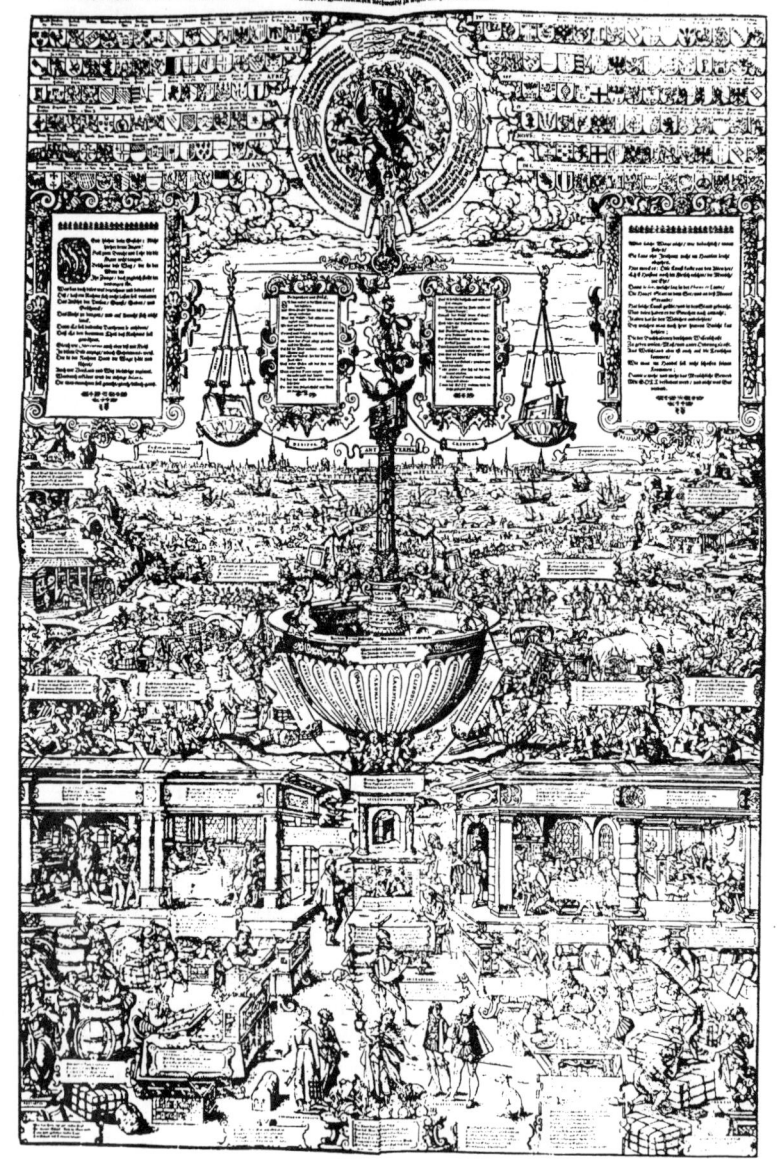

Figure 2.1 Allegory of Commerce.

institutional ties to the Catholic Church. Catholic observance ceased; Catholic foundations closed; Catholic clergy emigrated. Beginning in the sixteenth century, the 'politics of sin' had placed new powers in the hands of the City Council and had expanded the city's bureaucracy.[81] The City Council reserved to itself the appointment of Protestant clergy and custodians and new organizations enforced Augsburg's religious and moral regime.[82] This was particularly apparent in the control of morals and the provision of charity. Matheus played an active role in both.

In 1675 the Lutheran *Stadtpfleger* and members of the Secret Council appointed him to replace Marx Hübner as Associate (*Beisitzer*) to the Marriage Court (*Ehegericht*).[83] Augsburg had established its Marriage Court upon the specific recommendation of Martin Bucer, who insisted on the necessity of a civil tribunal to remedy all irregularity and immorality in the holy estate of matrimony.[84] Beginning on 13 September 1537, eight judges, all of whom were members of the City Court and, therefore, the Secret Council, met on Monday and Wednesday mornings to hear marital disputes, lodged by plaintiffs before the court.[85] A court secretary recorded the proceedings, and four bailiffs (*Waibel*) served as advocates. By December 1537, the City Council decreed the obligatory presence of one of the city's legal counselors to advise the judges in complex cases.[86] In this form, the Marriage Court met regularly until 1548, when the Caroline Constitution dissolved it and transferred its jurisdiction to the Official's Court of the Diocese of Augsburg. Not until 1632, with the city in the hands of a Swedish garrison, was the Marriage Court restored as part of the magistrates' disciplinary regime. Matheus's specific duties on the reconstituted court are unspecified. His memoir offers no explanation, and no court records survive from his tenure. Neither the court constitution (*Ehegerichtsordnung*) nor the Discipline Ordinance (*Zuchtordnung*) refer specifically to the office of *Beisitzer*. In general parlance, the term indicates a representative or representatives of the community charged with general administrative functions.[87] This suggests that Matheus may have been involved in the court's management, that is, in such matters as the regular payment of fees and salaries and the scheduling of hearings and inquiries. He may also have been a non-voting member of the tribunal, one who attended and observed its cases. Certainly, he took no active part in legal or disciplinary issues.

Matheus was far more actively involved in charitable offices. These were also confessional in nature. Unlike the Marital Court, however, Augsburg's public charity drew no direct inspiration from the introduction of Protestantism. 'Its [the alms ordinance] original impetus was civic rather than evangelical.'[88] In part, the City Council responded to increased vagrancy, poverty and begging in the fifteenth and sixteenth centuries. In part, they attempted to bring order to the welter of private and ecclesiastical charities that had emerged over time.[89] And, of course, they sought simply to expand their authority into all areas of public life.

The lists of Augsburg officials record a Matheus Miller as Bursar (*Austeiler*) of Alms from 1659 to 1661.[90] The Alms Office (*Almosenamt*), founded in 1522, gathered most of the non-ecclesiastical, social foundations of medieval Augsburg under its supervision.[91] It divided the city into thirds and assigned to each district two Alms Lords (*Almosenherren*).[92] Originally, these offices were filled by members of the Small Council, as was the case with all other, important administrative posts. By Matheus's time, an alms lord and a bursar, drawn from the ranks of the merchant corporation (*Kaufleuteschaft*), policed each district. Assisted by a number of servants (*Almosenknechte*), they visited and examined the poor at home, collected and distributed such alms as the law allowed, and reported and accounted to the City Council. Matheus's memoir makes no mention of this office. He would have been quite young, just 35 years of age, to occupy so important a position. The list may refer to another person of the same name; Augsburg contained no less than six Matheus Millers. At least one, a notary and City Secretary, has been occasionally confused with Matheus Miller the merchant. That said, the bursar and the merchant may have been one and the same. The joined functions of treasurer and distributor required the skills of a successful and conscientious merchant. Moreover, the office of bursar was held by many associates and friends of Matheus, among others his father in 1633 and his future brother-in-law, Anton Christoph Schorer, in 1659. Whether Matheus served the Alms Office remains unclear.

Such doubt raises, once again, the question of Matheus's reticence. If he served two years as a high official, why did he not mention it in his memoir? Why does he wait to record the series of lesser appointments that began in 1673? The period between 1673 and 1675, noteworthy for Matheus's active engagement in public affairs, coincides with great events in his private life. His family's fortunes were approaching their zenith. Between 1667 and 1674, his tax liability nearly tripled, rising from fl. 30 kr. 10 to fl. 83 kr. 40, indicating an increase in wealth from as little as fl. 6,000 to as much fl. 33,200.[93] Matheus's business acumen had born substantial fruit. His family also experienced a series of dramatic changes. His mother, Sibilla Miller, born Hopfer, died on 23 February 1673. His second wife, Helena Miller, born Schorer, died a year later, on 31 January 1674. Two days afterward he took up his commission in the militia. On 14 February 1674, he purchased for his family's use the Schorer crypt, located in the cloister of the Lutheran Church of St Anna, in which he buried Helena.[94] He settled his late wife's estate on 3 April 1674. Confronted with a business and family in need of substantial attention, he married Johanna Katharina Miller on 7 May 1674, an apparently controversial event that prompted the anonymous publication of Matheus's *Flowery Wedding Celebration*. Later that year, on 5 November 1674, his son Philip Jakob married Anna Maria Mehrer, daughter of the late Hieronymus Mehrer, the head of a prominent family of Lutheran merchants.[95] These negotiations brought Matheus into renewed contact with Augsburg's Lutheran elite; the patricians, Otto Lauginger and David von Stetten, were Anna Maria's guardians (*Beistand*). All of these events – the official, the commercial and the domestic – brought Matheus into the public eye. His growing success and stature, tinged as they were by the hint of scandal, may have inspired him to continue the memoir. He would have returned to it both as a vindication of his struggles and as a testimonial to his triumph. His repeated encounters with death may have reminded him of the transience of human life. As the older generation passed away, a generation familiar with his tale, Matheus would have turned to his children and grandchildren as the bearers of memory. They were the ones who needed to recite his litany of offices, to hear his experiences, and to learn his ethic.

Matheus never makes explicit his grounds for including certain events and excluding others. Certainly, he recorded what he happened to remember and what he thought to be important. There can be no doubt, therefore, that he held charity in high regard. Matheus served as Council-appointed trustee for several private, charitable foundations. In Augsburg, individuals and families of every status, from middling artisans and shopkeepers to elite merchants and patricians, created private charities that in sheer numbers may be unique in the history of late medieval and early modern poor relief.[96] Many of these, named for the person or family who founded them, offered food to beggars, dowries to maidens, apprenticeships to youths and stipends to scholars. Others offered shelter, furnishing a deserving recipient with residence (*Seelgeräte* and *Pfründe*) in a specified establishment. Altogether more ambitious were those that met the physical and spiritual needs of certain elderly or infirm persons, by founding a private, secular community (*Seelhaus*) similar to a monastery. Before 1500, Augsburg claimed no less than seven of these, housing at least 70 residents, to say nothing of the hundreds of smaller, private charities. And the numbers rose as the centuries progressed.

Beginning as early as 1659 and continuing until his death in 1685, Matheus served as administrator (*Verwalter*) of the Anna Raiser Foundation (*Stiftung*).[97] It has an interesting history, in many ways emblematic of the Reformation in Augsburg.[98] Anna Raiser was a conventual in the Dominican Convent of St Margaretha in Augsburg. During the early years of the Reformation, she abandoned the convent to live in a communal house with two of her sisters from St Margaretha. The City Council supported her with an annual pension of fl. 100. She converted to Lutheranism and devoted herself to helping the needy. In a will, created in 1563, she established a Foundation that would provide poor Lutheran girls with dowries of fl. 8, 10 or 12, depending on the annual proceeds from the investment of her property. When she died in 1576, that property proved extensive; an inventory valued it at fl. 5,955 of which fl. 2,467 went to her Foundation. In 1641, the Catholic-dominated City Council ordered the Anna Raiser Foundation to support Catholic as well as Lutheran girls. To ensure compliance, it appointed a Catholic and a Lutheran trustee, the latter of whom was Michael Miller, Matheus's father.

Given the significance Matheus attached to charity, as well as his family's connection to this Foundation, it is odd that his appointment to the Anna Raiser Foundation received no mention in his memoir. Foundation documents, however, indicate that Matheus routinely oversaw the provision of dowries to needy Lutheran and Catholic girls. In 1672, for example, the Foundation paid fl. 20 in dowries to an unspecified number of honorable poor (*haußarmen Leute*) as well as another fl. 20 to the trustees as a *Deputat*.[99] As administrator, he rendered annual accounts to the Small Council. He also defended the financial interests of the Foundation. When, in 1659, the heirs of Adam Hartman refused to repay a loan of fl. 300 plus interest of fl. 15, extended to them by the Anna Raiser Foundation, Matheus sent them a written warning that further delay would result in the seizure of their property.[100] His various tasks recall the merchant in his counting house.

The Reformation encouraged an increase in charitable donations that transformed not only the quantity but also the quality of giving. Private charities, such as the Anna Raiser Foundation, bore the marks of confessional tension. During the sixteenth century, well-to-do Augsburgers contributed fl. 303,457 in 56 separate donations to various foundations and organizations.[101] More than half were confessionally specific: 14 donations were limited to needy Lutherans; 15 donations were specifically dedicated to Catholics. And the proportion rose with the level of antagonism. From 1555 to 1586, from the Religious Peace to the Calendar Conflict, 61 percent of all charity was specifically reserved for the benefit of a single confession. Between 1584 and 1650, 91 percent of all charity was confession-specific, a consequence of the religious tensions further strained by the Calendar Conflict and the Thirty Years' War.[102] Only after the cessation of open hostilities in the peace of exhaustion did confession become a somewhat less urgent consideration. Between 1651 and 1699, 55 percent of all charity specified confession.

Matheus participated in what might be called the politics of charity. On behalf of the Anna Raiser Foundation, he administered funds that, despite their Lutheran origins, succored the poor of both confessions. In 1675, he became an administrator (*Administratoris*) of the Johann Georg Österreich Foundation, which he served until his death a decade later.[103] Here, charity was more narrowly understood. The scion of one of Augsburg's most ancient patrician families, Johann Georg Österreich, devoted 75 percent of his estate to the creation of an aggressively Lutheran foundation in 1656.[104] Though the uses of its charity were to be flexible, in accordance with the availability of funds and the needs of the times, in one matter it was unyielding: only needy Lutherans could enjoy its support. Should the Augsburg Confession be suppressed, as had been attempted in 1629, or should the endowment come into Catholic hands, as had befallen the Anna Raiser Foundation, the administrators were instructed to transfer the Foundation to another, securely Lutheran, location.

It never came to that extreme during Matheus's tenure. Rather, under his guidance, the Foundation regularly provided stipends for the sons of Augsburg's Lutheran families to study theology. One of these, Matthias Friderich Beck, sent Matheus a personal letter of congratulation on his appointment to the Foundation. Johann Paulus Mees pursued his studies at Leipzig with the aid of an Österreich stipend.[105] Also among the beneficiaries were Johann Marcus Goebelin, who received fl. 23 in 1677 to study at Tübingen and the younger Jeremias Peer, also at Tübingen, who received fl. 10 in 1678.[106] Nor were students the only persons to receive assistance. In 1678, Anna Sabina Garreis, born Österreich, a needy widow living in Nuremberg, received fl. 10 from the Foundation.[107] Like the Anna Raiser Foundation, Johann Georg Österreich's charity was enmeshed in local and regional capital markets.[108] In 1675 and 1676, Johann Wankmüller and Hans Conrad Rehm, both of Ulm, acting for Georg Heinrich von und zu Wertenstein und Dallmaßingen, paid the Foundation fl. 100 in overdue interest on a capital of fl. 400.[109] In 1678 and 1679, the Foundation paid interest on a capital of fl. 1,000 invested by the Zobel family, one of the city's premier merchant dynasties.[110] In the event of nonpayment of debt, the administrators of charitable foundations proceeded much as heads of commercial firms. Matheus empowered foreign merchants to seize the goods of debtors in default to his business. In 1678, acting on behalf of the Österreich Foundation, he authorized the firm of Nicolas Wöllerein's Heirs to arrange the arrest of persons and goods of certain *debitores* during the Corpus Christi Fair at Bolzano in Tirol.[111] Matheus even appraised works of art on behalf of the Foundation.[112] Clearly, the worldly wisdom and multiple talents of a businessman stood the Foundation and the city-state in good stead. Despite his varied engagements on behalf of the needy, his memoir bears nothing more than a terse remark: 'Year 1675 the 19th December I was asked by Dr. Wolfgang Sulzer and Heinrich Langenmantel to join them as an administrator of the Johann Georg Österreich Foundation in place of the deceased Otto Lauginger, which I accepted.'[113] Though the mere fact of his administration suited his purpose in writing, and though such service was memorable, Matheus seems to have found such matters unremarkable.

His final record of public office furnishes a different aspect. In 1676, Matheus accepted election as custodian of the Lutheran Holy Cross Church.[114] Custodian (*Zechpfleger*) was an important lay assignment of all in Augsburg's Lutheran community. And Holy Cross was a particularly important parish. Yet, neither of these facts accounts for Matheus's detailed discussion of his particular experience, the most lengthy and penetrating of the memoir. At Holy Cross he was plunged directly into scandal that provided an opportunity for reflection. The custodianship proved an ideal stage for the articulation of his particular notion of public morality and its relationship with private utility.

Understood in spiritual terms, as congregations of the faithful, churches were material communities nonetheless. They depended on the generosity of their members for their existence. *Zeche* refers to property and money, donated for such pious purposes as providing charity, supporting education, founding altars or funding observances. This capital required supervision to assure its proper use. The earliest documentation of laymen providing such supervision in Augsburg comes from the parish of St Ulrich in the year 1284.[115] Custodianships (*Zechpflegschaften*) were soon established in most of the city's ecclesiastical foundations, especially cloisters and hospitals, as well as in all of its parishes. The responsibilities of this office gradually extended beyond the simple administration of property. Because most of the parish churches of Augsburg were associated with a monastery, cloister, or collegiate church, parish worship occurred in conjunction with a special community altar (*Leutpriesteraltar*). The custodians were able to bring these altars, and the payment of the priests who served them, under their control. The same applied to other church functions that immediately affected the parish, such as schools, cemeteries and buildings. As the duties of custodian expanded beyond financial matters to include legal and political issues, the Council established its oversight of them and, so, gradually drew them into its jurisdiction.[116] The custodians provided the means by which the City won a degree of control over all ecclesiastical foundations within its walls and the burgher gained influence over churches in their neighborhoods.

Like the Anna Raiser Foundation, the Holy Cross Church captured the currents of reform in Augsburg. It was founded in the mid-twelfth century as a priory of Augustinian canons. Its Chapel of St Ottmar served as a parish church from 1445; the City Council granted Protestants access to it as early as 1525. Rather than tolerate the flowing tide of Reformation and the Council's claims to spiritual as well as political supremacy, the canons went into exile in 1537. The city took charge of the monastic property, but the Protestants apparently forsook the Romanesque church. They continued to use the smaller chapel, which was first expanded to accommodate the congregation through the addition of a wooden shed in 1549 and then enclosed with wall and roof in 1560–62.[117] In the wake of the Edict of Restitution, the Prelate of the restored Augustinian community had the Lutheran Holy Cross Church demolished. During the Swedish occupation of 1634, Gustavus Adolphus ordered the priory to indemnify the Lutheran parish through a payment of fl. 2,500 toward the construction of a new church. The rebuilding commenced in 1652, after the Treaty of Westphalia, and became a political event that attracted the attention and support of princes and commoners across southern Germany. Though not the most important of Augsburg's Lutheran churches, a dignity reserved to the Anna Church in the prosperous *Oberstadt* district, Holy Cross embodied Lutheran endurance and resistance. Its custodians enjoyed a certain importance as well.

Matheus was doubtless aware of the representative stature of his parish, but he made no particular mention of it. The rebuilding, to which he probably contributed, had been completed some 20 years earlier. Holy Cross's heroic age, and that of the Lutheran community generally, had passed. Matheus concerned himself less with the transcendent aspects of his church and his office than with the human ones. Parish and custodianship were beset by scandal, which he identified with fellow custodian Jerg Mair – Hans Georg Mair according to church accounts.[118] He also named a predecessor, Jerg's brother Hans Christoph Mair.[119] The two had, according to the memoir, very different approaches to the duties of their office, which eventually brought them into conflict with Matheus.

The contention may have been more than official; the Mairs and the Millers may have been economic and social competitors. Both families numbered among their members powerful merchants who strove for prestige within Augsburg's Lutheran community. In 1675, when he shared the custodianship of Holy Cross with Matheus, Jerg was likely one of Augsburg's wealthiest burghers and a member of one of its great families.[120] He rendered a tax of fl. 147 kr. 30 in 1674. Hans Christoph was wealthier still, paying a tax of fl. 172. By comparison, Matheus was still a man on the make; he paid a tax of fl. 84.[121] By 1681, however, this amount would rise to fl. 115. These differences in position and trajectory may explain in part their differences in office.

Matheus had earlier enjoyed extensive contact, of a much friendlier, more accommodative sort, with the Mairs. They were closely connected to the family of his first wife, Anna Maria, born Warmberger. Matheus's first mother-in-law, Susanna Warmberger, born Wild, had served as godmother to the children of Christoph Jörg Mair, one of whom was Christoph Jörg the Younger.[122] When she died, an inheritance dispute, of which more later, arose between Matheus and Hans Jerg Rauhwolff, the husband of the deceased's sister.[123] Christoph Jörg the Younger, who established his family's fortune, figured prominently in Matheus's efforts to defend his interests. As it happened, Rauhwolff's wife Sara, the aunt of Matheus's first wife, was also the godmother of his sons, Philip Jakob and Matheus the Younger. When their mother died in 1654, Matheus had named Rauhwolff a trustee (*Scheinpfleger*) of the sons' maternal inheritance because he represented deceased's family. This was typical in Augsburg after the death of a spouse and before the remarriage of the survivor; trustees were named to secure the inheritances and protect the interests of the children. The dispute with Rauhwolff created such tensions within the family, however, that Matheus decided to replace him. In Rauhwolff's stead, he appointed Hans Christoph Mair, the son of Christoph Jörg the Younger and his future adversary at Holy Cross.

Anna Maria's death may have attenuated Matheus's contact with the Mair family. Moreover, the appointment may have caused conflict with them, specifically with Hans Christoph. The maternal inheritance of Philip Jakob and Matheus the Younger was substantial and its terms complex.[124] Involving capital worth at least fl. 21,300, it contained arrangements for the settlement of the estate and detailed the rights and responsibilities of all parties. As the representative of the heirs' interests, the trustee occupied a position of power within the family, where he might mediate economic and filial relations between Matheus and his sons. As father, Matheus retained usufruct of their inheritance until they came of age. He bore the responsibility of educating them and arranging suitable marriages for them. Though he mentions no specific disagreement with Hans Christoph over these or other provisions, the potential for interference and conflict was very real nonetheless. While Matheus's appointment of Mair signaled his esteem for the man and his acknowledgment of the family's stature, it may have contributed to their eventual falling-out.

The causes of the rupture remain unclear, but relations between the Millers and the Mairs became less cordial and cooperative. In describing his experiences as custodian, which began in November 1675, Matheus complained that Jerg 'had arranged those matters of church business that were to be arranged and let me know little'.[125] Custodians served staggered, two-year terms. When Matheus was first elected, Jerg was beginning his second year in office. As the official in the senior position (*eltere Stelle*), he kept the church accounts, as Matheus would the following year. Matheus seems to have found aspects of this working relationship objectionable. According to his memoir, Jerg frequently acted without consulting him. Matheus objected 'pro memoria' to such practices. As events make clear, Matheus expected to share official responsibility and authority. Because custodians served in tandem, this seemed the proper procedure. He also voices a more personal grievance: 'It did not please me that one possessed authority alone.'[126] Though he had once been beholden to, even dependent upon, the Mairs, conditions had changed. He had risen high in the world and would rise higher still. He disliked being treated as a subordinate.

Among the duties of custodian was the management of donations to the parish. The 13 collection boxes in Holy Cross had to be emptied and the moneys counted on a regular basis, for which task the keys were divided among the custodians. Both men were expected to be present for the purposes of security and accuracy. On Christmas Eve in

1675, Jerg and Matheus emptied the collection box but left the proceeds uncounted because the time was too short.[127] They decided that Jerg would keep the funds in a sealed bag until the opportunity for an accounting arose. Matheus left his signet ring as a token of his agreement. Before the money could be counted, however, Jerg and the sacristan (*Meßner*) removed a certain sum from the bag. Though Matheus received a receipt accounting for the total taken and believed that it was accurate (*fideliter*), still he objected that 'it did not occur with my knowledge...it is not right because it is not fitting for him alone but rather should occur in common because of the consequences'.[128] Again, Matheus's criticism has two distinct aspects that were inseparable in his thinking. First, Jerg's action offended his sense of his own dignity. He should have been told; he should have been present. Second, Jerg's action violated his sense of proper procedures. Matheus knew 'what evil things' could creep into church affairs were routines not observed.

Collection boxes were emptied four times annually as a rule: on the eves of Christmas, Easter, Pentecost and the Peace Festival (*Friedensfest*).[129] A quick review of church accounts reveals that collections during Jerg's term of office were substantially lower than during the terms preceding or following, including Matheus's. In 1676, Jerg recorded total donations worth fl. 477 kr. 2; in 1677, Matheus reported fl. 668 kr. 25.[130] Annual discrepancies may be attributable to nothing more than chance variation in the charitable imperative. They may have awakened Matheus's suspicions, however, in much the same way that irregular procedures provoked his disapproval.

In addition to donations from the congregation, returns from a variety of investments helped to cover the expenses of the Holy Cross Church. Both Jerg and Matheus listed four investments in fixed capital, primarily houses, worth fl. 890, that provided an annual income of fl. 44 kr. 30, and four loans in the form of circulating capital, worth fl. 2,300, that yielded an annual return of fl. 115.[131] Three defaulted loans generated payments of fl. 147 kr. 30 in 1676 and fl. 171 in 1677. One of these, a debt of fl. 150 plus interest, owed by Melchior Stain, was discharged by Matheus himself. Was Stain Matheus's friend or client? Did the payment indicate some official responsibility for the debt? Neither account nor memoir offers any explanation. Nonetheless, the simple fact suggests the potentially complex interrelationship between private connections and public responsibilities.

Indeed, the lines of demarcation between private and public were rarely clear. On 4 March 1676, Jerg recorded an expenditure of fl. 171

kr. 51, nearly 10 percent of the church's annual resources.[132] The sum had paid for the purchase of 100 *Reichstaler*, presented in a satin bag with silver buttons as a wedding gift for the newly remarried pastor Georg Philip Riß.[133] Matheus had covered the expense out of his own pocket and received reimbursement from church funds. Such expenditures were expected of the custodians, especially the junior officials, as the records make clear. In 1677, Hans Jakob Baur would extend fl. 34 for repairs to the stucco on the interior of the choir, for which he was duly repaid. Building repairs and wedding gifts both constituted legitimate uses of church funds, a fact that confounds in itself the modern distinction between public and private. Though probably intended as a gift on behalf of the entire congregation, 100 silver coins in a satin bag remains a princely gift and an unusual use of the money.

Matheus voiced no explicit objection to the wedding gift for Pastor Riß. The same cannot be said about other expenditures. Irregularities could lead to malfeasance. 'What evil things could arise from such practices was made plain to me when matters became manifest of which I had no knowledge but recognized that a misuse had crept in.'[134] Earlier in the decade, during the custodianship of Hans Christoph Mair and Priester Goldschmit, each had taken fl. 12 from uncounted church funds to provide a celebration for the congregation (*der gemein bei der wahl ein Trunkh zu geben*), probably limited to the male members.[135] Because these festivities occurred when the senior custodian left office, it remained for the successor to balance the account. As a courtesy to his predecessor, the new senior custodian described it as an expense incurred to provide a decoration for the church (*hinterließ einer Jedesmals dem andern zue gebrauch einer Zierot der Kürchen*). Although it had become common usage ever since, Matheus found no evidence that it had occurred at any previous time. He objected not to the use of the money but specifically to the fact that the funds were never formally accounted as money received or paid. 'What one receives ought to be properly written down, and what one properly spends properly should be noted as an expenditure and not otherwise.'[136] What made the gift to Pastor Riß proper and the festivity for the custodian otherwise was the simple keeping of an account. In this case, however, Matheus seems to be insisting on more than an exact list of monetary transactions. His predecessors had clearly noted the spending of fl. 12. An accurate record of events was also essential. Custodians were required not only to render accounts but also, and more importantly, to explain events. They had to be answerable. And, indeed, Matheus balked at anything less. Jerg's closing balance was short the expected fl. 12. Refusing to record a fictive expenditure, Matheus rendered an explicit account: 'First December, note a shortfall in the fl. 322 kr. 16. transferred by Hans Jerg Mair, to no more than fl. 310 kr. 16, which upon reminder that he had to answer for it and take it upon himself, was set as an expense, fl. 12, pending his agreement.'[137] A philosophical temperament, in Cicero's sense of the term, one that sought the good of the state without regard for personal gain, no longer sufficed to ensure public morality and to protect the *res publica*. An individual might have a moral compass – the entire memoir gives testimony to Matheus's faith in such things – but it had to be externalized, abstracted and attested. For Matheus, therefore, public morality required a formal accountability.

Nor were farewell celebrations for senior custodians the only abuses that Matheus decried. During an earlier custodianship, Hans Christoph Mair claimed that a local artist, Joseph Werner, had promised to donate to the church a set of paintings, probably a five-panelled altarpiece that would be placed in the choir.[138] There was, as Matheus wrote, 'much more to this excess that seemed to me careless and impractical and will properly be acknowledged as wrong'.[139] Another artist, Johann Spillberg, had donated a similar painting on time and without recompense. Werner's painting finally appeared in 1676 but with two panels instead of the expected five. It was hung above the pulpit, next to the cross, and Pastor Riß offered effusive thanks before the congregation. These gifts were, he said, things that 'the noble artist had freely donated as evidence of his pure faith and love of the church'.[140] Matheus points out, however, that the congregation did not know that 'the canvas and paint had been purchased and, beyond that, the community had given 30 *Reichstaler* from the collection boxes and a further fl. 55, in total fl. 100, to honor the donor'.[141] In fact, accounts from 1676 list only the fl. 45 honorarium 'given to Joseph Werner of Augsburg, as was given to Heüser of Memmingen, because of his donated, beautiful painting in the choir of the Last Supper of Christ'.[142] Matheus's predecessors, Steuden, Beck and Jerg Mair, had regularly laundered money, siphoning the remaining fl. 55 out of the church. Jerg told Matheus that he should 'make it up from uncounted funds'.[143] Matheus could disguise the shortfall by reporting 'the proceeds of the collection boxes as fl. 139 rather than fl. 159'.[144] He refused these dubious bits of bookkeeping, as noted, and recorded as missing the fl. 12 that was Jerg's share. Not only numbers but also explanations had to add up. Accounts were embedded in value judgments and social relations. What constituted a proper expenditure was by no means fixed according to objective standards. Matheus interpreted such matters narrowly. In his memoir he remarks only that 'the kind of business that comes from righteous people is amazing'.[145]

In December 1676, Jerg Mair ended his term of office, and Matheus succeeded him as senior custodian. That Jerg viewed the custodianship of Holy Cross as a source of profit and patronage became clear 'in the proceedings during the falsified election upon Mair's retirement'.[146] As Matheus was careful to point out, he was kept in ignorance of the proceedings, told only how and whether to appear.[147] At the last possible moment, Jerg nominated as his replacement a man named Teller, supposedly the candidate preferred by Pastor Riß. In the ensuing debate, Matheus objected that, according to custom, the next custodian had to be elected from a suburb (*Vorstadt*). Jerg, joined at this point by his brother Hans Christoph, noted that 'one needn't be bound by [that point]' and immediately cast their votes for Teller, as did all those 'who feared the pastor and preferred to set the old order aside'.[148] Jerg counted the votes and 'by the time he finished there were more ballots than people present'.[149] When he realized that the Mairs intended to rig the election, Matheus cast his own and Deacon Laub's votes for an alternative candidate, who already had 'non-partisan support', the goldsmith Baur.[150] Challenged on whose orders he cast Laub's vote, Matheus replied, 'I will answer for it.'[151] With that, Baur became the new junior custodian. The Mairs complained to Pastor Riß that the 'business had miscarried despite all their efforts and advantages'.[152] Laub admitted that he had not given Matheus specific permission to vote in his name, but, because the sacristan had acted similarly, 'so could the custodian, his cousin [*Veter*], cast his vote and protect his rights'.[153] According to Matheus, Pastor Riß had instructed the sacristan to ask Laub to cast his vote for Teller. Somehow the message miscarried. Not knowing the candidates, Laub decided on his own to vote with the majority. Thus, concludes Matheus, 'because the sacristan kept silent, I unwittingly told the truth and did not lie as do those so accustomed to lying'.[154]

His account of the election at Holy Cross constitutes the memoir's longest single anecdote on public office. The specificity of Matheus's memory suggests its importance to him; it captures all the elements of his notion of public office and public morality: dignity, propriety and accountability. His manipulation of the election certainly struck the Mairs as unethical, but Matheus wishes to argue that his actions were proper under the circumstances. And, those circumstances had social as well as ethical facets. From the beginning, Matheus bridled at Jerg's treatment of him as a subordinate. It was inimical to his dignity as a successful merchant and as an elected official. Thus, his actions contained an element of social rebelliousness insofar as he directed them against a former patron in order to establish his own stature. They retain an ethical character insofar as he justifies them in terms of some recognizable standard of propriety. It is not the fraudulent election that strikes him as improper – indeed, he participates in it, though the tortured logic of his final remark captures his enduring unease with the fact – but the violation of public procedures for private ends. Proceedings, in this case legitimated by established, traditional usage, therefore, provide the framework for his notion of accountability. Due process must govern conduct; conduct must be explained; explanations must add up. Matheus locates public morality not in an abstract standard of right but rather in a empirical gauge of transparency.

The memoir falls silent after the election of 1677. For the next year, Matheus served as senior custodian at Holy Cross, the official finally responsible for the church's administration. Not surprisingly, perhaps, he conducted its affairs without noteworthy incident. Matheus's memoir contains no mention of the mundane duties of his custodianship. Rather, it is a retelling of distressing and instructive events. They are distressing because they depart from the expected behavior of important officials; they are instructive because they reveal the appropriate response. If Jerg's tenure exemplifies official conduct to be exposed and condemned, his own captures public morality in action.

Yet, crises and scandals absorbed little of his official attention. He devoted his energies to the normal business of the church. Its funds paid for liturgical expenses. A local publican and member of the congregation, Georg Sedelmair, did a brisk business providing Holy Cross with communion wine. In 1677, he made fifteen deliveries worth fl. 150 kr. 59.[155] Moreover, the church adorned its worship with music. Holy Cross employed the cantor Georg Schmezer, the organist Jakob Ehinger, and the soloist Caspar Grot. Each received a quarterly stipend of fl. 10 plus honoraria for special performances or services.[156] They were supported by a ten-voice choir, which included two boy sopranos and an assortment of instrumentalists. Such richly furnished services befitted one of the city's wealthy and prestigious churches. Church funds also provided compensation for its pastor, deacon and sacristan. Pastor Riß and Deacon Laub led worship services and directed religious education, for which they received a salary from the city but transportation and accommodation from Holy Cross. Their expenses amounted to fl. 129 kr. 55 in 1677.[157] Sacristan Reischlin bore responsibility for the maintenance of the church building. He received a quarterly stipend of fl. 10 and submitted receipts that shed light on the material life of an early modern church and the official concerns of its custodians.[158] He paid quarterly fees to the bell-ringer, the grave-digger, the altar-keeper and the street-sweeper. He facilitated the pastor's office of preaching by maintaining adequate supplies of paper, quills and ink, an hourglass to time sermons, as well as sundries referred to as 'important things' (*krefftige Sachen*). He provided light and heat, in the form of candles, oil and wood. He paid for the cleaning of the church and purchased the necessary supplies, such as brooms, cloths, sand and sawdust. Normal maintenance of the building and its functions required over fl. 112 in 1677, a considerable sum of money in countless small transactions.[159] Matheus described all such dealings in painstaking detail, including the goods and services purchased, the persons involved and the amounts tendered. In this, his accounts distinguish themselves from those of all other custodians.

Such attention to the most trivial sums might seem unnecessarily obsessive – his colleagues did not feel themselves so bound – but is totally consistent with Matheus's notion of accountability. Nor were all transactions small. In major building projects, the custodians came into their own, not merely keeping the books but managing the projects. Holy Cross underwent extensive repairs to its exterior walls and doors as well as to its gables and eaves in 1677, the year in which Matheus served as senior custodian.[160] It fell to him to negotiate costs, contract labor, purchase materials, control quality, pay bills and keep accounts. Such tasks required a merchant with knowledge of markets and experience in trade. At its height, from the beginning of August to the middle of October, the work required the services of five masons, three apprentices, and a day-laborer. Because the work could only be carried out on scaffolding with 'dangerous, careful effort', they demanded no less than kr. 32 per day for skilled hands, an unusually high wage.[161] Total labor costs for the masonry alone came to more than fl. 150. Materials amounted to fl. 165 kr. 35. To repair and replace roofing and eaves, nearly 1,000 *Pfund* of copper had to be purchased at a cost of fl. 161.[162] Here, too, labor was unusually expensive. Coppersmith Tobias Wideman demanded kr. 5 per *Pfund* of copper installed, rather than the customary kr. 3, 'because much more effort was required than is usual for the covering of a roof, although one usually paid kr. 3, in this case he would not accept less than kr. 5'.[163] He pocketed fl. 62 kr. 26 for the entire job. Matheus noted skeptically that the smith claimed he 'often installed less than 10 to 12 *Pfund* in an entire day'.[164] He was unable to force the price down, but accountability dictated that he record his efforts.

Indeed, accountability could set a very high standard of conduct in public office. Toward the end of his tenure, Matheus recorded an expenditure of fl. 20 for Pater Esaias, a Capuchin priest and preacher who had recently converted to Lutheranism.[165] Some five months earlier, in July 1677, Pastor Riß had recommended that money be taken from the church's collection boxes to help Esaias travel secretly (*jn Stille*) to Hamburg. The expense, for what should have been a moral as well as a propagandistic triumph, one that would have been celebrated throughout Augsburg, had not been recorded promptly. Matheus's account suggests that the loan, as he described it, may have been improper and that those responsible – the pastor and, perhaps, himself – may have hoped donations would cover it. Were this the case, his actions would recall those of Jerg Mair and other custodians, who misused church funds and disguised the fact with creative bookkeeping. But Matheus sets the record straight. Because such support was not forthcoming and the end of the fiscal year was at hand, he finally contributed fl. 3 out of his own pocket. By so doing, he asserted his official dignity and demonstrates his moral probity. Despite the unusual, possibly guilty, circumstances, Matheus left a detailed account that listed a net expenditure of fl. 17. Adhering to correct procedures in this way, he established the propriety of his actions. The official record of church expenditures explained what might have been an embarrassing deficit and justified what might have been a scandalous incident. By falling back on accountability, Matheus conformed to his own notion of public morality.

After 1677, the memoir ceases to record Matheus's official experiences. His custodianship lasted another year, however. His commission in the militia and his administration of charity extended to the end of his life. Despite the silence, his official duties continued, sometimes with interesting and illuminating twists and turns. Yet, Matheus had made his point. He had left a list of his assignments; he had explained their significance. In private life as in public office, he had exercised accountability.

Handed down by Augsburg's highest authorities or decided upon by its Lutheran community, Matheus's appointments and elections represent a crowning achievement. Coming in the final decade of his life, they signaled the successful conclusion of that private struggle, which inspired the writing of his memoir. Given their place in his story, at the end of his familial history, they certified his personal propriety and his social stature.

Yet, Matheus does not savor his hard-fought recognition. Public service played a secondary role in his life. His recollections are few and selective, devoted to certain illustrative details that allow him to reflect on his actions and his values. Even when he describes the misconduct of others, he directs attention ever to his own. In this sense, he remains fundamentally a private individual. He resisted public office initially, preferring to attend to his own domestic and commercial affairs. At that time, he argued that any service should reflect not only one's station but also one's expertise. Although this line of reasoning did not convince the magistrates to set aside his captaincy, at least it was consistent with his other appointments. Indeed, the magistrates would not have disagreed in principle. To function properly, the city-state relied upon the services and skills of its subjects. The offices of court associate, foundation administrator or church custodian required not only the stature of a prominent burgher but also the expertise of a successful merchant. Once in office, Matheus began to delineate a public morality that derived from principles of private conduct. Dignity, propriety and accountability, which he attributes to his entire career but which figure most explicitly in his discussion of the custodianship, are nothing less than standards derived from the household and the marketplace. Matheus seems to suggest, therefore, that public life could not be separated from private life.

As Matheus's public career began to unfold in 1675, the Lutheran *Stadtpfleger* and members of the Secret Council appointed him a deputy of the *Rodwesen*, that is, the public office charged with the maintenance of transalpine passes and transportation for the city's merchants.[166] As events transpired, it proved an abortive assignment. Within a year, the authorities released Matheus from service. According to the memoir, previous deputies had not exercised their authority in the best interest of the city's merchants (*für die Kaufmannshafft besten nit guberniert*). Among the guilty were Hans Christoph Mair. In the year of his appointment, an investigation implicated the brothers Mair and Miller, presumably uncles Gabriel and Hans Jakob Miller. Matheus felt unable to remain in office without the support of the authorities (*ohne erleuterte obrigkeitlich assistenz*). A commission of *Burgomaster* was impaneled to examine the matter and recommended replacing all the current deputies. Matheus claims at this point that the commission wished to retain him but that the 'Papisten' opposed him. As in other branches of the government, parity dictated a strict division of the deputies between Catholics and Protestants. Whereas he might have taken a dim view of Catholic machinations, he interprets the opposition positively in that it released him from further service.[167] Matheus objects not to his Catholic opponents but rather to those Lutheran deputies who misused public office. He notes, 'Deeds that damage the common substance (*gemeinen wesen*) cannot finally be hidden from God; and city and community reap shame as their reward, as people will see.'[168]

Matheus's description is both cryptic and revealing. He never makes clear the actual abuses of office that led to the appointment of a high commission and the dismissal of all deputies. Indeed, he did little more than observe events, entering and leaving the scene upon command. His interest was not passive, however. When his family was implicated in the scandal, Matheus prepared to abdicate office. Their involvement cast doubt upon his integrity, making it impossible for him to continue without the particular support of higher authority. His reputation as a worthy man and honest official was at risk.[169] In the memoir, he applauds the restoration of order, involving both the exposure of old abuses and the prevention of new ones. 'Such misuses and inconveniences must be exposed so that they not be neglected and ignored.'[170] Propriety, in the form of established procedures, and accountability, in the sense of demonstrable explanations, constitute the basis of a public morality restored. As the extent of the scandal is revealed, Matheus can only voice relief at having escaped involvement. It would have damaged his reputation even as it undermined the city-state.

In this instance, as throughout the memoir, Matheus did not write a history of daily life. Rather, he self-consciously selected events to make a particular point. Thus, as he recounts his public career, he reveals his notions of public office, good works, public morality and the autonomous citizen. Public office includes all the appointments and elections by which Augsburg called Matheus to service. Yet, he reserved particular attention for those that were specifically Lutheran in content or character. Recall that he was commissioned in the militia, appointed to charities, elected to the custodianship, and removed from the *Rodwesen* because he was Lutheran. His Lutheran upbringing might have encouraged him to associate public office with good works. Certainly, as Luther taught, all Christians must devote themselves to the welfare of others or, as Matheus put it, to the common substance. Public service constituted a good work; this was its literal meaning. For Matheus, however, it had metaphorical and moral connotations as well. His public career reflected and confirmed the on-going process of vindication that moved him to write his memoir in the first place. And, his conduct in office demonstrated a public morality, composed of dignity, propriety and accountability. Though the essence of official integrity in this particular context, they were appropriated from Matheus's – indeed, from any merchant's – private experience. Thus, he created a standard of conduct, at once rationally abstract from its empirical basis and universally applicable to all public office. This, finally, was the essence of the autonomous citizen. He participated in public life, through the exercise of administrative office, he reflected critically upon the exercise, and he applied his own standard in judgment. For Matheus, dignity, propriety and accountability were the essence of credibility and creditworthiness. The 'perfect businessman' employed knowledge, experience, prudence and caution as keys to his success; he not only manifested these qualities through his profit but also demonstrated them through honest dealings, keen judgment, and careful bookkeeping.[171] Here, then, were the ideal qualities through which private interests and personal utility were pursued and achieved. Here, also, were the ideal standards by which the *res publica* was established and defended. Matheus, the successful merchant and householder, defined public morality as the application of private virtues to public life.

In the public sphere, as Matheus understood it, morality and utility were not separate but rather contiguous entities. They reinforced one another. The humanist, who agreed with Cicero that public life should be freed from private interests, set an irrational standard of conduct. The patricians, who tacitly admitted with Alberti that public life should be exploited for private interests, destroyed the 'common substance' of political society. Not a member of Augsburg's patriciate, Matheus was excluded from the ruthless exploitation of the city-state. Yet, as a functionary, he administered the city-state and, as such, engaged in its political life. Viewing these tasks with detachment, he brought a set of values, born of his experience in the household and the marketplace. His public ideology lends a bourgeois sensibility to the business of statecraft.

3
Sociability and Social Structure

Matheus Miller was a sociable man. Every New Year's Day, he honored certain acquaintances with gifts of cash. The entries in his memoir are little more than accountings of funds paid; they offer neither reasons for the gifts nor details about the recipients. The first such record listed more than fl. 50 given to some 33 people in 1658.[1] The rest must be reconstructed from other passages and other documents. These sources reveal that Matheus gave to members of his household: his wife, his three children and his three servants.[2] He included his father and his father's maid, suggesting that the elder Miller was somehow dependent on the younger. He remembered his favorite nieces and nephews.[3] He even extended generosity to a few of his many godchildren, the sons and daughters of Thomas Hopfer, at that time pastor of Holy Cross and Senior Pastor of Augsburg's Lutheran community.[4] The largest portion of his annual gift-giving, and the bulk of the list, he devoted to the Lutheran *ministerium*, every pastor, deacon and sacristan in the city.[5] Similar lists appear for every year following until 1685, the year Matheus died. That New Year's Day, he followed a pattern of giving that, if somewhat narrower than in his youth, had become traditional over a lifetime.[6] He gave, as he had every year, to his household, to his family and to his pastors. And he recorded the fact, as he had every year, in his memoir. These lists expose an element of Matheus's life, hitherto unaddressed in the memoir but essential to its purpose, a wider world of personal associations and social solidarities. Here were people he knew, people he supported, people he valued.

That they appear without annotation suggests that these relationships needed no explanation. They were on-going and self-evident. They were also, as the memoir makes clear, multivalent. No single term in modern parlance captures this complexity. But, in early modern

Europe, the word 'friend' did so. It had broader implications than are customary today. Justus Menius, in his *Oeconomia Christiana*, described friends (*Freundschaften*) as 'an external, physical community through which one helps another at need to the best of his ability'.[7] Hence, friendship applied to anyone, related or unrelated, whose acquaintance offered physical or spiritual assistance.

Borrowing from Aristotle and the Stoics, especially Cicero, humanists recognized three kinds of friendship.[8] In addition to the sort that Menius describes, based on utility, there were also friendships based on pleasure and on virtue. Alberti addresses the topic in Book IV of his *Libri della Famiglia*. Piero, an elder statesman of the family, tells the tale of three princes, each of whom cultivated friends for different reasons. Lionardo and Adovardo immediately recognize the Aristotelian tropes and enter into a dialogue on amity.[9] Adovardo points out that 'not every sort of familiar acquaintance nor every sort of affection of spirit that is kindled brings true friendship into life'.[10] Some people offer affection in the pursuit of advantage; others do so in the expectation of amusement. 'But no love is greater than that of the person who is not moved by some lovely and desired thing obtained or hoped for from you, or by some benefit which your generosity provides or promises him, but who reveres and honors you – who prizes and delights in your character and in your honorable conduct'.[11] Thus, virtue inspires the purest form of friendship because it is supposedly free from selfish motives. Adovardo recognizes, however, that friendships involve exchange and advantage. Who best deserves friendship but those 'who have reciprocated their older friendships well and constantly'?[12] Cicero maintains that 'what we enjoy in a friend is not the profit but the affection'.[13] Yet, Adovardo understands that affection has a practical purpose: to 'make us acceptable and well liked by everyone' and to 'attach the spirit of men to ourselves'.[14] To this end, it may, indeed must, be manipulated. 'Diverse arts' have their place: 'it is important to know how to present oneself as honorable, modest, pleasant, friendly, joyful, temperate, conscientious, kind, as lively of spirit as constant, as well as illustrious in name and fame'.[15] Cicero acknowledges that 'advantage does, it is true, grow out of friendship, whether you have intentionally pursued such a benefit or not'.[16] But this is 'another matter'.[17] Not so for Adovardo and the Alberti. 'What the necessary attributes of friendship are, we have already made clear: a true, simple, and open affection, pleasant intimacy and converse in which are honorably shared the interest, opinion, and fortunes of both friends, and, to cement all this, every kind of ready service'.[18] Far from being of different sorts, therefore, friendship combines the three disparate elements: virtue, pleasure and utility. But utility, at least according to Alberti, is the adhesive that binds the elements, makes them tangible, and gives them meaning.

Piero, the experienced diplomat, gives the matter a succinct, practical turn: the ultimate purpose of friendship – its utility – is 'to increase the name and repute, the dignity and standing of our kinsmen, and to exalt the family'.[19] Relationships of this sort might reside in a dynamic of recognition and esteem between two people, the open affection to which Adovardo feelingly refers. For an elite family, however, especially one living in exile, friendship necessarily assumed an instrumental quality. It was the means to acquire and articulate power. It was essential for self-preservation. As an exile within his own family, Leon Battista Alberti would probably have agreed with Cicero that 'real friendship is even more potent than kinship; for the latter may exist without goodwill, whereas friendship can do no such thing'.[20] Ties of affection might prove more reliable – and, therefore, more useful – than those of blood. For this reason, friendship was a matter of the first importance.

Like Alberti, in his youth Matheus was something of an exile within his own family. He remembered his youth in similar terms. Members of his family counseled against employing him in the Miller counting house and encouraged his father to send him into foreign service. To them he was a 'thorn in the eye', one they would indenture for ten years in an arch-Catholic community rather than admit to the family business.[21] Like Alberti's book, which served as a reproach to the family that expelled him, Matheus's memoir answered the reservations implicit in the actions of his family. It recorded the fact that Matheus made something of himself: he became a successful member of Augsburg's merchant community; he became the head of an affluent household; he became a holder of public offices. All of these achievements testified to a propriety that his youthful excesses placed in doubt. In all, his family had been as much a hindrance as a help. Matheus had relied on his own efforts and on the assistance of friends.

Such solidarities, based on principles of reciprocity and mutuality, were essential to life in early modern Augsburg.[22] Friendships, in the broad, early modern sense of the word, oriented individuals in larger networks of obligation and advantage. They extended and strengthened families and households by involving the members in exchanges of spiritual and material resources. Likewise, they contained and conditioned families and households, by enmeshing the members in systems of authority and power. Friends and neighbors assured survival in a world of scarcity and encouraged harmony in a world of tension. Yet, friendships were not only social institutions that constrained or disciplined families. They were also relationships that enriched and enabled individuals. As Menius and Alberti made clear, early modern city-dwellers used the term to cover a broad spectrum of relationships, in which the components – utility, pleasure, virtue – varied according to the social, economic and political relations of the city. Those components also varied according to each individual's specific situation. Hence, friendship, based as it is on a unique combination of affection and calculation, can be abstracted only imprecisely from the persons involved.

When Matheus listed his annual giving, recording both the gift and the recipient, he situated himself in a network of relationships based on utility as well as affection, interest as well as emotion. Without describing or categorizing, nonetheless, he recognized the fact of the friendship and his reliance upon it. He acknowledged participation in a system of mutual rights and responsibilities. He documented the achievement of social stature and guaranteed its maintenance. Finally, he demonstrated his own virtue to those who might read the memoir, especially his heirs. For them, Matheus's account of his friendships was a kind of social patrimony, an extension of the business records and capital reserves that were their inheritance. It indicated the friends who had served the family in the past and would do so in the future. It described social behavior that would secure status, promote prosperity and proclaim propriety. And it opened a window on a wider world of associations, all located in the city of Augsburg. The record of his relationships offers a key to Matheus's social identity and social purpose, how he understood who he was and what he wanted. It fixes his exact position in and provides a map to his political and social landscape.

How did that landscape look? In Augsburg, urban society mirrored urban topography.[23] Rich and poor lived as neighbors, but they were not equally distributed throughout the city.[24] Nearly 60 percent of the patrician and mercantile elite, but less than 4 percent of the artisanal population, lived in the Upper City (*Oberstadt*), the central area west of the main thoroughfare. Here Matheus made his home. East of the main thoroughfare and south of the City Hall lay the Lech Quarter (*Lechviertel*), the city's most densely populated district, home to one-third of the city's taxpayers and most of its industries. Still further east, between the Lech Quarter and the Lech River stood the St James' Suburb (*Jakobervorstadt*), the poorest section of Augsburg. North of the Upper City lay the Lady Suburb (*Frauenvorstadt*), where nearly half of Augsburg's textile-workers lived and labored, the poorest of whom huddled miserably between the cathedral and the northern wall. Place of residence, reflecting wealth, lifestyle and status, is one objective symbol that identifies the standing of its possessor and distinguishes him from his superiors and inferiors. With Augsburg's most powerful inhabitants enthroned on the high street and in the Upper City, geographic distance from these centers signaled a social distance from the elite. Augsburg assumed a stratified appearance, therefore.

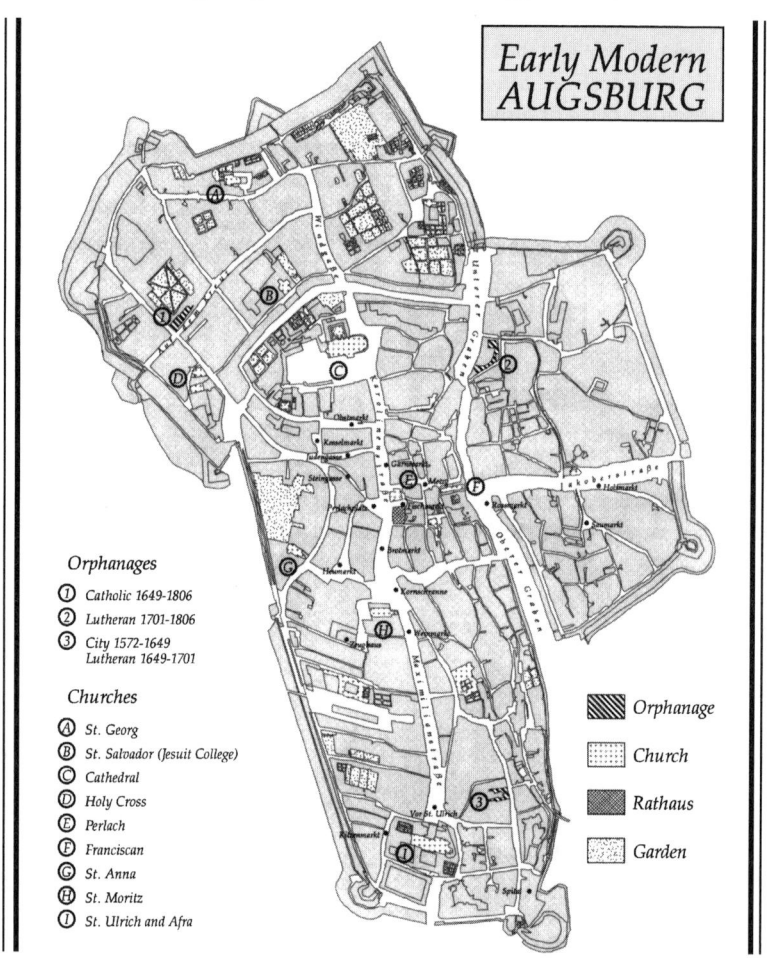

Figure 3.1 Map of early modern Augsburg.

In general, social stratification exists when clear distinctions of status are visible in a society.[25] The concept of ranked orders (*ordinis*, *Stände*) was a commonplace of medieval and early modern Europe. Sources from the early Middle Ages reveal a stratified society, consistent with relatively simple, feudal and agrarian realities. The poles of *potens* and *pauper* established a vertical hierarchy, distinguishing those who exercised power over property and people from those who had no such right.[26] With the growth of the population and the development of the economy, contemporary models became more complex.[27] Later schema involved three or even four strata: those who pray, those who fight and those who work; or those who pray, those who fight, those who trade and those who work.[28] Cities introduced new elements, substituting for political and legal inequalities social and economic distinctions.[29] By the late fifteenth century, the free imperial city of Nuremberg had developed a social hierarchy composed of five strata: patricians, large-scale merchants, middling merchants, small-scale merchants, artisans.[30] A 1683 sumptuary law (*Policey-Ordnung*) in Augsburg organized the city into five somewhat different orders: patricians, merchants, substantial masters, ordinary masters, and laborer.[31] Thus, depending on the defining principle, traditional hierarchical societies resolved themselves into orders defined by legal status, political power, or economic function.[32] Birthright or sanction determined an individual's place in a specific order of that hierarchy. Born a merchant of Augsburg, Matheus expected to remain a merchant of Augsburg and organized his life and his family accordingly. Thus, he strove not only for propriety but also for perpetuity. As important as it was to demonstrate his own ethical worth, it was no less important to establish himself and his family over generations within the city's mercantile elite.

An individual's position in society was understood to be permanent, not given to change. Social models upheld an ideal of stability, indeed eternity, because hierarchies reflected divine ordination. As the Herborn philosopher, Johann Heinrich Alsted, wrote in 1630:

> Nothing is more beautiful, nothing more fruitful than order. Order establishes the worth and rank of all things in the great theater of the world. Order is the nerve of the mystical body (*corpus mysticum*) in the church of God. Order is the strongest bond in the life of the family and of the state.[33]

One was born into a fixed place in the world, a place that brought with it specific behavioral expectations and limitations. Opportunities for initiative and mobility were severely limited.[34] All social, cultural, and legal norms obliged individuals to behave honorably, that is, in a manner consistent with their station. As such, society perceived mobility as a form of deviance, a violation of the social and natural order.

Premodern stability seemed most pronounced when compared to modern mobility. Considering the bases of social stratification, Max Weber juxtaposed orders and classes, noting that the former involves the monopoly of spiritual and material goods by a specific 'status group'.[35] Class-based societies arise under specific circumstances: when a majority of people enjoy similar opportunities; when those opportunities are determined largely by economic factors, such as wealth or occupation; and when those economic factors are distributed according to market conditions.[36] 'The market and its processes knows no personal distinctions'.[37] It might also be said that the market knows no stability, as it is subject to constantly changing conditions of supply and demand. Against the economic force of markets, orders pose the social pretensions of honor, which emphasize the exclusivity of each status group through specific conventions of lifestyle or behavior.[38] They constitute a barrier to the development of modern, class-based social structures, therefore. Because orders come into existence not through market-based activities but rather through lifestyle and heredity, their claims to status are understood as permanent.

Yet, attempts to define and describe traditional hierarchies and orders remain simplified caricatures of ambiguous realities. The weight given to particular qualities and, therefore, the boundaries between social strata tended to be fluid, varying from person to person and family to family. Membership in the patriciate, which formed the political leadership of most free imperial cities by the second half of the sixteenth century, commonly involved a complex set of factors: birthright, honor, marriage, wealth, occupation, lifestyle, association and office.[39] Nonetheless, Augsburg sheltered both impoverished patricians, who enjoyed the prerogatives of their status despite their inability to lead an appropriately aristocratic lifestyle, and wealthy merchants, such as Matheus, who were excluded from the rank and power of the patriciate despite their economic potency and elite bearing.[40] More importantly, the ideal of stability never captured the dynamic reality. Mobility occurred constantly. It was, in fact, never irreconcilable with hierarchy. Pitirim Sorokin has argued that all societies offer the means to mobility.[41] Permanent, universal factors of mobility exist that constantly shift the distribution of individuals across social strata. In early modern

Europe, the sale of office provided one such avenue of advancement. Service supplied another. Marriage yet another. Social mobility also presupposed such conditions as wealth, opportunity and progeny.[42] It depended on production and reproduction. Economic and demographic factors constantly shifted the social structure, making possible advancement within orders and, occasionally, between orders. The process never ceased but was at points more marked.

Between the fifteenth and the nineteenth century, Augsburg's traditional, hierarchical society slowly evolved toward a class society. To borrow Weber's formulation, structures based on patterns of consumption, reflected in modes of behavior that were specific to different social strata, gradually yielded to structures based on relations of production.[43] Cities had long been the crucibles of social change. They offered relatively greater opportunities for vertical or horizontal social mobility because status was reinforced but not fixed by law. Because their economies were more complex, based on industry and commerce as well as on agriculture, they offered greater social variety. In the early modern period, however, demographic expansion, collapse and recovery encouraged capital concentration, technology investment and monopoly formation, all of which loosened the traditional social structure and strengthened the degree to which wealth and occupation competed with honor and birthright to determine status and define stratification. The Miller family in general, and Matheus in particular, were beneficiaries of these economic and social forces.

The institutions of Augsburg's social hierarchy emerged shortly after the Guild Rising of 1368. Deprived of their monopoly on political power, patrician families closed ranks to defend their social exclusivity. They reorganized themselves into a corporate body centered on a meeting hall, the *Herrenstube*, and limited membership to male descendants of the city's 51 original ruling families.[44] Beginning in the early fifteenth century, however, Augsburg entered a period of growth, based on the production of fustian, a cloth woven from linen and cotton.[45] This transformation strained social stratification: it created a new community of self-made merchant-entrepreneurs; it concentrated wealth in the hands of a few; and it increased the distance between elites and commons.[46] Between 1396 and 1492, the city's population rose from 12,000 to 19,000.[47] According to city tax registers, 2.4 percent of the population controlled 49 percent of the taxable wealth in 1396. A century later, in 1492, the concentration of wealth stood at 80 percent of taxable property in the hands of 4.7 percent of the taxpayers.[48] Parvenus sought their economic fortunes and laboriously climbed the social ladder, a struggle Lucas Rem captured in his autobiography.[49] The newly rich built urban palaces throughout the Upper City. Those who could, married into the old patriciate. Two centuries later, Matheus would find himself in a similar situation. Scion of a rising, merchant family, he would seek ways to establish his fortune and fame. For him, however, access to the elite had long since been limited by the institutions that guarded its exclusivity. In 1478, those wealthy merchants with patrician relations formed the *Gesellschaft der Mehrer*.[50] Founded as a bridge of sorts between the group from which they came and the one to which they aspired, the association granted to its members heightened social status without real political influence.[51] Its essential purpose, however, was to underscore their corporate exclusivity with regard both to merchants and to patricians. As Augsburg's economy began to generate new wealth, new opportunities and new mobility, therefore, its political and economic elite moved to limit the social consequences.

Augsburg built upon these foundations. In the long sixteenth century, the economy continued to expand, despite occasional recessions, and the elite continued to consolidate, despite new wealth. This was the city's golden age. Its population rose to approximately 40,000. Its artisans produced goods bound for marketplaces throughout the world. Its financiers set the pace of economic and political events. Its cityscape served as a stage for the history of the period. And its economic elite expanded with the economy. According to tax returns from 1610, 7.5 percent of the city's taxpayers controlled 86 percent of its taxable property.[52] Yet, their distance from the political elite was no less great than their distance from the poor. Merchants dominated the office of *Burgomaster* from 1368 until 1548, but the patriciate steadfastly resisted incorporating *nouveau riche* families. It paid a price for its exclusivity. By 1538, only 7 of the original 51 families survived: Herwart, Hofmaier, Ilsung, Langenmantel, Ravensburger, Rehlinger and Welser.[53] Of these, only the Herwart, Rehlinger and Welser remained both wealthy and powerful. To replenish the ranks of the patriciate, Emperor Charles V elevated 38 families from the *Mehrer*, including the Fugger, Arzt, Baumgartner, Lauginger, Rem and von Stetten. In response to this strengthening of the elite and their allies, around 1540 Augsburg's merchants formed their own exclusive corporation, the *Gesellschaft von der Kaufleutestube*.[54] Yet such maneuvers proved vain. Because a closing of the city's merchant community could have dire consequences for the city's economy, the City Council insisted that the merchant guild (*Kaufleutezunft*) remain open to all applicants rather than insist on a hereditary birthright for membership. Augsburg's established merchants could form an association, if they wished, but they could not prevent non-members from engaging in commerce. When the Caroline Constitution restored a virtual monopoly of political power by the patricians in 1548, it effectively closed the most important avenue of social advancement and foiled the social aspirations of Augsburg's merchants. Matheus's identity and trajectory would be marked by these events. Perforce, he would situate himself in the straitened world of Augsburg's mercantile elite, excluded from any real political power, restricted to its own social corporation. The gap between economic and political elites became unbridgeable, but the mobility within these orders never ceased.

The series of calamities that marked the history of Augsburg between 1622 and 1635 ended its economic expansion. By the year of Matheus's birth, the city no longer possessed its former greatness. Its population fell 75 percent; industrial productivity declined 85 percent.[55] A study of the city's property taxes indicates that economic loss had the greatest impact on the top and bottom of the social hierarchy.[56] While the proportion of taxpayers rendering fl. 1 or less in property taxes held constant at 75 percent, and those rendering between fl. 1 and fl. 100 increased from 23.1 percent to 23.7 percent, the have-naughts decreased from 48.5 percent to 37.2 percent, and the wealthiest Augsburgers, those taxed in excess of fl. 100, decreased from 1.4 percent in 1618 to 0.5 percent in 1646.[57] The number of plutocrats declined from 142 in 1618, to 80 in 1632, to 23 in 1646.[58] Most of the survivors experienced catastrophic losses of property. Over 90 percent of the capital held by the city's economic elite was destroyed.[59] By contrast, its political elite remained demographically stable. The confessionally motivated elevations of 1628 and 1632, intended to raise the number of Catholic or Lutheran patricians respectively, were largely undone after 1648 and had few lasting effects. The patricians needed no further recruitment from the *Mehrer*.[60] Their political monopoly and social exclusivity emerged from the crisis largely intact.

Matheus's personal history begins at precisely this point. The winnowing of the economic elite created an opportunity for the Miller family to rise in the economic and social hierarchy. His uncles, Gabriel and Hans Jakob, made their fortunes while others were collapsing. His father, Michael, suffered a series of reverses that had potential consequences for Matheus. A merchant's apprentice, Matheus learned his profession in these uncertain times. His life and his memoir can only be understood in this context of mutability and mobility.

After 1650, Augsburg's economy began slowly to grow again. The process was not steady, but the results were real. By 1670, Augsburg had recovered from many of the direct economic effects of the Thirty Years' War. This achievement, as noted, must be attributed both to a fiscal policy that stopped the loss of city resources and to a renewal of trade that generated new wealth.[61] Despite economic and demographic recovery, however, Augsburg society remained highly stratified. The 1688 property tax assessed 5,186 taxpayers of whom 24.3 percent paid the rate of have-naughts and 4.0 percent rendered taxes of fl. 100 or more.[62] By 1712 the number of taxpayers had risen to 5,474, and the proportions of poor and rich had increased to 27.3 and 4.1 percent respectively. Recovery also brought renewed mobility for the economic elite. Those who paid fl. 100 or more in property taxes slowly increased in number from 21 in 1660 to 31 in 1717, and the average assessment of this group grew from fl. 182 to fl. 266.[63] Yet, the patriciate's political monopoly was constitutionally unassailable, and its social exclusivity endured into the nineteenth century.[64] No further elevations followed those of the Thirty Years' War. Furthermore, sumptuary laws, such as that of 1683, reinforced the differences in status between Augsburg's social orders with behavioral restrictions. Noting that 'an excessive luxury and expense among all orders [of society]...had taken control, such that one no longer knew to distinguish the orders', the magistrates divided society into five strata and enjoined each 'in dress and demeanor to behave in accordance with their order'.[65] They then proceeded to list in considerable detail not only what constituted appropriate 'dress and demeanor' for each strata but also what constituted appropriate manners of transportation, marriage, baptism and burial. The ordinance projects the image of an elite on the defensive. As the economy forged new wealth and encouraged new mobility, the patriciate responded with renewed insistence upon their unique honor and stability.

Matheus's memoir concerns itself with this period. In many ways, his history reflects that of his hometown. As a merchant, he participates in Augsburg's economic recovery, accumulates considerable wealth and joins the economic elite. He enters a series of advantageous marriage alliances with substantial merchant families that solidify his position and status. He heads a large household in a prestigious neighborhood, surrounded by family members and business associates. He occupies a series of offices, suitable to a man of his station and distinction. Social structure provided the ligaments of his social identity. Matheus knows himself and shapes his destiny in Augsburg. Its institutions help to explain his purpose. His entire life testifies to social mobility in a world that will have none of it. He passes to his heirs, therefore, a patrimony that will allow them to perpetuate his achievement.

In Augsburg, mobility resulted from a constant process of social selection. As change and crisis left their marks on society, established political and economic elites were exhausted and new leadership had to be recruited. Yet, mobility violated social norms. Against unrelenting pressure from below, elites strove, with greater or lesser success, to preserve their exclusivity and dominance. Because it was constant, even within a ranked society of orders, and because it was constantly opposed to the values of that society, mobility has been treated by historians as consistently self-conscious. Moreover, they apparently have adopted Alberti's notion that utility is the common bond that explains all.

Both mobility and stability called for strategic thinking and self-conscious planning. The acquisition of sufficient wealth, the achievement of an appropriate education, the completion of an advantageous marriage, the largesse of a powerful patron, or the performance of a notable service promoted the slow process of advancement that, as a rule, required generations to complete. By the same token, a loss of property, a dishonorable action, or a powerful opponent could mean the loss of social standing and a plunge into disgrace and obscurity. Under such circumstances, which could set property, status and even survival at risk, the players used all the social, cultural, economic and political means at their disposal.[66] Aspiring parvenus and established elites alike understood how to represent and reorganize themselves, in order to reach a higher station or defend their social status.[67] An image of deliberate, persistent social striving emerges.

Furthermore, stability and mobility both involved transactions between social strata – exchange and cooperation between elites and commons – that yielded greater cohesion among those most immediately concerned. Patronage, in all its various forms, is a good example. Recent studies have shifted attention from sociologically homogeneous groups to socially connected groups. These connections emphasize the interactions by which political and economic elites maintain their ascendancy and replenish their ranks.[68] As such, they fostered vertical as well as horizontal linkages, allowing oligarchs to cull and curry their members and dependents and merchants to cultivate their patrons and recruit associates.[69] Beyond the reciprocities of patron and client or colleague and colleague, social interactions created networks of families, connected by ties of mutual dependence and shared ambition that transformed them into communities of interest and action.[70] These networks are the friendships that Alberti extolled and Matheus recorded.

Yet, for Matheus, the friendships in his life seem remarkably unselfconscious. In his memoir, at least, he never calculates the price of his affection. He never explains why certain people merit the title of friend or the generosity of a gift. These things were understood by his readers. He never selects his friends to facilitate his family's eventual ascendancy into the ranks of the elite. It is a goal for ever beyond his reach and beside his thought. He never rails against the social or political tyranny of his betters. They remain his 'gracious lords'. Thus, he seems to be completely at ease within the ranked society of orders – understandably so, if those orders reflect the divine hierarchy – even as he strives for such advancement as it has to offer. The implicit tension between stability and mobility, hierarchy and equality, appears not to involve him even as it shapes his life. How, then, did Matheus understand and observe the social hierarchy of his day? Closed to him, the world of high politics and aristocratic connections apparently held no attraction. He limited his ambitions, insofar as his memoir reveals them, to the marketplace, the neighborhood, the church and the household, spheres that so occupied his attention. And his friendships seem well adapted to his purposes. As a merchant, then, Matheus aspired to establish his reputation, create a business, found a family, accumulate wealth, and pass it to an heir. Such goals were consistent with the old, ranked society of orders and the new, fluid society of classes, both of which were evident in the Augsburg of his day. Matheus had a foot in each world.

His memoir reveals little of Matheus's sociability. Missing are the descriptions of daily life that grace other autobiographical sources.[71] It records none of his mundane routines: walking the streets, greeting his neighbors, associating with his peers, entertaining his friends. It records only select instances. The gifts he gave every New Year's Day, for example, given his particular attention to them and the reciprocity implicit in them, seem to circumscribe an inner circle of 'friends'. How, then, did Matheus understand the word?

Neither utility, nor pleasure, nor virtue fully capture his notion of friendship. As memorialized in the lists of gifts, at least, Matheus apparently did not indulge in the classical tropes. The name of Hans

Christoph Mair never appears, despite his utility. Closely connected to the family of Matheus's first wife, he assisted Matheus in resolving an inheritance dispute and served as trustee to Matheus's sons, Philip Jakob and Matheus the Younger, as well as godparent to the latter.[72] Likewise missing is the name of Anton Christoph Schorer the Younger, Matheus's affection for him notwithstanding. With this brother of his second wife, Matheus enjoyed such intimacy that Schorer could speak directly – 'vex' him, as Matheus put it – about the need for a wife.[73] Nor, for that matter, does Matheus honor Zacharias Schoap, despite his esteem for the Nuremberger merchant's virtue. He took an early hand in Matheus's training and did as much as any 'flesh-and-blood father' could to make a successful businessman of him.[74] Social relationships of the sort that Cicero and Alberti understood as friendships, involving people outside the circle of the family, are largely absent.

That the members of his household – his wives, children, and servants – comprised the majority of recipients, year in and year out, indicates that most of those to whom Matheus gave were the people closest to him either emotionally or physically. His wives received 4, later 8, Reichstaler; his children and servants each received 1 *Reichstaler*. Such gifts were marks of uncalculated affection or, as is more likely in the case of servants, acknowledgments of loyalty. This continued, even after his children married and formed households of their own. In 1672 and 1673, when Philip Jakob was a single, young man, living on his own, Matheus gave him 2 *Reichstaler*.[75] When Philip Jakob married Anna Maria Mehrer in 1674, Matheus recorded the event and promptly added her to his list of gift recipients. Beginning in 1675, each received 1 *Reichstaler*.[76] As their children were born, Matheus's giving reflected the fact. When Philip Jakob's first child arrived in 1678, his grandfather gave him 1 *Reichstaler*.[77] The pattern held for each of his subsequent three children. Though he does not preserve their marriages in his memoir – an honor reserved for his heir – Matheus treated his other children, children-in-law and grandchildren similarly: Helena and Jakob Habisreitinger (1679) with their three children; Matheus the Younger and Anna Barbara Mehrer (1680) and their two children; Sibilla and Wolfgang Störr (1683) and their child.[78] In short, he gave regularly and systematically to all those who viewed him as a father figure.

If gifts mark some of his most intimate relationships, however, the defining principle is paternalism with a twist. Matheus also remembered his parents and siblings – or, to be specific, their servants and children respectively – on New Year's Day. Unlike the members of his household, however, these relations appear inconsistently in his lists. Matheus never remembers brother Michael the Younger, with whom he formed his first business venture. His father's maid and the children of his two brothers, Daniel and Thomas, received small gifts in 1658, the first year such giving was recorded. No list appears for 1659; the list of 1660 excludes all but Matheus's household and the Lutheran clergy. By 1661, giving became more liberal; father Michael's maid, brother Daniel's children, and sister Peirler's children were added to the list. Matheus remembered them annually until 1665, when the record was interrupted again. It resumed in 1667 with the addition of mother Sibilla's maid. Matheus's father falls from the list in 1669, but his brother Thomas's children reappear in 1672. Daniel's children are removed in 1674; mother's maid and sister's children disappear in 1676. Only Thomas's children remain from 1676 until 1682, when his widow is added. After that year, all references to siblings and parents cease.

Matheus's parents and their servants may have been members of his household or otherwise dependent upon him. Father and maid appear regularly in the lists from 1658 onward, allowing for the omission in 1660 and the lacunae in 1665 and 1666. Though his father died in 1664, his father's servant received a gift annually until 1669. Recall that the elder Michael joined his son's firm after the senior partners in his former association decided to reorganize their business without him.[79] Indeed, the boy was father to the man both in terms of seniority and in terms of wealth. It is possible, moreover, that Michael later lived under his son's roof. On 20 August 1652, Michael purchased for fl. 3,000 a house adjacent to the corner house in the Steingasse, where he had lived since Matheus's birth in 1625.[80] By 1660, however, city records listed Matheus as resident taxpayer in his father's two houses, now joined into a single dwelling.[81] The father probably lived there still, despite the fact that Matheus was the acknowledged head of household. Though the memoir offers less information about the mother, like the father she may have been financially dependent on Matheus and even lived in his household. Sibilla's maid appears in the lists from 1667 until 1676, though her mistress died in 1673. The patterns suggest that Matheus, as eldest son, somehow supported his parents in their old age and that he sustained their servants as long-term family retainers. They suggest further that not only physical and spiritual proximity but also financial dependence and, perhaps, material need inspired Matheus's gift-giving.

Though his younger siblings and their children were not members of Matheus's immediate household, subordination or reliance may have bound them to him, nonetheless. The memoir reveals nothing about sister Peirlerin's circumstances, but the brothers Thomas and Daniel figure in it and other documents.

Matheus gave Thomas 1 *Reichstaler* on New Year's Day 1658. He then disappeared from the list until 1672. Matheus offered no explanation; it must have been obvious to the members of his family. As the eventual readers of his journal, they would have known of any change in the brothers' relationship. He remained a member of the family. In 1660, Thomas served as godfather to Matheus's twin daughters, one of whom was stillborn and the other of whom survived but fourteen days.[82] In 1674, he participated in the negotiations surrounding the marriage of Philip Jakob to Anna Maria Mehrer.[83] If they had become estranged, then the rift was neither immediate nor complete.

That the gift-giving resumed in 1672 may have had something to do with Thomas's marriage to Sabina Wachter, daughter of Johann Wachter, a patrician and high official (*Stadtamman*) of Memmingen, on 25 October 1671.[84] The union brought Thomas a degree of financial security that seems to have eluded him as a merchant. His tax assessment rose from kr. 40 in 1667 to fl. 35 kr. 10 in 1674, reflecting an increase in worth from as little as fl. 130 to as much as fl. 1,400.[85] He appears to have inherited the property in the Steingasse, originally purchased by Michael and later used by Matheus, but never to have achieved the same stature as his elder brother.[86]

Yet, he stood high in Matheus's affections. Thomas is the only sibling whose death merited mention in the memoir.[87] Returning from business in Bozen, Tirol, he was struck down on Good Friday 1678 by physical weakness (*Leibes shwachheit*), quite possibly a stroke. By Monday he was unable to leave his bed, and by the following Sunday he was dead. Though the incident does not involve wrenching deathbed descriptions, such as adorn the records of other deaths in the family, Matheus remembered his brother with a warmth that is all the more eloquent therefore: 'I have lost a good brother in this world and the entire circle of friends (*freuntschaft*) a pillar and adornment (*stüze und Zieren*).'

The use of the term 'freuntschaft' suggests that Matheus understood friends not as some external community but as a group of people both related by blood and marriage and bound by ties of property and interest. It was a circle, centered on but not limited to the family, intimate but not inward-looking. Both as a collective and as individuals, it required the confirmation of a larger community. Matheus clearly associated the ethical quality of the man with broader notions of propriety: Thomas had been a solid support to family and friends; these qualities gave him stature in the broader community; he was, therefore, a good brother.

Such qualities, made tangible by actions, created obligations. So, Matheus reciprocated. He served as guardian (*Pfleger*) of Thomas' two daughters and bore responsibility for the secure administration of their paternal inheritance.[88] This had grown in the last years of Thomas's life to a comfortable, if by no means spectacular, estate of fl. 4,000 in real property and fl. 9,800 in cash.[89] Because she was not a burgher, Susanna could make no claim on her late husband's fortune. As such, some accommodation had to be made for her support as well as the children's future. Matheus proved instrumental in a compromise that accounted for both.[90] And he continued to give small gifts to each of Thomas's daughters until 1682, in which year he remembered the widow as well. That the giving ceased may have had something to do with Susanna's remarriage, which occurred in 1683 or 1684.[91] With that agreement in place, she and her children passed into the care of her new husband. As was the case with Matheus's parents, therefore, kinship and dependency seem to have guided his generosity.

About brother Daniel, the memoir has even less to say. Apart from annual gifts of one-quarter *Reichstaler* (kr. 15) to each of his five children, beginning in 1658 and continuing until 1673, it neither records his relationship to his elder brother nor reveals their feelings for one another. Yet, kinship and dependency bound him and his family more tightly than any other sibling to Matheus.

On 9 November 1666, Daniel's widow, Maria Stemmer, sued her brother-in-law.[92] Her husband had disappeared while traveling on business in 1658, leaving his affairs in disarray. Eight years later, the presumed widow accused Matheus of withholding her property. Maria claimed that Matheus had used her dowry of fl. 1,000 to pay her late husband's business debts, despite the fact that the money had not been invested in the firm. She wanted to exercise her womanly freedom (*weibliche Freiheit*) – that is, to assert her status as a privileged creditor and have her claims against her husband honored before all others – but Matheus refused to compensate her or even to render an account. Maria demanded that the City Council intervene on her behalf.

In his defense, Matheus told a somewhat different story.[93] Maria's dowry had been invested originally in his firm, of which Daniel was a salaried employee.[94] Determined to form his own business, Daniel reinvested his wife's property and took as partners his father Michael and father-in-law Georg Stemmer the Elder. As Matheus put it, his brother 'understood so little that they had to help him often with advances of their own means'.[95] By 1658, Daniel owed Matheus fl. 1,110 kr. 28 and his father-in-law a further fl. 3,060. Aware of this precarious situation, Matheus and Daniel's partners withheld their demands in order to satisfy the creditors. They agreed above all that they had to prevent insult, ridicule and bankruptcy.[96] Daniel departed Augsburg with the understanding that his father-in-law and wife would dispose of his debts in his absence. He disappeared without a trace and never returned.

Matheus offered detailed extracts from Daniel's books to substantiate his argument.[97] Accounts receivable and commercial wares, valued at fl. 1,472 kr. 7, had been used to discharge fl. 1,584 in accounts payable at Leipzig and Amsterdam. Capital worth fl. 3,241 remained, from which local debts and childcare costs were discharged. A balance of fl. 1,495 remained to Daniel's firm, more than enough to cover Maria's claim. Matheus expressed astonishment that she had not, in fact, collected her dowry. Moreover, he noted that she had waited eight years to bring forward her complaint against him. He insisted that he had acted with the agreement of all parties and in the best interests of the firm and the family.

The exercise in accountability proved compelling. The magistrates agreed with Matheus.[98] They found no evidence of impropriety on his part and ruled that Maria had delayed far too long to demand compensation. That notwithstanding, some gesture was needed to restore harmony between the Stemmer and Miller families. Matheus agreed voluntarily to pay fl. 300 with the understanding that it expressed neither guilt nor obligation on his part, that it would be used solely to support Daniel's five children, and that it would discharge for ever all claims against him and his family. With this agreement, the dispute was formally resolved.

Interestingly, the memoir makes no mention of this incident, despite the fact that it would have served Matheus's apologetic purposes quite well. After all, he was publicly exonerated of all wrong-doing in such a way that proclaimed his acumen, propriety and generosity. That notwithstanding, it must have remained a painful and embarrassing memory. It compelled him to reveal his late brother's lack of shrewdness (to say nothing of possible dishonesty) and to publicize details of family business. Moreover, it was an ugly conflict that exposed the entire family to disgrace. The magistrates noted often that the parties 'went at one another hotly' (*dz die parteien jnn zweyen ersten Sessionen gaar hitzig an einander kommen*). Be that as it may, bitter disputes did not lessen Matheus's sense of responsibility for Daniel's widow and children. The gift-giving continued until 1673, by which time the children must have reached their majorities. In 1679, Matheus joined Andreas Stemmer, a brewer and burgher of Augsburg, as a trustee (*Pfleger*) of Daniel's estate.[99] In an agreement, probably necessitated by the remarriage of his widow, his children's inheritances were secured. Maria surrendered all claims to her late husband's estate but offered no further support to his children. Instead, each of them – Georg, Sibilla, Daniel, Felicitas and Johann – would immediately receive equal shares of their father's estate, valued at fl. 25. In addition to the fl. 5, each son would receive a further fl. 25 to pay for an appropriate apprenticeship, and each daughter would receive an unspecified settlement (*Ausfertigung*) to serve as a dowry. The projected settlement nearly equals the fl. 300 paid by Matheus in 1667. Whatever his feelings about the conflict, Matheus's commitment to his brother's family, the result of their kinship and need, apparently surmounted disagreements.

His lists of New Year's gifts portray Matheus as pater and patron, first and foremost within the limited circle of a kinship group. His social landscape takes the form of a cluster of households, related by blood and marriage. Matheus refers by name only to his parents, siblings, wives and children. All others are merely the spouses or offspring, widow or orphans, servants or retainers of an extended Miller clan. From the perspective of his gift-giving, Matheus was at the center of this circle. He provides largesse to those who are economically dependent on him, his own household. He provides largesse as well for those who are legally dependent upon him, his official wards. And he provides largesse for those who are ethically dependent upon him, his needy relations. Yet, theirs are not simply the shared ties of relationship or necessity, important as these are for Matheus. They share as well common interests, a common stake in the family's fortunes. The fame or infamy of one reflects on them all; the success or failure of one affects them all. It seems that Matheus tried to foster a solidarity that had been missing in his father's generation and an esteem that had been missing in his own youth.

Paternalism and patronage also explain the outsiders in the lists. In fact, Matheus gave to many people who would not have deferred to him as a paterfamilias. Among these were Augsburg's Lutheran clergy. Each member of the *ministerium* received a gift every New Year's Day, a considerable expense that mounted annually to about fl. 30.[100] With the members of his household, the pastors comprise the most important group of associates listed in Matheus's memoir. They participate in the momentous events in the lifecycle of every family, to which the memoir is largely devoted. They marry Matheus and his wives; they baptize his children; they bury his dead. This alone might be enough to justify the gifts: they reflect Matheus's personal estimation of the importance of such transitions; and they express a conventional, but – as will become clear – not untroubled, Lutheran identity. So important are the Lutheran clergy that Matheus remembers each by name and describes the parts they played. Yet, his relationship to each of them as private persons, rather than as office-holders, is far from clear. He is their patron. With but two exceptions, they appear only as passive recipients of his annual largesse, about whom he offers no further details.

The two exceptions were both pastors of his parish, Holy Cross Church. Georg Philip Riß, who figured prominently in Matheus's troubled tenure as custodian, preached from 1661 to 1684.[101] His predecessor, Thomas Hopfer, served from 1648 until 1661.[102] Both were firebrand preachers, zealous critics of Augsburg's Catholics and tireless opponents of any accommodation with them. In their correspondence and sermons they frequently attacked Catholic theology and liturgy and urged their congregations to steadfast antagonism against their non-Lutheran neighbors. This brought both men into regular contact with the City Council, whose policy it was to maintain public order by avoiding open confrontation and hostility between the two confessions. They were frequently questioned about their preaching and warned to moderate their sentiments. The admonitions had little effect. Riß was repeatedly censured for his unbridled enmity toward Augsburg's Catholics, but rose through the ranks of the the city's ministerium to end his days as senior and pastor at St Anna. Hopfer refused to surrender to the authorities certain correspondence that pertained to the local Lutheran community and was released from office in 1661. He eventually settled in Württemberg, where he served as pastor to several communities before his death in 1678.

For all their similarities, the two men had very different relationships to Matheus. The memoir suggests that Riß was not a close friend, despite the fact that the men associated frequently in matters of church business. Indeed, Matheus is obliquely critical of him at several points. That notwithstanding, Riß received the annual consideration without exception. Indeed, he received twice the normal sum, 2 *Reichstaler* each New Year's Day, probably because he was Matheus's own pastor. Hopfer received twice that sum, 4 *Reichstaler*, and his four children each received one-half *Reichstaler*. Kinship and dependency explain the difference.

Matheus's mother Sibilla was Thomas Hopfer's sister. Both were the children of Matheus Hopfer the Elder, who numbered among the great merchants of Augsburg before his death in 1624.[103] Yet, the Hopfer fortunes went into eclipse thereafter. True, the widow Hopfer remained a wealthy woman by virtue of her late husband's estate.[104] By 1646, however, no Hopfer was included among Augsburg's economic elite. They had fallen from the mercantile firmament, while Matheus had begun his rise.

Different trajectories strengthened the ties that linked the Miller and Hopfer families. Matheus's first wife, Anna Maria, born Warmberger, stood as godmother to Thomas Hopfer's four children, all of whom were remembered by Matheus on every New Year's Day until the end of his life. In turn, Hopfer baptized two of Matheus's children by his second wife, Helena, born Schorer: Matheus the Younger in 1658 and Sibilla in 1660, for whom he also stood as godparent.[105] Matheus also associated with a number of his mother's other siblings. In 1655, he commissioned a portrait of his second father-in-law, Anton Christoph Schorer the Elder, from Bartholomeus Hopfer, an aspiring artist in the city of Worms. That same year, he loaned fl. 1,500 to another of her brothers, Matheus Hopfer the Younger.[106] His fortunes waxing, Matheus, though younger, had become a patron to the Hopfer family. Connected by marriage and, it seems safe to assume, affection, he aided them in a variety of ways, serving their interests and his own. Paternalism, as well as patronage, shaped their relationship.

The loan to Matheus Hopfer prompted a complex and revealing series of transactions. Collateral took the form of Hopfer's 25-percent interest in his late father's house, of which Matheus already owned 47.5 percent, most likely acquired through his mother.[107] When Matheus called the debt in 1659, Hopfer's inability to pay principal and interest gave rise to negotiation and compromise.[108] Matheus granted a three-month extension, at which time Hopfer would pay loan and interest, rounded to fl. 1,620, as well as surrender his share of the house, worth fl. 1,250. Failure to meet the new terms would result in the immediate transfer of complete ownership of the house and all its furnishings to Matheus. Though no direct evidence testifies to the fact, Hopfer must have paid his debt. The day after the deadline, on 4 November 1661, Matheus sold his interest in the house, which now included his own share as well as Hopfer's, back to Hopfer for fl. 3,125.[109] Now the owner, Hopfer used the house as collateral to secure fl. 4,675 in new debt, including fl. 875 from brother Bartholomeus and fl. 260 from Matheus.[110] One year later, on 21 November 1662,

Hopfer sold the property in its entirety back to Matheus for fl. 5,300. With this sum Hopfer discharged his obligations.[111] Despite his financial interest in the house, Matheus had no desire to live there. Less than two months after buying it, on 12 January 1663, he sold it to David von Stetten for fl. 5,000.[112] What had been the gage in a convoluted financial scheme between merchants became a villa for a patrician.

The Hopfer property provided the means to several ends. Most immediately, it served as collateral for a series of credit transactions. Yet, in a world of nascent capitalism, where loans floated and capital flowed, it supported more ambitious plans. Matheus used it as leverage. The house had no value as a dwelling for him, but it enabled him to assist a related family on the outs and to profit handsomely for his efforts. Hopfer's distress was evident. He failed to repay a sum that his father would have scorned. Using the house to secure the loan and to hide the default, Matheus propped up his mother's brother without depriving him of either his honor or his independence. What might have been an act of largesse or patronage remained, nonetheless, justifiable from a purely commercial perspective. In return for the loan of fl. 1,500, Matheus netted fl. 1,370 in profit, that is, his interest from the loan combined with Hopfer's share of the house. He resold their combined shares at the proclaimed market value of fl. 625, for a total of fl. 3,125. Though timing and price indicate that he always intended to support Hopfer's ownership, Matheus still booked a tidily positive cash flow. Finally, he sold the house at fl. 5,300 against a cost of fl. 5,000, that left him with a net gain of about fl. 4,000 and may have curried the favor of the von Stetten family as well. Nor did Hopfer suffer. He walked away from the entire deal with a comfortable profit of fl. 675, all of his debts paid, and his honor entirely intact. Matheus had become a protector and friend of the Hopfer family. And, he had proved himself to be a shrewd one. Yet, his shrewdness should not obscure the fact he also acted out of a sense of familial solidarity and personal profit, a combination that posed no intrinsic contradiction in terms. For Matheus, friendship could not be parsed into convenient categories such as utility, pleasure or virtue. Nor could it be explained in terms of interest or emotion. Such theoretical constructs assume a Hobbesian individuality that sets all against all. Matheus understood these things as indissolubly connected, however. His friendships might serve his self-interest, as canonical works urge and scholarly literature argues, but that self-interest was not at odds with a larger framework of relationships. He achieved his own gain through his friends and family, through his honor and propriety, through his acumen and ability.

It is no surprise, therefore, that Thomas Hopfer placed his children under the guardianship of Matheus, rather than take them into exile with him in 1661.[113] Matheus was the natural choice: his mother was one of their own; the Hopfer considered him to be a friend. In their need, they turned to him for support and shelter; he assisted them to the best of his ability. To Hopfer's children, he consistently gave one-half *Reichstaler*.[114] When their father went into exile, Matheus shouldered the burdens of guardianship and added Hopfer to his New Year's list. Despite his residence in Württemberg, Thomas Hopfer received 2 *Reichstaler* beginning in 1663 and 4 *Reichstaler* from 1670 until his death in 1678.[115] Clearly, Matheus acknowledged the responsibilities that went with even the most distant of family ties. To the Hopfer, as to his siblings, he offered paternalism and patronage.

Yet, Matheus offered such support to other people. The Hopfer family was related to the Miller family both conjugally, through the marriage of Matheus's mother and father, and spiritually, through the godparentage of Matheus's wife and Thomas Hopfer. They also had interests in common. Property facilitated a collaboration that promoted mutual advantage. Yet, kinship, property and necessity applied to people who never found their way onto Matheus's lists.

Matheus served as a legally appointed trustee or guardian to several of his relatives.[116] The memoir notes six of them without comment for the most part. None apparently involved the exchange of gifts or any indication of social obligation. They might, however, have required considerable effort or expense on his part. In 1673, Matheus and Gabriel Schorer were appointed *Beistand* to the widow of Jakob Schorer, Regina Bocklerin.[117] The Schorer family was related to Matheus by his marriage to Helena, and they occupied a special place in his affections. In this instance, however, the duties of legal representative cost him 'much and great effort' (*so mir vil und grose mühe verursacht*). He does not elaborate. Four years later, Matheus became a trustee of Jakob Schorer's estate, when his widow remarried.[118] Again, he was responsible for securing the paternal inheritances of Schorer's children. The agreement assumed the standard form. Renouncing all rights to the estate, the widow promised to raise and support the children, Christoph Jakob and Euphrosina Regina, until they came of age or married. At that time, each would receive an inheritance of fl. 150, half their father's personal property, and a settlement of fl. 30 to provide an apprenticeship for Christoph or to serve as a dowry for Euphrosina. Such services as these, whether for relatives or for strangers, resemble official duties rather than familial responsibilities. They lack the devotion implicit in the regular giving of gifts.

Thus, the lists mark an important group of relationships rather than describe exclusive modes of behavior. Matheus demonstrated great solicitude and solidarity for people to whom he never gave a penny on New Year's Day. His diary records one such instance: 'In the year 1656 on 8 April died Philip Warmberger...I bore the burial costs because of his arrangement with the house as recorded in my accounts.'[119] That cryptic remark obscures a world of transaction, compensation and accommodation.

Hans Philip Warmberger, the uncle of Matheus's first wife, was a merchant of no particular substance.[120] The Warmberger family may have been victims of the mid-century crisis. His brother, Matheus's father-in-law, had loaned a capital of fl. 20,000 to the imperial city of Kempten in 1638. In the wake of war, most city governments suspended payment on such debts in the desperate struggle to preserve solvency. So it may have happened in this case. In 1648, Matheus and Anna Maria bought out Hans Philip's share of the investment, nominally worth fl. 10,000, for a mere fl. 1,400.[121] The transaction signaled the declining fortunes of the Warmberger and the rising estate of Matheus. Given the improbability of recovering even a part of the capital, the purchase was a thinly disguised act of charity on the younger man's part. Nor was it the only such instance. In 1653, Hans Philip sold his house in the Heiligkreuzstraße to Matheus and Anna Maria for fl. 2,000.[122] The contract of sale refers to his 'destitute condition and acknowledged need' (*kümmerlichen Zuestandt und bekandter noth*), in which Matheus and Anna Maria had repeatedly lent a hand. He had failed to pay his city taxes and his servants' wages in recent years. In light of these facts, the contract established a kind of receivership. Matheus would not pay the sale price of the house to Hans Philip but, rather, would use it to discharge his uncle-in-law's obligations. Hans Philip would continue to reside in the house until his death, during which time he would receive a monthly stipend of fl. 10 to provide clothing, food, heat and light. When Hans Philip died, Matheus would assume all costs of a Christian burial, which he duly paid.[123] Should that occur before Matheus had rendered the full fl. 2,000, the balance would be forgiven and the house and furnishings would convey to Matheus. From the year of the sale until the year of his death, Hans Philip paid no tax.[124] He had become Matheus's dependant and remained so, even after his niece's death and Matheus's remarriage, until the end of his days.

For Matheus, property was more than a form of wealth, a means to status. It underwrote familial solidarity by permitting members to assist one another. He used a house to preserve the honor and estate of his mother's family, the Hopfer. He repeated that strategy for his first wife's family, the Warmberger. Yet, this was not simple charity. He did not reduce his partners to dependency and, thus, deprive them of their dignity. Hopfer and Warmberger each provided the capital to fuel their transactions; each bore his part in fair exchanges. Nor did he fail to profit. His support for impecunious relatives demonstrated a sharp-eyed sense of value. Interest and emotion underwrote one another. That they did so established Matheus's stature in his family and in the world.

Marriage and property, kinship and dependence, also divided individuals and families against each other, even as they created ties and encouraged mutual assistance. The ambivalence of these ties helps to explain the bitterness of internecine property disputes. They violated the convergent and concurrent ties of interest and emotion. They reduced Matheus to fury and invective decades after the fact.

One person, in whom the strands of interest and emotion were tightly interwoven, was Matheus's first mother-in-law, Susanna Warmberger, born Wild. Their particular circumstances worked to create a bond between them that endured long after Matheus's first marriage had ended. Susanna lived in her son-in-law's household while her daughter was alive. After Anna Maria's death, she took over his housekeeping.[125] He described the situation as mutually satisfactory (*mit Jhrer und meiner seits gueten contento*), despite unnamed but predictable difficulties with the servants.[126] He had given thought to some provision for his mother-in-law that would provide her with a measure of peace and security in her old age but had done nothing at the time. As he put it: 'the dear Lord knew what we would have to do according to his divine will' (*der Liebe Gott wuste woll selber was beede nach seinem Götlichen Willen Thuen wurden müeßen*). When Helena Schorer became his wife in 1654, Susanna initially objected to the unseemly haste of the wedding but eventually 'showed herself willing and did as much as she could to assist' him.[127] Out of gratitude and obligation, Matheus located an independent dwelling and a reliable servant for Susanna at his own expense. These mutually agreeable arrangements justified Matheus's claim that they 'parted from one another in love and peace...after we lived seven and one-half years together and got on well with one another, in joy and sorrow, despite the various hard knocks that came our way'. His affection endured. Upon her death, he wrote with feeling: 'I received many good deeds in every way from this good and honorable woman.'[128] Had she lived longer, her name might have appeared on Matheus's first list of New Year's gifts.

On 17 October 1655, after a walk with her grandsons, Philip Jakob and Matheus the Younger, Susanna began to complain of fatigue (*Matigkeit*).[129] She took to her bed, thus initiating a struggle to gain influence over her and her estate. Her sister, the wife of Hans Jerg Rauhwolff, convinced Susanna to consult a new physician. They intended, so wrote, Matheus, to demonstrate that the old woman 'no longer remembered but had forgotten the old pledges'. Moreover, she pressed Susanna to prepare a formal testament.[130] The dying woman initially resisted, but her sister threatened to abandon her. Fearing a contested estate, Susanna finally relented and agreed to create a will.

During a visit with Matheus and his sons, she told him of her plan, as yet unrealized, to leave her sister fl. 1,000 and her corner house.[131] Matheus argued that the sister had no claim on the estate (*Jch sagte hete der Fraw hierin nix einzuereden*). He urged Susanna to remember her grandsons, saying she knew what her means were and how to dispose of them but that his sons would have many needs before they came of age. She insisted that, apart from making her sister universal heir, she would leave only small legacies to the Lutheran pastors and the Lutheran Poor House. With that, she refused to divulge any further particulars.

Matheus reassured Susanna that he would do as she wished but asked whether she had discussed this matter with her trustee (*Beistand*), Christoff Georg Mair.[132] When she expressed a wish to do so, he fetched Mair and notary Weienmair. On the way back, they were joined by a Hopfer, who served as witness. Meeting Rauhwolff and wife at Susanna's door, Matheus accused them of selfishly intimidating the old woman into forgetting her family's needs and her own responsibilities.[133] He expressed amazement that they would hurt the interests of his children (and their godchildren) in this manner. Susanna must struggle with her own conscience, said Matheus, because she knows her estate should not be divided in this manner. On the one hand she has natural heirs (the children of her daughter, Matheus's late wife); on the other hand, it is no affair of her sister (*Rauhwölffin*) to interfere in the estate. Matheus claimed that he hoped to spare Susanna further care and to preserve the friendship of the Rauhwolff family by reaching an amicable compromise. He offered them fl. 1,000 in installments from the value of the estate; they demanded fl. 1,000 at once or Susanna's house on Katzenstadel. When no agreement proved mutually acceptable, Matheus gave up his efforts. Meanwhile, Hopfer and Mair were inside with Susanna, who refused to discuss the matter of her testament.[134] Later that night, the Rauhwolffs called the notary once again. Susanna spoke with him about various matters, only one of which concerned her estate: she disinherited her sister (*darauff het sie nun ferners nix thon lassen dann abwolen die Rauchwölffin*). All those present urged her to consult a notary. Matheus promised again that he would comply with any arrangements she chose to make. Susanna only responded that she 'had two dear grandchildren'. Realizing that the inheritance was slipping from his grasp, Rauhwolff offered to accept Matheus's compromise. Matheus replied that the lady could speak but chose not to do so. He would agree to nothing that Susanna did not wish. So the dispute ended.

Her worldly affairs ordered, Susanna turned to her spiritual needs. She asked to receive the sacrament. Matheus sent for a pastor, who talked privately to the old woman for some time.[135] She made her confession, received absolution and took the sacrament. The pastor ordered those in attendance not to trouble the old woman further but rather to assist her by reading and praying. Matheus notes particularly that the Rauhwolff family abandoned the deathbed when they realized that no testament would be made in their favor. Despite all pleas to see Susanna before she died, they did not return. In the presence of Matheus and his sons, she made a Christian end.[136]

> The good woman weakened steadily from that hour onward, suffered some pain but never complained. On Sunday she recommended the children to my care and wished me good fortune in all my doings. She died gently and spiritually on Monday, 8 November, during the morning sermon and amid the prayers of those around her.

Her final serene moments contrast starkly with the uneasy days that preceded it.

This was not merely some tawdry dispute over property. A large estate could cause considerable ambition and animosity. It was, however, a crucial moment in the life of a family. The devolution of property confirmed the affective and material connections between its members. Moreover, the transfer of property to the appropriate persons constituted a moral obligation. When Rauhwolff intervened in this process, she set the emotional, economic and ethical underpinnings of Matheus's household at risk. This explains his engagement. He remembered the events in considerable detail, recreating conversations and revealing personalities as if he were arguing the correctness of his behavior. He was. It was not just a matter of money but rather a confirmation of Susanna's affection for him and his sons and an affirmation of their collective propriety. It was a striking scene: an inheritance dispute, fought in the presence and over the head of the testatrix. He defended his sons' interests in the estate of their late mother. He recalled Susanna to her moral responsibility not to neglect her 'natural heirs', by which he meant the succeeding generations, that is, her daughter's and his own children. In the end, the testament was never written. By pressing her case, Rauhwolff ruined her chances. By dying intestate, Susanna left her property to Matheus's sons. By submitting to Susanna's wishes – supporting her decision not to create a will – he promoted his interests and acted appropriately. Ironically, in the midst of conflict, Matheus gave her that peace he had long intended.

In the matter of Susanna Warmberger's estate, as in the other relationships and associations recorded in his memoir, Matheus cast himself in a particular light. He appeared always the capable, charitable father-figure, the pater and patron of a network of related, interdependent households. Spiritual and physical proximity, based on common residence and ties of blood and marriage, gave rise to tight-knit interests and emotions. These are his central concern. Larger ambitions were hardly realistic. Marriage alliances with the patriciate and high office within the city-state, both of which promised social advancement and political power, remained beyond his reach. The arenas within which he could achieve a degree of greatness were the marketplace and the household. The absence of a self-conscious instrumentality, as ascribed to early modern sociability, is not surprising. By recording instances that revealed both his business acumen and his familial solidarity, Matheus conveyed characteristics that spoke to his quality and promised success in both settings. His memoir constitutes a form of social patrimony, not only an ethical justification but also a social compass. Matheus explicitly wished to leave his children and heirs something of his life.[137] Its most important lessons, like the lists of New Year's gifts, were drawn from a wider world of experience and applied to the inner circle of his friends, his family.

Matheus devoted the final section of his memoir to a list of a different sort. Fully one-third of its entire length contained the names of his godchildren. To judge by the space alone, godparentage was one of the most important social relationships in Matheus's life. Not only did he list with great care the godparents chosen for his own children but he also kept careful record of those children for whom he was chosen godparent. Yet, again like the gift lists, he offered almost no explanatory detail. His readers would have understood both the meaning of the larger institution and the significance of the specific relationships.

Both Catholic and Lutheran churches viewed the responsibilities of godparents as highly significant.[138] The classical Lutheran position retained Catholic liturgical and educational functions virtually unchanged. After the parents, godparents served as witnesses to the fact of infant baptism and were entrusted with the spiritual growth of the child, its education and development as a Christian. During the baptism, they were required to swear as much. Whereas Lutheran theologians generally recognized that these functions lacked scriptural justification, they argued for their retention on the grounds that they were pious and useful.[139] Thus, in principle, moral reputation played a considerable role in the selection of godparents.

Nor were the bonds between godparent and godchild limited to matters of religious instruction and life. In practice, a godparent might be expected, even required, to contribute to any and all of the godchild's material support in the event that its parents proved unable to do so alone. In the course of the godchild's growth they might be consulted in matters pertaining to its secular education and training, asked to recommend a tutor or master. Eventually, the godparents might take a role in the arrangement of marriages for their godchildren. Not surprisingly, therefore, godparents served as a conduit for patronage and, accordingly, were also chosen on the basis of their social stature.

Neither moral nor social calculations figured in the selection of godparents for Matheus's children, however. He followed a regular pattern: a member of his own family; a member of his wife's family; and a member of the Lutheran *ministerium*.[140] These three individuals varied from child to child but were, with very few exceptions, culled from the same three groups. The godparents of Matheus's eldest son, Philip Jakob, offer a case in point.[141] They were Matheus's wealthy, reputable, and, at one time, critical uncle Hans Jakob, his wife's cousin Sara Rauhwolff, and the Senior Pastor Philip Weber. Occasionally Matheus added a fourth person to the list of godparents. For this purpose, he usually turned to business colleagues and associates. Thus, Gabriel Hopfer, a Nuremberger merchant and distant relative of his first wife, joined the sponsors of Philip Jakob, while Baltas Schnurbein, who served as Matheus's master in 1641, served as godparent to his children, Susanna in 1654 and Marcus in 1653. At the birth of his last child, Johanna Katharina, he chose Georg Laub, Assistant Pastor at

Holy Cross, Sabina Miller, his sister-in-law, and the wife of Jakob Füll, his third wife's cousin.[142] The consistency with which Matheus selected godparents for his children suggests a no less consistent strategy. Though mindful of the need for powerful patronage as a means to temporal success, still he preferred to foster solidarity between the branches of his family and affinity with the Lutheran clergy. This matches almost exactly the pattern of his gift-giving.

Matheus served as godfather often. His memoir listed no fewer than 41 godchildren. Yet, the strategy that applied so consistently to the sponsors of his own children does not seem to have applied to Matheus. Barely one-third of his godchildren were family members, related by blood or marriage to him or to his wife. Most were outsiders; their specific relationships to him are unclear; the memoir seldom offers the least hint. In most instances, Matheus does little more than note the birth and baptism along with a quick, epigrammatic invocation, 'G. G. G.', God give grace (*Gott geb Gnad*). At one point, Matheus recalls serving as godfather to Johannes Ehinger: 'Because of the many services I received from the father, I gave him a silver knife and spoon case upon which was engraved: "God has told you what is good; and what is it that the Lord asks of you? Only to act justly, to love loyalty, and to walk wisely before your God."'[143] The nature of the service – even the father's identity – remain obscure. As a group, Matheus's godchildren were the sons and daughters of Augsburger pastors, merchants and artisans. They came from all sectors of the economy and all parts of the city. Most were poorer than Matheus, but some boasted considerable property and bore venerable names. They have in common only their Lutheran confession.

Etienne François has argued that baptism was a crucial moment in the social life of Augsburg's Lutheran and Catholic communities.[144] It defined initially and usually indelibly the infant's affiliation. As such, it belongs to an array of identifying objects, symbols and ceremonies that proliferated in the late seventeenth century to bind individuals to religious groups. Convinced that baptism rendered newborn children impervious to conversion, quite apart from other imperatives, pastors and priests rushed to perform the ceremony as early as possible. Certainly, much evidence exists to support increased confessional identity in early modern Augsburg.

Yet, it seems to have affected Matheus's sociability only unevenly. Though he associated with his Catholic neighbors, as his militia service revealed and his business activities required, they never numbered among his friends. His lists and reminiscences awaken the impression that confession set the framework for his sociability. The Lutheran Church received his services, Lutheran pastors received his patronage, and Lutheran children received his sponsorship. His identity as a Lutheran encouraged him to do so. These were, after all, acts of Christian love, incumbent upon all members of the community. If confession motivated his sociability, however, it was but one source and not necessarily the most important. Matheus consistently stressed the importance of family connections, whether by blood or by marriage. These stood at the absolute center of his household, his business and his world. His dealings with people in all these spheres were sparked by a certain paternalism, the readiness of a well-to-do pater or patron to stand by families less fortunate than his own. He indicates also a sense of reciprocity, a conviction that services should be recompensed not merely in cash but more essentially in kind.

His friendships served his purposes, but his purposes conform only inexactly to standard theories. In the literary canon, friends are abstract relationships, based on virtue, pleasure and utility. Yet, Matheus did not explicitly incorporate Cicero's projection of a metaphysical virtue. Nor did he openly advocate Alberti's pursuit of political advantage. In the scholarly canon, social relations are understood instrumentally because they exist only to promote political, social and economic ends. Though Matheus strove for and achieved a degree of power, stature and wealth, the fruits of which were obvious to all, his friendships and associations were not obviously the means to these ends. They appear free of abstraction and calculation. The memoir maps a different, more complex, reality.

During the preceding century, the traditional purpose and trajectory of a successful Augsburg merchant had changed. New wealth had sought and found ways to rise above its station: marrying into the patriciate; investing in land; offering service to city or prince; pursuing patents of nobility.[145] Constitutional change and economic retrenchment fostered a social exclusivity that rendered such advancement all but impossible in Matheus's lifetime. Moreover, Augsburg's loss of political and economic influence limited opportunities to achieve the same ends on a broader stage or a grander scale. Though doubtless wealthy, Matheus lacked the resources to overcome such obstacles. His reach was shorter, his world more parochial and his goals more humble. His memoir suggests that, with the slow erosion of traditional urban society, doubts emerged not over the nature of community or of citizenship but rather over the location of the self.[146] Less interested in social mobility or social status as these things slip from his grasp,

Matheus sought to shape his social identity, to perpetuate his personal reputation for propriety.

His memoir documented this purpose, even as his associations incorporated it. Matheus cultivated protégés, all of whom were commoners of economic and social standing equal to or lower than his own. He was not consciously calculating at every turn; his generosity often followed his affections. In the end, his sociability was a flexible practice, defined by the specificities of his life, person by person and situation by situation. Yet, his purpose remained, and patronage and reciprocity proved most useful to this end. His wealth allowed him to engage in largesse of a work-a-day sort. Not for him were the great endowments and foundations. He relied instead on more modest, more individualized, gifts and services. They permitted him to acquire social debt without seeming to aspire to social prestige. And, they testified not only to his stature but also, and more importantly, to his generosity, affection and virtue.

For Matheus, propriety embodied the characteristics of a successful merchant: experience, astuteness, prudence, honesty, and, at need, generosity. He demonstrated these qualities as were appropriate to business dealings and social relations in his hometown. Local knowledge was the foundation of local reputation. So conceived, it was ideally suited for a world of limited opportunities and ambitions.

4
Death and Confession

Matheus Miller was a pious man. As he recorded the noteworthy events of his life, he scored his memoir with prayers to God and reflections on Providence. Some of these invocations were rather brief and distant – at least to modern ears. On the occasion of his first marriage in 1647, he noted that the arrangements were concluded 'with good peace and content for which praise and thanks to the All Highest; may He further give the assured, divine blessings'.[1] Other entries were more fulsome appeals for divine aid or retribution. After an inheritance dispute, he consigned his opponents to a justice higher than his own: 'God will unerringly arrange it and direct Satan, who arrogantly bustles about in small, fleshly form; God rebuke and beset you, Satan, and give peace and unity, trustworthy honorableness without self-seeking desire or lust.'[2] Still other reflections expressed bewilderment at the mystery of God's will. When his daughter died, Matheus groaned: 'Now see the hand of God that touched me once more with righteous zeal and mercy...and once again tore open my wounds.'[3] Through his private devotions, he marked the boundary between the natural and the supernatural, between the limited world of human efficacy and the infinite realm of superhuman agency.

Matheus was also a church man. Raised in the Lutheran Church, educated at a Lutheran academy, befriended by Lutheran clergy, he occupied numerous Lutheran offices. From 1664 to 1684 he served as trustee of the Anna Raiser Foundation, a private Lutheran charity.[4] From 1673 until his death in 1685, he commanded the First Burgher Company of Infantry, a post reserved for a Lutheran citizen.[5] In 1675, he served as an associate (*Beisitzer*) of the Augsburg Marriage Court, a Lutheran tribunal.[6] That same year, he accepted the trusteeship of the Hans Georg Österreicher Foundation, another Lutheran charity.[7] From

1676 to 1678 he served as custodian of the then recently rebuilt Lutheran Church of the Holy Cross.[8] In a long and varied career of public service, Matheus always acted as a representative of his confession.

But Matheus was a profoundly private man. In his memoir, he distinguished between public, religious observance and personal, pious expression. Prayers and offices, friends and enemies all testified to a life informed by the Lutheran Church and the Augsburg Confession. Yet, the silences are no less expressive. He never reflected on the larger historical events of his day, events often born of confessional animosity. He never excoriated the Catholics who lived all around him, a constant challenge to his Lutheran conviction. He never accepted unquestioningly the workings of divine Providence, so much a part of early modern religion. Matheus acknowledged as well not only the sacred but also the secular functions of confessionally influenced religious observance. Private devotions and public worship testified not only to his personal religiosity but also to his social status. They strengthened his social relations. Once again, the silences are no less telling. Even as he reflected on the devotion of others, he held a mirror up to his own propriety and his family's solidarity. Recalling moments of great spiritual meaning, he all but ignored the role of the church and its clergy. Concerned for the salvation of his soul, he understood that religion served his worldly aspirations. The written and unwritten aspects of Matheus's life permit, therefore, an exploration of one person's religious sensibilities in an age of confessionalization.

Confessionalization refers to two related but distinct historical processes.[9] It describes the gradual emergence of confessions as self-conscious groups, defined by distinctive modes of devotion and behavior, that began as early as the 1520s. It also describes the politicization of Protestant and Catholic Reformations that resulted from the Religious Peace of Augsburg in 1555. Both of these elements of confessionalization – the internal and the external – and the tensions between them left their traces in Matheus's memoir. His repeated appeals to God and his constant concern with Providence constitute the markings of a religious *habitus*.[10] His life as a Lutheran citizen and his service as a Lutheran official were shaped by the social and political relations between confessions.

The Religious Peace of Augsburg provided the framework for these relations in Augsburg and throughout the empire. It afforded legal recognition and protection to Lutherans and Catholics while denying them to all other confessions. Its name notwithstanding, the Religious Peace was no religious peace but rather a political arrangement that recognized a temporary division in the Christian Church as an emergency measure that would guarantee freedom and security to both great confessions until unity could be restored.[11] It also legitimized the construction of state churches in which civic and territorial rulers insisted that clergy adhere to uniform confessional formulae and that laity conform to sanctioned religious observance. Social order and political policy set renewed emphasis upon religious unity.

Civic magistrates in imperial cities such as Augsburg could not rely on princely power to enforce religious conformity. Their authority rested instead on a common commitment to certain broadly shared principles that constrained individual interests and integrated community members.[12] The Reformation challenged that common commitment, especially in cities where the balance of power between Catholics and Protestants prevented either from dominating the other. It created conflicting loyalties that encouraged citizens to act against their neighbors and to defy their magistrates. Diaries, such as that kept by Matheus, expose the contours of these divided councils and conflicted loyalties as personal, lived experience.

Augsburg was a multi-confessional city.[13] In the early years of the Reformation, its walls harbored many sects and confessions, among which the Anabaptists, Schwenkfeldians, Zwinglians, Lutherans and Catholics were all well represented. In 1537, the process of reform, which had been cautiously controlled by the City Council since the early 1520s, entered a decisive stage. The election of two Zwinglian patricians, Mang Seitz and Hans Welser, to the office of *Burgomaster* signaled an end to restraint. The Reformation Ordinance of that same year decreed the banishment of 'popish idolatry' (*die papistische Abgötterei*) from the city.[14] Catholic worship ceased, and Protestant pastors took over the churches. Catholic clergy and nuns chose either to accept the authority of the Council or to suffer exile from the city. A wave of iconoclasm followed, by which 'each and every image, whether painted, carved, or cast, from altars or wherever ... [were] to be taken and removed orderly and unbroken and to be preserved until a future [ecumenical] council or national assembly'.[15] Very little ecclesiastical art survived.

That a Catholic minority persisted despite the combined hostility of the City Council and the Protestant majority had much to do with the firmness of their faith, the stature of their members, the steadfastness of their clergy, and the proximity of their allies. Among the leaders were some of the wealthiest and most powerful patrician families of the city, including the Fugger, the Welser, the Rehlinger and the Baumgartner. They were supported by forceful and influential Catholic neighbors just beyond the city's walls: the Wittelsbach Duchy of Bavaria to the east; the Habsburg County of Burgau to the west; and the political territories (*Hochstift*) of the Diocese of Augsburg to the north and south. Political realities necessitated caution, compromise, and concession within the walls and without.

When policies failed to reflect realities, the city paid a heavy price. Catholic and imperial forces defeated the combined armies of Protestant princes and cities, to which forces Augsburg contributed, in 1547. That summer, the Bishop of Augsburg demanded the restoration of Catholic worship and the return of Catholic property. One year later, a victorious emperor forced the City Council to accept the Augsburg Interim, an agreement that re-established Catholic worship and limited Protestant observance. Moreover, that observance would conform to the Augsburg Confession, despite the fact that most of Augsburg's Protestants were Zwinglian rather than Lutheran.[16] The emperor also struck at what he considered to be the root of the problem, a constitution that opened city government to radical influences. To prevent further disorder, he imposed a new structure that set two *Stadtpfleger*, one Catholic and one Protestant, at the head of the government, supported by a Secret Council of four Catholics and one Protestant and a Small Council of twenty-one Catholics and twenty Protestants. Swept aside was representation by the guilds; installed was government by an oligarchy.

A narrow Catholic majority ruled the councils of Augsburg from 1555 until 1648. It determined the fates of the city's population, roughly 90 percent of which was Protestant, and maintained a tenuous hold on power by steering a middle course in confessional politics.[17] The Religious Peace provided a point of departure of sorts. The City Article (Article 27) specifically excepted Augsburg and a few other cities with substantial religious minorities from uniformity of religion, a principle later made famous by the formula, *cuius regio, eius religio*. Instead, it provided a limited, legal toleration for Catholics and Lutherans: non-religious, civil rights of citizens were governed according to equality; religious expression was limited by previous practice and precedent; possession of religious property was returned to the status quo of the Interim.[18] Here was a framework within which the two confessions could live beside if not with one another.

The Council's efforts notwithstanding, conflict erupted frequently in the period between the two great peace treaties, the Religious Peace of 1555 and the Treaty of Westphalia in 1648, that mark the supposed boundaries of the age of confessionalization. Insofar as historians are correct in their assumption that external crises were the forge of confessional identity and solidarity, then the generations that lived through these times developed strong religious loyalties.[19] Men like Matheus inherited that sense of affiliation and commitment.

In Augsburg, small irritations formed the stuff of daily life.[20] Catholic clergy missed no opportunity to challenge Lutheran beliefs and practices from the pulpit and in pamphlets. Inflamed Lutherans mocked and disrupted Catholic processions as they wound through the streets. In parishes where Catholics and Lutherans worshiped in close proximity, as in the monasteries of Holy Cross, St Georg and St Ulrich, arguments often arose over the location of property lines, the use of church clocks and the ringing of church bells. Even the employment of servants or workers of one faith by mistresses or masters of another gave rise to city-wide controversy and contention. One particularly notorious example was Peter Canisius' exorcism and subsequent conversion of Susanna Roschmann, a Lutheran maid employed by the newly converted and enthusiastically Catholic Ursula Fugger.[21] Such controversies generated constant friction between confessions despite a superficial peace.

Larger, more serious conflicts periodically threatened the social and political order. Sharply heightened tensions resulted from the expansion of Catholic foundations in Augsburg: the founding of the Jesuit College of St Salvador, 1579–82, and the settlement of religious orders, the Franciscans in 1609 and the Discalced Carmelites in 1629. Augsburg's Lutheran community opposed still more explosively the introduction of the Gregorian calendar, proposed in 1582. The Calendar Conflict caused years of litigation and confrontation that reached its peak in 1586 with the banishment from Augsburg of the entire Lutheran clergy and an armed confrontation between a Lutheran mob and the city's militia. It ended with a formal compromise between Lutheran Church and City Council only in 1591. Far more disastrous for the Lutheran community, however, was the Edict of Restitution of 1629, which restored all ecclesiastical properties and incomes to the Catholic Church, stripped all Lutheran magistrates of their offices, and banished all Lutheran ministers from the city. For the next twenty years, with a few brief exceptions, Augsburg's Lutherans would worship without benefit of clergy and without shelter from the elements.

By 1648, they lost two-thirds of their membership to the horrors of war, an experience that threatened their physical existence as a community and their spiritual relationship to their confession.[22] Endurance and sacrifice proved the common stock of Augsburgers regardless of confession over the ensuing decades of the Thirty Years' War, as siege and occupation repeatedly demonstrated the city's political impotence and ruined its economic base.

Matheus was 23 years old at the time and already heir to a powerful heritage of endurance and sacrifice. As a boy, he had observed the destruction of his hometown. Shortly thereafter, he had left Augsburg to be schooled, first in the classics and then in commerce. Apart from brief visits, he had not returned to Augsburg until 1646, when he decided to go into business for himself. Thus, he experienced directly but never recorded explicitly the high tide of confessional strife – the nadir for Augsburg's Lutherans – and its end in 1648.

The institution of parity, as spelled out in the Treaty of Westphalia, ended the conflict and provided a basis for peace. Article 5, sections 4 through 10 of the *Instrumenta Pacis Osnabrugense* dictated an exact constitutional equality between the confessions.[23] They paid particular attention to Augsburg and other imperial cities with bi-confessional populations, where they specifically regulated the sharing of political office. At the highest levels of power, the Secret and Small Councils, Catholics received four of seven and 23 of 45 seats respectively with the balance reserved for Lutherans.[24] Where uneven numbers of magistrates exercised a particular office, the treaty held that the odd position would transfer in alternating years between a Catholic and a Lutheran.[25] The same division of office extended to every level of the city government and bureaucracy. These complicated provisions had the effect of splitting Augsburg's government and, indeed, the entire city into two separate but essentially equal parts, neither able to dominate the other.

The treaty divided competencies as well as offices. Though the Lutheran and Catholic governments conducted jointly all matters of common interest, each was prohibited from interference in the religious affairs of the other.[26] According to the principle of *itio in partes*, each part of Augsburg's government received sole responsibility for the religious affairs of its own confession.[27] This extended from the churches themselves to religious foundations, such as schools and charities.

Lutherans in Augsburg greeted the provisions and guarantees of the Treaty of Westphalia with undisguised joy.[28] These not only restored their right to worship but also assured their share of power, both long jeopardized by the political might of the Catholic opposition. For their part, Catholics resisted implementation of the treaty. For months the executors of the Peace struggled with a recalcitrant City Council 'worse than with pesky solicitors'.[29] The struggle spread to other areas of public life and captured the attention of contemporary observers and latter-day historians.

Obviously, policy alone could not regulate hostilities between confessions. Nor could it control underlying social and economic forces that exacerbated the tensions. Widespread destruction of the city's industrial base necessitated a consequent effort to rebuild. Anxious to increase the number of taxpayers and provide Augsburg with needed skills, the patrician-controlled City Council encouraged immigration by granting citizenship liberally after 1648.[30] Catholics and Lutherans alike wandered to Augsburg, the former coming from the neighboring Catholic hinterlands, the latter traveling from distant Protestant cities and territories.[31] Typically seeking employment as day-laborers, mill workers, or domestic servants, unskilled rural Catholics tended to fill the lower strata of Augsburg's society. Trained and educated urban Lutherans, on the other hand, entered the city's professions, trades and crafts. Thus, a disproportionate number of Catholics were trapped at the bottom of the social hierarchy while Lutherans dominated its economic elite.[32] Confession joined wealth and honor as determinants of social status in early modern Augsburg. Immigration gradually altered not only the city's social but also its demographic structure.[33] Around 1750, two centuries of Protestant plurality ended, and a Catholic majority emerged. Such disparities of faith, wealth and station were not new; they had characterized urban society throughout the early modern period. Similar findings in other cities, notably Kaufbeuren and Colmar, suggest that material inequalities may have chilled already cool relations between confessions or delayed a reconciliation between them in seventeenth- and eighteenth-century Germany.[34] Hence, growth compromised parity. A durable, political balance had been struck, but confessional tensions continued to complicate social relations in Augsburg.

The consequences of this politicization of religious difference on the development of confessional identities has long been a topic of speculation. The intellectual father of the study of confessionalization, Ernst Walter Zeeden, believed that 1648 marked the end of the age of confession, the point in time from which confessional issues retreated from the historical consciousness.[35] The notion is counter-intuitive when applied to Augsburg specifically and to Germany generally. Controversial literature, preached and printed in the later seventeenth century by Catholic and Lutheran clergy, all intent on attacking their adversaries and inflaming their allies, creates the impression that hostility defined confessional relations into the modern age.[36] That such presumed antagonisms shaped social relations in Augsburg became the stuff of popular wisdom in the eighteenth century. Parity, with its constitutionally mandated separation of confessions, prompted little sympathy in the age of Enlightened tolerance. One cosmopolitan observer described Augsburg as a 'city of Catholic and Protestant pig sties'.[37] The Berliner philosopher, Friedrich Nikolai, a keen if no more penetrating observer, captured the irony of the situation in his travel diary: 'On the one hand, one bakes tolerance pastries; on the other hand, one holds balls where only Catholics or Protestants dance, or one creates contracts in which the renter must first show whether he believes what the church believes.'[38] Both recognized that social and cultural hostility persisted within a stable and equitable political framework. Bernd Roeck apparently agrees and redefines the period from 1555 to 1648 as a 'time of incubation for confessional differences'.[39] Etienne François demonstrates that the boundaries between Lutherans and Catholics remained evident and complex at least into the eighteenth century.[40] Thomas Nipperdey insists that confessional dualism is 'one of the fundamental, daily, vital truths of [modern] German life'.[41] Among the majority of historians, a consciousness of confession and confessional difference forms one of the constitutive elements of a modern mentality.

It seems reasonable to conclude, therefore, that religious observance in the seventeenth and eighteenth centuries became formal, and confessional commitments hardened. Confronted with horrific suffering, each confession turned in upon itself and sought strength in renewed devotion.[42] The loss of life and property prompted efforts at consolidation and recovery, not only to repair churches but also to fill them with devoted congregations. Shifting economic and demographic relations further irritated what had always been a ticklish situation. Yet, such conclusions are based largely on references to prescriptive literature and confessional conflict, evidence that distorts quotidian behavior. The perspective of personal history, of confessionalization as lived experience, remains unexamined. Yet, personal history requires context, not merely the larger framework of conflict and concord between confessions but also, and more importantly, the framework of observance and meaning within which that personal history most immediately occurred.

Matheus's memoir ignored larger, worldly events. Rather, it accounted for a human life and a soul's progress, as stated explicitly on the title page.[43]

> Oh reader, think of me that I must die and that my days are numbered. And that I must live those days as the Lord did, must die as the Lord did, thus living and dying as the Lord did. Christian living sanctifies one and gains a holy death and eternal joy. God help us gain all three.

Matheus drew a close connection between a Christian life and eternal salvation, one that necessitated the recording of his life to document his struggle and justify his reward. Consistent with its exemplary purpose, the memorialized life would also reveal the workings of Providence at every turn. Petitions to God and invocations of the divine appear, therefore, throughout the text. Over the course of the memoir, they reveal more than the author's Christian comportment. They expose internal complexities as well. The progress of Matheus's soul was not uncontested. His religiosity was beset by misgivings, the result of the irreconcilability of God's mercy and the world's cruelty, especially in the face of death. Such misgivings found their voice not only in his devotions but also in his public recollections. Matheus increasingly adopted a private spirituality, shorn of its overt connections to the Lutheran Church and confession.

Matheus prayed at all times and in all circumstances. He summoned divine judgment and retribution on his enemies. He also sought divine favor and acknowledged an inscrutable Providence in his enterprises: 'Begun in the name of God the Father, the Son and the Holy Spirit on 2 April 1654; the Holy Trinity grant fortune and blessing just as almighty God in wondrous ways has guided me against all human reason'.[44] Such reflections were, however, relatively uncommon in Matheus's memoir. The hand of God showed itself most unmistakably neither in the courthouse nor in the marketplace but rather in the household.

His religious devotion emphasized the lifecycle of his family. Without scientific advances to reduce the wonder of it, birth and death in early modern Europe possessed a timeless, miraculous and ominous quality. Life was uncertain. Confronting its beginning and ending, a Christian could only plead for God's guidance and assistance. To judge from the attention he devoted to it, death particularly captured Matheus's imagination and challenged his beliefs. He rationalized it in terms of divine omnipotence and human frailty; he sheltered from it as an end of suffering and the promise of eternal life. Such things proved cold comfort.

Death has recently, and quite justly, been described as 'ubiquitous' in early modern Europe.[45] Despite the general lack of reliable mortality statistics for the sixteenth and seventeenth centuries, scholars agree that mortality rates were staggeringly high and life expectancies correspondingly short. Ordinarily, in cities such as Augsburg, death removed 3 percent of the population per year, a figure that could climb to 10 percent in times of crisis.[46] Normal mortality in Europe today stands at about 1 percent. Arguments that the frequency of untimely death opened emotional distance within families have inspired vigorous protests. As will become apparent, that thesis receives no support from Matheus's memoir. Undeniably, however, death constituted a perilous moment in the lifecycle of the family. It uniquely jeopardized the biological and economical unit. Moreover, it became generally contested ground in early modern Europe.[47] The Reformation transformed the observance of death more profoundly than any other religious ritual, making it a flashpoint of confessional tension. The state regulated death in order to discipline its subjects, making it a source of political conflict. Elites used death to reproduce the social order and assert social status, making it a measure of social distinctions. Matheus's memoir captures all of these elements. Thus, death offers not only a benchmark for assessing confessional identity but also a vantage point for observing cultural change.

Lutheran orthodoxy altered the traditional relationship between the living and the dead.[48] Prayers for the dead had been an integral part of Christian observance since the second century.[49] The notion of a Purgatory, which arose during the High Middle Ages, combined this intercession by the living with the concept of purification after death and with the localization of that process.[50] Without completely rejecting the existence, in space and time, of a place where the dead awaited final judgment, Luther argued that Purgatory was a place of purification rather than satisfaction.[51] Pain and suffering rather than prayers and rituals provided such redemption as their sins demanded. The intercession of the living had not the least effect on the souls of the dead. By the time his theology of salvation was fully formed, Luther had totally rejected both the existence of Purgatory and the possibility of post-mortem purification.[52] The gulf between the living and the dead had become absolute; the fates of souls were in God's hands. Prayers for the souls of the dead had been reduced to prayers of submission to God's will.

Matheus's devotions accord, at least outwardly, with this description. When his first child died in infancy, he expressed resignation.[53]

> But it pleased God the almighty, according to his divine will, to take this child quickly out of this vale of tears, for it returned gently and piously to sleep in the Lord on 7 April between 6:00 and 7:00 in the evening. Was buried on 9 April in the Zacharias Wild grave in St. Stephen's Cemetery. May the Lord God grant us all a sanctified end and a joyous resurrection in His time.

When the child's mother, Anna Maria, died in childbirth six years later, Matheus recalled her passing in terms that captured not only resignation but also grief and yearning.[54]

> Finally she said, 'I have emptied my heart and thank my dear Lord for the grace to have done so. Now I will die softly and piously in God's name. May God keep me. And you, my dear Miller, give me your hand and stay with me.' The doctors had given her a soothing drink [*Herztrünkhlein*]. This she drank and laid herself on her side with my arm in hers and her hands clasped and began to drift away, though she retained her sight, hearing, and understanding. Her speech failed but she indicated with mouth and hands that we should pray. She looked at me, turned her eyes toward heaven, and slept blessedly in the Lord, soft and still; God help us all in his time so to do. Amen, amen, amen. This occurred on Sunday, 7 June 1654, at 7:00 in the evening.

He orchestrates Anna Maria's final moments in such a way as to testify both to their submission to God's will and to their faith in His grace. She passed away surrounded by loved ones, in the midst of prayer, 'blessedly in the Lord, soft and still'. Hers was a model death; his was a model attendance; both were recorded for purposes of instruction and inspiration.

Matheus's prayers reflect the didactic purpose of his memoir. Occurring at immutable points in the human lifecycle, at those points where the hand of God was most tangible, they indicate the proper spirit of Christian devotion. Their author reduced that spirit to three fixed imperatives, fixed insofar as they appeared regularly and reliably in every prayer and invocation he uttered: the Christian submitted with gratitude and contrition to the will of God; the Christian acknowledged God's constant mercy; the Christian recalled the promise of eternal life. That was all. The dead were beyond all human assistance, the living could consider only their own spiritual state. Insofar as Matheus's devotions reflected these principles, they upheld, at least formally, a strict Lutheran orthodoxy.

Yet, consistently expressed resignation could not mask a growing unease. His memoir, particularly in its reflections on death, gives voice to an intense, if troubled, religiosity. Even as he surrendered to God's will and sought God's aid, Matheus betrayed certain misgivings. Constant repetition confirms the importance of prayer for Matheus; it also opens that importance to doubt. With but cosmetic changes he copied and recopied these prayers throughout a memoir that spans 60 years. Twenty years after the death of his first wife, he stood at the deathbed of his second, Helena, and offered virtually the same formula: '[She died] softly and piously amid the prayers of all her beloved family... May God help us all in His time to eternal life and preserve us in His grace until then.'[55] This invocation appears repeatedly: at the deaths of wives and children; at the deaths of parents and parents-in-law; even at the deaths of more distant relatives and acquaintances. It becomes part of a private litany, unchanging through the storms and seasons of his life, mechanical but not meaningless. Physical and spiritual comfort – the end of suffering, the promise of redemption, and the hope of reunion – are the balm that soothes the sting of death. It avows a profound faith, even as it suggests, quite possibly, a growing ambivalence.

A clear change of voice occurs early in the memoir. The young Matheus is filled with a certain naive optimism at the many ways in which God works for the faithful or, more specifically, for him. When he enters his first partnership with his father, and so avoids employment with another firm that would have sent him to Vienna, he attributes the sudden change in his fortunes to the fact that 'God did not want it but worked instead a wondrous change'.[56] Likewise, the provisions for his first marriage, in which 'all parties were completely willing' must be ascribed to 'God's special ordinance'.[57] Nine months later, he acknowledges the birth of his first son as a divine blessing. When Michael dies within 24 hours, however, an obviously distraught father points to the inscrutability of a Providence that removed the infant from 'this vale of tears'.[58] These are modest changes. Yet, they occur when Matheus first confronts life's hard realities and become standard usages thereafter, attending triumphs as well as tragedies over the course of the memoir. After his first recorded experience of death, Matheus admits explicitly that the world is a place of sorrow. Only then does he perceive a discrepancy between divine Providence and worldly misfortune.

When his daughter Susanna dies, six months after the death of her mother, Anna Maria, the ambivalence between submission to divine ordinance and objection to unbearable loss rises to the surface. The death becomes a sign of God's righteousness toward the bereaved.[59] It accords with his 'just will and holy pleasure' that an infant, deprived of proper nourishment and nurturing by the death of its mother, should thrive initially before sickening and dying. The father 'must suffer great pain and according to God's will take comfort that his daughter now knows eternal joy in the presence of her Savior and her mother and that she has avoided much danger and sorrow'. But, through the death of a child, 'God has torn open the father's old wounds.' 'May He spare the rest of my family and through his beloved son Jesus Christ forgive my sins and justify me once again.' The juxtaposition of divine Providence, an innocent's death and a father's grief lends this long reflection an air of anguish, even inquisition, rather than resignation. Still, he closes on the usual note: 'Now may the dear Lord grant the body blessed peace and all of us in his time a pious departure and, a joyful resurrection with all faithful Christians on that great day.'[60] Never directly acknowledged, nonetheless the tension between God's mercy and man's suffering seems to trouble him.

These sentiments achieve their fullest expression in the entry devoted to the death in 1674 of his second wife, Helena. It would be the last death he recorded in his memoir. At the time, Matheus would have been accounted an old man. He was 49 years of age and had outlived two wives and five of 13 children. He had lived 20 years, most of his adult life, with the deceased; his sense of disappointment and injustice would not be denied. He begins with the remark that the 'dear God' showed him *'ein hartes'*.[61] The choice of words is particularly interesting here; it can be translated as either 'severity' or 'harshness', the one suggesting a just discipline, the other implying an arbitrary cruelty. Such ambiguity infects Matheus's references to God more and more over time. He worries how much he and his children need his wife but turns reluctantly from such worldly problems to a dutiful gratitude for the reminder that the only concern of a Christian is to die a pious death and achieve eternal life.[62] Yet, he cannot escape his grief so easily. The memory of a 'genuinely friendly and loving' life over 20 years demands acknowledgment.[63] He remembers her frequent illnesses, a pattern of frailty extending over 14 years: 'Oh my God how many heart-rending cries of pain have I with an aching heart heard; oh how often have I stood by in loyalty and sympathy and prayed to God that he would be gracious to us.'[64] Matheus did not rely on God alone but 'used every possible means' to extend her life. At this point, he makes an unexpected observation: 'Nothing chanced according to our wish for a timely improvement, but God strengthened our hope through many repeated hours of vigor so that we hoped for an eventual improvement and lived our lives in hope and fear.'[65] After his wife's death, Matheus can only conclude that 'God showed mercy in that he gave us hope as well as patience and grace in that he ended the advancing disease before the pain worsened.'[66] The palpable tension derived from a conflict between Matheus's emotional attachment and God's inscrutable purpose. The tale of false hopes and disappointed expectations evinces puzzlement that God would permit suffering and withhold recovery over so long a period of time. It even comes perilously close to imputing malice to God. That would, however, be too much for him to state directly.

Perplexity and disenchantment become leitmotifs of Matheus's private devotions. Though they never overthrow his religious convictions, they force him to question his religious assumptions. They increasingly complicate his attempts to maintain a Christian attitude. Matheus believed that Providence played a role in human affairs, and he prayed constantly and earnestly for guidance and comfort. Yet, these sensibilities were compromised by a growing apprehension. The hand of God, present though it doubtless was, failed to explain and justify the many tragedies that beset him. And Matheus needed explanations for these events. Providence seemed capricious, even threatening. Matheus struggled to see the beneficent hand of God in the events of this world; he strove to witness God's mercy manifest in the tragedies of his personal experience. His devotions indicate that his confession provided little reassurance.

In this anxiety, so human in the face of personal tragedy, the Lutheran Church offered no comfort. Matheus wrote gruelling, detailed accounts of the deaths of his wives. Every pain and symptom, every word and gesture, every visitor and mourner received careful attention. The clergy must have been among those present, leading the prayers, offering the sacrament, but they virtually disappear from these scenes. They played their formal roles. They officiated at the funerals, as demonstrated by Matheus's brief references to funeral sermons. They laid to rest in sanctified ground the bodies of his wives and children, his parents and siblings, his friends and associates. Yet, Matheus makes no mention of clergy or church otherwise. Rather, those friends and family who gathered to attend death turned directly to God. They prayed. They read the Bible. Miller recorded it all in precise detail. He retold the deaths – refashioned them, orchestrated them – as a reflection on his piety and as a memorial to the departed.

The keeping of a memoir is an act of recollection. It is the compilation, preservation and propagation of things that, for one reason or another, are needful to know. In Matheus's case, the contents of his memoir served principally to capture his actions and demonstrate their propriety. Yet, they served a more general purpose as well. His memoir comprised part of the collective memory of his family. It revealed not only who he was but also who they were. Hence, the record of saintly deaths quickened the dead. It called their lives to mind. It gave their fortitude, patience and piety new life. It permitted them, through their examples, to inspire and instruct the living. Only in the context of formal worship were 'the souls of the dead...irrevocably cut off from the world of the living'.[67] The so-called 'economy of salvation' had been transformed by changes in Lutheran theology and liturgy.[68] Rather than separating the living from the dead, however, Lutheran orthodoxy altered the relationship between them. Prayers for the dead had served not only as acts of intercession and satisfaction but also, and no less importantly, as acts of reminiscence and piety. These functions were transferred out of the church and its rituals into the more private realms of household and memory. Insofar as the dead provided examples of Christian comportment, strengthening the faith of families and friends, it was they who now assisted – and, effectively, interceded for – the living.

In remembrance, with all its rich connotations of identification, idealization and instruction, the Lutheran Church and confession played no part. They appear as little more than *obiter dicta* in the narratives of Matheus's memoir. His spiritual reflections become increasingly freighted and cryptic. His attention turns instead to the living and the dying; his memoir documents their spiritual and social stature.

Consider once again the death of his first wife, Anna Maria. It is the longest, most detailed, and most harrowing deathbed scene in the entire memoir, extending over 12 manuscript pages. After the birth of her daughter, Susanna, Anna Maria began to experience pain in the abdomen, thought to stem from the uterus (*Muter*), accompanied by vomiting or diarrhea.[69] Matheus consulted a physician, Dr Kneilin, as well as his mother and the wife of Daniel Österreicher. They applied an enema (*Klistier*), which encouraged a discharge of some material (*materia*) but did nothing for her discomfort. A second application so dramatically increased her pain that 'it would be impossible to describe to those who had not seen it'. It continued throughout the following day, causing great sadness (*grosem betauern*) to those who witnessed it. Here is the first reference to those who accompanied the death, a circle probably limited at this point to Matheus, the physician and the aforementioned women. The symptoms perplexed Dr Kneilin. Although Anna Maria suffered no fever, a cold sweat soaked her hands and feet. Her head remained warm, and her urine appeared normal. By the end of the second day, he prescribed a sedative (*Herz und Schmerz Trünklen*), to ease her pain and help her sleep, and a salve to rub on her stomach. She became progressively weaker, to the point that she could neither sit up nor roll over.[70] Around midday on the third day Anna Maria began to vomit a gall-like fluid. A terrible, uncontrollable pain returned such that she 'cried aloud and begged God for help and support'.[71] Matheus consulted a second doctor, all in vain. The fourth day passed with unrelenting vomiting and pain. Anna Maria finally died on the evening of the fifth day, Sunday 7 June 1654.

Even as she died a painful and protracted death, Matheus seemed fascinated by the symptoms of the fatal disease and reserved particular attention for the details of her suffering. The question arises why he gave them this extended treatment. He could have been moved by a personal interest in natural phenomena. Possibly, the vividness of the memory of a loved one's death found expression in an exceptionally precise recollection. Yet, there is an element of calculation in Matheus's memoir. Though his grief and pity were geniune, Matheus recreated the scene deliberately and purposefully. Events were retold – and, probably, rearranged – to emphasize certain themes. Amid the largely futile efforts of the physicians, he observed repeated that 'we always hoped it would be better' (*wir hofften inn sonderheit es sollte immer besser werden*). The stage was set for a leave-taking that would emphasize not only the spiritual but also the social functions of death.

On the fourth day, Anna Maria received word of an unexpected visit by Matheus Hopfer the Younger, the same man whose economic interests Matheus would promote five years later.[72] She immediately called for the commemorative gift (*Gevater Pfennig*) she intended to give his youngest son, Augustin, whom she sponsored at baptism. No trival object, it was a book, elegantly bound in tortoiseshell, with a silver clasp and inscribed silver nameplate. The odd detail of the book suggests an awareness of its symbolic value, on the part of Anna Maria and Matheus. The *Gevater Pfennig* manifested the spiritual bond that existed between sponsor and child. She bore a certain responsibility for his

Christian upbringing. It also attested to the social relationship between two families. Godparents were often sought among families related by blood, marriage or friendship, and served to reinforce ties. Thus, the book served as a reminder of the spiritual affinity, to say nothing of the conjugal unity and social solidarity, between the families. As it happened, Hopfer canceled his visit, not knowing the seriousness of Anna Maria's condition, and the exchange was left incomplete.

In the evening of the same day, Anna Maria realized she was dying. She asked that her sickbed be made anew. She could neither embrace God's will nor leave her family in a bed soiled by her violent illness. As soon as this was accomplished, she began to pray earnestly. Those around her joined in these prayers and read passages from the Bible. The proper devotions were essential to focus the spirit of the dying on the promise of divine mercy and to comfort the spirits of the living with the promise of eternal life. Once she had composed her soul, Anna Maria took leave of family and friends one by one. She bade Matheus a 'friendly farewell' (*freüntlich Abshid*), in which she thanked him for his loyalty and kindness, commended their children into his keeping, and begged forgiveness for any misconduct on her part.[73] She specifically asked that he care for her widowed mother, a request he did his utmost to fulfill. Observing that they 'had lived together as they had hoped to answer before God and as would provide a good example to other Christians', she kissed him goodbye and concluded, 'Now my dearest treasure, we will not see one another any more in this world, but we will find one another again in eternal life.' Matheus could only recall that he was so heavy hearted that he could not speak. Words failed him. His grief was indescribable. Anna Maria addressed each of those present in much the same terms. To her mother, her parents-in-law, her siblings, her siblings-in-law and her friends she said goodbye, thanked them for their friendship (*freuntschafft*), begged their forgiveness, and commended each to the others. Last came her children, Philip Jakob and Matheus the Younger. She kissed them, urged them to be obedient and faithful toward their father, and commended them to God's care.[74] Having left her world in order, Anna Maria prepared to enter the next. She returned to her prayers and died the following evening.

According to Matheus, those who witnessed Anna Maria's final hours were amazed at her courage and joy. 'Her farewell to me, which lasted a quarter of an hour, filled those around us with great wonder, including older folk who had witnessed many deaths but had never seen such a courageous, joyful mood on the part of the dying.'[75] The observation is itself ambiguous. It can be read as a reflection on the strength of Anna Maria's faith, an exortation to Christian life. She confronted her death calmly, even joyously, in the certain knowledge of the salvation of her soul and her resurrection to eternal life. It can also be read as a testimonial to the strength of Anna Maria's character, an extension of her social identity. In her final hours she turned her attention to her family and evoked the relationships that would sustain it. Death became a means of strengthening social solidarity within the family, and the remembrance of death functioned to recall and renew that commonality.

Did the sacred and the secular uses of death collide and conflict? Koslofsky has noted that 'tension existed between Christian ritual and social display', between the need to incorporate Lutheran doctrine and the opportunity to demonstrate social status in funeral rituals.[76] The uneasy balance between observance and representation manifested itself in funeral sermons that grew in importance from the middle of the sixteenth century but became increasingly biographical and secular from the middle of the seventeenth century. Likewise, funeral ceremonies were gradually stripped of their religious elements and transformed into moments of social replication. Against this secularization of death the Lutheran Church of the seventeenth century struggled mightily and vainly.

Matheus's memoir suggests that, in death as in life, the sacred and the secular were indivisible, perhaps indistinguishable. In his descriptions of death, the comportment of the dying and the surviving testifies not only to their spiritual but also to their social stature. Anna Maria's calm courage demonstrated both a Christian faith and a social presence. The sympathy and solidarity of her companions confirmed their upright souls as well as their social identities. Each was reflected and magnified in the other. They were inseparable. Hence, the dichotomy of sacred and secular may be too crude an instrument to examine the complex religiosity of the seventeenth century. What seems clear, however, is that this religiosity found its place, at least in part, apart from church and confession.

Matheus only sketchily describes funeral rituals. For Anna Maria, he offers a cryptic record.[77]

> On 11 June, the body was borne to the Wagner house in Holy Cross Alley, where we lived at the time. The funeral sermon was spoken by Master Thomas Hopfer in Holy Cross [Church]. The burial occurred that afternoon in the Zacharias Wild grave in St Stephen's Cemetery amid a large crowd. And the penalty [*leicht tax*] was rendered.

It seems to indicate, albeit indirectly at points, that Anna Maria died outside her household, perhaps in her mother's house. Her body had to be carried home to be mourned and, then, prepared for burial. From there, it was borne to the church, where a funeral sermon was read. Finally, it was buried in a separate place, St Stephen's Cemetery. The entire ceremony must have involved two or three public processions. Matheus refers to a large crowd and the *'leicht tax'*, the fine paid for violations of the city's sumptuary laws. Hence, more than sixty mourners, the legal limit for members of Augsburg's merchant corporation [*Kaufleuteschaft*], followed Anna Maria to her final resting place.[78] For their daughter, Susanna, whose death followed that of her mother and touched her father so deeply, Matheus listed funeral expenses.[79] These offer a somewhat more detailed impression of the burial rites. Matheus offered payment to the midwife who attended both mother and child. The maids of his and his father's households received gratuities, too, whether for their service as mourners or for the cost of mourning dress remains unclear. His household servant bore the infant on a byre covered with a burial cloth to its grave. He paid a cantor, probably for his role in the funeral service, and offered gratuities to the officers of the peace (*Gassenknecht*) and of the alms (*Säckelknecht*), all of which indicate a public procession that included the poor. These expenses Matheus duly recorded. Hence, like her mother, Susanna was mourned at home, borne to the church, laid to rest in a cemetery, probably in her mother's family's grave, and honored with alms, all more or less standard features of a Lutheran funeral. No direct mention is made of a service in church or the presence of clergy, though both doubtless applied. Yet, this brief record indicates a clear consciousness of the representative functions of a funeral, even that of a child. These things had to be done properly, in keeping with Matheus's stature.

Another important means of expressing social stature was the funeral sermon. It became, between 1550 and 1650, the most important element in any Lutheran funeral and a popular literary genre.[80] It provided the clergy with an opportunity to elevate a life to the level of allegory, making of the dead a medium for the Christian revelation and a memorial to the Christian life. It provided the laity with an opportunity to recall a life lived, remembering the dead as an individual of flesh and spirit and as a burgher invested with stature and association. Aware of both functions, Matheus carefully noted the sermons that marked the passage of his family. In some instances, such as the funeral sermon of Anton Christoff Schorer the Elder, he helped to write them and recalled passages in his memoir.

On St Bartholomew's Day, 24 August 1655, Schorer, the father of Matheus's second wife, Helena, took to his bed. He complained of difficulty and discomfort when moving his left foot. Four days later, on 28 August, he died. Matheus noted these events with the same careful attention to detail that he gave to the death of his first wife.[81] Schorer must have been an important figure in Matheus's life; such passages in the memoir were usually reserved for members of Matheus's immediate family.

The two death scenes – indeed, all death scenes in the memoir – evince notable similarities. The symptoms are recorded. Schorer experienced difficulty moving his feet and hot and cold flashes but was otherwise relatively free of pain. The indications suggest a stroke. Although doctors were consulted and no therapy left untried, his condition steadily worsened. As Matheus noted: 'The dear Lord did not wish to give his blessing to [his recovery] but rather, according to his divine will and Schorer's pleas and supplications, to take him out of this sorrowful world unto everlasting, joyous life.'[82] The fortitude of the dying was captured as well. Because Schorer experienced no real pain he did not believe himself to be dangerously ill and expressed the hope that 'he would soon go about his business'. As he steadily weakened, those in attendance called for the pastor of St Ulrich, M. Heinrich Faber, to visit the sufferer, hear his confession and offer him the sacrament. This being done, Schorer remained silent and absorbed, whether the result of his piety or of a paroxysm, Matheus was uncertain. He made clear, however, through turning his eyes toward heaven and mouthing words of devotion, that he wished to pray, and those around him willingly joined in.[83] Matheus noted with wonder that there was little leave-taking.[84]

> During the entire time no one spoke about dying. Nor was leave taken, which was not to be wondered at in this case because he had for some time previously spoken, prayed, and sung, particularly with his wife and also with all his children about his death so that each of them would have enough to think about in fear of the Lord. And he must have thought, 'What more should I say? Whoever wishes to follow my example will have heard what I said and will now recall that this must be.'

And, so, Schorer slipped quietly away, accompanied by the prayers of those about him. The death scene differs only in degree from those of family members.

Schorer was more than relative or friend, however. Recall that Matheus had arranged for a portrait of him by Bartholomeus Hopfer, a unique distinction, of which he kept a copy for himself.[85] Here was a man to be memorialized in life and in death. The passage in the memoir ends with a singular biographical – and autobiographical – note. The memoir synopsizes the *pia defuncti memoria* of Pastor Faber's funeral sermon at St Anna's Church, which Matheus himself wrote.[86]

> But no one could say other than that he was a very courageous, honest, and forthright man of worth [*biderman*], who gave good satisfaction in his manner and means, succoured widows and orphans, and set such an example for his children that it were desirable more would follow him. He loved God's word and was zealous in prayer in that he set aside an hour for private devotion daily, held to his devotion as much as human weakness permitted, and gained greatly from God as a result. What more shall I say, my dears, to you who will read this? Let it suffice that this Anton Christoff Schorer the Elder of sainted memory was a most pious man of worth, whom God loved and on whom he bestowed physical and spiritual blessings. He had his cross to bear and great sadness in a variety of things. But these belong to the love of Christ.

His father-in-law embodied Matheus's ideal of propriety. He was the patriarch, who ruled by example. He was the burgher, who acted righteously and honestly. He was the neighbor, who assisted the less fortunate. He was the Christian who exercised his faith in word and deed. The sacred and the secular cannot be separated in this image. They belong together, strengthen one another. Yet, these qualities transcend confession: they required the mediation neither of church nor of clergy; they depended formally neither on liturgy nor on theology. Rather, they communicated more directly with the divine. As Matheus said, '[Schorer] was a pious man of worth, whom God loved.'

The Lutheran Church could not assuage his grief; it did not ease his doubt. Moreover, it seemed to provide no satisfying medium for remembrance. Matheus's memoir suggests that such things moved out of the church and into the household, into the circle of the family. That does not mean they became private, however. He paid discreet attention to such representative forms of expression as funeral processions and funeral sermons. These, like the memoir itself, served the purpose of remembrance, with its sacred and social functions.

Death and remembrance could emphasize and strengthen family solidarity. They could also expose domestic tensions or leave an image of filial ambivalence. When his father died in 1664, Matheus noted the fact succinctly.[87]

> In the year 1664 on 10 March, in the sixtieth year of his age, my beloved father Michael Miller slept blessedly in the Lord Jesus Christ. The funeral sermon was read by Pastor Fustennegger at Holy Cross in the new church. There he was buried in the choir before the altar. The funeral text was taken from Psalms, 'Commit thy way onto the Lord; trust also in him; and he shall bring it to pass.' I wrote his biography and gave it to Pastor Fustennegger, who read it word for word. I have appended a copy hereafter.

That is all. He noted cryptically that his father was buried in a place of high honor, in the choir before the altar. That distinction, usually reserved for members of the clergy or patrons of the church, signaled Michael's close association with Holy Cross. Though a merchant of no particular prominence, he had nonetheless served as a member of the delegation that sought to raise funds for the rebuilding of the Lutheran church in 1648. That duty had taken him as supplicant to courts of Europe's Lutheran princes and had proven highly controversial at the time. Yet, Matheus did not commemorate this singular, diplomatic foray. Nor did he record a death scene. The memoir gives no description of Michael's suffering. It offers no evidence of his piety. It records no demonstrations of the family's grief. Compared to other deaths, Michael might have died alone, unmarked and unmourned.

Why did Matheus not mark his father's death in the manner, standard throughout his memoir? Perhaps Michael died suddenly, without suffering or leave-taking for his son to record. Perhaps they were estranged despite – or because of – their close association and partnership. Yet, these possibilities accord poorly with his earlier recollections. Michael had been his son's steadfast advocate within the family, especially against the opposition of his brothers. He had helped young Matheus over numerous difficulties early in his career, not least his employment difficulties in St Gall. Eventually, Michael ended his involvement in the family firm and began a new partnership with Matheus, creating the impression that he helped his son start his first business. Such steadfast cooperation, to say nothing of intimacy, would seem to merit some kind of commemoration at the end. Nothing of the sort occurred. It is impossible to reach a conclusion; Matheus wrote too little.

Yet, he wrote just enough. The funeral text was drawn from Psalm 37: 4–5: 'Commit thy way unto the Lord; trust also in him; and he shall bring it to pass.'[88] If Matheus had a hand in choosing it, that particular passage might have been an epigraph of his father's life as presented in the memoir. Had Michael not languished as a lesser member of a successful family? Had he not striven on his son's behalf against the censure of his brothers? Had he not abandoned their business in order to join in partnership with his eldest son? Had his son not risen in the world as a result? These deeds might have seemed to Matheus, perhaps a bit self-consciously, to be acts of genuine paternal responsibility, the way of true righteousness. The passage would have been no less apposite, if applied to Matheus's own life. Had he not striven against the disapproval of his uncles, been a 'thorn' in their eyes, as he put it? Had he not struck out on his own in business, without the support of any member of his family, other than his father? Had he not succeeded, as a result, and become a successful merchant, one of Augsburg's economic elite? The Psalm, to say nothing of the funeral sermon no longer extant, was the ultimate act of remembrance and commemoration, encapsulating in pious form a life of sacrifice, suffering and sanctity, combining secular and sacred purposes in a single thought.

Nor was the funeral sermon, however apt, the only commemorative act to attend the passing of Michael Miller. Shortly after his death, a nephew Benedict Hopfer, penned a mourning poem (*Traur-Gedicht*) to honor the dead and comfort the living.[89] This type of occasional verse, a genre that was popular in seventeenth-century Germany, was commonplace, the fact that it has been little studied notwithstanding. Hopfer's is an unremarkable example that combines humanistic and evangelical sentiments. It begins with a lament that the death of Michael Miller could not be prevented but admits that 'here can neither shield nor defense suffice, even one of hardest steel and diamond, to turn aside that sharpened lance.'[90] Yet, there is no need for sorrow: 'Still fame does not pale; only the fragile body breaks.'[91] Michael was at all times a man of 'German faith and honesty,' one who fled all fickleness and flattery. He manifested his Christian convictions in charity and patriotism. Indeed, his love of fatherland was such that he 'traveled distant paths, where the cold north wind rules, and so achieved not without pain that which pious 'Cross hearts' long desired.'[92] But virtue cannot stay death. Therefore one should embrace it, knowing that God sets sorrow, fear and suffering on all those he truly loves. 'Whoever does not patiently bear such things should not be called a servant of Christ.'[93] Yet, even as he offers the cross to those he loves, God offers them comfort of eternal life as well. Michael has left a world 'ruled by evils without number' and achieved the joys of heaven. Thus, the body, subject to suffering and decay, reaches its end, but reputation lends it an immortality not unlike that of the pious soul. This poem was a particularly public effort to assure that Michael's fame would survive him.

A similar composition accompanied the death of Matheus's second wife, Helena Schorer, in 1674.[94] The sentiments resemble those of Hopfer's poem, but the situation in which it was written suggests an interestingly secular interpretation. The first eight stanzas compare the soul in life to a ship at sea, tossed by sin and misfortune.[95] The voyage is certain only where faith is the boat, love the Pole Star, and prayer the sail. These things alone bring the soul to that desired shore. So it was for the devout (*Gott-ergebnen*) Helena. 'The master of her ship has received her and given her the desired place that she may now share the joy of angels after such a bitter journey.'[96] The final four stanzas turn to Matheus, urging him to resignation. 'But you Miller, most sorrowful man, because God himself stands in the middle, take on the widower's title with a submissive will and remember that he who ended the journey arranges everything to the best for us.'[97] Matheus ought not to mourn too much, for, however short her life may seem, Helena has replaced it with eternity. The Almighty often summons the best souls early to heaven 'because our senses join with them there, where their treasure has traveled'. It is the dead, through emotion and memory, who 'intercede' for the living and draw them to eternal life.

These are orthodox Lutheran sentiments. The dead depart this life piously; the living submit to God's will hopefully. Yet, the specific context of Matheus's life at this point implies that worldly ends might have been served as well. As a widower, he confronted the impossibility of managing a business and keeping a household alone. On her deathbed, his late wife had recognized the problem, urged him to remarry quickly and even named the prospective bride.[98] Less than three months later, therefore, he began formal negotiations to marry Johanna Katharina Miller, who became his third wife on 7 May 1674. This violated acceptable patterns of mourning, forcing him to the unusual expedient of publishing a thinly veiled apologia, *The Flowery Wedding Celebration*. Among the several objections addressed in it was the way in which his hasty remarriage had cast doubt on his feelings for Helena. Fililla asks Nymfe, the bride-to-be, directly, 'Would it please you, had the one who held your heart forgotten so quickly and behaved like a bachelor with your body still warm?'[99] Interestingly, Nymfe later justifies Matheus's quick decision by adopting the metaphor of life as a ship a sea. A sailor does not wait for the last blow of the storm to destroy his ship but rather takes such action as is necessary to reach safe harbor. *The Life-Voyage*, written to commemorate Helena, can also be read as a response to this accusation. The authors acknowledge Matheus's patronage on the title page, indicating that the poem was published at his behest. Insofar as it serves his purposes and reflects his sentiments, therefore, it testifies publicly, without speaking directly to the question of his remarriage, to Matheus's devotion to his late wife and the propriety of his mourning. He casts her life as a stormy and dangerous voyage, now safely and piously ended. He evinces his grief and resignation, as befits a faithful Lutheran. He anticipates his eventual reunion with her in eternity. Meanwhile, however, he must attend to his responsibilities in this world. Like funeral sermons and ceremonies, mourning poems served sacred and secular purposes: they memorialized the dead; and they upheld the living.

The depiction of Helena's death in the memoir serves the same purposes.[100] It is more economical than Anna Maria's – though far less so than Michael's – but contains all the usual elements. It describes Helena's symptoms, provides examples of fortitude and faith, testifies to the solidarity of the dying and the living, and records a pious ending. As an act of remembrance, it would inspire its readers to emulate the faith of the dying and identify with the living.

Personally, as noted, Matheus reacted to this tragedy with something like despair and bitterness. Small wonder. Helena had been his companion and partner for 20 years. Her suffering lasted nearly 18 weeks until death released her. Matheus was bereft with a business and household, including unmarried children, to manage alone. As a result, social difficulties compounded his spiritual turmoil and forced him to justify his actions publicly. It brought him near a spiritual crisis. It brought to the foreground the tension in his memoir between an implicit faith in a world directed by Providence and a dawning awareness of nature as unpredictable. On the one hand, he retained a profoundly Lutheran piety, one that sees the hand of God in the course of human existence. All details reveal the divine presence. On the other hand, Providence neither predicted nor protected. It remained a part of his cosmology but no longer explained all occurrences, answered all questions or relieved all uncertainty. So, he vacillated quietly. As his prayers became increasingly formulaic, even desperate, they gave tongue to a pessimistic fatalism born of repeated catastrophes. Though by no means agnostic, Matheus seems to have experienced a certain distance between himself and his faith. He prayed and worshiped assiduously, as was expected of a householder in the seventeenth century, but his words and deeds suggest a helplessness that his confession, born of political and theological conflict, could not overcome.

Yet, at precisely this point in his life, Matheus apparently reconciled the sacred and social functions of death and remembrance. He purchased a family crypt.[101]

> This, my beloved housewife deceased, is buried at St Anna in the cemetery in a crypt that I purchased from Gabriel Beg. It had belonged to Maximilian Mair, whose seal in metal was on the stone. I will order a new one set there. The contract of sale is properly drawn. There were expenses beyond the fl. 27 purchase price. But the crypt is my own. Upon opening it appears completely new without a single bone in it.

The transaction itself was more complicated and revealing than Matheus indicated. Gabriel Beg, a hosteller in Augsburg, acquired the Mair tomb from Hieronymus Schorer, who had lived his final years under Beg's roof, a not unusual arrangement for the private care of the elderly.[102] The tomb served, therefore, as compensation for expenses incurred in sheltering and feeding a member of Helena's own family. Beg, in turn, sold it to Matheus. Hence, Helena came to rest in the tomb that had housed the bones of her own family and would *mutatis mutandis* continue to do so.

The purchase price was neither the sole nor the greatest expense, however. Matheus paid a further fl. 46 to have his family crest carved and mounted on it and, by so doing, transform it into a representative symbol of his family's social stature. The investment merely increased the economic and social value of what was already a prestigious possession. Since the early sixteenth century, German cities, Augsburg included, had begun to close churchyards and expand cemeteries outside the city's walls, in part due to concerns about hygiene and in part as a response to over-crowding.[103] The move had met with some popular resistance because many wished both to exercise their prerogative to choose their burial place and to benefit from the reassurance of traditional, sanctified ground. Interment in the new graveyards smacked of dishonorable burial. Matheus's newly purchased crypt not only stood within the city walls but more expressly within the church itself. The cemetery (*Gottesacker*) to which he referred was not the churchyard but rather the cloister. Moreover, the bones of his family would mingle with no others. Clearly, it was important for Matheus to establish this crypt as his own in every possible way. It was the quintessential act of remembrance, a memoir in stone, as permanent as the stuff of which it was made, as the building of which it was part, that testified to the piety, unity and stature of his entire family across generations and would do so for all time to come.

The purchase of a crypt, at considerable expense, is an excellent metaphor for the sacred and social aspects of death. It stood on hallowed ground, where Augsburg merchants had buried their dead for centuries. It stood at the very center of Augsburg's Lutheran community; St Anna's was possibly the largest and certainly the most prestigious of the city's evangelical churches, a place Luther himself had visited. It stood, therefore, in close proximity to and spiritual solidarity with the religious and political fate of the *Confessio Augustana*. At the same time, a crypt in St Anna's constituted a permanent and powerful social symbol. It expressed the prestige of the Miller family. It commemorated the members of that family. It represented the propriety of the family's head. For all these reasons, it was a worldly demonstration of social identity and solidarity within the confines of the church and its confession. Like the crypt in the cloister, the secular and the sacred were inseparable in death.

For Matheus, memory established identity. Confessions fostered identity otherwise, by strengthening the consciousness of difference. Instrumental in this process were sermons, whether preached at funerals or on Sundays. How they impressed Lutheran laymen is another matter. An examination of word and response might amplify the story of a city, its confessions and its citizens. It might further clarify the relationship between the confessional politics of Augsburg and the personal piety of a single Augsburger.

Most of his adult life, Matheus worshiped at the Lutheran Church of the Holy Cross. Its pastor, Georg Philip Riß, was a controversial figure in the confessional history of Augsburg. According to his biographer, he was a man of God. 'Because he showed great zeal in his office, particularly in punishing opponents of truth, he endured much adversity.'[104] The reality is more colorful. According to the records, Riß was the wrath of God. At the Church of the Holy Cross, in the decades that followed the Treaty of Westphalia, he heaped hatred and scorn on the Catholic Church. He preached repeatedly against the doctrine, liturgy and behavior of the papists. He recounted their lies and iniquities in lurid detail. He spoke, even when ordered to be silent. Against the accusation that he disturbed the peace and defied authority, Riß insisted that his office, formed in a heroic tradition, required him to preach Lutheran truth against Catholic falsehood.

> According to praiseworthy and well-founded examples that lit the Church of God... [the opponents of truth] must be attacked on the basis of Scripture and... on behalf of God's honor and human salvation, which I have done with suitable earnestness and zeal... for the papist teachers spare no energy with their written and oral lies to make the simple doubt[105]

He saw no contradiction, therefore, between the politics of confession and the care of souls.

Conflicts between Catholics and Lutherans were not uncommon in seventeenth-century Augsburg. Pastors were regularly called to task for preaching sermons that seemed too incendiary, that might incite violence. Between 1650 and 1700, three Lutheran clergymen were released from office, including Thomas Hopfer, Riß's predecessor as pastor of Holy Cross and Matheus's relative by marriage.[106]

Riß had comrades in controversy, but he was a singular figure. His picture shows a large man in the black robe and white ruff of his calling.[107] His expression is formidable. A widow's peak rests above a high forehead and wrinkled brow. Broadly set eyes narrow as if in doubt or anger. A tightly pursed mouth is set above heavy jowls. The image awakens the impression of a choleric individual. Certainly, Riß fought longer, more determined and more bitter battles with his enemies than did any other Lutheran pastor of his day in Augsburg.

Those battles began upon his arrival in Augsburg and persisted regularly until the end of his career. On 26 July 1661, for example, the Vicar General of the Diocese of Augsburg complained to the Lutheran magistracy that a Catholic woman had been harassed during a Corpus Christi procession.[108] He attributed the disturbance to the preaching of Georg Philip Riß. In a recent sermon, Riß had insulted various articles of the Catholic faith and called processions idolatry. He had likened Catholics to heathens and compared the many saints of the former to the multiple gods of the latter. He had referred to the Host as a 'god of dough' (*pappeten Herrgott*) and told the story of a mouse that had to be dissected in order to recover the contents of its stomach after it invaded a monstrance and ate the Host. He had claimed that the Catholic Church replaced the eternal Trinity of God the Father, Son and Holy Ghost with a new trinity of Joseph, Mary and Jesus, and warned that prayers to Mary were idolatrous. He had defamed religious orders and said their houses should all be consumed in the fire of Sodom and Gomorrah. And he had called the Pope Antichrist. Here were cause and effect: incendiary preaching resulted in a violation of the religious peace. Riß had to be silenced.

Yet, to silence a pastor was itself a violation of the Treaty of Westphalia insofar as it deprived his congregation of the Word. Riß knew how to use the provisions of parity to his own advantage. He dutifully submitted his sermons for examination and wrote a detailed response in which he admitted every statement attributed to him by the Vicar General.[109] In his own defense, he referred not to the Bible or to the Church Fathers but rather to confessional tracts, above all the Augsburg Confession, the Articles of Schmalkalden, and the Large and Small Catechisms of Luther. The tale of the mouse originated in a legal proceeding adjudicated by Pope Gregory XI in 1371, was retold by Gabriel Biel, and had been published most recently in a 1593 pamphlet by Wilhelm Holder entitled *Mus exenteratus*.[110] This was a new scholasticism, the defense of truth through a marshalling of human opinion rather than of divine testimony. It had one signal advantage, to which Riß called particular attention. Insofar as he taught nothing except that which was to be found in standard works of the Lutheran faith, he could claim that his preaching conformed to the standard content of Lutheranism, a content specifically sanctioned and protected by the Peace of Augsburg of 1555 and the Treaty of Westphalia of 1648. Riß's justification apparently convinced the magistrates, who took no action against him.

Matheus mentions none of these events in his memoir. Even the magistrates, immediately involved as they were, took a practical view of them. Rather than resolve the dispute, they warned both sides to maintain discipline. Conscious of the city's recent history, especially its disastrous experiences in the Thirty Years' War, they wished to be perceived as capable of maintaining a balance between confessions, and so avoid the involvement of foreign or imperial powers.

Protected by the provisions of peace and parity, which assured the exercise of the Lutheran faith without interference, Riß pressed his assault relentlessly. And he broadened it to include not only the articles of the Catholic faith but also its religious and secular leaders.[111] He even reprimanded Lutheran authorities who were lax in defense or practice of the faith. Public criticism of secular authority – Catholic or Lutheran, foreign or domestic – was not specifically sanctioned by the religious peace. Nor could it be tolerated in an age that was sensitive to the potential for rebellion. Sedition finally forced the Lutheran authorities to take a stand against Riß.

In 1663 the administrators of the Lutheran Church of Augsburg met in council to consider the latest charges against their controversial pastor. The electoral government of Bavaria had accused Riß of blasphemy against God and His saints and of direct slanders of the Elector and House of Bavaria in a recently delivered funeral sermon.[112] Lutheran leaders worried that these charges were common knowledge (*stadtkundig*); Matheus said nothing about them. More important than the reaction of this or that Augsburger, in the eyes of the magistrates, were the actions of the city's most powerful neighbor. Bavaria demanded a 'palpable demonstration' (*wohlempfindliche Demonstration*) against Riß. Were the blasphemy proven, he should be removed from office. Were the slanders corroborated, he should be sentenced to prison. The magistrates decided that forceful measures would have to be taken to satisfy the Bavarians. The usual examination of the text would not be sufficient. They would interrogate prominent Lutherans to establish the truth of these charges.[113] The outcome of this investigation would determine their course of action.

Thirty-one Lutheran burghers – Matheus not among them – responded to a series of seventeen questions. These fell into five general categories, according to the charges lodged against Riß.[114] Had he blasphemed or encouraged others to blaspheme against God and His saints? Had he slandered or encouraged others to slander the Catholic estates of the Empire? Had he engaged or encouraged others to engage in impious acts? Had he disparaged or encouraged others to disparage the honor of the Elector and House of Bavaria? Finally, had he doubted or encouraged others to doubt the sanctity of the recently canonized Thomas de Vio Cardinal Cajetan? Although only 13 heard Riß deliver the sermon in question, all respondents stated that they attended at least some of his services and could, therefore, discuss the general content and tone of his preaching.[115] Their responses were unanimously negative. No one had ever heard Riß blaspheme God and His saints; they would not listen to such sermons. No one had ever heard Riß slander the Catholic estates; all claimed that Riß held them in high esteem. No one had ever seen or heard Riß engage in impious acts; the respondents cast off the accusation without further thought or comment. No one had ever heard Riß disparage the honor of Bavaria; most could not remember his mentioning the House or the Elector at all. Finally, nearly everyone admitted that he had mentioned Cardinal

Cajetan; no one ever heard Riß doubt the man's sanctity. Not surprisingly, the Lutheran pastor had done no wrong in the eyes of his Lutheran congregants.

That he had done no wrong should not be taken to mean that he had done right. The magistracy took no action against Riß. He continued to preach the Augsburg Confession, remained pastor at Holy Cross, and became Senior the following year. The terms of confessionalization in Augsburg protected Riß and freed him to attack Catholicism. It also provided a means by which the magistrates could assess and control him. But it left the laity silent in 1663. Like Matheus, they had little to say about Riß's conduct or his preaching. While they refused to indict him, they also refused to defend him. They knew his reputation as a controversialist, heard similar sentiments on various occasions, and recognized the direction of the magistrates' questions. None adopted the line of the authorities in defense of the clergy, that is, none stated that Riß merely preached as he had always done, as all Lutheran pastors had always done. Neither magistracy nor laity contended that Riß upheld the truth. None seemed to care. Those matters of greatest moment to Riß – the struggle to resist Catholicism, the politics of confession – they passed in silence.

Silence can have many meanings. To discover – even to speculate – how people might have responded to Riß and his sermons, or to examine their conscious identification with his ideas, we need a more immediate, personal source. These polemics elicit no mention in Matheus's memoir. Its contents betray no engagement in confessional politics. Nor do they express openly anti-Catholic sentiments. In this regard, Matheus maintained the same silence in his memoir as the witnesses before the magistracy. Yet, he heard Riß's sermons as a member of the congregation at Holy Cross, knew of the scandals as an active figure in the Lutheran Church. What connection existed between the strident confessionalization of the Lutheran Church in Augsburg and the muted confessional sensibilities of this Augsburg Lutheran?

Matheus Miller was caught between two worlds, one of private misgiving and memory and one of public conformity and commemoration. In his devotions, as in his offices and relationships, the tensions between these two worlds found expression. Confessional identity became lost between them. This may have been nothing more than a function of parity. Confessional lines and antagonisms were so drawn in Augsburg that life took shape within them, internalized them without acknowledging them.[116] That said, magistracy, clergy and laity imputed different meanings to confession. Officials seized it as an instrument of order; pastors argued from it as a bulwark of truth; people like Matheus ignored it as irrelevant to their concerns.

The Peace of Augsburg and the Treaty of Westphalia afforded specific legal protection to Catholicism and Lutheranism predicated upon a maintenance of established doctrines and practices. Thus, these two faiths institutionalized religious polemic by setting limits within which it might proceed unhindered. By the same token, however, they established a benchmark against which conflict could be measured and mediated. Ultimately, they provided the state with a means to control religious expression. Confessionalization was more than a political process; it was a political instrument.

As it set political and religious authorities at odds with one another, confessionalization separated clergy from laity. Confessional issues touched Matheus directly, both as a prominent Lutheran layman and as a Lutheran official in a bi-confessional city, but it seemed to find no place in his reflections on his life. If his memoir contains the things about which he cared, then confessional politics, as represented by the activities of Pastor Riß, was not one of them. Miller is not unique in this regard. Bernd Roeck cites the case of David Altenstetter, a literate Augsburg goldsmith who refused involvement in institutional religion in favor of a personal and private piety during the second half of the sixteenth century.[117] Such behavior illustrates one possible consequence of confessional tension, a politique Nicodemism. Without arguing that Matheus remained publicly involved in the Lutheran affairs while espousing privately a supra-confessional Christianity, it is at least clear that he avoided the rough and tumble of religious conflict.

Scholars have long associated confessionalization with conviction and passion. Certainly the controversial literature preached and printed by Catholic and Lutheran clergy, intent on attacking their adversaries and inflaming their allies, awakens this impression. In this regard, the scandal surrounding Pastor Riß and the echoes resonating in the testimony of Lutheran laity suggest a paradox. Confessionalization is the transfer of religion from the realm of private conviction to the arena of public order. As a political instrument, wielded by magistracy and clergy for specific, not always congruous purposes, confession failed to provide a satisfying outlet for the piety of Matheus and, perhaps, many of his neighbors. His misgivings, manifested in the appearance of distance between himself and his church, may have had less to do with the demands of confession than with his own desire to grieve and remember. Matheus wished to preserve the memories of his dead in private and to commemorate their lives in public. For these ends, the confessional church, with its emphasis on conformity and controversy, was not a satisfying medium. The disjuncture between private piety and public discipline, which erupted at the beginning of the Reformation, may help explain the escape into pietism and quietism and the retreat into conservatism and reaction at its end.

Conclusion

Matheus Miller was a bourgeois in the strict sense of the term. He was a burgher of Augsburg, a townsman who drew his sustenance and his identity from his participation in and close association with a specific place. Yet, Matheus was a bourgeois of a different stripe. Rather than a captive rentier, living conservatively within his means and according to expectations, he shaped and changed his life in Augsburg. Through well-laid schemes, he created an ordered existence that was both rational and irrational, born of public engagements in commercial and political affairs but shaped by family ties and personal prejudices.

Not only did he self-consciously shape his world but he reshaped it for the purpose of his memoir. It can be read as an allegory for the rise of the bourgeoisie. Its organization moves in an orderly and logical manner from productive enterprise, the source of his wealth and distinction, to political office, the point of departure for social advancement, to social status, the supposed goal and ideal of all early modern bourgeois. Yet, mobility was not foremost in Matheus's mind. His memoir preserved the history of his life and achievement for future generations. Matheus wrote to assure continuity.

His eldest son and heir, Philip Jakob, was born on 25 July 1650. The momentous event prompted nothing more than a laconic entry, typical of the father and his memoir.

> In the year 1650 the 25th of June at a quarter after two on the Feast of James my aforementioned beloved wife bore for the second time into the vale of lamentation that is this world a son who was baptized by Master [Philip Weber, TMS] and received the name Philip Jakob that same day in the afternoon after the evening sermon at the Lutheran Church of St. Anna. The godparents were Master

Philip Weber, Pastor and Senior at St. Anna, Master Hans Jakob Miller the Elder, and Gabriel Hopfer from Nuremberg in addition to the aforementioned Sara [the wife of] Hans Jerg Rauhwolff, all in person.[1]

That is all. Rituals were observed with proper care. Godparents were chosen from the usual circles. Matheus had nothing more to say about his son until he began his education.

In 1655, Philip Jakob received his first schooling from Gabriel Vogel, a 'good, industrious man and recommended to me by Cousin [*Veter*] Hopfer', who would teach the boy for one hour each day.[2] He transferred, in 1656, to a Latin school run by Tobias Kriegsdorffer and, in 1661, to the Collegium St Anna.[3] Despite the fact that he was still in Augsburg, Philip Jakob boarded with Rector Mathias Wilhelm at a weekly rate of 1 *Reichstaler*. In 1663, in a move reminiscent of his father's youth, Philip Jakob left home for Memmingen, where he attended the Lutheran academy of J. Conrad Hörmann, 'a truly fine and pious man', who charged fl. 45 per year for instruction, room and board.[4] He was 13 years old; Matheus had quit school at 14 years of age. By 1667, when Philip Jakob left Memmingen, the cost of his education had reached approximately fl. 280.[5] Matheus was scrupulous about these expenses; it is the only insight he offered into his domestic economy. They suggest that, like his father before him, he valued education and that, again like his father before him, he might have had cause to complain about its expense. Whether Philip Jakob continued his education at a university or sought training with a series of merchant-masters after 1667, the memoir falls silent. Apart from the similarity between father and son, it offers nothing more.

Once he came of age and established himself, in 1674, Philip Jakob married Anna Maria, the daughter of the late Hieronymus Mehrer.[6] As in the case of Matheus's own marriages, this one constituted a consolidation within rather than a move up the social hierarchy. Matheus sounded out the guardians, Otto Lauginger and David von Stetten, both leading members of Augsburg's Lutheran patriciate. They agreed to the marriage and arranged the matter quickly. Matheus's father-in-law and brother, Balthas and Thomas Miller, carried the formal request after the details had been negotiated by Matheus and the guardians. In short, preliminary arrangements followed much the same, scrupulously correct ritual as did those for Matheus's marriages.

About those arrangements the settlement of the father's estate gives some indication.[7] Hieronymus Mehrer died on 5 August 1657 and was survived by his widow, Sibilla Pimmel, and four daughters, including Anna Maria. His property was modest by the time his daughter married Matheus's son.[8] She had received fl. 500 as her share of the paternal inheritance. Those funds had been invested in their father's business, now operated by his brother, Marx Christoph Mehrer. In return, he had promised to support and house the children and their mother and to pay the children fl. 200 per annum, 100 as interest and 100 as a usufructuary fee on their investment. This agreement had been superceded in 1661 by a new one, according to which the fl. 2,000 principal and fl. 600 accumulated interest were removed from the business and invested in a 'House on the Haymarket' (*Behausung am Heumarkt*) that became the property of the four daughters. Marx would continue to pay annual interest (fl. 100) until all four girls married. It was typical of Matheus's marriages that he sought connections to reputable merchant families, whose economic resources seldom exceeded his own. Such had been the case with the Warmberger, Schorer and Miller. Such seems to have been the case with the Mehrer.

Anna Maria was, however, evidently better dowered than her paternal inheritance indicated. When she died in 1686, she left Philip Jakob a son named Thomas, whose maternal inheritance had to be secured in the usual contract of agreement.[9] Matheus and Hans Jakob Habisreitinger served as guardians for the boy. Philip Jakob promised to raise and support the boy until he came of age or married, at which time he would give him his maternal inheritance of fl. 4,000 in cash and his mother's personal property of worked gold and silver. Insofar as her son's expectation matched the independent means of the deceased parent, in accordance with traditional practice in Augsburg, Anna Maria's dowry must have brought Philip Jakob as much as fl. 4,000. Viewed as capital, it corresponds roughly to those received by Matheus.

The marriage festivities followed. Wedding and feast took place at the Lauginger house on the first two days after the marriage contract was concluded.[10] This is the only mention Matheus makes of any celebration, a terse reference that reveals its unimportance in his thought or, perhaps better put, its irrelevance to his image.[11] The purpose of his memoir did not extend to public externalities such as social status or mobility. Rather, it served private and internal ends. Thus, he took pains to choreograph the private marriage negotiation and passed in silence over the public wedding celebration. Opportunities for conspicuous display and consumption were immaterial. From the initial suggestion to the detailed consultation to the formal courtship to the final agreement, he provided his reader a sketch of the appropriate decorum and ceremony that applied to his son's marriage as well as his own.

Philip Jakob rose quickly in the world of his father. At the time of his marriage, his tax assessment stood at fl. 10 kr. 10.[12] A decade later, by the time his father died, it had risen to fl. 45 kr. 5, reflecting an increase in wealth from as little as fl. 2,000 to as much as fl. 18,000.[13] That same year, he acquired two of his father's properties, the houses at Annastraße 3 and Steingaße 11, by paying fl. 5,000 to his brothers and sisters.[14] Philip Jakob occupied several public offices, including those of custodian (*Zechpfleger*) of Holy Cross Church in 1688, and administrator (*Pfleger*) of the Georg Regel Foundation in 1691.[15] He was a merchant and *stubenfähig*, that is, qualified by birth to be a member of the Augsburg merchant association, but no records survive from his business. A few details can be reconstructed from a property dispute between Philip Jakob and the guardians of his son, Thomas.[16] The documents, which are fragmentary and disclose neither the dispute's cause nor its resolution, include an extract from Philip Jakob's account books. He had entered a partnership with Zacharias Lang, a son of another established Augsburg mercantile family. On 20 February 1686, the firm claimed fl. 57,670 in assets, most important among which were fl. 28,057 in accounts receivable, as opposed to fl. 27,816 in liabilities. Though the exact nature of the business remains obscure, the inventory reveals stockpiles of agricultural products, commercial connections in Tirol and, surprisingly, credit relations with the Catholic Church. How Matheus might have reacted to this last aspect of his son's affairs cannot be reconstructed. In every other particular, however, Philip Jakob seems to have modeled his own career so closely on that of his father that there could hardly have been room for complaint. In his eldest son, therefore, Matheus would appear to have achieved the wished-for continuity.

But, was Matheus satisfied with this achievement? Did he rest from his labors, as his end approached, confident that his business, his property, and his reputation were in good hands? The memoir gives clear evidence that Philip Jakob held a singular position in the thoughts of his father. None of the other eight surviving children receive as much attention. Yet, Matheus offered no insight into his personal relationship with his eldest son. Philip Jakob inherited his father's position in Augsburg, and Matheus was evidently satisfied with that position.

The organization and texture of his memoir leave little doubt as to his complacency. After recording the struggles of his early days, he chronicled only his accomplishments and victories: his harmonious marriages; his growing family; his solid associations; his public services; his private benevolence. In all, he consistently maintained his propriety. As a patriarch he managed his household mildly, adapting to circumstances and consulting with relatives. As an official he held to standards of probity but was not above mild collusion in a good cause. As a friend he demonstrated an open-handed paternalism that could be both selfless and self-serving. As a Lutheran he clung externally to the trappings of an orthodox piety even as he grappled internally with his faith. All of these things admitted him to that charmed circle of proper merchants and householders which his uncles would have denied him. Matheus revealed no reason why he should not be at peace with his life and his success.

Certainly, he rose from an unpromising, perhaps disreputable, youth to achieve a degree of fortune and fame. The archival records testify unmistakably to it. Despite the topsy-turvy state of his world at the end of a period of extreme crisis – and because of it – Matheus achieved settled success. Through his enterprises and his marriages, he established himself and his family in the merchant community of Augsburg. By the end of his life, he rendered a property tax in excess of fl. 100 and, therewith, could justly have claimed membership in the city's economic elite. He occupied offices that, if not at the pinnacle of Augsburg's state apparatus, were as near the apex of power as merchants could aspire to approach. Moreover, such offices as captain of militia, associate of the marriage court, administrator of charity and custodian of the church, conferred a public visibility that reflected and enhanced Matheus's private achievement. Within the confining circle of Augsburg's walls, fortune and fame were his.

Yet, in the memoir he valued the former less than the latter. He seldom referred to his business and revealed little of his means. Important as these things were, they were immaterial to this account. Fame meant much more than the acclaim that follows the conquest of fortune through one's 'unshakeable spirit, constant mind, energetic intelligence, indefatigable industry and art'.[17] The struggles and insecurities of illegitimacy drove Alberti to seek public acclaim and vindication. Not so Matheus. For him, public reputation merely underscored a man's private propriety, his personal stature. A merchant's fortune was more than the sum of an annual balance. Wealth served to underscore a merchant's credibility and creditworthiness, those qualities by which private interests and personal utility were sought and secured. Manifested in financial accounting, they derived from the commercial training and experience of merchants, their *habitus* of keeping detailed, accurate records not only to summarize their fortunes but to foster their growth. Thus, accounts recorded more than the ebb and flow of property. They demonstrated the character of the merchant, his honesty and his acumen.

Far from abandoning productive enterprise in favor of offices and rentes, a charge frequently leveled at the early modern bourgeois, Matheus drew from it a discipline that shaped all else.[18] Accountability extended well beyond the counting house and the marketplace. It assured stable relationships and reliable transactions in all spheres of life; it demonstrated the acumen and probity of the accountant; it became the tool by which Matheus sought to justify and vindicate his life. The order and rationality of commercial life could not be separated from those of the domestic sphere. In his marriages, he presented a solid, reputable face to the world. He intended his negotiations and agreements to testify not only to his social stature but also to his ethical fiber. When conditions required it, as on the occasion of his third marriage, he even rendered account to the community at large. What emerged was the image of a firm, yet flexible, patriarch and a householder at once caring and calculating. In his offices, Matheus cast public life as a rational extension not of private interest but rather of private virtues. Accordingly, he drew upon his own background and experience to fashion a public morality based on established procedures and accurate accounts. The result is a portrait of himself as state servant and autonomous burgher at one and the same time. In his friendships, Matheus demonstrated a paternal benevolence to the members of his extended family, assisting those people for whom he felt a spontaneous affection and those people from whom he expected some reciprocity. Not simply a means to social mobility, friendship expressed genuine sympathy even as it fostered familial solidarity and demonstrated personal stature. His upward trajectory notwithstanding, he revealed himself to be a man of complex affinities and aspirations. In his encounters with death, Matheus mourned the passing of loved ones and honored their memories, celebrating their Christian fortitude and commemorating their personal accomplishments. The church – its offices, rituals and beliefs – provided a context for grief and remembrance without completely defining them. In his own retelling, he upheld his faith but avoided the trammels of confession. His account of his life, like an account of his business, reorganized and summarized events in ways that underscored his quality – his propriety – to himself and to his posterity.

It demonstrated his mastery as well. Worldly events may be ineluctable and inscrutable, but the human remains free to respond properly or otherwise to these turnings of fate. The individual retains his or her dignity, even as God's omnipotence is upheld. Thus, in his memoir Matheus seemed to reconcile the ideals of Renaissance humanism with those of Lutheran orthodoxy. He tempered honor, power and freedom with modesty, obedience and service. As he looked back into his own past and forward to his family's future, this was his claim to fame. Propriety and, finally, mastery were the essence of the social patrimony that accompanied the fortune he bequeathed to his children.

Yet, this crafted self – this image of propriety and mastery – remains a facade of sorts, not unlike Alberti's articulation of the bourgeois family. It should not obscure Matheus's constant struggle to reconcile traditional institutions with personal circumstances. He seldom evinced the defensive, parochial chauvinism of the German townsman, but he remained grounded in Augsburg.[19] He represented himself not only as the product of individual effort and achievement but also as the beneficiary of a particular social estate and status. He embraced the assumptions of household patriarchy but found it difficult to reconcile with his changing circumstances. He engaged in forms of personal patronage even as he rejected it in public life. He conformed to the religious precepts of the *Confessio Augustana* while lacking confidence in some of its most fundamental, theological precepts. The result was a series of tensions and conflicts – between the general and the particular, the old and the new, the social and the personal, the sacred and the secular – that remain, at best, imperfectly resolved. Though they accord uneasily with the testimony of his memoir, the interplay of such opposing tendencies reveal his individuality, his complexity, and, ultimately, his humanity.

Propriety and mastery notwithstanding, Matheus sought divine guidance and assistance, in 1655, when Philip Jakob began his education.[20] It is the most remarkable devotional moment in a memoir filled with invocations, supplications and benedictions. Spontaneously and confidently, Matheus prayed for the thing he had struggled a lifetime to obtain, his son's success.

He begins by quoting the Gospel, John 16: 23: 'In very truth I tell you, if you ask the Father for anything in my name, he will give it you.'[21] Unlike those prayers in which he struggled to accept God's will, here Matheus expresses certainty that faith in the next world will have its reward in this one. He asks that the grace of the Holy Spirit inspire his son and all his children with the fear of God, 'which is the beginning of all wisdom and wit', and that it keep them from idolatry and falsehood. After connecting human intelligence with heavenly wisdom, he focuses more directly on the kind of qualities he hopes Philip Jakob will achieve, the kind of man he hopes Philip Jakob – and all his children – will become.[22]

> Give them a devout, obedient and modest heart, also the proper wisdom and understanding that they grow and increase in wisdom, age and grace before God and men. Plant in their hearts the love of your godly word that they are pious in prayer and worship; respectful toward the servants of the word and toward everyone; upright in their dealings; modest in manner; disciplined in morals; truthful in words; true in works; industrious in business; fortunate in the conduct of their profession and office; knowledgeable in affairs; proper in all things; gentle and friendly toward all men. Preserve them from all misfortune of this world, so filled with misfortune that they not be led astray by evil company. Let them not fall into gluttony [*shlemmen*] and immorality that they waste their lives and offend others. Protect them from dangers that they not die untimely. Grant me not dishonor and shame but rather joy and honor in them that they increase your kingdom and enlarge the numbers of the faithful and that they sit at your table in heaven, like the heavenly olive branch, and with all the saints honor, praise, and glorify you.

This prayer – more heartfelt than any of the others – captured the life Matheus hoped he had lived, the portrait he had sketched in his memoir. Philip Jakob and his siblings should take up not only their father's possessions and dignities but also his virtues and values, and incorporate them into their own lives.

These qualities form, in fact, an elaborate set of what would be recognized by the eighteenth century as bourgeois virtues (*bürgerliche Tugende*). Nearly a century later, in his treatment 'Concerning Bourgeois Virtues', Johann Heinrich Gottlob von Justi would speak in almost identical terms of the virtues, or obligations, owed by all burghers to the state, the virtues owed by all burghers to one another, and the virtues owed by all burghers to themselves.[23] Whereas Justi's three-part division betrays his secular orientation, however, Matheus couched his reflections in the language of an orthodox piety. The sacred and the secular were inextricably linked. Virtues in the one applied unquestionably to the other. If these virtues spoke of economic success and business morality, they applied with no less force to all arenas of human exchange and interaction. Finally, apt as they were for the promotion of political order or social mobility – and bourgeois virtues have been applied to both of these, occasionally contradictory, ends – their purpose remained more universally the strengthening of individual or personal qualities. They formed a catalogue of early modern propriety. They sought moral probity and material success in a world open to human endeavor and achievement but circumscribed by divine will and ordinance. They are emblematic of Matheus's memoir, the story of his life.

Matheus Miller died in 1685. His memoir ceases without a conclusion, as if he walked away from it and never returned. That is as it should be; in a sense it could not be finished. Though the memoir reconciled past and present – memory and actuality – it also projected a future. It was Matheus's voice to his children, his call for continuity.

Notes

The following abbreviations are used in the Notes:

EWA	Evangelisches Wesensarchiv
StaatsAA	Staatsarchiv Augsburg
StadtAA	Stadtarchiv Augsburg
StadtAMM	Stadtarchiv Memmingen
StadtBA	Stadt- und Staatsbibliothek Augsburg
UK	Urkunden

Preface

1 StadtAA, EWA 59, Miller Tagebuch, p. 1: 'Inn disem Büchlein allerleÿ sachen / verzeichnet / So mich Matheo Miller Inn Augspurg / betreffen / Vonn meiner Geburt ann So lang mir Got das Leben unnd / die Genade verlihen dises zue continuieren / Ist mit wenigem darum verzeichnet umb die / meinigen da Got die Gnade verlihe etwan zue verlassen solhes nach mir finden.'

Introduction

1 StadtAA, EWA 59, Miller Tagebuch, p. 3: 'Ist doch mein / inclination auch lust mehrers zuer Hantlung gewesen mein / geliebter Vater auch inn Gueter Hofnung gestanden wann Er / mich zue der Hantlung solte wollen gebrauhen Jnn seinen / aignen negotio mir mit der Zeit woll wurde dienen können / mich demnach nach Hauß kommen lassen.'
2 StadtAA, EWA 59, Miller Tagebuch, p. 2.
3 Ibid.: 'Ob nun wohl mein geliebte unnd geehrte Eltern hernach Järlich / andere Kinder bekommen unnd grosen fleiss unnd sorg zuer / Mühe gehabt unns sovill Jnen Jmmer moglich Jnn der Forcht / Gotes zue auferziehen inn geringsten nix erwinden lassen / wan sie Jmmer vermeinet dz wir etwas erlehrnen könnten / massen sie es mit grosem uncosten genuegsam werden Erfaren / haben so Got inn Gnaden anderwerts ersetzen wolle.'
4 StadtAA, Steuerbücher, 1625, 97c; 1635, 98a. The common coinage of early modern Augsburg was the Rhenish *Gulden*, abbreviated 'fl.', a silver piece worth roughly 1.75 DM or $0.95 today. Its subdivisions were the *Kreutzer* (kr.) and *Heller* (hl.). The following equivalency applied as a rule: 1 *Gulden* (fl.) = 60 *Kreutzer* (kr.) = 420 *Heller* (hl.). Some sense of the market value of the *Gulden* can be derived from the accounts provided to the City Council by the Bakers' Guild in 1596. According to these estimates, an artisanal household paid fl. 1 kr. 30 for a week's supply of bread or beef (12 pounds). As cited in B. Roeck, *Bäcker, Brot und Getreide in Augsburg: Zur Geschichte der Bäckerhandwerk und zur Versorgungspolitik der Reichsstadt im Zeitalter der Dreißigjährigen Kreiges* (Sigmaringen, 1987), p. 27.

5 Augsburg taxed the total of real and moveable property, the value of which can be calculated as the product of tax assessment and tax rate. Because it used two rates – 0.25 percent (0.0025) for real property and 0.50 percent (0.0050) for moveable property – but listed only a single, undifferentiated figure as the liability of a given taxpayer, the result is a range rather than a specific value. See C.-P. Clasen, *Die Augsburger Steuerbücher um 1600* (Augsburg, 1976), pp. 7–9; A. Mayr, *Die großen Augsburger Vermögen in der Zeit von 1618 bis 1717* (Augsburg, 1931), pp. 5–9.

6 An assessment of the tax registers for 1610 indicates that only 719 of 9,599 taxpayers rendered taxes in excess of fl. 10. By 1618, the proportions had changed minimally. Of all taxpayers, 6.6 percent paid taxes in the fl. 1–100 range. Cf. C.-P. Clasen, 'Arm und Reich in Augsburg vor dem Dreißigjährigen Krieg,', in G. Gottlieb *et al.* (eds), *Geschichte der Stadt Augsburg: 2000 Jahren von der Römerzeit bis zur Gegenwart* (Stuttgart, 1985), p. 318; B. Roeck, *Eine Stadt in Krieg und Frieden: Studien zur Geschichte der Reichsstadt Augsburg zwischen Kalendarstreit und Parität* (Gottingen, 1989), Vol. I, p. 398. Even Blendinger's early attempt to reconstruct the middle strata of early modern Augsburg society placed Michael on the cusp between middle and upper levels. See F. Blendinger, 'Versuch einer Bestimmung der Mittleschicht in der Reichsstadt Augsburg vom Ende des 14. bis zum Anfange des 18. Jahrhunderts' in E. Maschke and J. Sydow (eds), *Städtische Mittelschichten* (Stuttgart, 1972), p. 71.

7 The *Literaverzeichnis*, a combination of letter and number, was the system used to identify houses in Augsburg. Created by order of the City Senate, on 19 June 1781, in conjunction with administrative measures for the new Poor House (*Armenanstalt*), it divided the city into eight districts, A–H, and assigned numbers to the houses within each of them. It remained in effect until 1 April 1938, when the city instituted the current system, based on street name and house number. StaatsAA, Grundbücher der Reichsstadt Augsburg, Index, pp. 710–11.

8 A. Mayr, *Die großen Augsburger Vermögen*, p. 116.

9 Ibid., p. 118.

10 K. Sieh-Burens, *Oligarchie, Konfession und Politik im 16. Jahrhundert: Zur sozialen Verflechtung der Augsburger Bürgermeister und Stadtpfleger, 1518–1618* (Munich, 1986), passim.

11 Ibid., pp. 190–1.

12 StadtAA, EWA 59, Miller Tagebuch, p. 2: 'so / habe doch selbige inn sonderheit auf mich grose uncosten ergehen / lassen'.

13 Unlike Augsburg, which also possessed an extensive system of walls and towers, the medieval fortifications of Ulm were modernized to the latest standards of military architecture in the first decades of the seventeenth century. It proved a safe haven from violence, if not from famine and disease, throughout the Thirty Years' War. G. Zillhardt, *Der Dreißigjährige Krieg in zeitgenössischer Darstellung: Hans Heberles 'Zeytregister' (1618–1672): Aufzeichnungen aus dem Ulmer Territorium. Ein Beitrag zu Geschichtsschreibung und Geschichtsverständnis der Unterschichten* (Ulm, 1975), p. 14.

14 StadtAA, EWA 59, Miller Tagebuch, p. 3: 'Anno 1639 nach Veronam Jtem / geshikt worden zue dem Jnacentio Tomasini inn das / Hauß alda ich nahent eine Jaar gewesen unnd die Sprach / zimmlich ergriffen mein geliebter vater

hernach vermeinet solte / mir noch besser taugen wann Jch Jtem auch ein mehrers lehrnete / unnd mich demnach nach Florentz geshibt ueber venedig alda / Jch mit Veter Anthoni Stenglin inn dem Teütshen Hauß / bei Einem Evangelishen Herrn Prediger Comuniciert. Zue Florentz / habe mich bei denn Herrn Georg und David Wolff aufgehalten / unnd wann Jnn Jrer shreibstube nix anders verrichten / können zue hr. anto. gallacino oder auch lorentio franescko gehen / dürfen die mich zum andictieren der brf. gern gebraucht.'

15 J. Riebartsch, *Augsburger Handelsgesellschaften des 15. und 16. Jahrhunderts* (Cologne, 1987), pp. 27–9.
16 StadtAA, EWA 59, Miller Tagebuch, p. 4: 'Ob Jch nun wol gern lenger darr gewesen were, So ist es doch / meinem Lieben Vater nit lenger gefällig gewesen wegen / tewren Costgelts unnd andern speci die ann solhen orten Jmmer / mehrers aufgehen. Mich demnach abermallen uber Venedig / nach Hauß citiert.'
17 Ibid.: 'Jch hate aber gelegenheit zuevor Pistoia / Pisa Lucca Livorno und Siena mit gueter compa. zuversehen. / also nach verrichter selbiger lustigen spazier reiß mich mit / dem Poten eillendts nach Venedig gemacht vonn daar mit / Herrn Sigmund Deiboldt auf Verona unnd fördres nach Augspurg / also nit länger als ungefer 3/4 Jaar Zue Florentz mich befunden.'
18 Ibid.: 'bei meiner anheims konfft verhoffte meine gl. Vater mich gleich / andern Vetern inn der shreibstuben unnd geschäfften zugebrauhen / aber dz glüben wolte nit sondern Einer unnd andere rathete / Jmmer mich ferners zue vershicken unnd inn fremte Kaufleuths / dienste mich zue obligkiern die wolten sich aber nit gleich / presentiern. dz urtell fälte mann entlich mit Herrn Baltas / Shnuerpeins leuten 1641 inn die frankfurter Herbstmess mich zue / versenden inn denn vorhaben da einige glegenheit zu diensten / sich erzeigte.'
19 Ibid.: 'binn etlichen alhier / Ein Dorn inn den Augen gewesen unnd inn dem gueten / Estimo bei denn nechsten dz all Jhr rath nun immer gangen / ob Jch gleich nach Cöln als inn das erzt Catholishe orth kommen solte / unnd mich 10 Jaar verobligkieren müeste solte es nix bedeuten / damit Jch nun die Millerishe shreibstuben nit dörffte betreten.'
20 Ibid.: 'warum aber es Got also verhenget Jst imme ann dem besten bewust / anderseits aber ist es aus privat aigennutz erfolget'.
21 A. Mayr, *Die großen Augsburger Vermögen*, pp. 13–26.
22 P. Fassl, *Konfession, Wirtshaft und Politik: Von der Reichsstadt zur Industriestadt, Augsburg 1750–1850* (Sigmaringen, 1988), pp. 42–3.
23 B. Greiff, 'Tagebuch des Lucas Rem aus den Jahren 1494–1541: Ein Beitrag zur Handelsgeschichte der Stadt Augsburg', *Jahresbericht des historischen Vereins für Schwaben und Neuburg* 27 (1861), pp. 18–20: 'Erfand, daz Antonio Welser und geselschaft Ir General-Rechnong 8 tag darvor beschlossen, tag, fil von der nacht gesessen onmas fast geeilt hetten, untriulich, gefarlich und unerber, al ding ring angeschlagen, um dz Si al gelt mit 1/3 abkünden, Jacobo Welser und fil ander urlauben wolten. Hetten den Schulden durchaus 10 pro Cento a Kapo abrochen, fil guot bös gmacht, schentlich hendel darin giept. Also auf 17 Nov. verwis und zaiget ich gar drutzig und aigentlich an – wz Antonio & Bartolomeo Welser, Peter & Hans Hainzel, Narcis Lauginger, Simon Seitz, Hans Vöhlin – verwis Inen Ir misdat, zaigtet

In mit der kreidt, redt In an Ir eer, luos Inen nichtz dahinten, treet ihnen ich wiste ales, des ich Si zich, bezuigen mit Iren selbs schrifften … ir antwurt was, Si hetten nit geirrt, noch nictz vergessen, redlich mit der merern stimm die anschläg getan, darbey wurd und miest es belieben – Darauf bat ich Si um vrlaub. Die schmechwort litten Si, aber kainswegs wolten Si mir vrlaub geben … Aber kaineswegs wolt ich bey diser unerberkait bleiben,' etc.

24 The Great Ravensburger Company, which involved over 120 families between 1380 and 1520, is the exception that proves the rule. See J. Riebatsch, *Augsburger Handelsgesellschaften*, p. 215.
25 Ibid., p. 218.
26 F. Blendinger, 'Augsburger Handel im Dreißigjährigen Krieg nach Konzepten von Fedi di Sanità, Politen, Attesten u. ä.' in H. Kellenbenz and J. Schneider (eds), *Beiträge zur Wirtschaftsgeschichte* (Stuttgart, 1978), Vol. V, p. 294.
27 A. Mayr, *Die großen Augsburger Vermögen*, pp. 118–19: Gabriel paid fl. 112 kr. 30 on property valued between fl. 22,500 and fl. 45,000; Hans Jakob paid fl. 125 on a gross worth between fl. 25,000 and fl. 50,000.
28 StadtAA, Reichsstadt Akten, Stadtkanzlei, s.a., s.d., UK 274.
29 F. Blendinger, 'Augsburger Handel im Dreißigjährigen Krieg nach Konzepten von Fedi die Sanità, Politen, Attesten ü. a.,' pp. 303–4.
30 StadtAA, Reichsstadt Akten, Stadtkanzlei, s.a., s.d., UK 373a, 383, 392, 404, 406, 408, 410, 412, 458, 459, 486, 488, 490, 498, 502, 504, 506.
31 StadtAA, EWA 59, Miller Tagebuch, pp. 4–5: 'wie Jch / nun zue frankfurt allerhand conditiones gesucht hat Got doch / nirgents etwas annemlich erblüken lassen sondern muste / damit Ja nit nach Augspurg komme auf Nürmberg auß sonderbarn / Schikung Gotes zue dem Herrn Zacharias Shoap deme mein geliebter / vater dz Cost gelt zue geben sich anerboten biß etwan uns Liebe Got / andere dienste ordnete'.
32 Ibid., p. 5: 'bei disem Herrn Shoapen bin Jch ankommen / dem Monat Oktober 1641 unnd vonn Jme dermassen zue der Hantlung / unnd dergleichen verrichtungen mit solhem embsigen aifer / angehalten worden dz Jch mir woll zue sonderbar dankbarem / Ehrn und Jme zum ruhm nach sagen kann ein leiblicher Vater / mehrers nit woll thuen könnte als Er gegen mir fremte gethon / da Jch dann anlaß bekommen die sachen auff ein und andern weis / fleisiger unnd ernstlicher nahzudenken auch nah deme er mir / die Handelsbücher anfangen vertrawen allerlei grose patientin / mit mir gehabt inn underweissung allerhandt Kauffmans ausszug / brief unnd wexelbrief zue formieren'.
33 Ibid.: 'hat Got wunderlich / Eine condition erblübhen lassen bei Herrn Hanns Schlumpffen / vonn St Gallen der damalen auch seine Casata in Nürmberg / unnd zuem complimentario seinen Sohn Hans Caspar hate / mich demnach zue dem selben inn dienst zuer prob eingeloßen / unnd vom Jme nach St Gallen nah dem bei 14 Tage bei Jne / zue Nürnberg gewesen zue seinem Vater befürdert alwoh Jch / Anno 1642 ershinen mich entlich dahin obligirt uff $6\frac{1}{2}$ Jaar / neben meinem freyen tish mir Järlich fl. 43 zue solario reihent / darauß abzunemmen wie genaw wegen der langen Zeit / unnd hingegen des geringen solvey bei meinem damaligen Herrn / gesehen worden'.
34 Ibid., pp. 5–6: 'nun es ließ sich der dienst beiderseits fein ann / auch über 2 Jaar dabei Jch nun Scritura halten die Cassa versehen / unnd dem verkaufen abwarten müesen sowoll als auch andere briefe / verantwurten. So Jch alles

so guet möglich nach meinen Jugent verrichte / unnd meinem Herrn alle Jaar zue Zürcher markht helfen versehen / Alles mit beidersiets guetem Condento'.

35 J. A. Comenius, *Informatorivm maternvm, Der Mutter Schul* (Nuremberg, 1636) as cited in P. Münch, *Lebensformen der frühen Neuzeit, 1500 bis 1800* (Berlin, 1992), p. 233.
36 B. Greiff, 'Tagebuch des Lucas Rem', pp. 5–6.
37 StadtAA, EWA 59, Miller Tagebuch, p. 6: 'balt nach Zweien Jaarn starb / meinem Herrn seine Hausfraw wordurch dz Haushaben von tag zue / tag inn mehrere ohnordnung gerathen darauff zwischen unns / beeden undershidtliche disgusti entstanten das ich entlich als gesehen / kein ander mitel vorhanden die feintseeligkait so von tag zu tag / gewaxen unnd über $1\frac{1}{2}$ jaar continuiert bei zue legen ich komme / dann gaar vonn Jme als ersuchte meinen l. Vater shrifftlich / mir ann die hant zue gehen'.
38 Ibid.: 'worauff er balt zue St Gallen ershinen / unnd nach dem es vill unnd grose mühe gebraucht mich entlich / losgemacht. so geshehen dem Oktober Anno 1645 ich müste aber damallen / versprechen zue bleiben biß Anno 1646 inn Febrer.'
39 Ibid.: 'inn diser zeit wurde / ich entlich mal gebeten lenger zue verbleiben aber mein Jntent / ist förders gewesen inn sonderheit weillen guete annleutung / hate im zueruggreisen zue Leükürch einer witfr. Tochter / so vonn guetem vermögen sein sollen zue heuraten weswegen / dann meine zueruggreis nit lang aufgeshoben sondern nach dem / inn guetr freundlichkeit vonn meinem Patron urlaub hate / unnd Jme denn Billanzo durchgehent ordenlich übergeben / unnd meine dienste quitiert.'
40 Ibid.: 'binn vonn villen gueten / bekannten bis nach Lindaw begleitet worden als Jch vonn daar / nach Leükürch kommen finde die gelegenheit nit wie Jch es erhofft / derowegen meine Heüratsgedanken widerum endern müsse'.
41 B. Greiff, 'Tagebuch des Lucas Rem', p. 43: 'Auf fil, lang und ernstlich anhaltten meiner Ersamen muoter, brieder und ander fil vertraut fraind und guot günner, adi 14 May 1518 ward mein heyrott durch Lucas Welser und Bartolomeo Rem mit Marx Echäin und Conrat Relinger abgerett, und adi 17 ditto, montag zwischen 1 und 2 ur endlich beschlossen zwischen mir, Lucaz Rem, und Junckfraw Anna Echäinin, weilendtt Jerg Echäins und Anna Endorferin eeliche docter.'
42 StadtAMM, A327/9, Tagebuch des Handelsherrn Caspar Koch, geboren 1576, gestorben 1620, pp. 2–5.
43 StadtAA, EWA 59, Miller Tagebuch, p. 6: 'als Jch nach Haus kommen wolte sich doch vonn annders nix / reden lassen als widerum dienste zue seuchen dann inn meines / Vetern schreibstuben wolte kein mensh nit nemmen. duch solchs / mitels wurde auch andererwerts vershlagen niemanden wüste / warum mich die Herrn Millerischen nit annemmen / wolte'.
44 Ibid.: 'das / mein Geliebter Vater wiewoll es Jn vormals offt shweer / ankommen etwas aignes anzuefangen doch entlich auch das / Herz angenommen unnd gerathen mit wenig baumwoll / gegen webern etwas zue negotirn'.
45 L. B. Alberti, *The Family in Renaissance Florence: I Libri della Famiglia*, R. N. Watkins, trans. (Columbia, S.C., 1969), p. 1.
46 Ibid., p. 12.

47 These relations come to light in Alberti's *Vita anonymi* in L. A. Muratori (ed.), *Rerum italicarum scriptores* (Milan, 1723–51), Vol. XXV. Cited in L. B. Alberti, *The Family in Renaissance Florence*, pp. 1–20.
48 Fletcher maintains that civility rises in the void replaced by the decline of honor as a social concept. It is civility, therefore, that organizes relations in a class society. Matheus, however, seems to have identified a different principle. See A. Fletcher, *Gender, Sex and Subordination in England, 1500–1800* (New Haven, 1995), p. 142.
49 G. Mancini, *Vita de Leon Battista Alberti* (Florence, 1911) as cited in L. B. Alberti, *The Family in Renaissance Florence*, p. 3.
50 L. B. Alberti, *The Family in Renaissance Florence*, p. 3.
51 My colleague, Anthea Waleson, first supposed that the common element between Matheus and Alberti might have been cultural and intellectual rather than archival, that is, that their educations predisposed them to view their writings in similar terms. I thank her for the suggestion.
52 F. Copleston, SJ, *A History of Philosophy*, Vol. I (Garden City, N.Y., 1962), pp. 428–31. Cf. C. Trinkaus, *In Our Likeness and Image: Humanity and Divinity in Italian Humanist Thought* (Chicago, 1970), passim.
53 All citations are from R. McKeon (ed.), *The Basic Works of Aristotle* (New York, 1941).
54 *Politics*, Bk. I, Ch. 2.
55 *Nicomachean Ethics*, Bk. VII, Ch. 1.
56 StadtAA, EWA 59, Miller Tagebuch, p. 1: 'Ach Herr Lehse mich bedenken das Jch sterben muss und / mein Leben Ein Zihl hat. und Jch davon / muss leben so leben wie dem Herrn Sterben so sterben wie dem Herrn / darumb wie lebeben [sic] oder sterben so sein wie des / Herrn. / Christlich leben macht Selig Seelig sterben und Ewige freud Ererben. / Ach Gott Hilft uns alle Dreij Stukh Erwerben.'
57 A similar sentiment can be found in 'Ein Deutsches Requiem' by Johannes Brahms:

> Herr, lehre doch mich, daß ein
> Ende mit mir habe muß, und
> mein Leben ein Ziel hat, und
> ich davon muß.

I wish to thank Anthea Waleson for both references.
58 Psalms 39: 5. This and all other biblical references are to *The New English Bible with the Apocrypha* (Oxford, 1970).
59 P. Boerner, *Tagebuch* (Stuttgart, 1969), p. 16; A. Macfarlane, *The Family Life of Ralph Josselin* (Cambridge, Eng., 1970), p. 5; P. Seaver, *Wallington's World* (Stanford, 1985), p. 6; K. von Greyerz, *Vorsehungsglaube und Kosmologie* (Göttingen, 1990), pp. 19–20.
60 StadtAA, EWA 59, Miller Tagebuch, p. 1: 'umb die / meinigen da Got die gnade verlihe etwan zue / verlassen solches nach mir finden'.
61 The origins of autobiographical writings in German-speaking regions extend at least to the thirteenth and fourteenth centuries. Cf. M. Buchholz, *Die Anfänge des deutschen Tagebuchschreibung* (Münster, 1981); T. Klaiber, *Die deutsche Selbstbiographie: Beschreibungen des eigenen Lebens, Memoiren, Tagebücher* (Stuttgart, 1921); W. Mahrholz, *Deutsche Selbstbekenntnisse: Ein*

Beitrag zur Geschichte der Selbstbiographie von der Mystik zum Pietismus (Berlin, 1919); H. Wenzel (ed.), *Die Autobiographie des späten Mittelalters und der frühen Neuzeit*, 2 vols (Munich, 1980).
62 G. Misch, *Geschichte der Autobiographie*, (Frankfurt/M, 1969), Vol. IV, p. 583; M. Phillips, *The Memoir of Marco Parenti* (Princeton, 1987), p. 241; von Greyerz, *Vorsehungsglaube und Kosmologie*, pp. 39–46.
63 H. Wenzel (ed.), *Die Autobiographie*, Vol. II, p. 8.
64 H. Wenzel (ed.), *Die Autobiographie*, Vol. I, p. 14.
65 The argument that Italian merchants and, by extension, all businessmen of the early modern period conflated public and private affairs in their commercial dealings and, more importantly, in their commercial writings fundamentally misinterprets their understanding of their own interests and involvements. Cf. S. Jed, *Chaste Thinking* (Bloomington, 1989), pp. 74–120.
66 Social historians have found little to praise in the autobiographical writings of the Baroque Period; it has variously been described as 'tedious, narrow, crude, and obscure', a kind of petty-bourgeois, family chronicle, especially when compared to the great examples of the sixteenth century. Cf. T. Klaiber, *Die deutsche Selbstbiographie*, p. 55; W. Mahrholz, *Deutsche Selbstbekenntnisse*, pp. 78–89, citation, p. 87; K. von Greyerz, *Vorsehungsglaube und Kosmologie*, pp. 42–3.
67 Matheus's memoir certainly does not conform to an observation made by E. von Ranke, 'Der Interessenkreis des deutschen Bürgers im 16. Jahrhundert (aufgrund von Selbstbiographien und Briefen)', *Vierteljahrsschrift für Sozial- und Wirtschaftsgeschichte* 20 (1928): 447–90: 'the citizen of the sixteenth century knew at every moment that his life was in God's hands. God determined the hours of birth and of death, the shape of the body, the selection of spouses, sent sickness and infestation, riches and poverty, good and bad markets, holocaust, peace, good and bad weather; even the virtue, industry, and boldness of a human being were His works.' Cf. K. von Greyerz, 'Religion in the Life of German and Swiss Autobiographers (Sixteenth and Early Seventeenth Centuries)' in idem (ed.), *Religion and Society in Early Modern Europe, 1500–1800* (London, 1984), pp. 1–14; idem, *Vorsehungsglaube und Kosmologie*, p. 42.
68 This quality clearly distinguishes Matheus's memoir from the spiritual diaries of his day. Cf. P. Seaver, *Wallington's World*, pp. 9–10; K. von Greyerz, *Vorsehungsglaube und Kosmologie,* passim.
69 Recent literature distinguishes early from modern autobiography in that the former elevates the event over the self. This is certainly not the case with Matheus's memoir, a fact that sets it apart from most of its contemporaries. Cf. K. von Greyerz, *Vorsehungsglaube und Kosmologie*, p. 46; H. Wenzel (ed.), *Die Autobiographie*, Vol. II, pp. 8–9.
70 S. Jed, *Chaste Thinking*, pp. 94–108.
71 J. Presser, 'Memoires als geschiedbron', *Winkler Prins Encyclopedie*, Vol. VIII (Amsterdam, 1958), pp. 208–10; idem, *Uit het werk van dr. J. Presser* (Amsterdam, 1969), esp. pp. 277–82; R. M. Dekker, R. Lindeman and Y. Scherf, 'Verstopte bronnen: egodocumenten van Noord-Nederlanders uit de 16de tot 18de eeuw', *Nederlands Archieven Blad* 86 (1982), pp. 226–35; R. M. Dekker, 'Egodocumenten: Een literatuuroverzicht', *Tijdschrift voor Geschiedenis* 101 (1988), pp. 161–89; idem, 'Ego-Documents in the Netherlands,

1500–1814', *Dutch Crossing* 39 (1989), pp. 61–72; idem, 'Ego-Dokumente in den Niederlanden vom 16. Bis zum 17. Jahrhundert', in W. Schulze (ed.), *Ego-Dokumente: Annäherung an den Menschen in der Geschichte* (Berlin, 1996), pp. 33–58.
72 In addition to those works already cited from the vast bibliography on 'ego-documents', see: K. Barkin, 'Autobiography and History', *Societas* 6 (1976), pp. 83–108; D. Bertaux (ed.), *Biography and Society: The Life History Approach in the Social Sciences* (London, 1981); P. Delany, *British Autobiography in the Seventeenth Century* (London, 1969); J. Kronsbein, *Autobiographisches Erzählen: Die narrativen Strukturen der Autobiographie* (Munich, 1984); P. Lejeune, *L'histoire de l'autobiographie en France* (Paris, 1971); G. Niggl (ed.), *Die Autobiographie: Zu Form und Geschichte einer literarischen Gattung* (Darmstadt, 1989).
73 To this discussion, see W. Schulze, 'Ego-Dokumente: Annäherung an den Menschen in der Geschichte? Vorüberlegung für die Tagung "Ego-Dokumente"' in idem (ed.), *Ego-Dokumente: Annäherung an den Menschen in der Geschichte* (Berlin, 1996), pp. 11–32.
74 K. von Greyerz, *Vorsehungsglaube und Kosmologie*, p. 31.

1 Marriage and Patriarchy

1 StadtAA, EWA 59, Miller Tagebuch, pp. 7–8: 'Jnn disem meinem angefangenen Ehe Standt hat Got der / Almechtige meine Liebe Hausfraw auch mit Leibes Erben / gesegnet unnd Jst dz Erste inn dise Welt Geboren worden / Anno 1648 denn 22 Merzen nachst umb 12 uhr Einn Sohnlein / jst denn 23 Merzen Sontags Mitag Jnn dem Evangelishen / collegio vonn dem Herrn M. Paullo Jenisch Getaufft worden / unnd Jme dem Nahmen Michael gegeben. die Gevatern wahren Herr Hanns Jacob Miller der alte Herr Mag. Philip Weber / / Pfarherr unnd Senior unnd Fraw Saara Hanns Jerg Rauhwölfin / eine Geborene Wildin alss meiner Fr. Shwiger Shwester. / Got dem Almechtigen aber hat Es gefallen nach seinem Götlichen / wüllen dises Kintlein auß disem Jammerthal balt wegg / zuenemmen dann denn 7 Apprill abents zwishen 6 und 7 uhr / sanfft unnd Seelig wider Jnn dem Herrn entshlaffen. / denn 9 Apprill Jnn St Stephans Gots Aker begraben worden inn / des Zacharias Wilden begrabnuß. Got der Herr verleihe unns / seiner zeit auch allen Ein Seeliges Ende unnd neben Jme Eins / frölice Auferstehung. die uncosten der Täfen und Leicht seze / nun hierein umb inn das kommende deren sich zubedienen. /

	fl.
des Hebammen Sara. 3 Taller	4.30
der Afthauserin	2.00
dem Herrn M. Jenisch	1.30
dem Mesner	0.30
inn die Stökh der Täfsagerin geben	0.30
denn Armen leuten d do	0.12
der Amenin Täfsagerin fur Jr lohen	1.30
[Total]	10.42
bey der Leicht	
der Kintbet Kellerin veehrt	1.30

der Magt	2.30
dem Teller so das Kint getragen	1.30
der Ammemin so die leichtzusagen / und dz Kind ein zu nehen	2.00
der Krantzmacherin	0.48
den Toden Gräbern	1.00
für dz bährlen	0.48
dem Samuel so gebetet nach der begreb.	0.40
Almuesen	2.00
[Total]	12.36

2 StadtAA, EWA 59, Miller Tagebuch, p. 9: 'Anno 1650 denn 25 Julli ann dem Tage Jacobi hat mir vor ehrngedahte / meine Liebe Hausehr Zum Andern Mall Einn Sohnlein gebohrn'.
3 Concerned with the disciplinary aspect of patriarchy, Lyndal Roper insists that mastery over a woman defined masculinity and patriarchy. See L. Roper, *Oedipus and the Devil: Witchcraft, Sexuality and Religion in Early Modern Europe* (London, 1994), p. 46. Cf. A. Fletcher, *Gender, Sex and Subordination*, p. 89.
4 See P. Münch, *Lebensformen in der frühen Neuzeit*, pp. 191–232.
5 Cf. L. Roper, *The Holy Household: Women and Morals in Reformation Augsburg* (Oxford, 1989); M. Wiesner, *Working Women in Renaissance Germany* (New Brunswick, 1986).
6 C. Spangenberg, *Catechismus: Die Funff Heuptstuck der Christlichen Lehre Sampt der haußtaffel und dem Morgen und Abendt Gebet, Benedicte und Gratias etc.* (Erfurt, 1567).
7 J. Coler, *Calendarum perpetuum et Libri Oeconomici: Das ist ein sietwerender Calendar darzu sehr nutzliche und notige Hausbücher* (Wittenberg, 1592), p. 5.
8 Ibid., p. 4: 'Die Oeconomia is eine Monarchia ... nur einer herrschet.'
9 Recent scholarship insists that patriarchy carried a 'whiff of marital violence' because of its reliance on dominance and submission. The prescriptive literature, however, suggests an alternative reading, a basis in authority and obedience, reciprocal and, to an extent, voluntary relations. Cf. A. Fletcher, *Gender, Sex and Subordination*, p. 202; L. Roper, *Oedipus and the Devil*, p. 107.
10 StadtAA, EWA 59, Miller Tagebuch, p. 9: 'uncosten bey der Tauff /

	fl.
der Hebammen Saara 3 Taller	4.30
Affhauserin	2.40
dem Herrn so das Kint getaufft	3.00
der Täftsägerin	1.30
dem Knecht so die Täfer gefürt	0.30
dem Meßner	0.30
inn die stökh 30 unnd 12	0.42
Trinkgelt	0.10
dem Balbierer so die Jungen gelöß	0.30

11 H. Medick and D. W. Sabean (eds), *Interest and Emotion: Essays on the Study of Family and Kinship* (Cambridge, Eng., 1984), passim. This collection addresses in detail the reciprocities between social processes and domestic relations. It insists throughout that interests and emotions are mutually defined rather than fundamentally separate.

12 *Collection des Voyages des Souverains des Pays-Bas* (Brussels, 1882), Vol. IV, pp. 457–562 as cited in H. Dussler, OSB, *Reisen und Reisende im Bayerisch-Schwaben* (Weissenhorn, 1974), Vol. II, p. 68: 'Sie ist groß, reich, schön und hat kostspielige Bauten.'

13 *Voyage du Duc de Rohan faict en l'an 1600 en Italie, Allemaigne, Pays-bas uni, Angleterr et l'Escosse* (Amsterdam 1646) as cited in H. Dussler, OSB, *Reise und Reisende in Bayerisch-Schwaben*, Vol. II, p. 72: 'hat sich mehr und mehr vergrößert und verschönert in dem Maße, daß es heute zu den beachtenswertesten Städten ganz Deutschlands zählt'.

14 *Hodoeporicon Itineris Veneti, Romani, Helvetici et Rhenani* (Rostock, 1586) as cited in H. Dussler, OSB, *Reise und Reisende in Bayerisch-Schwaben*, Vol. II, p. 54:

> Hinc ditem Augustam itamus, quo Caesare divo
> praesente innumeri, terrarum lumina, reges,
> de summis habuere recens comitia rebus.
> Heic, ut perventum est, placide nos excepit ambos,
> haeresium terror, fidei lux, enthea Christi
> buccina, vir longo MYLIUS dignissimus aevo:
> ostenditque domos, minitantes vertice coelo
> et late depicta novis asarota figuris
> multiplicesque Midas, patresque aetate verendos
> et murum gyros, et, qui siphonibus altis
> turris ad excelsae ducti fastigia fontes.
> Quis memor est Croesi, quis devitiis Narcissi
> pollentes cives, domum luxum, aenea tecta
> redentesque auro, quas struxit Fuggerus aedes
> et, quae nec stibium, nec consuluere cerussam,
> Effigies Veneris, concinnno lumine pupas?

15 B. Rajkay, 'Die Bevölkerungsentwicklung von 1500 bis 1648' in G. Gottlieb *et al.* (eds), *Geschichte der Stadt Augsburg: 2000 Jahren von der Römerzeit bis zur Gegenwart* (Stuttgart, 1985), pp. 252–8.

16 H. Kellenbenz, 'Wirtschaftsleben der Blütezeit' in G. Gottlieb *et al.* (eds) *Geschichte der Stadt Augsburg: 2000 Jahren von der Römerzeit bis zur Gegenwart* (Stuttgart, 1985), p. 290. The differing assessment rates for moveable and real property necessitates the use of ranges rather than specific valuations. Cf. n. 5 in Introduction, above.

17 B. Roeck, 'Wirtschaftliche und soziale Voraussetzungen der Augsburger Baukunst', *Architectura* 14 (1984), pp. 119–38; idem, *Elias Holl: Architekt einer europäischen Stadt* (Regensburg, 1984), pp. 83–8, 172–85; idem, *Eine Stadt in Krieg und Frieden: Studien zur Geschichte der Reichsstadt Augsburg zwischen Kalenderstreit und Parität* (Gottingen, 1989), Vol. I, pp. 193–200. Cf. R. A. Goldthwaite, *The Building of Renaissance Florence: An Economic and Social History* (Baltimore, 1980), pp. 29–112.

18 Kellenbenz, 'Wirtschaftsleben der Blütezeit', pp. 295–7.

19 Ibid., p. 270.

20 StadtAA, EWA 48, Poetische Beschreibung der Teuerung, 1571–2: 'Die Kauffleutt hielten sie so cluegg / Gaben jnn dann echt nit genuegg / Das mueßten sie groß Saumnus han / Sehr lang offt umb die woll anston. Dann mueßt spinnen offt

mann weib und kindt / Kundten nit furderen das gesindt / Mueßten derhalb mit großern haufen / Spueler mägde und knappen laßen laufen. Darann hernach gar vill verdorben / erfroren und gar hunger sturben.'
21 Letter dated 23 July 1582 to Graf von Salm as cited in L. Lenk, *Augsburger Bürgertum im Späthumanismus und Frühbarock (1580–1700)* (Augsburg, 1968), p. 15: 'Es ist in summa alles in Abnehmung und erzeigen sich leider alle Sachen mehr zur Böserung als zur Besserung.'
22 Cf. M. L. King, *The Death of the Child Valerio Marcello* (Chicago, 1994), esp. pp. 180–4.
23 B. Roeck, *Eine Stadt in Krieg und Frieden*, Vol. I, pp. 553–603.
24 StadtAA, EWA 448/II; C.-P. Clasen, *Die Augsburger Weber. Leistungen und Krise des Textilgewerbes um 1600* (Augsburg, 1981), p. 21; P. Fassl, 'Wirtschaft, Handel und Sozialstruktur, 1648–1806' in G. Gottlieb *et al.* (eds), *Geschichte der Stadt Augsburg: 2000 Jahren von der Römerzeit bis zur Gegenwart* (Stuttgart, 1985), p. 468; W. Zorn, *Augsburg: Geschichte einer deutschen Stadt* (Augsburg, 1972), p. 40.
25 StadtAA, EWA 448/II; P. Fassl, 'Wirtschaft, Handel und Sozialstruktur, 1648–1806', p. 468.
26 P. Fassl, 'Wirtschaft, Handel und Sozialstruktur, 1648–1806', p. 468.
27 StadtAA, Bestand des historischen Vereins für Schwaben 98; P. Fassl, 'Wirtschaft, Handel und Sozialstruktur, 1648–1806', p. 468.
28 StadtAA, Einnehmerbuch 1649–1650; P. Fassl, 'Wirtschaft, Handel und Sozialstruktur 1648–1806', p. 468; W. Zorn, *Augsburg*, p. 216.
29 P. Clasen, *Die Augsburger Weber*, pp. 20ff., 437; P. Fassl, 'Wirtschaft, Handel und Sozialstruktur 1648–1806', pp. 468–9.
30 P. Fassl, 'Wirtschaft, Handel und Sozialstruktur 1648–1806', p. 468.
31 StadtAA, Steuerbücher 1625, 97c.
32 A. Mayr, *Die großen Augsburger Vermögen*, pp. 118–19.
33 StadtAA, Steuerbücher 1639, 90b, 96a.
34 StadtAA, Steuerbücher 1640, 89a, 94b; 1646, 80b, 84a; 1647, 79a, 82d. Mayr lists the 1640 tax paid by Hans Jakob at fl. 229 and that paid by Gabriel at fl. 216. I am unable to locate the source of the discrepancy. Cf. Mayr, *Die großen Augsburger Vermögen*, pp. 119–20.
35 The population of Augsburg has been a matter of debate since the eighteenth century. See: F. Blendinger, 'Versuch einer Bestimmung der Mittelschicht in der Reichsstadt Augsburg vom Ende des 14. bis zum Anfang des 18. Jahrhunderts' in E. Maschke and J. Sydow (eds), *Städtische Mittelschichten* (Stuttgart, 1972), pp. 32–67; A. Buff, *Augsburg in der Renaissancezeit* (Bamberg, 1893); P. Dirr, *Augsburg* (Leipzig, 1913); H. Eberlein, *Augsburg* (Berlin, 1939); P. Fassl, *Konfession, Wirtschaft und Politik: Von der Reichsstadt zur Industriestadt, Augsburg 1750–1850* (Sigmaringen, 1988), pp. 17–26; J. Jahn, 'Augsburger Einwohnerzahl im 16. Jahrhundert – ein statistischer Versuch', *Zeitschrift bayerischer Landesgeschichte* 39 (1976); B. Rajkay, 'Die Bevölkerungsentwicklung von 1500 bis 1648' in G. Gottlieb *et al.* (eds), *Geschichte der Stadt Augsburg von der Römerzeit bis zur Gegenwart* (Stuttgart, 1984), pp. 252–8; B. Roeck, *Brot, Bäcker und Getreide in Augsburg: Zur Geschichte des Bäckerhandwerks und zur Versorgungspolitik der Reichsstadt im Zeitalter des Dreißigjährigen Krieges* (Sigmaringen, 1987); H. Rost, 'Die Bevölkerungszahl der Stadt Augsburg bis zum Jahre 1900', *Der schwäbische Postbote. Feuilleton zur Neuen Augsburger Zeitung* 110–22 (1905); A. Schreiber,

'Die Entwicklung der Augsburger Bevölkerung vom Ende des 14. bis zum Beginn des 19. Jahrhunderts', diss., Erlangen, 1922; J. P. Süssmilch, *Die göttliche Ordnung in den Veränderungen des menschlichen Geschlechts, aus der Geburt, dem Tode und der Fortpflanzung desselben erwiesen* (Berlin, 1788); W. Zorn, *Augsburg: Geschichte einer deutschen Stadt* (Augsburg, 1972).
36. StadtAA, Bestand Statistik, EWA 448/II, Schätze 37; P. Fassl, *Konfession, Wirtschaft und Politik*, pp. 17–26; B. Rajkay, 'Die Bevölkerungsentwicklung von 1500 bis 1648'.
37. P. Fassl, *Konfession, Wirtschaft und Politik*, p. 18.
38. StadtBA, Einblattdruck 142; B. Rajkay, 'Die Bevölkerungsentwicklung von 1500 bis 1648', p. 253.
39. P. Fassl, *Konfession, Wirtschaft und Politik*, p. 18
40. Ibid., pp. 19–20. Fassl calculated 3.41 births per marriage in the period, 1701–50.
41. P. Fassl, *Konfession, Wirtschaft und Politik*, p. 22. Fassl estimated total population size by multiplying the aggregated deaths for each year by a stable coefficient (0.44) and calculating the average for each decade.
42. A. Hämmerle, *Erstes Hochzeitsbuch der evangelischen Pfarrei St. Anna in Augsburg, 1596–1629* (Munich, 1938), p. 138.
43. I. Bátori, 'Reichsstädtisches Regiment, Finanzen, und bürgerliche Opposition' in G. Gottlieb *et al.* (eds), *Geschichte der Stadt Augsburg: 2000 Jahren von der Römerzeit bis zur Gegenwart* (Stuttgart, 1984), pp. 457–60.
44. P. Fassl, 'Wirtschaft, Handel und Sozialstruktur', p. 469.
45. StadtAA, EWA 59, Miller Tagebuch, p. 7: 'Das / mein Geliebter Vater wiewoll es Jn vormals offt shweer / ankommen etwas aignes anzuefangen doch entlich auch das / Herz angenommen unnd gerathen mit wenig baumwoll / gegen webern etwas zue negotiern Got der Almechtige / hat seine Seegen darzue geben'.
46. F. Blendinger, 'Augsburger Handel im Dreißigjährigen Krieg', p. 304.
47. StadtAA, Reichsstadt Akten, Stadtkanzlei, UK 347, 370.
48. Ibid., UK 376, 380, 384.
49. Ibid., UK 378: 'unum dolium stanno repletun, sub numero 5: item unicam Lagenam, in qua panni linei Ulmenses continentur, sub numero 4'.
50. Ibid., UK 347, 426: 'unum dolium variis pellibus impletum sub numero 3'.
51. StadtAA, EWA 59, Miller Tagebuch, p. 12: 'Hingegen mein Gel[iebter] Vater und br. Michael / Miller der Jünger zue mir inn mein negotio ge / tretten. Jm Nahmen Gottes Des Vatters Sohns und / Hailligen Gaistes denn 2 Aprill 1654 der Anfang / genommen.'
52. StadtAA, Reichsstadt Akten, Stadtkanzlei, UK 675, 1 July 1666.
53. Ibid., UK 344, 7 August 1674.
54. C.-P. Clasen, *Textilherstellung in Augsburg in der frühen Neuzeit* (Augsburg, 1995), Vol. II, p. 354.
55. He refers to the fact that Thomas was returning from Bozen, the heart of the Tirolean mining industry, when felled by the illness that ultimately killed him. StadtAA, EWA 59, Miller Tagebuch, p. 114.
56. StadtAA, Steuerbücher 1646, 1647, 1669, 1667, 1774, 1681, 1684.
57. O. Brandt, *Die Fugger: Geschichte eines deutschen Handelshauses* (Jena, 1928); G. Brucker, *Two Memoirs of Renaissance Florence: The Diaries of Buonaccorso Pitti and Gregorio Dati* (New York, 1967); R. de Roover, *The Rise and Decline of the*

Medici Bank, 1397–1494 (New York, 1966); R. Eirich, *Memmingens Wirtschaft und Patriziat, 1347–1551* (Wießenhorn, 1971); R. A. Goldthwaite, *Private Wealth in Renaissance Florence: A Study of Four Families* (Princeton, 1968); D. Herlihy, *The Family in Renaissance Italy* (St Louis, 1974); B. Kedar, *Merchants in Crisis: Genoese and Venetian Men of Affairs and the Fourteenth Century Depression* (New Haven, 1976); F. W. Kent, *Household and Lineage in Renaissance Florence: The Family Life of the Caponi, Ginori, and Rucellai* (Princeton, 1977); E. Lutz, *Die rechtlichen Strukturen süddeutscher Handelsgesellschaften in der Zeit der Fugger* (Tubingen, 1976); R. Mandrou, *Les Fugger, propriétaires fonciers en Souabe, 1560–1618: Étude de comportements socio-économiques à la fin du XVIe siècle* (Paris, 1969); L. Martines, *The Social World of the Florentine Humanists, 1390–1460* (Princeton, 1963); G. Freiherr von Pölnitz, *Die Fugger* (Frankfurt/M, 1960); idem, *Anton Fugger*, 4 vols (Tubingen, 1958–71); J. Riebartsch, *Augsburger Handelsgesellschaften des 15. und 16. Jahrhunderts*; A. Sapori, *The Italian Merchant in the Middle Ages* (New York, 1970); G. Seibold, *Die Manlich: Geschichte einer Augsburger Kaufmannsfamilie* (Sigmaringen, 1995); J. Strieder, *Zur Genesis des modernen Kapitalismus: Forschungen zur Entstehung der großen bürgerlichen Kapitalvermögen am Ausgange des Mittelalters und zu Beginn der Neuzeit, zunächst in Augsburg* (Munich, 1935); W. Sombart, *Der moderne Kapitalismus*, 2 vols (Leipzig, 1902–22).

58 O. Brunner, 'Das "ganze Haus" und das alteuropäische Ökonomik' in idem, *Neue Wege der Sozialgeschichte* (Göttingen, 1968); L. Davidoff and C. Hall, *Family Fortunes: Men and Women of the English Middle Class, 1780–1850* (Chicago, 1977); J.-L. Flandrin, *Families in Former Times: Kinship, Household and Sexuality* (Cambridge, Eng., 1979); J. Goody, J. Thirsk and E. P. Thompson (eds), *Family and Inheritance: Rural Society in Western Europe, 1200–1800* (Cambridge, Eng., 1976); B. A. Hanawalt, *The Ties that Bound: Peasant Families in Medieval England* (Oxford, 1986); R. Houlbrooke, *The English Family, 1450–1700* (London, 1984); A. Imhof, *Die verlorene Welten: Alltagsbewältigung durch unsere Vorfahren und Weshalb wir uns heute so schwer damit tun* (Munich, 1984); P. Kriedte, H. Medick and J. Schlumbohm (eds), *Industrialization before Industrialization* (Cambridge, Eng., 1977); P. Laslett and R. Wall (eds), *Household and Family in Past Times: Comparative Studies in the Size and Structure of the Domestic Group over the Last Three Centuries in England, France, Serbia, Japan and Colonial North America with Further Materials from Western Europe* (Cambridge, Eng., 1972); D. Levine, 'Production, Reproduction, and the Proletarian Family in England, 1500–1851' in idem (ed.), *Proletarianization and Family History* (Orlando, 1984); idem, *Reproducing Families: The Political Economy of English Population History* (Cambridge, Eng., 1987); H. Medick and D. W. Sabean (eds), *Interest and Emotion: Essays on the Study of Family and Kinship* (Cambridge, Eng., 1984); M. Mitterauer and R. Sieder, *The European Family: From Patriarchy to Partnership* (Chicago, 1982); M. Mitterauer, *Grundtypen alteuropäischer Sozialformen* (Stuttgart, 1979); D. C. Quinlan and J. A. Shackelford, 'Economy and English Families, 1500–1850', *Journal of Interdisciplinary History* 24 (1994), pp. 431–63; T. Robisheaux, *Rural Society and the Search for Order in Early Modern Germany* (Cambridge, Eng., 1989); D. W. Sabean, *Property, Production, and Family in Neckarshausen, 1700–1870* (Cambridge, Eng., 1991); L. Stone, *The Crisis of the Aristocracy, 1558–1641* (Oxford, 1965); idem, 'Family

History in the 1980s: Past Achievements and Future Trends', *Journal of Interdisciplinary History* 12 (1981), pp. 51–6; I. Weber-Kellermann, *Die Deutsche Familie* (Frankfurt, 1974); K. Wrightson and D. Levine, *Poverty and Piety in an English Village* (New York, 1979); K. Wrightson, *English Society, 1580–1680* (New Brunswick, 1982).

59 Two leading figures in what might be called the great transformation of modern historical scholarship, the rejection of the base–superstructure dichotomy in favor of an independent cultural model, were Natalie Zemon Davis and Edward P. Thompson. See N. Z. Davis, *Society and Culture in Early Modern France* (Stanford, 1965) and E. P. Thompson, *The Making of the English Working Class* (London, 1963).

60 W. J. Goode, *World Revolution and Family Patterns* (New York, 1970); D. I. Kertzer and D. P. Hogan, 'Family Structure, Individual Lives, and Societal Change' in M. W. Riley (ed.), *Social Structures and Human Lives* (Newbury Park, 1988); M. Segalen, *Historical Anthropology of the Family* (Cambridge, Eng., 1986); D. S. Smith, 'The Curious History of Theorizing about the History of the Western Nuclear Family', *Social Science History* 17 (1993), pp. 325–53.

61 M. Anderson, *Approaches to the History of the Western Family, 1500–1914* (London, 1980); C. N. Degler, *At Odds: Women and the Family in America from the Revolution to the Present* (Oxford, 1980); A. Macfarlane, *The Origins of English Individualism: The Family, Property and Social Transition* (New York, 1979); idem, *Marriage and Love in England, 1300–1840* (Oxford, 1986); E. Shorter, *The Making of the Modern Family* (New York, 1975); L. Stone, *The Family, Sex and Marriage in England, 1500–1800* (New York, 1977); E. Todd, *The Explanation of Ideology: Family Structures and Social Systems* (Oxford, 1985); J. R. Watt, *The Making of Modern Marriage: Matrimonial Control and the Rise of Sentiment in Neuchâtel, 1550–1800* (Ithaca, 1992).

62 Studies by the Cambridge Group for the History of Population and Social Structure played a key role in revising the myth of the modern family. Among the many, these few: P. Laslett, *The World We have Lost: England before the Industrial Revolution* (New York, 1965); P. Laslett and R. Wall (eds), *Household and Family in Past Time* (Cambridge, Eng., 1972); D. Levine, *Family Formation in an Age of Nascent Capitalism* (New York, 1977); D. Levine and K. Wrightson, *The Making of an Industrial Society: Whickham, 1560–1765* (Oxford, 1991); E. A. Wrigley and R. S. Schofield, *The Population History of England, 1541–1871* (Cambridge, Mass., 1981).

63 D. S. Smith, 'The Curious History of Theorizing about the History of the Western Nuclear Family', p. 342.

64 M. Foucault, *Discipline and Punish: The Birth of the Prison* (New York, 1979); idem, *The History of Sexuality, vol. 1: An Introduction* (New York, 1980).

65 S. D. Amussen, *An Ordered Society: Gender and Class in Early Modern England* (London, 1988); I. V. Hull, *Sexuality, State, and Civil Society in Germany, 1700–1815* (Ithaca, 1996); M. E. Perry, *Gender and Disorder in Early Modern Seville* (Princeton, 1990); L. Roper, *The Holy Household*; M. Segalen, *Love and Power in the Peasant Family* (Oxford, 1983).

66 W. H. Sewell, Jr, 'History in the Paranoic Mode?', *International Labor and Working Class History* 39 (1991): 21–4.

67 P. Münch, *Lebensformen in der frühen Neuzeit, 1500 bis 1800* (Berlin, 1992), p. 199: 'Die existentielle Notwendigkeit der Aufgabenteilung im

patriarchalischen System hat partnerschaftliche, oder besser: kollegiale, Verhaltensformen wahrscheinlich sogar vielfach erzwungen, und zwar gegen alle rechtlichen Einschränkungen und traditionalen Begründungen, welche der Frau lediglich eine generell vom Mann abhängige Position einräumen wollten und ihr jede originäre Gewalt absprachen.'

68 D. Levine, 'Punctuated Equilibrium: The Modernization of the Proletarian Family in the Age of Ascendant Capitalism', *International Labor and Working Class History* 39 (1991), pp. 3–20.
69 Exemplary in this regard is A. Fletcher, *Gender, Sex and Subordination*.
70 A. Fletcher, *Gender, Sex, and Subordination*, pp. 172, 190–1.
71 W. H. Sewell, Jr, 'History in the Paranoic Mode?', p. 22.
72 R. Jütte, 'Household and Family Life in Late Sixteenth-Century Cologne: The Weinsberg Family', *Sixteenth Century Journal* 17 (1986), p. 166. See also: *Das Buch Weinsberg, Kölner Denkwürdigkeiten aus dem 16. Jahrhundert* 5 vols (Leipzig, 1886/1926); S. Ozment, *When Fathers Ruled: Family Life in Reformation Europe* (Cambridge, Eng., 1983); J. Stein, 'Hermann Weinsberg als Mensch und Historiker', *Jahrbuch des Kölnischen Geschichtsvereins* 4 (1917), pp. 109–69.
73 Most merchants' diaries combine household events with business records. For example, see: B. Greiff (ed.), 'Tagebuch des Lucas Rem aus den Jahren 1494–1541: Ein Beitrag zur Handelsgeschichte der Stadt Augsburg', *Jahresbericht des historischen Vereins für Schwaben und Neuburg* 27 (1861), pp. 1–110; StadtAMM A327/9, Tagebuch des Handelsherrn Caspar Koch, geboren 1576, gestorben 1620.
74 StadtAA, EWA 59, Miller Tagebuch, p. 7: 'Got der Almechtige / hat seine Seegen darzue geben dz entlich widerum gedankhen / auff dz heürathen gewendet unnd mich umbgesehen nach der / Junghfr. Anna Maria einen gebornen Warmbergerin der Herr Vater / See. gewesen Johann Warmberger vonn seiner andern ehee erzeigt / nemmlich derer noch lebenten Fr. Müter Susanna eine gebornen / Wildin unnd hernachmals Herrn Elias Shröckhen see. hinderlassnen / Witib dern einige Tochter meine Liebste ware als nun / meinerseits nix erwunden lassen sowoll Jhre gunst zu / erlangen als meiner unnd Jhrer geehrten Eltern consenso / so sich alles gantz unnd gaar willig erzeigt worauf Gotes / sonderbaare shikung abzuenemmen. Jst entlich der / hochzeitliche Ehrntag benambset worden meinerseits / sein die Werber gewesen Herr Hanns Jacob Miller elter / unnd die Hochzeit ware denn 30 Juli Anno 1647 / Alles mit guetem Fridt unnd Conntento dem Hochsten sein / darvon Lob unnd Dankh.'
75 Joel Harrington has argued convincingly that all reformers – secular or religious, Protestant or Catholic – shared the same vision of the ideal marriage. It must be stable and consensual, holy and enforceable. See J. Harrington, *Reordering Marriage and Society in Reformation Germany* (Cambridge, Eng., 1995), pp. 10–17.
76 B. von Freiburg, *Summa Confessorum* (Augsburg, 1472) as cited by M. Dallapiazza (ed.), *Wie ein Mann ein fromm Weib soll machen* (Frankfurt/M, 1984), p. 45.
77 A. von Eyb, *Ob einem Manne sey zunemen ein eelichs weyb oder nicht* (Darmstadt, 1982), p. 10.

78 C. Spangenberg, *Ehespiegel: Das ist Alles was vom heyligen Ehestande nützliches, nötiges, und tröstliches mag gesagt werden. In sibentzig Brautpredigten zusammen verfasst* (Strasbourg, 1563), p. 203v.
79 Ibid., p. 38v.
80 Ibid., p. 38r: 'wie soll er sie dann lieben? Er soll ir pflegen wie sein selbst, soll ir narung unnd herberge, essen und trincken, schuch, kleidern und dergleichen notturfft verschaffen, für allem frävel unnd mutwillen böser menschen schützen unnd zu forderst auch Geystlich mit Gottes wort versorgen, zu Gottes erkandtnuß und zu allem was der Seelen heyl und Seligkeyt belanget bringen unnd halten.'
81 StadtAA, EWA 59, Miller Tagebuch, p. 37: 'Denn 13. 9bris 1654 habe ich der Stat Gebrauch nach Alß / Zue der andern Ehe Jm Nahmen Gotes geshriten. bei / dem Lobl. ober pfleg Amt meinen beeden Büeblein / Erster Ehe Sheinpfleger vorgestelt unnd darzue / Erbeten Meinen Gel[iebten] Vater Herr Michael Miller / unnd Herrn Hanns Jerg Rauhwolff die auch ordenlicher / weisse sein eingeshriben worden.'
82 StadtAA, Reichsstadt Akten, Stadtkanzlei, UK 277, 10 November 1654.
83 Ibid.: '... Studium, erlernung der sprachen oder anderwerttigen ehrlicher Handtierung worzue sie lust haben und tauglich sein werden'.
84 StadtAA, Reichsstadt Akten, Stadtkanzlei, UK 261, 30 July 1648.
85 L. Roper, *The Holy Household*, pp. 148–9.
86 A. Haemmerle, *Die Hochzeitsbücher der Augsburger Bürgerstube und Kaufleutestube bis zum Ende der Reichsfreiheit* (Munich, 1936), p. 212.
87 StadtAA, EWA 59, Miller Tagebuch, pp. 32–3: 'Jn dem Monnath 9bris 1654 Hat mein Br. Michael Miller / meiner seiner Haußfr. samt seinem shwagern Hr. Anton Christoff / Shorer Jüngern mich mit sich nach / Haußstetten spazie gefürth / unnd under anderm mich anfangen vexieren muste wider / Ein weib haben. Jch zwaar ware damallen noh nit / inn solhen gedanken, doh Jst mein Herz geh verendert / worden unnd als Jch sagte werde nit wol Eine vor / handen sein die vor mich taugte nanten sie mir vill / mit Nammen, aber der shorer wolt sein Jfr. shwester nit nennen / unnd Jch ursach bekam Zue fragen warum die selb nit / auh benambst hete darüber er compliment gebrauht / die Jch aber Kurz inn shimpff unnd Ernst verantwurt / dz Er woll spüren müste. Jch hingegen auh spüren könte / dz balt von Einander kommen möchten. Jch bekame / ursach hernach mit denn meinigen zue reden Er / gleichermassen mit denn seinigen wurden auch / inn kurzem so Einig dz einen gewissen Tag bestelt. / Einmall Zuesammen Zue kommen so dz Erstemall / inn dem Stat Garten beshehen. da Jch Jr Ein Ring / verehrt nemmlich den Ehrn unnd vill Tugentreichen Jfr. Helena / Shorerin. / Sie mir aber hingegen folgendts ann dem / Tag des Apostels Mathei auch Einen shönen Diamantring / verehrt so das Jch auch ann Jhrer geliebter Eltern affectio / geringstens nit zue Zweiflen gehabt. deswegen / dann meinen Gel[iebten] Vater Ersucht dz Er mit dem Herrn / Anton Christoff Shorer dem Eltern selbsten rede. so auh / beshehen unnd alles dahin vermitelt worden / dz der Hochzeitliche Ehrntag auff denn 23 9bris 1654 / bestelt unnd geordnet worden. So auh Gotlob / mit guetem belieben unnd condento männiglihs / glüklich unnd woll volzogen unnd vollendet / worden.'
88 'When we encounter young men passing up fat dowries to wed their hearts' desire, we shall know we're standing before romance.' E. Shorter,

The Making of the Modern Family, p. 17. Shorter's classic assessment has assumed a lamentably durable place in the history of the family. Despite its over-simplification of emotion in the premodern family and its over-generalization of it in the modern family, the notion that love is somehow modern has been taken up by other scholars. Cf. L. Stone, *The Family, Sex and Marriage in England* and J. Watt, *The Making of Modern Marriage*.

89   Caspar Koch, for example, listed his wives' dowries among the annual accounts of his business. Cf. StadtAMM, A 327/9, Tagebuch des Handelsherrn Caspar Koch, geboren 1576, gestorben 1620, p. 14.

90   StadtAA, EWA 59, Miller Tagebuch, p. 93: 'Nach dem Seeligen Absterben meiner anderen geliebten Hauß- / frawen Hellena geborner Shorerin sel. habe ich balt erfaren / dz wegen meiner Sterken Haußhaltung nit geraten sein würde / mich in dem Wütib stende lang aufzuehalten. Denn / mit 6 Kindern alle ledig standes und noch jung und un- / erfaren drei Ehehelten ein Costgeij offene Behauss wegen / der shreibstuben und alles anders bedenken hat nit / gut geheisen ohne Hausmeisterin die sache also angehen / zulossen.'

91   Ibid.: 'es hate benebenst auch / mein gemüth errindert die mehrmalige Trewherzige / freuntlich errinderung meiner geliebten Haußfr. sel. / beshehen Jnn Jhrer letstern / shweren Krankheit sowoll / ann mir selber Jnn guter vertrawen also auch gegen / die Kinder selbsten derer Jntent dahingegangen wann sie / Je der Liebe Got Jnn diser welt nit lenger lassen wolte / und Jch dardurch mit meinen 6 Kindern zum Wütibstands / geraten wurde Jch Ja nit lang darin verbleiben solte / sondern den Kindern und dem Haußwesen zum besten / balt denn Ehestand anzutreten und zwaar meine gedanken / auf Herrn Baltas Miller Eltere Jfr. Tochter richten / solle was ich mir Jren rat wurde gefallen lassen.'

92   Ibid., p. 94: 'obwolen Jch dem gewonlichen weg noch wollenger hete werden / sollen. So Jst doch viller ursachen willen und fürnemlich nach / reifer Beherzigung unnd Anrufung des Lieben Gotes Hülff / rath und beistand mein Resolution dahin gegangen dz / Jch Jnn Gotes Namen denn 5 Mertzen 1674 denn Herrn / Baltas Miller selbsten angeredet und Jmme meines / Herzen gedanken geoffenberet dabei gebeten wann er / auch solhes für gut befinde Er mir seine Liebe Jungfraw / Tochter Johanna Catharina zue meiner Liebsten Haußehr / und Ehegaten vertrawen solle. Worauf er bedenkh / zeit genommen und den 12 Merzen mir Jn Gotes / Namen bedeutet dz Ers für seine Person herzlich gerne / sehen wolte auch leiden möchte dz Jch mit / der Jungfr. Tochter mich selbsten besprechen möchte. so auch / denn selben tag in seinem hauß beshehen. durch Gotes / Genädigen gefallen auch mit beederseits Condento uns verainiget / mit unsern befreunten zue beeden Teilen desentwegen uns auch / zu besprechen so meinestheils auch beshehen.'

93   Ibid., pp. 94–5: 'also dz Jch / folgenden / tag mit der Frau Shorerin als meine Gel. Fr. / Shweher wie auch mit meiner Shwester Peirlerin und anderen / der sachen halber geredet die alle Jhren guter will ganz / gerne darein gegeben und sich die gefaste Resolutio höchlich / erfrewet. Also dz Jnn Gotes Namen gleich folgende / tag den sachen völlige richtigkeit gemecht und also / mit allerseits Condento denn Heurat beshlossen darauff / Jm Namen Gotes denn 7 Mai dz Hochzeitliche Ehrnfest / Jnn Herrn Baltas Millers Behausung Ehrlich volzogen / die Copulation in deß Heuß auch beshehen auf die / erlangte Erlaubtnus.'

94 StadtBA, 40S Leichenpredigten 269, Nr. 9, *Blumen-Reiches Hochzeits-Fest / des / Wol-Ehrnvest und Wol-Fürnehmen Herrn / Mattäus Miller / Wittiber / beruhmten Kauff-Herrn allhier / mit der / Wol-Ehrn und Vil-Tugendreichen Jungfer / Johanna Katharina / deß auch allhier / Wol-Ehrnvesten und Wol-Fürnehmen Herrn / Balthasar Miller / wolbenahmten Handels-hern / Ehren-Tochter / in der Freude des Herrn zu Augsburg in / Jahr 1674 den 7. May Ehrlich und Christlich / begangen / und mit nachfolgenden Glükwunschungen / beziert* (Augsburg, 1674).

95 Lenk referred to *Gelegenheitsdichtungen* that became a kind of *panegyrische Verkaufsware*. He had no high opinion of the genre of that age and indicated as much by describing the literary climate of Augsburg as *echter Dichtung abhold*. L. Lenk, *Augsburger Bürgertum*, pp. 146–7.

96 Ibid., pp. 150, 152.

97 Ibid., p. 152.

98 Ibid., p. 126.

99 StadtAA, EWA 59, Miller Tagebuch, pp. 80–1.

100 Ibid., passim. Cf. J. F. Rein, *Das gesamte augspurgische Evangelische Ministerium in Bilder und Schrifften von den ersten Jahren der Reformation Lutheri bis auf Anno 1748* (Augsburg, 1749), pp. 142, 152.

101 StadtAA, EWA 59, Miller Tagebuch, p. 17.

102 StadtBA, 40s Leichenpredigten 269, Nr. 9, *Blumen-reiches Hochzeits-Fest*, III: 'O was für gesunde Lufft / muß Jhr Bett und Haus betauen! Auf deß Winters Frost und Schneyen / muß der Mayan sie erfreuen.'

103 Ibid., IV.: 'Nun wird sein Jungfer Braut Jhm seyn ein Regenbogen / Der gegen Morgen sich am Himmel aufgezogen: Nun werden Wolcken / Wind / und Regen hören auf / und zeigen sich die Sonn mit unverdecktem Lauff.'

104 Ibid., VI: 'Das Muhl-Werk gehe fort / ohn hemmende Beschwerden. Der Segen bringe reiche Beut! Die Kasten Seyen immer voll! Die neue Millerin hauß mit dem Miller wol!'

105 Ibid., X: 'Lebt mit dem Vatter so / der Euer Mann wird seyn / Daß über unserm Hauß die Gluckes-Sonne schein.'

106 Ibid., XI: 'So wird uns widerum beywohnen Freud und Wonne.'

107 Ibid., XII: 'Gesegnet sey die Stund / und bringe Wolfahrt mit / Da Eur Fuß unser Haus das erste mal betritt.'

108 Ibid., XIII: 'Vertreuliches Gespräch einer guten Freundin / mit der Jungfrau Hochzeiterin wegen Jhres Heuraths. Samt der entscheidenden Adelfia.'

109 Ibid.: 'Was solt ich sagen / Nein?'

110 Ibid.: 'Der / so solche wolt bescheren / gibt dem Hasen nechsten den Gras.'

111 Ibid.: 'Seine Hauses-halb Gottinne / hab erwisen alle Treu / Die nur Mensch und möglich sey? Hat er ihrer nicht gepfleget / und gewartet Tag und Nacht?'

112 Ibid.: 'Männer habe kein Erfahrung / recht zu schalten in dem Haus.'

113 Ibid.: 'N: Hat Jhm dises nicht gerathen / Sein gewesene Augens-Lust? Glaub mir / Sie hat Jren Lieben nicht nur einmal angetriben / Daß er bald sine Haus verseh / Mit den dritten Band der Eh. F: Und / villeicht / hat sie dich selber / Jhm / in Jhre statt vermacht.'

114 Ibid.: 'Doch / weil sie selb / aufs best / sich verantwortet hat / Ists unvonnöthen / daß mein Red hier finde Statt.'

115 Ibid.: 'Er ist ein Weiber=Mann / und kan nicht ohn Sie leben / Drum kont Er sich deß Weibs aufs längest nicht begeben. Nicht nur / damit sein Haus / welchs sehr weitläuffig ist / bestellt werden möcht / und wider eingerüst / Mit einer tauglichen und häuslichen Hausmutter / Die Jhm / den Kindern / dem Gesind verschaff Jhr Futter / Und alle Hausgebühr: Als / weil das Einsam seyn / Ihm fast unmöglich fiel.'

116 Steven Ozment explores these issues in the correspondence of Balthasar and Magdalena Paumgartner. A too-brief waiting period or too great disparity of age provoked disapproving comment from this husband and wife of sixteenth-century Nuremberg. Yet, they also understood the social and psychological forces that drove people, especially widows and widowers, to remarry. Evidently, these were gray areas for which no hard-and-fast rules applied. See S. Ozment, *Magdalena and Balthasar: An Intimate Portrait of Life in Sixteenth-Century Europe Revealed in the Letters of a Nuremberg Husband and Wife* (New York, 1986), pp. 85–8.

117 See T. M. Safley, *Let No Man Put Asunder: The Control of Marriage in the German Southwest, 1550–1620* (Kirksville, Mo., 1981), pp. 33–7.

118 Rough music refers to noisy demonstrations that mocked, among other things, married couples in which a gross disparity of age separated bride and groom. See: N. Z. Davis, 'The Reasons of Misrule' in idem, *Society and Culture in Early Modern France* (Stanford, 1965), pp. 97–123.

119 Johann Philipp Warmberger payed a tax of fl. 7 kr. 40. StadtAA, Steuerbücher 1646, p. 71c.

120 The elder Schorer was assessed fl. 28 in 1653, more than twice the worth of Matheus. By the time of his death in 1660, his tax had risen to fl. 61 kr. 10. StadtAA, Steuerbücher 1653, p. 93d; 1660, p. 94b.

121 Baltas paid fl. 40 kr. 10 in taxes in 1667 and again in 1674. His wealth, though considerable, was less than half that of Matheus, who paid fl. 84 in 1674. StadtAA, Steuerbücher 1667, p. 95d; 1664, p. 98a.

122. As a single example one could cite the relationship between Marco Parenti and members of his wife's family, the Strozzi. See M. Phillips, *The Memoir of Marco Parenti*, passim.

123 L. B. Alberti, *The Family in Renaissance Florence*, p. 98.

124 Ibid., p.115.

125 Ibid., p. 101.

126 Ibid., p. 180.

127 Ibid., p. 115.

128 H. H. Gerth and C. W. Mills (eds), *From Max Weber: Essays in Sociology* (New York, 1946), p. 296.

129 Ibid., pp. 186–91.

130 Ibid., p. 181.

131 P. Bourdieu, *Outline of a Theory of Practice* (Cambridge, Eng., 1977), pp. 10–15.

2 Public Office and the Public Sphere

1 StadtAA, EWA 59, Miller Tagebuch, p. 90: 'Anno 1673 ungefehr in denn 8ber wurde Jch / vonn dem Herrn Statpfleger David vonn Steten Herr Aman und / Herrn Weiß in dz Evangel. Collegio gefordert / die mir zue verstehen geben was gestalt ein wol Edler / Magistrat alhier resolviert vonn

der lieben Burgershafft / von ein mal 4 copagnio zue Fuß zu armieren / umb selbe in allem notfall zuer Deffension der / Stat zue gebrauchen weillen die zimliche fract. / Trublen auch uns nit ohne gefahr shinen. Heten / demnach auch beshlossen mir eine Capitan Stelle / zue vertrawen Jnn der guten Zueversicht Jch / wurde dz gegen mir damit bezeugende gute / vertrawen erkennen und mich zu solcher Chargen [sic] / willig erkleren.'

2 Cicero, *On Duties* (Cambridge, Eng., 1991): 'A brave and great spirit is in general seen in two things. One lies in disdain for things external, in the conviction that a man should admire, should choose, should pursue nothing except what is honourable and seemly, and should yield to no man, nor to agitation of the spirit, nor to fortune. The second thing is that you should, in the spirit I have described, do deeds which are great, certainly, but above all beneficial, and you should vigorously undertake difficult and laborious tasks which endanger both life itself and much that concerns life... Those, on the other hand, who have adapted themselves to great achievements in the service of the political community, lead lives more profitable to mankind and more suited to grandeur and fame... those who are equipped by nature to administer affairs must abandon any hesitation over winning office and engage in public life. For only in this way can either the city be ruled or greatness of spirit be displayed' (pp. 27–9); 'It is, then, the particular function of a magistrate to realize that he assumes the role of the city and ought to sustain its standing and its seemliness, to preserve the laws, to administer justice, and to be mindful of the things that have been entrusted to his good faith' (pp. 48–9).

3 L. Bruni, 'Panegyric to the City of Florence' as quoted in B. G. Kohl, R. G. Witt and E. B. Welles (eds), *The Earthly Republic: Italian Humanists on Government and Society* (Philadelphia, 1978), p. 169.

4 P. Bracciolini, 'On Avarice' as quoted in B. Kohl, R. Witt and E. Welles (eds), *The Earthly Republic: Italian Humanists on Government and Society*, p. 270.

5 Ibid., p. 251.

6 L. B. Alberti, *The Family in Renaissance Florence*, p. 175.

7 Ibid. This observation would not have been lost on the many officials and administrators, who, like Niccolo Macchiavelli, were deprived of office because of the policies of their superiors. Waley makes clear that part-time civic employment of the citizen formed the essence of the city republic. Given their deep and completely ubiquitous internal divisions, changes of government and exile for the losers were commonplace. See D. Waley, *The Italian City-Republics* (New York, 1969), pp. 164–220.

8 Ibid. Alberti's procurator, Marco Parenti, a man much taken up by the politics of his day, might have agreed. His engagement on behalf of the Strozzi absorbed much of his active life. See M. Phillips, *The Memoir of Marco Parenti: A Life in Medici Florence* (Princeton, 1987), passim.

9 Ibid., p. 176. This sentiment seems thoroughly consistent with Bracciolini's aversion to avarice in public office.

10 Ibid., p. 177.

11 Ibid., p. 178.

12 Ibid., p. 149.

13 The argument that Luther provided an important theoretical justification for totalitarianism is well known and much debated. Cf. Q. Skinner, *The*

Foundations of Modern Political Thought (Cambridge, Eng., 1978), Vol. II; W. D. J. Cargill Thompson, *The Political Thought of Martin Luther* (Hassocks, 1984).

14. Cf. E. J. Carlson, 'Marriage and the English Reformation', Ph.D diss., Harvard University, 1987; B. Gottlieb, 'Getting Married in Pre-Reformation Europe: The Doctrine of Clandestine Marriage and Court Cases in Fifteenth-Century Champagne', Ph.D diss., Columbia University, 1974; J. Harrington, *Reordering Marriage and Society in Reformation Germany* (Cambridge, Eng., 1995); M. Ingram, *Church Courts, Sex and Marriage in England, 1570–1640* (London, 1987); W. Kohler, *Zürcher Ehegericht und Genfer Konsistorium*, 2 vols (Leipzig, 1933–42); A. Lefebvre-Teillard, *Les Officialités à la Veille du Concile de Trente* (Paris, 1973); K. Lindner, 'Courtship and the Courts: Marriage and Law in Southern Germany, 1350–1550', Th.D diss., Harvard University, 1988; A. Lottin, *La désunion du couple sous l'ancien régime: L'exemple du Nord* (Paris, 1985); A. Staehlin, *Die Einführung der Ehescheidung in Basel zur Zeit der Reformation* (Basel, 1957); T. M. Safley, *Let No Man Put Asunder: The Control of Marriage in the German Southwest, 1550–1620* (Kirksville, Mo., 1984); J. Watt, *The Making of Modern Marriage: Matrimonial Control and the Rise of Sentiment in Neuchâtel, 1550–1800* (Ithaca, 1992); R. Weigand, 'Die Rechtsprechung des Regensburger Gerichts in Ehesachen unter besonderer Berücksichtigung der bedingten Eheschliessung nach Gerichtsbüchern aus dem Ende des 15. Jahrhunderts', *Archiv für katholisches Kirchenrecht* 137 (1968), pp. 403–63; F. Wendel, *Le mariage à Strasbourg à l'epoque de la Réform, 1520–1692* (Strasbourg, 1928); R. Wunderli, *London Church Courts on the Eve of the Reformation* (Cambridge, Mass., 1981).
15. M. Luther, *Three Treatises* (Philadelphia, 1970), p. 304.
16. Ibid., p. 294.
17. Ibid., p. 297.
18. Ibid., p. 302.
19. StadtAA, EWA 59, Miller Tagebuch, p. 91: 'so wolte doch keine entshuldigung statfinden sondern / setzten mir alle drei so Starkh zue. Ermanet mich nit zue underlossen disen beruf den sie samtlich in gesamtem / Evangel. Magistrat woll erwagen in gute obacht zu / nemmen und mich darzue zue accomodieren.'
20. Ibid., p. 91: 'die ville umbständen so dabei vorgebracht wurde / auch ander bedenken dz gute werkh vor einmall / helfen zue befürdern macht mich resolvieren / die sach Jm Namen Gottes anzuenemmen'.
21. M. Weber used the term 'charismatic' to denote authority which derives from the personality of an individual such that the ruler is thought to possess exceptional, even superhuman, powers or qualities, obedience to which is the recognized duty of all subjects. See M. Weber, *Economy and Society* (Berkeley, 1978), Vol. I, pp. 241–5.
22. Weber, *Economy and Society*, Vol. II, pp. 973–80.
23. H. H. Gerth and C. W. Mills (eds), *From Max Weber: Essays in Sociology* (New York, 1946), pp. 296–8.
24. G. Kreuzer, 'Augsburg als Bischofsstadt unter den Saliern und Lothar III (1024–1133)' in G. Gottlieb et al. (eds), *Geschichte der Stadt Augsburg: 2000 Jahre von der Römerzeit bis zur Gegenwart* (Stuttgart, 1985) p. 125.

25 W. Baer, 'Das Stadtrecht vom Jahre 1156.' in G. Gottlieb *et al.* (eds), *Geschichte der Stadt Augsburg: 2000 Jahre von der Römerzeit bis zur Gegenwart* (Stuttgart, 1985), p. 132.
26 An example among many is the rebuilding of the city after it was sacked by imperial forces in 1132. See P. Fried, 'Augsburg unter der Staufern (1132–1268)' in G. Gottlieb *et al.* (eds), *Geschichte der Stadt Augsburg: 2000 Jahre von der Römerzeit bis zur Gegenwart* (Stuttgart, 1985), pp. 128–30.
27 W. Baer, 'Der Weg zur königlichen Bürgerstadt' in G. Gottlieb *et al.* (eds), *Geschichte der Stadt Augsburg: 2000 Jahre von der Römerzeit bis zur Gegenwart* (Stuttgart, 1985), p. 135.
28 M. Weber, *Economy and Society*, Vol. II, pp. 971–3.
29 Ibid., p. 968: 'Even though the full development of a money economy is thus not an indispensable precondition for bureaucratization, bureaucracy as a permanent structure is knit to the one presupposition of the availability of continuous revenues to maintain it. Where such income cannot be derived from private profits, as it is in the bureaucratic organization of modern enterprises, or from land rents, as in the manor, a stable system of *taxation* is the precondition for the permanent existence of bureaucratic administration. For well-known general reasons only a fully developed money economy offers a secure basis for such a taxation system. Hence the degree of administrative bureaucratization has in urban communities with fully developed money economies not infrequently been relatively greater than in the contemporaneous and much larger territorial states.'
30 F. Blendinger, 'Die Zunfterhebung von 1368' in G. Gottlieb *et al.* (eds), *Geschichte der Stadt Augsburg: 2000 Jahre von der Römerzeit bis zur Gegenwart* (Stuttgart, 1985), pp. 150–3; P. Dirr, 'Zur Geschichte der Augsburger Zunftverfassung', *Zeitschrift des historischen Vereins für Schwaben* 39 (1913), pp. 144–243; F. Frensdorf, 'Die Einführung der Zunftverfassung in Augsburg' in *Die Chroniken der deutschen Städte vom 14. bis in's 16. Jahrhundert*, Vol. IV (1862), pp. 129–49; W. Zorn, *Augsburg: Geschichte einer deutschen Stadt*, 2nd edn (Augsburg, 1972), pp. 131–5.
31 Augsburg followed a pattern typical of free imperial cities in southern Germany during the fourteenth century. Indeed, rebellious artisans sent embassies to neighboring cities to seek guidance in matters of constitutional change. See P. Eitel, *Die oberschwäbischen Reichsstädte im Zeitalter der Zunftherschaft* (Stuttgart, 1970), pp. 37–50.
32 Of 51 patrician families in Augsburg, a few joined the merchants' guild (*Kaufleutezunft*). The majority refused the new organization, continued to draw income from real estate, and eventually returned to their commercial enterprises. In 1383, they closed their ranks to outsiders and refused to accept new members. See F. Blendinger, 'Die Zunfterhebung von 1368', p. 151.
33 The *Steuermeister* were subject to the *Einnehmer*, who directed the activities of all those offices that administered the city's various sources of income.
34 I. Bátori, *Die Reichsstadt Augburg im. 18. Jahrhundert: Verfassung, Finanzen und Reformversuche* (Göttingen, 1969); idem, 'Reichsstädtisches Regiment, Finanzen und bürgerliche Opposition' in G. Gottlieb *et al.* (eds) *Geschichte der Stadt Augsburg: 2000 Jahre von der Römerzeit bis zur Gegenwart* (Stuttgart, 1985), pp. 457–68; B. Roeck, *Eine Stadt in Krieg und Frieden: Studien zur*

Geschichte der Reichsstadt Augsburg zwischen Kalendarstreit und Parität (Göttingen, 1989), esp. vol. I, pp. 209–69; F. Roth, *Augsburger Reformationsgeschichte*, vol. IV, pp. 189–99; P. Warmbrunn, *Zwei Konfessionen in einer Stadt: Das Zusammenleben von Katholiken und Protestanten in den paritätischen Reichsstädten Augsburg, Biberach, Ravenburg und Dinkelsbühl von 1548 bis 1648* (Wiesbaden, 1983), pp. 106ff; W. Zorn, *Augsburg: Geschichte einer deutschen Stadt* (Augsburg, 1972), pp. 190–2.

35 Council membership sank to 41, of whom 31 were patricians, 3 were *Mehrer*, 1 was a merchant, and 6 were artisans. An amendment in 1555 increased the total to 45 by adding an additional *Mehrer*, two merchants, and one artisan. Given that the number of patrician families in Augsburg remained essentially stable, at 27 to 28, the Caroline Constitution theoretically reserved one council seat to each of them. See I. Bátori, 'Reichsstädtisches Regiment, Finanzen und bürgerliche Opposition', p. 461.

36 M. Weber, *Economy and Society*, vol. II, pp. 956–8.

37 Ibid., pp. 958–63.

38 R. Kießling, 'Augsburg zwischen Mittelalter und Neuzeit' in G. Gottlieb *et al.* (eds), *Geschichte der Stadt Augsburg: 2000 Jahre von der Römerzeit bis zur Gegenwart* (Stuttgart, 1985), p. 242.

39 I. Bátori, *Die Reichsstadt Augsburg im 18. Jahrhundert*, p. 69. See also, B. Roeck, *Eine Stadt in Krieg und Frieden*, pp. 262–4.

40 Ibid.

41 L. B. Alberti, *The Family in Renaissance Florence*, p. 149.

42 Weber used the term as the perfect antonym of the modern bureaucrat. See S. N. Eisenstadt (ed.), *Max Weber on Charisma and Institution Building* (Chicago, 1968), p. 75.

43 I. Bátori, 'Reichsstädtisches Regiment, Finanzen und bürgerliche Opposition', p. 463: 'Bedenkt man, daß die meisten Ratsherren unter gewissen Einschränkungen jeweils mehrere Ämter gleichzeitig verwalteten und verschiedene Ämter eigene Einnahmen hatten, die nicht weitergeleitet wurden, so zum Beispiel die Strafgeldeinnahmen der Bürgermeister, so leuchtet ein, daß das Stadtregiment vom Patriziat als eine Art Versorgungsinstitut angesehen wurde.'

44 A. Etzioni, *The Active Society: A Theory of Social and Political Processes* (New York, 1968), p. 4. Ingrid Bátori and Erdmann Weyrauch identified officeholding as an index for active political engagement in early modern German city-states. See I. Bátori and E. Weyrauch, *Die bürgerliche Elite der Stadt Kitzingen: Studien zur Sozial- und Wirtschaftsgeschichte eine landesherrlichen Stadt im 16. Jahrhundert* (Stuttgart, 1982), p. 256.

45 M. Weber, *Economy and Society*, Vol. I, pp. 24–5.

46 Cicero, *On Duties*, p. 3.

47 W. Doyle, *Venality: The Sale of Offices in Eighteenth-Century France* (Oxford, 1996), pp. 1–25. Cf. R. Mousnier, *Les Institutions de la France, sous la monarchie absolue* (Paris, 1980), Vol. II, pp. 454–644. Mousnier has argued for a deep split in the ranks of the royal administration between venal and appointive officers. Whether one accepts his argument or not, it testifies to the pervasiveness of venality.

48 C. Jones, 'Bourgeois Revolution Revivified: 1789 and Social Change', in C. Lucas (ed.), *Rewriting the French Revolution* (Oxford, 1991), p. 72.

Cf. C. Lucas, 'Nobles, Bourgeois and the Origins of the French Revolution', *Past and Present* 60 (1973), p. 90; R. Mousnier, *Les institutions de la France*, Vol. I, pp. 214–25; S. Schama, *Citizens: A Chronology of the French Revolution* (London, 1989), p. xiv; L. Stone and J. C. F. Stone, *An Open Elite? England, 1540–1880* (New York, 1984).

49 D. Bien, 'Office, Corps and a System of State Credit: The Uses of Privilege under the Old Regime' in K. Baker (ed.), *The Political Culture of the Old Regime* (Oxford, 1987); J. F. Bosher, *French Finances, 1770–1795: From Business to Bureaucracy* (Cambridge, Eng., 1970); G. Bossenga, 'From Corps to Citizenship: The Bureau des Finances before the French Revolution', *Journal of Modern History* 58 (1986); idem, *The Politics of Privilege: Old Regime and Revolution in Lille* (Cambridge, Eng., 1991); C. Church, *Revolution and Red Tape: The French Ministerial Bureaucracy, 1770–1850* (Oxford, 1981); W. Doyle, *Venality*; R. Giesey, 'State-Building in Early Modern France: The Role of Royal Officialdom', *Journal of Modern History* 55 (1983); C. Jones, 'Bourgeois Revolution Revivified'; G. Matthews, *The Royal General Farms in the Eighteenth Century* (New York, 1958).

50 See especially G. Bossenga, *The Politics of Privilege*, pp. 89–112.

51 J. H. Hurstfield, 'The Revival of Feudalism in Early Tudor England', *History* 37 (1952), pp. 131–45; S. Kettering, *Patrons, Brokers and Clients in Seventeenth-Century France* (Oxford, 1986); P. Lefebvre, ' Aspects de la fidélité en France au XVIIe siècle: le cas des agents du prince de Condé', *Revue historique* 250 (1973), pp. 59–106; N. B. Lewis, 'The Organization of Indentured Retinues', *Transactions of the Royal Historical Society*, ser. IV, 27 (1945); B. D. Lyon, *From Fief to Indenture: The Transition from Feudal to Nonfeudal Contract in Western Europe* (Cambridge, Mass., 1957); K. B. McFarlane, 'Bastard Feudalism', *Bulletin of the Institute of Historical Research* 20 (1945), pp. 161–80; R. Mousnier, *Les Institutions de la France*, Vol. I, pp. 85–93; L. L. Peck, *Court Patronage and Corruption in Early Stuart England* (London, 1990); O. R. Ranum, *Richelieu and the Councillors of Louis XIII: A Study of the Secretaries of State and Superintendents of Finance in the Ministry of Richelieu, 1635–1642* (Oxford, 1963); W. Reinhard, 'Papa Pius: Prolegomena zu einer Sozialgeschichte des Papsttums' in R. Bäumer (ed.), *Von Konstanz nach Trient: Beiträge zur kirchengeschichte von den Reformkonzilien bis zum Tridentinum* (Paderborn, 1972), pp. 261–99; idem, 'Ämterlaufbahn und Familienstatus: Der Aufstieg des Hauses Borghese, 1537–1631', *Quellen und Forschung aus italienischen Archiven und Bibliotheken* 54 (1974), pp. 328–427; idem, *Papstfinanz und Nepotismus unter Paul V. (1605–1621)*, 2 vols (Stuttgart, 1974); idem, 'Nepotismus: Der Funktionswandel einer papstgeschichtlichen Konstanten', *Zeitschrift für Kirchengeschichte* 86 (1975), pp. 145–85; idem, 'Herkunft und Karriere der Päpste, 1417–1963: Beiträge zu einer historischen Soziologie der römischen Kurie', *Mededelingen van het Nederlands Instituut te Rome* 38 (1976), pp. 145–85; idem, *Freunde und Kreaturen: 'Verflechtung' als Konzept zur Erforschung historischer Führungsgruppen. Römische Oligarchie um 1600* (Munich, 1979).

52 J. Habermas, *Strukturwandel der Öffentlichkeit: Untersuchungen zu einer Kategorie der bürgerlichen Gesellschaft* (Frankfurt/M, 1990). See also C. Calhoun (ed.), *Habermas and the Public Sphere* (Cambridge, Mass., 1994).

53 J. Habermas, *Strukturwandel der Öffentlichkeit*, p. 66. The term, 'public', attaches only to the state, its rulers and servants.
54 Ibid., p. 86: 'Bürgerliche Öffentlichkeit läßt sich vorerst als die Sphäre der zum Publikum versammelten Privatleute begreifen; diese beanspruchen die obrigkeitlich reglementierte Öffentlichkeit alsbald gegen die öffentliche Gewalt selbst, um sich mit dieser über die allgemeinen Regeln des Verkehrs in der grundsätzlich privatisierten, aber öffentlich relevanten Sphäre des Warenverkehrs und der gesellschaftlichen Arbeit auseinanderzusetzen.'
55 Ibid., pp. 69–85.
56 Ibid., p. 75: '"Öffentlich" in diesem engeren Sinne wird synonym mit staatlich; das Attribut bezieht sich nicht mehr auf den repräsentativen "Hof" einer mit Autorität ausgestatteten Person, vielmehr auf den nach Kompetenzen geregelten Betrieb eines mit dem Monopol legitimer Gewaltanwendung ausgestatteten Apparats. Grundherrschaft verwandelt sich in "Polizei"; die ihr subsumierten Privatleute bilden, als die Adressaten der öffentlichen Gewalt, Publikum.'
57 Ibid., pp. 90–107.
58 Ibid., p. 83: 'Weil die dem Staat gegenübergetretene Gesellschaft einerseits von öffentlicher Gewalt einen privaten Bereich deutlich abgrenzt, andererseits aber die Reproduktion des Lebens über die Schranken privater Hausgewalt hinaus zu einer Angelegenheit öffentlicher Interesses erhebt, wird jene Zone des kontinuierlichen Verwaltungskontraktes zu einer "kritischen" auch in dem Sinne, daß sie die Kritik einer räsonierenden Publikums herausfordert.'
59 Ibid., pp. 139–40.
60 Habermas assumes that public discourse takes its place alongside state power and market economics as a coordinator of human life and social action. See C. Calhoun (ed.), *Habermas and the Public Sphere*, p. 6.
61 So understood, the bourgeois public sphere served as both reaction and counter-balance to the state bureaucratic structures that so fascinated Weber.
62 Cf. D. Zaret, 'Religion, Science and Printing in the Public Sphere in Seventeenth-Century England' in C. Calhoun (ed.), *Habermas and the Public Sphere*, p. 213.
63 C. Calhoun, 'Introduction: Habermas and the Public Sphere' in idem (ed.), *Habermas and the Public Sphere*, p. 35.
64 J. Waley, *The Italian City Republics*, p. 108.
65 E. Isenmann, *Die deutsche Stadt im Spätmittelalter* (Stuttgart, 1988), pp. 131–209.
66 J. Kraus, *Das Militärwesen der Reichsstadt Augsburg*, p. 94.
67 Ibid., p. 94.
68 Ibid., p. 106.
69 Ibid., p. 80.
70 Ibid., p. 137.
71 Ibid., p. 105. Matheus noted that the magistrates ordered the creation of four companies of militia 'in order to use them in defense of the city, while the troubled times seemed a danger to us'. It is one of the very few references, albeit indirect, to external affairs in his memoir.

72 Kraus describes Matheus's command in some detail. It was composed of 264 men from the following industries: 8 non-iron metalworkers; 37 animal-product workers; 12 ironworkers; 55 textile-workers; 69 food-workers; 14 wood-workers; 33 decoration-workers; 2 glass- and stone-workers; 10 paper-workers; 6 construction-workers; 18 mercantile workers. Clear is the fact that the soldiers of the company were not drawn from a particular industry, guild, neighborhood or confession. J. Kraus, *Das Militärwesen der Reichsstadt Augsburg*, p. 139.

73 StadtAA, EWA 59, Miller Tagebuch, pp. 105–06: 'Wie Jch mich nun grundtlich (neben danksagung / der erweissenden guten vertrawen) entshuldiget / dz Jch nit capable seie der gleichen stelle mit / verhofften Frucht zue versehen Jn deme meine / Profession nit gewest und noch nit seije / woll aber shuldig denn Vaterland nach vermögen zu / dienen jedoch in sachen wormit gedient sein können / darzue Jch mich auch nach allen Cräfften erbieten. / so wolte doch keine entshuldigung statfinden sondern / setzten mir alle drei so Starkh zue. Ermanet mich nit zue underlossen disen beruf den sie samtlich in gesamtem / Evangel. Magistrat woll erwagen in gute obacht zu / nemmen und mich darzue zue accomodieren.'

74 Ibid., pp. 105–06: 'dz Jch nit capable seie der gleichen stelle mit / verhofften Frucht zue versehen Jn deme meine / Profession nit gewest und noch nit seije'.

75 J. Kraus, *Das Militärwesen der Reichsstadt Augsburg*, pp. 160–1.

76 J. Kraus relates instances of celebrations that cost officers 80 fl. at a time. See ibid., p. 161.

77 I wish to thank Lee Palmer Wandel for calling this illustration to my attention.

78 The industrialist Johann Heinrich Schule, one of Augsburg's wealthiest men, paid fl. 750 to avoid service: J. Kraus, *Das Militärwesen der Reichsstadt Augsburg*.

79 The muster rolls of the militia indicate that Müller [sic] served as captain of the First Citizen Company (*Bürgerkompanie*) until 1695! Cited in C. Kraus, *Das Militärwesen der Reichsstadt Augsburg*, p. 394.

80 P. Broadhead, 'Internal Politics and Civic Society in Augsburg during the Era of the Early Reformation, 1518–1537', Ph.D diss., Kent, UK, 1981; H. Immenkötter, 'Kirche zwischen Reformation und Parität' in G. Gottlieb et al. (eds), *Geschichte der Stadt Augsburg: 2000 Jahre von der Römerzeit bis zur Gegenwart* (Stuttgart, 1985), pp. 391–412; F. Roth, *Augsburgs Reformationsgeschichte*, 4 vols (Munich, 1901/04–11); L. Roper, *The Holy Household: Women and Morals in Reformation Augsburg* (Oxford, 1989), pp. 56–88.

81 L. Roper, *The Holy Household*, pp. 56–88.

82 L. Roper, *The Holy Household*, passim.

83 StadtAA, EWA 59, Miller Tagebuch, p. 99: 'Anno 1675...bin ich von denen / wolloblichen Herrn Statpfleger und Geheimen Ratsherrn alhier / A.C. zue einem Beisitzer ann dem hochloblichen Ehegericht / alhie in Augspurg denominiert und bestelt / worden worauf wenig Tag hernach dz Juramentum abgelegt. Got gebe sein Gnad. An Marz Hübners ab- / getretne stelle.'

84 Bucer's expert opinion (*Gutachten*) on the situation in Augsburg was dated 13 July 1536. W. Kohler, *Zürcher Ehegericht und Genfer Konsistorium*

(Leipzig, 1942), Vol. II, pp. 280–322. See also L. Roper, *The Holy Household*, pp. 56–88.
85 W. Kohler, *Zürcher Ehegericht und Genfer Konsistorium*, p. 290–2.
86 Further changes were soon necessary. On 13 January 1543, the Council raised the number of Marital Court judges to twelve – as before, all were members of the City Court and, therefore, of the Small Council – and lowered the number of sessions to one each week, Monday. The decree indicates that the Wednesdays previously devoted to marital disputes were needed for the consideration of other legal matters by the City Court. W. Kohler, *Zürcher Ehegericht und Genfer Konsistorium*, p. 293, n. 63.
87 See E. Haberkern and J. F. Wallach (eds), *Hilfswörterbuch für Historiker*, 2 vols (Tubingen, 1980).
88 L. Roper, *The Holy Household*, p. 58.
89 The economic and political pressures on states to provide social services first in conjunction with and ultimately in place of churches is nowhere more competently examined than in R. Kießling, *Bürgerliche Gesellschaft und Kirche in Augsburg im Spätmittelalter* (Augsburg, 1971).
90 StadtAA, Repertorien 39, Augsburger Amterbesetzung, 1548–1806. The term *Austeiler* appears to have been applied originally to the six councillors appointed to head the *Almosenamt*. Beginning in 1568, however, a distinction is made between three *Almsherren*, who appear to have been patricians and councillors, and three *Austeiler*, the majority of whom were merchants without council membership. This internal division probably resulted from the constitutional changes of 1548. Whether functional distinction arose as well remains unclear.
91 C.-P. Clasen, 'Armenfürsorge im 16. Jahrhundert,' pp. 337–43; R. Kießling, *Bürgerliche Gesellschaft und Kirche*, pp. 234. See also: B. Roeck, *Eine Stadt in Krieg und Frieden*; T. M. Safley, *Charity and Economy in the Orphanages of Early Modern Augsburg* (Atlantic Highlands, N.J., 1996). From this central agency came funds and goods for a variety of charitable enterprises. It distributed cash, food, fuel and clothing directly to honorable local poor people (*Hausarme*) in their own dwellings. Only the deserving poor – those truly unable to support themselves – were permitted to receive relief, and they received it only in their own neighborhoods, where they and their situations were best known. The undeserving and the foreign poor had to find some kind of work and support themselves. The Alms Office also saw to the needs of those poor who could not maintain independent households; it administered several public institutions for these needy souls, most notably Augsburg's three sanataria, its hospital (*Spital*), its foundling home (*Findelhaus*), its lazarette (*Nothaus*), its poor house (*Almosenhaus*), and its orphanage (*Waisenhaus*). No longer content to encourage private or ecclesiastical charity, the city became the most important provider of relief and patron of the poor through the organization of the Alms Office.
92 B. Roeck, *Eine Stadt in Krieg und Frieden*, p. 607.
93 StadtAA, Steuerbücher, 1667, 1674.
94 StadtAA, EWA 614, Kaufbrief über eine Begräbnus, 1674.
95 StadtAA, EWA 59, Miller Tagebuch, p. 97; A. Hämmerle, *Hochzeitsbücher der Augsburger Bürgerstube und Kaufleutestube bis zum Ende der Reichsfreiheit* (Munich, 1936), p. 238.

Notes 185

96 Cf. R. Kießling, *Bürgerliche Gesellschaft und Kirche*, pp. 215–89; P. Lengle, 'Spitäler, Stiftungen und Bruderschaften', pp. 202–7; P. Clasen, 'Armenfürsorge im 16. Jahrhundert', pp. 337–42; T. Stark, 'Die christliche Wohltätigkeit im Mittelalter und in der Reformationszeit in der Ostschwäbischen Reichsstädten' PhD diss., Erlangen, 1926; A. Werner, *Die örtlichen Stiftungen für die Zwecke des Unterrichts und der Wohltätigkeit in der Stadt Augsburg* (Augsburg, 1899); M. Bisle, *Die öffentliche Armenpflege der Reichsstadt Augsburg mit Berücksichtung der einschlägigen Verhaltisse in anderen Reichsstädten Suddeutschland: ein Beitrag zur christlichen Kulturgeschichte* (Paderborn, 1904).
97 StadtBA, Augsburger Ämterbesetzung, 1548–1806. This list records Matheus as a trustee of the Anna-Raiserin Stiftung from 1664. Foundation records in his own hand indicate that he was a trustee from at least 1659. In 1685, Melchior Mattsperger replaced Matheus as trustee of the Anna-Raiserin Stiftung. See StadtAA, Stiftungen, Nr. 43, Anna-Raiserin Stiftung, 1645–1804.
98 F. Eugen Freiherr von Seida u. Landensberg, *Historisch-Statistische Beschreibung aller Kirchen-, Schul-, Erziehungs- und Wohlthätigkeits-Anstalten in Augsburg von ihrem Ursrpunge an bis auf die neuesten Zeiten*, 2 vols (Augsburg, 1813), pp. 668–70.
99 StadtAA, Stiftungen, Nr. 43, Anna-Raiserin Stiftung, 1645–1804. In addition to their personal liabilities both father Michael and son Matheus regularly paid taxes, a modest sum of fl. 1 kr. 45, equivalent to capital of fl. 45 to 90, on unspecified earnings from the Anna-Raiserin Stiftung.
100 StadtAA, Stiftungen, Nr. 43, Anna-Raiserin Stiftung, Fasc. II, Nr. 4.
101 The statistics for this discussion are derived from materials published by A. Werner, *Die örtlichen Stiftungen*.
102 Again, the exhaustive and authoritative treatment of this period in the history of Augsburg is B. Roeck, *Eine Stadt in Krieg und Frieden*, pp. 604–53.
103 StadtAA, EWA 59, Miller Tagebuch, p. 99.
104 Freiherr von Seida u. Landensberg, *Historisch-Statistische Beschreibung*, pp. 662–5.
105 StadtAA, EWA 1320, Johann Georg Österreich'sche Stiftung, Tom. 14.
106 StadtAA, EWA 1320, Johann Georg Österreich'sche Stiftung, Tom. 15.
107 Ibid. In a postscript, she asked after Frau Müllerin, probably a reference to Matheus' second wife, Helena Schorerin, who had died a few years earlier.
108 For the connections between early modern charity and capital, see T. M. Safley, *Charity and Economy in the Orphanages of Early Modern Augsburg*.
109 StadtAA, EWA 1320, Johann Georg Österreich'sche Stiftung, Tom. 14.
110 StadtAA, EWA 1320, Johann Georg Österreich'sche Stiftung, Tom. 15.
111 Ibid. Though the name Wöllerwein does not appear in the surviving, fragmentary records of his business, they may well have been commercial associates of Matheus. It would not be unusual for the administrators, merchants all, to rely on business associates for such services.
112 StadtAA, EWA 1321, Johann Georg Österreich'sche Stiftung, Tom. 1.
113 StadtAA, EWA 59, Miller Tagebuch, p. 99: 'Anno 1675 denn 19 Xber bin vonn dem Herrn Doctor / Wolfgang Sulzer und Hern Heinrich Langenmantel erbeten / worden zue einem Administratore der Hans Jerg Östreichishen Stifftung neben Jhnen beeden an stat / des abgestorbnen Herrn Oto Laugingers. So ich acct.'

114 StadtAA, EWA 59, Miller Tagebuch, pp. 101–7. Cf. StadtBA, Augsburger Ämterbesetzung, 1548–1806.
115 R. Kießling, *Bürgerliche Gesellschaft und Kirche*, p. 102.
116 Ibid., pp. 99–179. Cf. S. Schröcker, *Die Kirchenpflegschaft: Die Verwaltung der Niederkirchenvermögen durch Laien seit dem ausgehenden Mittelalter* (Paderborn, 1934).
117 Freiherr von Seida u. Landensberg, *Historisch-Statistische Beschreibung*, pp. 400–1.
118. Cf. StadtAA, EWA 59, Miller Tagebuch, p. 101; StadtAA, EWA 877, Zechpflegschaft Heiliger Creuz AC, 1675–78. The problem of identification is acute in this instance. According to Mayr, the name Jerg Mair appears on many sealed documents (*Urkunden*) and identifies the merchant, Christoph Jörg Mair (1591–1671), one of the city's wealthiest men. The date of his death excludes him from consideration, however. Later in his memoir, Matheus notes that Jerg is the brother of Hans Christoph Mair and, therefore, the son of Christoph Jörg. Again according to Mayr, however, Hans Christoph had only two brothers: Daniel the jurist and Hans Ulrich the painter and student of Rembrandt. It is further possible that Matheus's Jerg Mair is identical with Hans Georg Mair, likely a brother of Christoph Jörg or a cousin of Hans Christoph, whom Mayr lists as a the twelfth wealthiest merchant (*Handelsmann*) in Augsburg with property valued from fl. 34,400 to fl. 68,800. It is impossible to be certain. However that may be, the Jerg Mair of the memoir must have been a wealthy, powerful and, as the incidents make clear, self-assured man. See A. Mayr, *Die großen Augsburger Vermögen*, pp. 106, 120–1.
119 StadtAA, EWA 59, Miller Tagebuch, p. 103.
120 Again, the identity of Jerg influences any estimation of his wealth. Mayr notes that Hans Georg Mair was the twelfth wealthiest man in Augsburg according to the 1674 tax register. His total wealth was valued somewhere between fl. 29,000 and fl. 59,000. Though Mayr lists no Jerg Mair among Augsburg's plutocrats, he would still have been quite wealthy as the son and heir of Christoph Jörg Mayr. As of 1660, eleven years before his death, Christoph Jörg had amassed a fortune estimated at fl. 80,000 to fl. 160,000. Hans Christoph inherited his father's business and, it must be assumed, the lion's share of his wealth. By 1674, Hans Christoph was the ninth wealthiest man in Augsburg with property between fl. 34,000 and fl. 68,800. Younger siblings would have received generous settlements as well. See A. Mayr, *Die großen Augsburger Vermögen*, pp. 120–1.
121 StadtAA, Steuerbücher, 1674, 1681.
122 W. Reinhard, *Augsburger Eliten des 16. Jahrhunderts Prosopographie wirtschaftlicher und politischer Fuhrungsgruppen, 1550–1620* (Berlin, 1996), p. 485.
123 StadtAA, EWA 59, Miller Tagebuch, p. 35: 'Hernach als die alte Fraw Shrökhin meine geehrte / Fraw Shwiger Sel. auß disem zeitlihen leben abgeshiden / unnd Hanns Jerg Rauhwolff vermeinte eine / Praetension zue haben wie folgends zue sehen / doch aber mit Gotes Hülff nix erhalten wirdt / weills Jnn nit gebühret. / Alß ist meiner seits Resolution dahin gangen ein / andern sheinpfleger zue verordnen unnd denn / Rauhwolff abzueshaffen. so auh beshehen unnd / denn [] Jenner 1656 Herr Hans Christoff Mair / dessen Fraw Muter mit meiner Hausfr. Sel. / Geshwisterget

Kindt gewesen vorzustellen / der sih auh darzu erklert unnd vor dem Lobl. / oberpfleg Amt eingeshriben worden. G. G. G.'
124 StadtAA, UK 277, 10 November 1654. See the discussion in Chapter 1.
125 StadtAA, EWA 59, Miller Tagebuch, p. 101: 'Der hat zwar / die sachen was jnn dem Kürchen Geshäft zue verichten gewest ganz / allein verricht mich wenig wüssen lassen.'
126 Ibid.: 'under dessen habe doch pro memoria wollen notiern dz mir nit wolgefallen dz Einen denn Gewalt also allein / habe'.
127 StadtAA, EWA 59, Miller Tagebuch, p. 102: 'Wir haben zwaar zue denn Kürchen stöken die shlüßel halbiert / Einer die zue dem Menshlaß der ander zum Cästlen nun hat es sich / begeben dz auf zeit eines heill abents mit beederseits willen / die stökh gelehrt worden und weillen die zeit dabei zu kurz / wurde die paarshafft ungezehlt in ein sackh getan undt / von mir pitshiert [sic] mit meinem ring dem Hr Mair hinder lassen bis zue gelegenheit die eröfnung und zehlung vor / zu nemmen Hr Mair hats wenig Tag hernach mit dem / Mesner ohne mein beisein eröfnet und von einkommern genommen / mir mit seinem comodo auf mein bgern di nota des befinden übershikt.'
128 Ibid.: 'Allein Jst es nit mit meinem / wüssen erfolgt und solle darum nit recht sein eben / weillen es balt darauf nach Einmal also ergangen / wann Jch nun glauben will dz alles doch fideliter seie / zu gangen so Jsts aber nit recht in dem dz sichs nit Jme ge-/ bühret allein sondern es solle ins gemein beshehen / umb der consequenz willen. Welche gaar üble sachen / gebehren können gestalten mir dann selbsten darauf / sachen vor kommen darein Jch mich weniger als gaar nit / richten noch finden kann noch weiß Jnn dem / befinde dz ein mißbrauch einshleichen'.
129 *Friedensfest* is an Augsburg observance of the Treaty of Westphalia and the end of the Thirty Years' War. Begun as a solemn commemoration of the survival of the Lutheran community in 1649, it has evolved into a local children's festival.
130 StadtAA, EWA 877, Zechpflegschaft Heiliger Creuz AC.
131 Ibid.
132 Ibid.
133 Though less ubiquitous than the *Gulden*, the *Reichstaler* was a common coin of transaction in Augsburg. Its value fluctuated with the silver content of the *Gulden*. Thus, the *Reichstaler* rose in value from kr. 68 in 1566 to kr. 84 in 1600 as the *Gulden* declined from 22.9 grams to 18.6 grams of silver. By the end of the seventeenth century, given a total lack of archival sources on Augsburg money, the value of the *Reichstaler* is estimated to have been roughly twice that of the *Gulden*. Cf. M. J. Elsas, *Umriss einer Geschichte der Preise und Löhne in Deutschland Vom ausgehenden Mittelalter bis zum Beginn des neunzehnten Jahrhunderts*, 2 vols (Leiden, 1949), pp. 120–1.
134 StadtAA, EWA 59, Miller Tagebuch, p. 103: 'Welche gaar üble sachen / gebehren können gestalten mir dann selbsten darauf / sachen vor kommen darein Jch mich weniger als gaar nit / richten noch finden kann noch weiß Jnn dem / befinde dz ein mißbrauch einshleichen'.
135 Ibid., pp. 103–4: 'sovile / als Jch bishero warnemmen könen rest vonn der zeit / Anno 167[] als Her Hans Christoff Mair und Priester Goldshmit neben / einander Zechpfleger waren. Da Jeder vom ungezelten gelt / fl. 12

bei seinem Abtrit genomen und gebrauchen sollen Jrem / bedeiten nach der gemein bei der wahl ein Trunkh zue geben / Dz gelt namen sie heraus und hinderließ einer Jedesmals dem / andern Zue gebrauch einer Zierot der Kürchen welhes / also vonn selbiger zeit ann sovil jch wahr nemen Könen beshehen / allein vonn vorigen Zechpflegern. Der gleichen niemalen observiert / noch vill weniger begangen worden.'

136 Ibid., p. 103: 'Was man Empfangt / soll man redtlich aufshreiben und was man redtlich auf-/gibt redtlich wider für Ausgab notieren und anders nit / Dis were dennoch nit genug sondern vil mehr excess / darin welher mir gaar unvorsichtig noch unpracticirlich / gedunket auch nit unbillich für unrecht erkent wirdt.'

137 StadtAA, EWA 977, Zechpflegschaft Heiliger Creuz AC: 'Primero Xber befinde Abgang an denen vorstehenden von dem Herrn Hans Jerg Mair jnn seiner übergebnen rechnung benanten 322:16, die sich mehrers nit den 310:16 befunden, welch auf Errindern er selbsten zu verantworten über sich zu nehmen under dessen dacordi zu geben werdens für ein Außgab gesetzt, 12 fl.'

138 StadtAA, EWA 59, Miller Tagebuch, p. 103: 'Darum dz der Hr Joseph Werner Mahler laut Hr Hans Christoff / Mairs gewesten Zechpflegers Anno [ ] aigen Hantshrifft / versprochen in dz Chor der vierfelter Eines Ein gemähl / zue verehrn wie auch Hr. Johann Spillenberg welher / Hr. Spillberg es gleich Anno [] gehalten auch ohne einige / Recompens dahin verehret. Hr. Joseph Werner bringt den / seinige Anno 76 zwar kurz vor Hr. Mairs Abtrit'.

139 Ibid.: 'Dis were dennoch nit genug sondern vil mehr excess / darin welher mir gaar unvorsichtig noch unpracticirlich / gedunket auch nit unbillich für unrecht erkent wirdt.'

140 Ibid., p. 104: 'es / würdt Jn zweien falter auf der Canzel beim Creutz vom Hr. / Pfar Riß deswegen mächtig gedanket und der gemein angedeit dz diß / Nobl Chünstler zu bezeugung seines Reinen gleuben und liebe zue / diß Kürchen und gemein dises St[uck]. freiwillig verehret.'

141 Ibid.: 'also dz kein / mensh anderst gleuben noch wüssen kann wie dz drein ein / mißverstand sein möchte wann man aufgezeichnet finde dz / dz das Tuch so gar die Farb bezalt seie und über dz auch die / gemein aus denn stökhen 30 rt. verehren neben den selben / auch noch fl. 55 also zue samen 100 fl. seien genommen'.

142 StadtAA, EWA 877, Zechpflegschaft Heiliger Creuz AC: 'dem Herren Joseph Werner verehrt, gleich wie es Herren Heüser von Memmingen beshehen, wegen seines verehrten shönen gemelte so in das Chor von dem Abendmal Christi 45 fl.'

143 StadtAA, EWA 59, Miller Tagebuch, p. 104: '10 fl. so Steuden [sic] vonn ungezelten gelt 12 fl. so Hr. Bekh vonn / ungezelten gelt und 12 fl. so Hr. Mair vonn der paarshafft die er / mir hete übergeben sollen. sovil weniger aber zugestellt und / mich gewisen dz Jchs vonn Künfftigen ungezelten gelten / nemmen solle.'

144 Ibid.: 'so mutete Er mir zue dz Jch mein habende nota vonn dem / gefäll. des Kürchen stökh under [ ] betragent fl. 159 kr. / nun fl. 139 [und] kr. notiern solle damit die 100 fl. / dem Werner complet verehret und verbleibt die er Jme / geshenkt ehe Er mir die Rechnung übergeben.'

145 Ibid., p. 104: 'was nun / diß von Hendel vonn rechten verhofenden leuten sein. / Komt gaar wunderlich hervor.'

146 Ibid., pp. 105: 'Jch schreib diß alles mit / besturz und demuth ganz confuez insonderheit wan dabei / betrachten wie jn der erfelshten wahl bei Mairs abtretung / verfahren worden.'
147 Ibid.: 'Die wurde von Hr. mair allein angestelt ohne mein befragen / oder wüssen sondern mir wurde allein angesagt wie oder umb / zu ersheinen. Jch gie[n]ge ein gute stund vor der Rechten / Zeit und vermeinte er wurde mir die rechnung weisen undt / Jnformation übergeben aber wurde mit andern di Insti [sic] / erhalten bis alle beisamen. Da den mit wenig worten gesagt / weil die 2 Jar vorbei übergebe er hiemit Zech und seie der Einkommern / fl. [ ] die Ausgab fl. [ ] rest übergebe er mir. / und trete ab wolle dabei gebeten habe zu einer Wahl eins / Newen zue shreiten'.
148 Ibid.: 'Aber Hr. / Mair wie sein Hr. Br. Hans Chr. meldeten kurz man müste aber nit daran gebunden / sein. Konte gar woll Hr. Deller genommen werden massen / sie Jme dann gleich die Stim geben und alle ubrige so denn / Hr. Pfarer furchten und dabei die alte ordnung Ehender hinger an-/ setzen.'
149 Ibid.: 'Hr. Mair colligierte die Stimmen und war mit denn strichlen / fertig in dem Jn kürzer zeit weit mehr als / personen selbst vorhanden.'
150 Ibid., p. 106: 'Wie Jch vernomen dz Hr. / Pfarer und der Mesner ein stim haben so Jch nit gewust / so habe Jch weilen des Hr. M. Lauben sonsten niemand gedacht / ermelden Jch gebs für denn Hr. M. Laub dem Hr. Baur goltshmidt / der sonsten vil stimen gehabt von anderen unparteishe und / von mir auch.' Georg Laub was the son of the Augsburg merchant, Tobias. Born in 1626, he received his initial education in Ulm, where he was probably a schoolmate of Matheus's. He studied theology and philosophy at Strasbourg and Uppsala. In 1676 he returned to Augsburg, where he was appointed deacon at Holy Cross. Two years later he became pastor at St Ulrich's. Laub died in 1686. J. F. Rein, *Das gesamte augsburgische Evangelische Ministerium in Bildern und Schriften von den ersten Jahren der Reformation Lutheri bis auf Anno 1748* (Augsburg, 1749), p. 154.
151 Ibid.: ' Jch welts shon verantworten.'
152 Ibid.: 'wie der Handel bei allen gebrauchten Vorteil / und fleis mißlungen'.
153 Ibid.: 'Dem auch befragt worden und nit / andern so sagen könen dz Er mir nichts bevohen weillen / Jch vorhero nit mit Jhme geredet dz wurde Eine leerm / als ob Jch mit lugen umbgieng. Als aber Hr Laub auch / von mir vernomen dz Jch dise Stim erst dann entlehnt / gegeben also ich gehört dz Hr Ris und Mesner und werner / nit gegenwertig Jre Stimmen entbrachten so wurde es Ja / Hr Diacono durch den Zechpfleger seinen Veter konen freylich / gegeben werden damit Jme an seinem recht nix ver-/geben wurde.'
154 Ibid., p. 107: 'so Jch dz selbe anfenglich vorhero gewist hete Jch / demselben darum befragt womit ein gentz worden er Hr / Laub were vom Hr Riß durch dem Mesner ersucht und der dem / Teller die Stim zue geben deme er bevolen wiellen / er vernommen dz dismal einer in der Vorstat sein solle. Er / aber ainich die leith nit könne so wolle er die Stim seint- / wegen dem Jenigen geben der ohne dz die meist stimmen / habe. Weillen den der Mesner fein geshwigen so habe Jch / unwüssent dz recht geret und nit gelogen / als wie die sonst so dz liegen fast gewohnt.'
155 StadtAA, EWA 877, Zechpflegschaft Heiliger Creuz AC.
156 Ibid.

190 Notes

157 Ibid.
158 Ibid.
159 Ibid.
160 Ibid.
161 Ibid.: 'weillen dero arbeit von oben an dem Thuren und also auch hinden zue oberst ann dem Shiester mit villem Gerüst und gefärliche sorgsamen mühe erfolgen muessen, wolten sie nit weniger Taglohn als 32 kr. nemen, darbei brot und bier auch begrifen gewest'.
162 The *Pfund* measured approximately 0.491 kilograms in weight. See M. Elsas, *Umriss einer Geschichte der Preise und Löhne in Deutschland*, pp. 152–4.
163 Ibid.: 'weillen weit mehrer mühe damit angewand als sonsten mit bedeckung des Dachs obwol man sonsten 3 kr. bezalt diß orths aber under 5 kr. vom lb. nit nemen wollen'.
164 Ibid.: 'vorgebent er hete offtmal in einem gantzen Tag dises dunnen Kupfer über 10 bis 12 lb. nit anmachen und befertigen können'.
165 Ibid.: 'So ist auch bereit in dem Monat Juli dem obgemelt gewesten Kapuziner Pater Esaias genand sonsten des rechten Nahmens Johann Conrad Seiferts von Würzburg der hier erkantlich 6 Jaar bei den Kapuzinern Pfarrer gewest und hernach laut vorgewisnen Testimonien Evangel. worden auf Herrn Pfarrers recommendation auß diser Cassa hergelihen worden 20:00 damit er in Stille seine reiß nach Hamburg fortzetzen mocht und bei denen ermangleten Mitel und vorgehabt ofentlich samlung nit außgeförsht und etwas aufgefangen wurde mit vertrostung es wurden gute freunde solche helf ersetzen weillen ab bis dato darzu nix gelivert, wogegen nur schlechte speranza dz iezo erfolge gemacht wird so habe von den meinigen 3:00 beigelegt ubrig bringe zu conto und hoffe es solle durch andere gutherzliche leuth hinfuro desto reichlicher in die Stöcken davor gelegt werden, so einem oder anderem operte zu recommendieren ist, 12 fl.'
166 StadtAA, EWA 59, Miller Tagebuch, p. 99: 'Anno 1675 den [ ] bin auch von einer wolloblichen / Hr. Statpfleger und Geheimen Rath A. C. alhier / zu der Roth Ordnung per signaturam under disem dato deputiert worden. so aber noch / nit vollig auß seinen beweglichen ursag.' Cf. StadtBA, Augsburger Ämterbesetzung, 1548–1806.
167 Ibid., pp. 100–1: 'Jnn dem monat 9ber Anno 1676 Binn Jch des Rath wesen / vonn Herrn Statpfleger Weissen Gest[reng] und Herl[ich] / darum entlassen worden weillens Jchs niemahlen / völlig antreten wolle in deme befunden dz die / Jenigen ein zeit vorhero darbei geweste Deputirte Hr. / Hanns Christof Mair Hanns Adam Baumbgartner Jakob Heim und Hr. Paull / Beklin mit Außschluss des letsten Hern Beklin inn vill lange / Jaar für die Kaufmannshafft besten nit guberniert welhes / die acta so vom Anno 63 angeführt worden da die gesamte / Kaufmannshafft in specie darwider gehandelt und zwaar / fürnemlich die baumbgartner und heim dannach vermeint / betrofen. Anno 75 aber Jm ende verspüret und offenbaar / worden dz auch die Geb[rüder]. Miller und Mair sich zue denn / selben geshlagen bei welchem umbstenden davon die Acta gar / weitleufig reden ohne erleuterte oberkeitlich assistenz / Jch nit verbleiben können noch wollen weswegen dann ein / Commission von drei Bürgermeistern erkennet worden / die vermögt dz alle Acta müsten heraufgegeben werden / und die

ganz rod [Rat?] Deputation mit anderen bestelt wobei man / mich behalten und haben wolten. die Papisten aber mit lieb nit davon / gwelt. Jch werde dann auch davon bleiben / so Jst wider dero Willen mir gaar woll geholfen und gedient / worden damit Jch davon komen. Got lob.'
168 Ibid., p. 101: 'es bleibt entlich von Got nit verborgen solche Taten so dem / Gemeinen wesen zum shad laufen bekomen doch entlich / stat und gemeine shand zum lohn. Dz wird man noch erfahren.'
169 Ibid.: 'müßbreuch und ungelegenheiten ofenbaret werden möchte / die mir gewislich sonsten offenbarlich were underhanden / auch andern damit offentlich ins gesicht kommen.'
170 Ibid.: 'es / seie darum vonn denen vorigen also verleget worden damit nit mehr / versaumt und übersehene dem gemeinen wesen fast shädliche / müßbreuch und ungelegenheiten ofenbaret werden möchten'.
171 Cf. J. Savary, *Le parfait negociant ou instruction generale pour ce qui regarde le commerce* (Paris, 1675), esp. pp. 33–8.

3 Sociability and Social Structure

1 StadtAA, EWA 59, Miller Tagebuch, pp. 63–4: 'Specificatio Newen Jaar / Ehrungen / 1658'.
2 Ibid.:

	fl.
M. L. Hausfraw 4 taler	12.00
Phl. Jacob 1 r. taler	1.30
Math. 1 r. taler	1.30
Helleneli 1 r. taler	1.30
Teller 1 r. taler	1.30
2 mägt a 1 / 2 taler	1.30
des Vaters Magt	0.30
Veter [Vater?] Mich. Miller	0.45
[Total]	20.45

3 Ibid.:

	fl.
dem Br. Thomas 1 r taler:	1.30
Geb Daniels 5 Kinder a 1 / 4 r. taler	1.52
[Total]	3.22

4 Ibid.:

	fl.
Her. Mag. Hopfer 2 r. taler	3.00
seine 3 Kinder doten a 1 / 2 r taler	2.15
[Total]	5.15

5 Ibid.:

	fl.
dem Her Steclen 1 r taler	1.30
dem Hr. Furstrich 1 r taler	1.30
dem hr. Göbel 1 r taler	1.30
dem Hr. Weber 1 r taler	1.30
dem Hr. Riss 1 r taler	1.30

192 Notes

dem Hr. Vogel 1 r taler	1.30
dem Hr. Ehingen 1 r taler	1.30
dem Hr. Hilen 1 r taler	1.30
dem Hr. Christeiner 1 r taler	1.30
dem Hr. Veter 1 r taler	1.30
dem Hr. Pfanzelt 1 r taler	1.30
dem Hr. Faber 1 r taler	1.30
dem Hr. Steidner 1 r taler	1.30
dem Mag. Ölhofen 1 r taler	1.30
[Total]	21.00

6 Ibid., p. 117: 'Anno 1685 New Jaar'

					fl.
Phl Ja und seine Fr rt.	2	4 Kindern	Hr. Pfarer Ris		2.00
Habißreitinger	2	3 Kindern	Hr. Jung		2.00
Matheus	2	2 Kindern	Hr. Leopolt		2.00
Stör	2	1 Kind	Hr. M. Bekh		1.00
Anna Marili	1		Hr. M. Miller		1.00
Ant. Christoff	1		Hr. M. Tulla		1.00
Joh. Catarina	1		Hr. Mg. Übel		1.00
2 Mägt		2	Hr. Bekh		1.00
[Total]		31	Hr. Wieland		1.00
			Hr. M. Spizel		1.00
Jfr. Regina Peirlin	1/2 rt.		Hr. Ehinger		1.00
			Hr. Ehinger		1.00
			Hr. Pfarer Laub		4.00
			Hr. M. Baur		1.00
			Hr. Steidner		1.00
			[Total]		21.00

7 J. Menius, *An die hochgeborne Furstin/fraw Sibilla Hertzogin zu Sachsen/ Oeconomia Christiana / das ist von Christlier haushaltung Justi Menij. Mit einer schönen Vorrede D. Martini Lutheri* (Wittenberg, 1529): 'eine eusserliche und leibliche gemeinschafft / dadurch sich einer dem andern zu seiner nottorft / mit stetter handreichung / so viel er wol thun kan / zu dienen verwilliget'. As cited by P. Münch, *Lebensformen in der frühen Neuzeit, 1500 bis 1800* (Berlin, 1994), p. 276.

8 Aristotle, *Nicomachean Ethics*, Bk. VIII, Ch. 3; Cicero, 'Laelius: On Friendship' as cited in *On the Good Life* (London, 1971), pp. 172–227.

9 Adovardo's arguments are Ciceronian in inspiration.

10 L. B. Alberti, *The Family in Renaissance Florence*, p. 284.

11 Ibid., p. 285.

12 Ibid., p. 282.

13 Cicero, *On the Good Life*, pp. 203–4.

14 L. B. Alberti, *The Family in Renaissance Florence*, p. 275.

15 Ibid., p. 272.

16 Cicero, *On the Good Life*, p. 226.

17 Cicero argues elsewhere that mutual service is essential to friendship and a foundation of society. Cf. *On Duties*, Bk. II.

18 L. B. Alberti, *The Family in Renaissance Florence*, p. 287.

19 Ibid., p. 255.
20 Cicero, *On the Good Life*, p. 187.
21 StadtAA, EWA 59, Miller Tagebuch, p. 4: '...Einer unnd andere rathete / Jmmer mich ferners zue vershicken unnd inn fremte Kaufleuths / dienste mich zue obligkiern die wolten sich aber nit gleich / presentiern. dz urtell fälte mann entlich mit Herrn Baltas / Shnuerpeins leuten 1641 inn die frankfurter Herbstmess mich zue / versenden inn denn vorhaben da einige glegenheit zu diensten / sich erzeigte mich gleich hin zuegeben dann binn etlichen alhier / Ein Dorn inn den Augen gewesen unnd inn dem gueten / Estimo bei denn nechsten dz all Jhr rath nun immer gangen / ob Jch gleich nach Cöln als inn das erzt Catholishe orth kommen solte / unnd mich 10 Jaar verobligkieren müeste solte es nix bedeuten / damit Jch nun die Millerishe shreibstuben nit dörffte betreten.'
22 P. Münch, *Lebensformen in der frühen Neuzeit*, p. 281.
23 See E. Piper, *Der Stadtplan als Grundriß der Gesellschaft. Topographie und Sozialstruktur in Augsburg und Florenz um 1500* (Frankfurt/M, 1982); B. Roeck, *Eine Stadt in Krieg und Frieden*, pp. 384–433.
24 The distribution of population according to wealth and occupation is based on an analysis of tax records from 1610. See: C.-P. Clasen, 'Arm und Reich in Augsburg' in G. Gottlieb *et al.* (eds), *Geschichte der Stadt Augsburg: 2000 Jahre von der Römerzeit bis zur Gegenwart* (Stuttgart, 1985), pp. 312–36.
25 E. Isenmann, *Die deutsche Stadt im Spätmittelalter* (Stuttgart, 1988), pp. 250–67. See also: K. Bosl, 'Kasten, Stände, Klassen im mittelalterlichen Deutschland', *Zeitschrift für bayrische Landesgeschichte* 32 (1969), pp. 477–94; P. Dollinger, 'Die deutschen Städte im Mittelalter. Die sozialen Gruppierungen' in H. Stoob (ed.), *Altständisches Bürgertum* (Darmstadt, 1978), Vol. II, pp. 269–300; W. Ehrbrecht, 'Zu Ordnung und Selbstverständnis städtischer Gesellschaft im späten Mittelalter', *Blatt für deutschen Landesgeschichte* 110 (1974), pp. 83–103; J. Ellermeyer, 'Sozialgruppen, Selbstverständnis, Vermögen und städtische Verordnungen. Ein Diskussionsbeitrag zur Erforschung der spätmittelalterlichen Stadtgesellschaft', *Blatt für deutsche Landesgeschichte* 113 (1977), pp. 203–75; idem, ' "Schichtung" und "Sozialstruktur" in spätmittelalterlichen Städten', *Geschichte und Gesellschaft* 6 (1980), pp. 125–49; H. Jecht, 'Studien zur gesellschaftliche Struktur mittelalterlicher Städte', *Vierteljahresschrift für Sozial und Wirtschaftsgeschichte* 19 (1926), pp. 48–85; H. Kellenbenz, 'Die Gesellschaft in der mitteleuropäischen Stadt im 16. Jahrhundert. Tendenzen der Differenzierung', in W. Rausch (ed.), *Die Stadt an der Schwelle der Neuzeit* (Linz, 1980), pp. 1–20; L. Manz, *Der Ordogedanke. Ein Beitrag zur Frage des mittelalterlichen Standesgedankens* (Wiesbaden, 1937); E. Maschke, 'Die Schichtung der mittelalterlichen Stadtbevölkerung Deutschlands als Problem der Forschung' in idem (ed.), *Städten und Menschen* (Wiesbaden, 1980), pp. 157–69; idem, 'Die Unterschichten der mittelalterlichen' in E. Maschke and J. Sydow (eds), *Gesellschaftliche Unterschichten in den südwestdeutschen Städten* (Stuttgart, 1967), pp. 1–74; idem, 'Mittelschichten in deutschen Städten des Mittelalters' in E. Maschke and J. Sydow (eds), *Städtische Mittelschichten* (Stuttgart, 1972), pp. 1–31; M. Mitterauer, 'Probleme der Stratifikation in mittelalterlichen Gesellschaftssystemen', *Geschichte und Gesellschaft*, Sonderheft, 3 (1977),

pp. 13–43; H. Rüthing, *Höxter um 1500. Analyse einer Stadtgesellschaft* (Paderborn, 1986); W. Schnyder, 'Soziale Schichtung und Grundlagen der Vermögensbildung in den spätmittelalterlichen Städten der Eidgenossenschaft' in H. Stoob (ed.), *Altständisches Bürgertum* (Darmstadt, 1978), Vol. II, pp. 425–44; W. Schulze (ed.), *Ständische Gesellschaft und soziale Mobilität* (München, 1988); W. Schwer, *Stand und Ständeordnung im Weltbild des Mittelalters. Die geistes- und gesellschaftsgeschichtlichen Grundlagen der berufsständischen Idee* (1934); G. Vogler, 'Probleme der Klassenbildung in der Feudalgesellschaft. Betrachtungen über die Entwicklung des Bürgertums in Mittel- und Westeuropa vom 11. bis zum 18. Jahrhundert', *Zeitschrift für Geschichtswissenschaft* (1973), pp. 1182–208; E. Weyrauch, 'Über soziale Schichtung', in I. Bátori (ed.), *Städtische Gesellschaft und Reformation* (Stuttgart, 1980), pp. 5–57; G. Wunder, 'Sie soziale Struktur der Handwerkerschaft in unseren alten Städten' in E. Maschke and J. Sydow (eds), *Städtische Mittelschichten*, pp. 120–34; H. Wunder, 'Probleme der Stratifikation in mittelalterlichen Gesellschaftssystemen', *Geschichte und Gesellschaft* 4 (1978), pp. 542–50.

26 K. Bosl, 'Potens und Pauper: Begriffsgeschichtliche Studien zur gesellschaftlichen Differenzierung im frühen Mittelalter und zum "Pauperismus" des Hochmittelalters' in idem, *Frühformen der Gesellschaft im mittelalterlichen Europa* (Munich, 1964), pp. 106–34; idem, 'Macht und Arbeit als bestimmende Kräfte in der mittelalterlichen Gesellschaft' in *Geschichtliche Landeskunde V: Festschrift für L. Petry* (Wiesbaden, 1968), pp. 46–64; idem, 'Kasten, Stände, Klassen im mittelalterlichen Deutschland'; F. Irsigler, 'Divites und Pauperes in der Vita Meinwerci', *Vierteljahresschrift für Sozial- und Wirtschaftsgeschichte* 57 (1970), pp. 449–99.

27 W. Schulze, 'Die ständische Gesellschaft des 16./17. Jahrhunderts als Problem von Statik und Dynamik' in idem (ed.), *Ständische Gesellschaft und soziale Mobilität*, pp. 1–18.

28 P. Münch, *Lebensformen in der frühen Neuzeit*, pp. 65–124.

29 H. Planitz, *Die deutsche Stadt im Mittelalter* (Graz, 1954). Cf. F. Irsigler, 'Divites und Pauperes', p. 498.'

30 E. Isenmann, *Die deutsche Stadt im Spätmittelalter*, p. 249. Cf. I. Bog, 'Reichsverfassung und reichsstädtische Gesellschaft: Socialgeschichtliche Forschungen über reichsständische Residenten in den Freien Städten, insbesondere in Nürnberg', *Jahrbuch für frankische Landesforschung* 18 (1958), pp. 325–39.

31 StadtAA, EWA 265, *Erneuerte Policey-, Zierd-, Kleider-, Hochzeit-, Kind Tauf-, und Leich- Ordnung* (Augsburg, 1683).

32 This definition of a hierarchical society is developed at some length in W. Schulze, 'Die ständische Gesellschaft des 16./17. Jahrhunderts'. See also: J. Kocka, 'Stand, Klasse, Organization. Strukturen Sozialen Ungleichheit in Deutschland vom spaten 18. bis zum frühen 20. Jahrhundert im Ausriß', in H.-U. Wehler (ed.), *Klassen in der europaischen Sozialgeschichte* (Gottingen, 1979), pp. 137–65.

33 J. H. Alsted, *Encyclopaedia septem tomis distincta* (Herborn, 1630). As cited in Münch, *Lebensformen in der frühen Neuzeit*, p. 66: 'Nichts ist schöner, nichts ist fruchtbarer als die Ordnung. Die Ordnung verschafft auf dem riesigen Theater dieser Welt allen Dingen Wert und Rang. Die Ordnung ist in der

Kirche Gottes der Nerv des Corpus mysticum. Die Ordnung ist das stärkste Band im Staats- und Familienleben.'
34 Schulze and others have attributed limited mobility in hierarchical societies to limited resources. I would argue that a conviction of limited growth weighs no less than the consciousness of limited resources. W. Schulze, 'Die ständische Gesellschaft des 16./17. Jahrhunderts', p. 15. See also B. Balla, *Soziologie der Knappheit. Zum Verständnis individueller und gesellschaftlicher Mangelzustände* (Stuttgart, 1978) and G. M. Foster, 'Peasant Society and the Image of Limited Goods', *American Anthropologist* 67 (1965), pp. 293–315.
35 M. Weber, *Economy and Society* (Berkeley, 1978), Vol. II, p. 935. He posited that status groups (orders) came into being by virtue of their own lifestyle, their hereditary descent, and their political power. See M. Weber, *Economy and Society* (Berkeley, 1978), Vol. I , pp. 302–7.
36 Ibid., pp. 927–8. The use of the term 'class' is itself telling. It derives from the writings of eighteenth-century physiocrats, who were concerned to determine the extent to which differences in wealth and occupation transformed social stratification in early industrial societies of Britain and Holland. Hence, the concept of class draws from its historical context notions of mobility and change that were supposedly absent in earlier, ranked societies of orders.
37 Ibid., p. 936.
38 Ibid., p. 937.
39 E. Isenmann, *Die deutsche Stadt im Spätmittelalter*, p. 252.
40 F. Blendinger, 'Versuch einer Bestimmung der Mittelschicht in der Reichsstadt Augsburg vom Ende des 14. bis zum Anfang des 18. Jahrhunderts' in E. Maschke and J. Sydow (eds), *Städtische Mittelschichten*, pp. 32–78. Cf. W. Schultheiss, 'Die Mittelschichten Nürnbergs im Spätmittelalter' in E. Maschke and J. Sydow (eds), *Städtische Mittelschichten*, pp. 135–49; W. von Stromer, 'Reichtum und Ratswürde: Die wirtschaftliche Führungsschicht der Reichsstadt Nürnberg' in H. Helbig (ed.), *Führungskräfte der Wirtschaft in Mittelalter und Neuzeit, 1350–1850* (1973), pp. 1–50.
41 P. A. Sorokin, *Social and Cultural Mobility* (New York, 1927), pp. 133ff.
42 Compare the emphasis on economic success in R. Endres, 'Adel und Patriziat in Oberdeutschland' in W. Schulze (ed.), *Ständische Gesellschaft und soziale Mobilität*, pp. 221–38.
43 M. Weber, *Economy and Society*, Vol. II, p. 927.
44 O. Mörke and K. Sieh, 'Gesellschaftliche Führungsgruppen' in G. Gottlieb et al. (eds), *Geschichte der Stadt Augsburg: 2000 Jahre von der Römerzeit bis zur Gegenwart* (Stuttgart, 1985), pp. 302–5.
45 J. Jahn, 'Die Augsburger Sozialstruktur in 15. Jahrhundert' in G. Gottlieb et al. (eds), *Geschichte der Stadt Augsburg: 2000 Jahre von der Römerzeit bis zur Gegenwart* (Stuttgart, 1985), pp. 187–93. See also: U. Dirlmeier, *Untersuchungen zu Einkommensverhältnissen und Lebenshaltungskosten in oberdeutschen Städten des Spätmittelalters* (Heidelberg, 1978).
46 Ibid., passim.
47 Ibid., p. 188.
48 Kießling set the proportion of have-nothings in Augsburg between 45 and 65 percent from the late fourteenth to the mid-sixteenth century. See: R. Kießling, *Bürgerliche Gesellschaft und Kirche*, p. 216.

49 B. Greiff, 'Tagebuch des Lucas Rem aus den Jahren 1494–1541: Ein Beitrag zur Handelsgeschichte der Stadt Augsburg', *Jahresbericht des historischen Vereins für Schwaben und Neuburg* 27 (1861).
50 P. Dirr, 'Zur Geschichte der Augsburger Zunftverfassung,' *Zeitschrift des historischen Vereins für Schwaben* 39 (1913), pp. 144–243.
51 See F. Blendinger, 'Die wirtschaftliche Führungsschichten in Augsburg, 1430–1740' in H. Helbig (ed.), *Führungsfräfte der Wirtschaft in Mittelalter und Neuzeit, 1435–1850* (Limburg/Lahn, 1973), pp. 51–86; V. Press, Führungsgruppen in der deutschen Gesellschaft im Übergang zur Neuzeit (um 1500)' in H. H. Hofmann and G. Franz (eds), *Deutsche Führungsschichten in der Neuzeit. Eine Zwischenbilanz* (Boppard, 1980), pp. 29–77; W. Reinhard, *Freunde und Kreaturen. 'Verflechtung' als Konzept zur Erforschung historischer Führungsgruppen. Römische Oligarchie um 1600* (Munich, 1979); A. Rieber, 'Das Patriziat von Ulm, Augsburg, Ravensburg, Memmingen, Biberach' in H. Rößler (ed.), *Deutsches Patriziat, 1430–1740* (Limburg/Lahn, 1968), pp. 299–351.
52 C.-P. Clasen, *Die Augsburger Steuerbücher um 1600* (Augsburg, 1976), pp. 15–16.
53 StadtAA, Patrizier und Geschlechter, Nr. 47, fol. 47v as cited in Mörke and Sieh, 'Gesellschaftliche Führungsgruppen', p. 302.
54 P. Dirr, 'Kaufleutezunft und Kaufleutestube in Augsburg zur Zeit des Zunftegiments, 1368–1548', *Zeitschrift des historischen Vereins für Schwaben* 35 (1909), p. 138.
55 Estimates set the population at less than 17,000, down from 40,000. Textile production declined from 400,000 pieces per year to barely 60,000.
56 Roeck, *Eine Stadt in Krieg und Frieden*, pp. 905–9.
57 Ibid., p. 907. Changes within this group – the relative decrease in those paying kr. 15 or less and the relative increase in those paying between kr. 16 and 60 – have been explained in terms of the possibility that Augsburg tax officials increased assessments, sparing only the truly propertyless, in a desperate attempt to increase public revenue. They might also be attributed to attrition through death or migration, which would have struck the lower strata of Augsburg society with particular ferocity.
58 Mayr, *Die grosse Augsburger Vermögen*, pp. 115–20.
59 Fassl, 'Wirtschaft, Handel, Socialstruktur', p. 468.
60 Mörke and Sieh, 'Gesellschaftliche Führungsgruppen', p. 304.
61 P. Fassl, 'Wirtschaft, Handel und Sozialstruktur' in G. Gottlieb *et al.* (eds), *Geschichte der Stadt Augsburg: 2000 Jahre von der Römerzeit bis zur Gegenwart* (Stuttgart, 1985), p. 469.
62 P. Fassl, *Konfession, Wirtschaft und Politik. Von der Reichsstadt zur Industriestadt, Augsburg 1750–1850* (Sigmaringen, 1988), p. 95.
63 All calculations based on figures provided in Mayr, *Die grosse Augsburger Vermögen*, pp. 120–3.
64 I. Bátori, *Die Reichsstadt Augsburg im 18. Jahrhundert. Verfassung, Finanzen und Reformversuche* (Gottingen, 1969), pp. 20ff.
65 StadtAA, EWA 265, *Erneuerte Policey-, Zierd-, Kleider-, Hochzeit-, Kind Tauf-, und Leich- Ordnung* (Augsburg, 1683), p. 69: 'der übermässige Pracht und die Kostbarkeit bey allen Ständen...überhand genommen / daß man schier keinen Stand mehr zu unterscheiden gewußt'; p. 72: 'in ihren Kleidungen und Trachten sich ihrem Stand gemäß verhalten'.

66 J. Dewald, *The Formation of a Provincial Nobility: The Magistrates of the Parlement of Rouen, 1499–1610* (Princeton, 1980); idem, *Pont-St-Pierre, 1398–1789: Lordship, Community, and Capitalism in Early Modern France* (Berkeley, 1987); R. Forster, *The Nobility of Toulouse in the Eighteenth Century* (Baltimore, 1960); idem, 'The Nobility during the French Revolution', *Past and Present* 37 (1967); idem, *The House of Saulx-Tavanes: Versailles and Burgundy, 1700–1830* (Baltimore, 1971); idem, *Merchants, Landlords, and Magistrates: The Depont Family in Eighteenth-Century France* (Baltimore, 1980); G. W. Pedlow, *The Survival of the Hessian Nobility, 1770–1870* (Princeton, 1988); L. Stone, *The Crisis of the Aristocracy, 1558–1641* (Oxford, 1965); L. Stone and J. C. Fawtier Stone, *An Open Elite? England, 1540–1880* (Oxford, 1984).
67 Cf. T. M. Safley, 'Die Fuggerfaktoren Hörmann von und zu Gutenberg: Werte und Normen einer kaufmännischen Familie im Übergang zum Landadel' in J. Burkhardt (ed.), *Augsburger Handelshäuser in Wandel des historischen Urteils* (Tubingen, 1996).
68 W. Reinhard, *Freunde und Kreaturen*, p. 19. See also I. Mieck (ed.), *Soziale Schichtung und soziale Mobilität* (Berlin, 1984); W. Reinhard (ed.), *Augsburger Eliten des 16. Jahrhunderts: Prosopographie wirtschaftlicher und politischer Führungsgruppen, 1500–1620* (Berlin, 1996); W. Schutze, *Oligarchische Verflechtung und Konfession in der Reichsstadt Ravensburg, 1551/52–1648: Untersuchungen zur sozialen Verflechtung der Führungsschicht*, Ph.D diss., Augsburg, 1981; K. Sieh-Burens, *Oligarchie, Konfession und Politik im 16. Jahrhundert: Zur sozialen Verflechtung der Augsburger Bürgermeister und Stadtpfleger, 1518–1618* (Munich, 1986); P. Steuer, *Die Außenverflechtung der Augsburger Oligarchie von 1500 bis 1620: Studien zur sozialen Verflechtung der politischen Führungsschicht der Reichsstadt Augsburg* (Augsburg, 1988).
69 Brady argues that the 'sinews of Strasbourg's oligarchic regime were the institutions of life tenures and cooptation in the privy councils and in the ruling corporations of the guilds...The very hallmark of the system was the careful screening of politicians'. See T. A. Brady, Jr, *Ruling Class, Regime and Reformation at Strasbourg, 1520–55* (Leiden, 1978), pp. 173.
70 This is most clearly revealed in studies of individual families, e.g., J. Dewald, *Pont-St-Pierre, 1398–1789;* Forster, *Merchants, Landlords, Magistrates;* M. Phillips, *The Memoir of Marco Parenti*.
71 Cf. R. Jütte, 'Household and Family Life in Late Sixteenth-Century Cologne: The Weinsberg Family', *Sixteenth Century Journal* 17 (1986), pp. 166. See also: *Das Buch Weinsberg, Kölner Denkwürdigkeiten aus dem 16. Jahrhundert* 5 vols (Leipzig, 1886/1926); S. Ozment, *When Fathers Ruled: Family Life in Reformation Europe* (Cambridge, Eng., 1983); idem, *Magdalena and Balthasar: An Intimate Portrait of Life in Sixteenth-Century Europe Revealed in the Letters of a Nuremberg Husband and Wife* (New York, 1986).
72 See the discussion in Chapter 2. StadtAA, EWA 59, Miller Tagebuch, p. 35.
73 See the discussion in Chapter 1. StadtAA, EWA 59, Miller Tagebuch, pp. 32–3. 'Jn dem Monnath 9bris 1654 Hat mein Br. Michael Miller / meiner seiner Haußfr. samt seinem shwagern Hr. Anton Christoff / Shorer Jüngern mich mit sich nach / Haußstetten spazie gefürth / unnd under anderm mich anfangen vexieren muste wider / Ein weib haben.'
74 See the discussion in the introduction. StadtAA, EWA 59, Miller Tagebuch, p. 5: 'bei disem Herrn Shoapen bin Jch ankommen / dem Monat Oktober

198 Notes

1641 unnd vonn Jme dermassen zue der Hantlung / unnd dergleichen verrichtungen mit solhem embsigen aifer / angehalten worden dz Jch mir woll zue sonderbar dankbarem / Ehrn und Jme zum ruhm nach sagen kann ein leiblicher Vater / mehrers nit woll thuen könnte als Er gegen mir fremte gethon.'

75 StadtAA, EWA 59, Miller Tagebuch, p. 81.
76 Ibid.
77 Ibid., p. 109.
78 A. Hämmerle, *Hochzeitsbücher der Augsburger Bürgerstube und Kaufleutestube bis zum Ende der Reichsfreiheit* (Munich, 1936), pp. 238, 243, 246. See also StadtAA, EWA 59, Miller Tagebuch, p. 117.
79 StadtAA, EWA 59, Miller Tagebuch, p. 12.
80 StadtAA, Reichsstadt Akten 46, Stadtkanzlei, Kaufbriefe 1650–54, 20 August 1652. Cf. Steuerbücher 1625–47: Michael's residence was consistently given as 'Vom Rappolt ietzo Michael Millers Egghaus in der Steingasse'.
81 StadtAA, Steuerbuch, 1660.
82 StadtAA, EWA 59, Miller Tagebuch, pp. 68–9.
83 Ibid., pp. 97–8.
84 A. Hämmerle, *Hochzeitsbücher der Augsburger Bürgerstube und Kaufleutestube bis zum Ende der Reichsfreiheit*, nr. 3149. Given the improbability of a patrician marrying a merchant, especially an impecunious one, it seems likely that Susanna was an illegitimate daughter of Johannes Wachter (1610–93). He married three times: Philippine Engler in 1642, Anna Elisabeth Neubronner in 1646, and Barbara Hopfer in 1657. None of these unions produced legitimate heirs. See H.-U. Frhr. von Ruepprecht, 'Die Memminger Patrizier', *Memminger Geschichtsblätter* (1981/82), p. 40
85 StadtAA, Steuerbuch 1667, 87c; Steuerbuch 1674, 90d.
86 StadtAA, Steuerbuch, 1674, 90d.
87 StadtAA, EWA 59, Miller Tagebuch, pp. 114–15: 'Anno 1678 / den [ ] hat es dem Lieben Got gefallen meinen Lieben / Bruder Thomas Miller nach dem Er am Charfreitag / mit Veter Michael Miller vonn Bozen kommen mit etwas / Leibes shwachheit zue belegen. Da er denn Montags Frühe / umb Mittags Zeit sich nach Haus Jns bet bgeben. Die Matrigkeit / Anfangen Clagen. sich aber balt alles Zeitliches sorgen / entshlagen und gutentheils sich vermerken lassen / dz Er dis Zeitliche gerne verlasse dennoch mit seinem / Lieben Got sich also versehnet und auf dz New ver[ ] der Jme zue Leben und zue Sterben. Jn welchen / Ernstlich und Christlich ein Vorsatz bis ann sein Sel. Ende / verharret. So gewehret bis Somstags abend umb 5 uhr. dem / Dz er deme mit grosem frewdigem gemüth seinem Lieben Got seine Seele haim gegeben Jme seinem Alter [ ]. / Jch habe ainen guten Bruder auff diser Welt verlohren. / und die ganze freuntshafft ein stüze und Zieren. / Got wolle uns allen [ ] Seelig lassen hernach folgen / und nach seinem Heilligen wolgefallen uns ferners / zue seines Names lebend Ehren inn aller / wahrer Gotseligkeit Jnn seinen Gnaden väterlich erhalten.'
88 StadtAA, Reichsstadt Akten 281, Abkommenbriefe, 18 July 1679.
89 StadtAA, Steuerbuch 1681, 90c.
90 StadtAA, Reichsstadt Akten 262, Stadtkanzlei, Vergleiche 1670–99, 18 July 1679. Susanna Wachterin received an allowance (*Kostgeld*) of fl. 200 to provide her with food, clothing and shelter. From this money she would render

fl. 15 yearly toward maintenance of the house in the Steingasse, where she and her daughters would continue to live.
91 StaatsAA, Reichsstadt Augsburg, Lit. 562, Grundbuch, p. 308. After Thomas's death and Susanna's remarriage, Matheus purchased the dwelling in 1684. When he died in 1685, it became part of his estate and, eventually, home to his heir, Philip Jakob.
92 StadtAA, Reichsstadt Akten 675. Oberpflegamt Protokollbeilage, *Stemmer v. Miller*, 1658–67.
93 Ibid., 18 November 1666.
94 Ibid.: 'Es were fördrist zue wüssen dz Er seinen Bruder Daniel gleich anfangs zue sich genommen und saloriert'.
95 Ibid.: 'daß er eine aigene Hantlung angefangen, die er eben sowol nit verstanden sondern sie folgents hin gaar vill und offtmals mit fürshiessungen eigener Mitel jme helfen müessen'.
96 Ibid.: 'schimpf und spot ja falliment verhüeten wollen'.
97 Ibid., Bilanz 1658.
98 Ibid., 14 November 1667.
99 StadtAA, Reichsstadt Akten 280, Stadtkanzlei, Abkommenbriefe, 16 September 1679.
100 StadtAA, EWA 59, Miller Tagebuch, passim.
101 J. F. Rein, *Das gesamte augspurgische Evangelische Ministerium*, p. 142.
102 Ibid., p. 132.
103 Mayr estimates Hopfer's worth to have been between fl. 76,000 and fl. 152,000 in 1618, making him the 22nd wealthiest person in Augsburg. See A. Mayr, *Die grosse Augsburger Vermögen*, p. 115.
104 Mayr estimates her wealth to have been between fl. 38,600 and fl. 77,200 in 1632. See A. Mayr, *Die grosse Augsburger Vermögen*, p. 118.
105 StadtAA, EWA 59, Miller Tagebuch, pp. 63, 66.
106 StadtAA, Reichsstadt Akten 150, Stadtkanzlei, Schuldbriefe 1660–69, 4 February 1655.
107 The house was located in the Grottenau district of Augsburg's Upper City, an elite neighborhood of merchants and patricians.
108 StadtAA, Reichsstadt Akten 150, Stadtkanzlei, Schuldbriefe 1660–69, 3 May 1660.
109 StaatsAA, Reichsstadt Augsburg, Lit. 562, Grundbuch, fol. 239v.
110 Ibid. Bartholomeus Hopfer later transferred his brother's fl. 875 debt to Matheus and therewith signed over his interest in the Grottenau property as well. See also StadtAA, Reichsstadt Akten 226, Stadtskanzlei, Transport 9 August 1661.
111 StaatsAA, Reichsstadt Augsburg, Lit. 562, Grundbuch, fol. 239v.
112 Ibid., fol. 239r.
113 StadtAA, EWA 59, Miller Tagebuch, p. 74.
114 Ibid., passim.
115 Ibid., pp. 80, 81, 109, 118, 119.
116 Ibid., p. 74: 'Anno 1664 Adi 14 Apprill bin vonn der Fraw Michael / Millerin meines Gel[iebten] br[üder] Hausfraw ann stat des L. Vaters / see. zue Jhrem beistand neben dem Herr Gabriel / Miller erbeten worden. so hiemit bewilliget. / Got geb gnad und Seegen. / 1665 Jst den 31. Juli an stat Hr. Gabriel Vater / Christian zum beistand neben mir verordnet. / Anno

1664 di 5. Mai bin vonn den Jfr. Saara und / Veronica Hopferin erbeten worden zu Jhrem beistand / neben dem Herrn Matheus Gelb. so auch bewilliget. / Got geb Gnad und Seegen. / Anno 1665 den 31. Julli Jst Johan / Bapto. Peirlin neben mir meiner Gel[iebten] Muter / zum beiständen eingeshriben worden. Got Geb / Gnad und Seegen;' p. 83: 'Anno 1667 ist Hr. Christian Miller neben mir / und [ohne?] dem Weienmair den 24 Marti als des Veter / Michl Miller Pfleger vorgestelt und eingeshriben / worden. Got geb Gnad und Segen. / Anno 1676 bin Jch neben dem Herr Licentiat Thoman / zum beistand ordentlich eingeshriben worden / der Fraw Maria Sibilla / Gustav Adolf Zeilerin witib. / Got geb Gnad und Segen.'
117 Ibid., p. 83: 'Anno 1673 bin Jch neben Hern Gabriel Schorer der fraw / Jacob Schorerin witib beistand worden. / so mir vil und grose mühe verursacht. Got helfs auch / tragen.'
118 StadtAA, Reichsstadt Akten 281, Stadtkanzlei, Abkommenbrief, 19 January 1677.
119 StadtAA, EWA 59, Miller Tagebuch, p. 55: 'Anno 1656 adi 8. Aprill Jst Herr Philip Warmberger / Meines shweher Hans Warmberger See. Brueder Jnn St. / Stephans Gots Acker inn die Herwartishe begrabnuß be-/graben worden und gestorben denn 5. diss[elben] / mitwuchs morgens under der predig. sein Leichtpredig / hate gehalten Herr M. Leonhart Fussenger bei St. Anna. / Got gebe Jme aine fröliche aufferstehung uns allen / seine Zeit auch ein Seeliges Ende. / Die leicht uncosten habe Jch gehalten wegen des vonn / Jm erhandelten Haus wie Jnn meinen Büchern zue / sehen.'
120 StadtAA, Steuerbuch 1646, 85b. Warmberger paid only fl. 10 kr. 10 in taxes, roughly equivalent to property between fl. 2,000 and fl. 4,000.
121 StadtAA, Reichsstadt Akten 261, Stadtkanzlei, Vergleiche, 1640–69, 30 July 1648.
122 Ibid., 20 October 1653.
123 These costs he duly paid, when Hans Philip died in 1656. See StadtAA, EWA 59, Miller Tagebuch, p. 55: 'Anno 1656 adi 8. Aprill Jst Herr Philip Warmberger / Meines shweher Hans [=Johannes, TMS] Warmberger See. Brueder Jnn St. / Stephans Gots Acker inn die Herwartishe begrabnuß be- / graben worden und gestorben denn 5. diss[elben] / mitwuchs morgens under der predig. sein Leichtpredig / hate gehalten Herr M. Leonhart Fussenger bei St. Anna. / Got gebe Jme aine fröliche aufferstehung uns allen / seine Zeit auch ein Seeliges Ende. / Die leicht uncosten habe Jch gehalten wegen des vonn / Jm erhandelten Haus wie Jnn meinen Büchern zue / sehen.'
124 StadtAA, Steuerbuch 1553, p. 95a; Steuerbuch 1660; p. 95a.
125 StadtAA, EWA 59, Miller Tagebuch, pp. 31–2: 'nachdeme nun wie hievor nach Einander außfürlich ver / meldet unnd bericht worden Jch inn denn traurigen / wütibstannt gerathen habe mit meiner geehrten / Alten Fraw Shwiger, Susanna Wüldin Herrn Elias / Shröken Seel. Hinderlassnen Witib mich Fridtlich und / freuntlich betragen unnd mein Haußhaben gefürth / mit Jhrer unnd meiner seits gueten condento / doh nit ohne unser beeden beshwerden wegen dem / nix wertigen Ehehalten die vill beshwernuß / zue machen sich understanden doch auß Gotes Gnaden / Entlich auch mit gueter mannier beigelegt und / vonn unns selbsten ruhe geshafft worden. / welche unruhe mich gleichwoll dohin gedenken / machen wie meiner Fr.

Shwiger ruhe shoffen / möchte Zue Jhrem Zimmlich hochen Alter / doh binn ich meinen nach Sinnen nit besteet gewesen / denn der Liebe Gott wuste woll selber was wir / beede nach seinem Götlichen Willen Thuen wurden / müeßen'.

126 Her difficulties with the servants seems to confirm most prescriptive literature of that period, that is, that servants were a source of constant trouble and required constant supervision.

127 Ibid., pp. 33–4: 'Meiner Fraw Shwiger habe Jhrs nun Zeitlih / comunicirt unnd wie will Sie anfangs etwas / unwilligs sein wollen Jnn Jhrem Sinn vermeinet / es were noh Zue früeh Doch als Jch die occasion / unnd andere bewegliche motivi vorgeshüzt / aigentlich Sich gaar willig darzue erzeiget und / sovill Sie dabei Thuen können mit rath begegnet wir / hingegen Jch mich auch Jhrer angenommen unnd / durch Gotes Gnadt Eine guete gelegenliche behaußen / Jnn der Fr. Christlin Hauß bei St. Anna wie auch den / Annsehen unnd befinden nach einen Getrew Ehehalten / auch vor sie gefunden. so dz wir mit guetem lieb unnd / friden vonn Einander sheiden können. so 14 Tag vor / der Hochzeit beshehen nach deme wir bei 7 1/2 Jaar / fridtlich unnd freüntlich beisammen Gelebt unndt / unns woll mit Einander betragen haben Jn lieb unnd Leidt / dern auch undershidtliche harte Anstöß unns begegnet / sein.'

128 Ibid., p. 55: 'Vonn diser gueten Ehrlichen Fraw nun habe Jch vill gut That / auf allerlei weeg empfangen'.

129 Ibid., p. 47: 'Anno 1655 denn 17 October hat sich die alte Fraw Shrökhin / als meine Geehrte Fraw Shwiger nun mehr Seel. anfangen etwas / übelß auff befinden nach deme sie Zuvor mit Jhren zwey Enkhlin / als meinen Zwey Söhnlin spaziern gegangen unnd Jst die / Krankheit allein mit einer Matigkeit ann sie kommen so dz / Sie sich müesen zue bete halten doch balt Herrn Doctor Shrökhen / als Jhres stieff Sohns rath unnd arznei mitell gebrauchen / ongeacht sie sonsten denn Dr. Kneili pflegte zue gebrauchen / denn Shröken aber aigentlich dismall darum weillen die Hans / Jerg Rauhwölfin solhes gerathen uneer disem Pretext / damit die leüth sehen die fraw der alten pignus [sic] nit mehr / gedächte sondern vergessen hete.'

130 Ibid., p. 48: 'bei Ehrngedachter Frawen Seel. mit allem Eifer unnd Ernst sie / solte doh einn Testament machen Jhrer dabei gedenken mahen / auch denn bossen so braun dz weillen die Fraw am ersten nit / recht consentiert unnd auf Jhre mannier sih verlauten laßen wollen / Sie samtlich vonn Jhr gegangen unnd die gute Fraw dardurch / Zue fürchten gehapt wann sies nit thete unnd Jhr got wider / aufhelffen solte sie solhes vonn Jnen hart entgelten müste / demnah sich resolviert ein Testament zue machen'.

131 Ibid., p. 49: 'Als / Jch nun fragte was Gibt sie zuer antwurt es werde mir nit / zue wider sein dz sie Jhrer shwester wolle Tausent Guldin / unnd Jhr shöne wullene Huseggen vermachen. Jch sagte / hete der Fraw hierin nix einzuereden. Woll sie himit / aber Fr. gebeten unnd errindert haben Jhrer Enklen auh besser / zue gedenken unnd werde die fraw selbst ann das besten / auch wüssen woh Jhr vermögen seye was vor bewantnuß / darmit habe unnd dz die Kinderlin noh ein merkliches / dedarfen werden biß Zue Jhren Jaarn komen. Jch auh ann / meinem shuldigen fleiß nix werde erwinden lassen die / selbige ferners inn der forcht Gotes zue auferziehen unndt mit guetem

Exempell sovill möglich vorzuegehen / darüber replicierte die fraw damalen anders nix als under / denn herrn predigern sollt Jhr auch etwas verehrn wie auch / inn die arme heuser doch nur denn Evangelischen. Als ich gebete / die persona zue benembsen sagte sie Jr werdet Jme shon wüssen / recht zue thuen. Anders hate sie nun ferners nix zue sagen.'

132 Ibid., p. 49: 'als ich sagte ich ließ mirs gefallen wies die Fraw ordnete / doch wolte ich sie auch hiemit f[erne]r. gefragt haben ob sie mit / Jhrem lieben herrn beistand herrn Christoff Georg Maijr diser / sachen halber einmall geredet habe sagte sie nein iedoch / were Jhr lieb zuvor deswegen mit Jhme / zue reden solte Jne alsbalt hollen unnd den Notario / weienmair die sach zue verfertigen. das Jst nun erfolget. beede kamen den / selbigen abent mit mir hin unnd under weg trafen wir / denn Herr Hopfer ann. denn baten wir mit zue gehen / umb zuehören wie die sach ferners passiern werde'.

133 Ibid., pp. 49–50: 'Jch / sagte zue Jnen es wundere mich nit wenig dz sie meinen / Kindern mit erpracticierung dises testaments solhen shaden mögen / zuefuegen unnd zue vorderst auch die guete Fraw also betrüben / dann ich spüre ann Jr große last unnd bangigkeit so von disem / guten theils her rühren mueste unnd seie mir leidt dz man sie / also betrüben möge dann sie mueste mit Jrem gewissen kämpfen / wies theills werde sie betrachten dz sie solhes nit thon / solte weillens wollgefällige und natürliche erben hete und / andern Theills ein mal Jhrer shwester nit gebühr. / doh dessen alles ungeacht wolle Jch die Fraw ferners mit / der gleichen sachen zue vershonen sie mit diser gebeten haben unndt / damit sie sehen was gestalt Jch freuntshafft zu erhalten suche / wolle ich mich gleich ehe mann zue der fraw hinein komme / mit Jnen heraußen inn presentia des weienmairs vergleichen / und dz aber mit solher mannier dz Jnen zwar die fl. 1000 / bleiben sollen Jedoch nah rata portione vonn der Frawen / seel. verlossenshafft in qualitate wie es ist. Rauchwolff / unnd sein wieb beruhen sie wolten die 1000 fl. haben oder / die heuser am Katzenstadel darfür. Jch sagte hingegen / ein vergleich woll ich trefen wie obgemelt unnd tate / undershidtliche guete vorshläg aber keine wolt Jnen gefallen / so das ich entlich dem wasser denn Fluss zue lassen genötigt / worden.'

134 Ibid., p. 51: 'Jnterim aber ist Hr. Hopfer und Hr. Mair / bei der fraw inn der stuben gewesen die Jnen aber in dem / geringsten auff kein worth inn diser materia antwurten / wollen entlich auch der weienmair darzue kommen denn / sie auch kein wort geantwurth woll sich bedankt dz mann / bei Jr zue sprechen aber ferners nix geredt. so dz mann auch / zwei ganzen stundt damalen zue gebracht. Rauchwolff / unnd sein weib liesen hernach umb 10 uhr den notarium / zu nachts wider hollen sie redete undershidtliches mit Jme / aber vonn testaments sachen wolts nit ein worth anhören / sondern begibt sich gleich auff die seiten. darauff / het sie nun ferners nix thon lassen dann abwolen / die Rauchwölffin. Jch unnd andere umbstehende freunt- / lichst sie ersucht unnd gebeten sie solte doch dem Herrn Weien- / mair denn sie anfangs begert Jhr herz eröfnen. Jch seye / erbürtig wie sie bevellen werde die sach werkhstellig / zue machen wolte sie doch nit ein einiges wort ant- / wurten als nach langem errindern unnd piten Jst / dz Jhr ainige sag gewest Jch habe zwei liebe Enkhlin. / wie weienmair gesehen dz er nix richten kann nimt er / abshidt von Jhr die freuntlich danket dz er einkhert habe unnd wüntsht / Jme auch gut nacht. Rauchwolff sahe dz

zweifelhafft / sachen wolte unnd begerte demnach denn accord zue ergreifen. / Jch hingegen sache dz die Fraw woll reden konte aber / nit wolte unnd praesumirte dabei sie müste etwas anders bei Jhr beshlossen haben. Wolte auch deswegen kein accord / ferners annemmen sondern wies die Fraw mache seije es mir / beliebig. Wir namen samtlich gut nacht.'

135 Ibid., p. 52: 'Ersuchte Jch demnach den Hr. M. Kreüten mit / d. Fr. deswegen vertrewlich zue reden dz geshahe nun aber vonn / diser materia wolt sie kein einig worth antwurten sondern begerte / dz Heilige Nachtmall zu empfangen. Nachdem sie nun mit / Andacht Gebeicht unnd darauff die Absolutio folgendts / Dz Hohwürdige Sacrament empfangen mit grosem / Eifer unnd Andachten Herr Creut hat bevollen man soll sie / mit dem Zeitlichen nun förders nit mehr bekümmern sondern / mit lesen unnd beten Jhr die Zeit vertreiben … unnd wie die Rauchwölffin und er gesehen dz die Fraw Jhrer / mit verfertigung des angeregten Testaments nit begegnen / will haben sies verlassen sein auch nit mehr zu Jhr kommen / ungeacht ich etlich mall zu Jnen geshikt wann sies / niehmalen sehen wollen kommen sollen aber vergebens.'

136 Ibid., p. 53: 'Die gute Fraw nun hat vonn stundt ann krefften abgenomen / zwaar ainigen shmerzen niemalen geklagt. Mir / denn sontag unnd samstag nah [=Nacht, TMS] die kinder bevollen / unnd glükh unnd haill zu meinem Thon unnd Handl ge- / wüntshet. Jst sie darauff monntags denn 8. / 9bre morgens unnder der predig zwishen 8 und 9 Uhren / sannfft unnd Seelig inn dem Herrn enthlaffen unnder dem / gebet der Umbstehendten'.

137 StadtAA, EWA 59, Miller Tagebuch, p. 1: 'Ist mit wenigem, darum verzeichnet, umb die meinigen, da Got die Gnade verlihe, etwan zue verlassen, solches nach mir finden.'

138 The historiography on early modern godparentage is frustratingly thin. The author wishes to acknowledge with thanks the particular assistance of Terrance L. Dinovo, at the time Curator of Special Collections at Luther Seminary in St Paul, Minn., in gathering such information as exists on baptismal sponsorship during the Reformation. See H. Boesch, *Kinderleben in der deutschen Vergangenheit* (Leipzig, 1900), Vol. V, pp. 23–33; A. Berthet, 'Un réactif social: le parrainage. Du XVIe siècle à la Révolution: Nobles, bourgeois et paysans dans un bourg perché du Jura', *Annales. Economies, société, civilisation* 1 (1946), pp. 43–50; K. Fojtik, 'Die Inhalts- und Funktionswandlungen der Gevatterschaft in Böhmen, Mähren, und Schlesien vom XIV. Bis zum XX. Jahrhunder', *Kontakte und Grenzen: Festschrift für Gerhard Heilfurth zum 60. Geburtstag* (Gottingen, 1969), pp. 337–43; D. Sabean, 'Aspects of Kinship Behavior and Property in Rural Western Europe before 1800' in J. Goody, J. Thirsk and E. P. Thompson (eds), *Family and Inheritance: Rural Society in Western Europe 1200–1800* (Cambridge, Eng., 1976), pp. 96–111; J. H. Lynch, *Godparents and Kinship in Early Medieval Europe* (Princeton, 1986), pp. 20–31.

139 See M. Luther, *Taufbüchlein* (Wittemberg, 1523); J. Bugenhagen, *Von den unge born kindern, vnd von den kindern, die wir nicht teuffen können, vnd wolten doch gern, nach Christus befehl, vnd sonst von der Tauff, etc.* (Wittemberg, 1551); J. Gerhard, *Loci theologici* (Tubingen, 1768).

140 Three sponsors, two of the same sex and one of the opposite sex, seems to have become the norm among Protestants. By contrast, the Council of

Trent allows only one sponsor of the same sex or two of the opposite sex. See: 'Baptism', *The New Schaff-Herzog Encyclopedia of Religious Knowledge*, Vol. I (Grand Rapids, Mich., 1963–66), p. 446.
141 StadtAA, EWA 59, Miller Tagebuch, p. 10.
142 Ibid., p. 111.
143 Ibid., p. 129. The scriptural passage is Micah 6: 8.
144 E. François, *Die unsichtbare Grenze, Protestanten und Katholiken in Augsburg, 1648–1806* (Sigmaringen, 1991), pp. 178–81.
145 The city's history teems with examples of families that abandoned their merchant backgrounds to orient themselves on the aristocracy. Some of the better known instances are the Fugger, the Baumgartner and the Herbrot. Cf. M. Häberlein, *Brüder, Freunde und Betrüger: Soziale Beziehungen, Normen und Konflikte in der Augsburger Kaufmannschaft um die Mitte des 16. Jahrhunderts* (Berlin, 1998), pp. 224–43.
146 A growing consciousness and vitality on the part of the early modern bourgeoisie, understood here as the broad, diverse middle stratum of urban society, is usually attributed to the spread of capitalism in the seventeenth and eighteenth centuries. I would like to suggest the possibility that such changes in mentality, with their potentially revolutionary questions about the relationship between class and society or class and state, may have their roots in the social and political upheavals of an earlier age. Cf. C. Jones, 'Bourgeois Revolution Revivified: 1789 and Social Change' in C. Lucas (ed.) *Rewriting the French Revolution* (Oxford, 1991), pp. 69–118.

4 Death and Confession

1 StadtAA, EWA 59, Miller Tagebuch, p. 7: 'Alles mit guetem Fridt unnd Conntento dem Hochsten sein / darvon Lob unnd Dankh. der Gebe noch ferners denn / angefangenen versprochnen Göttlichen Seegen.'
2 Ibid., p. 82: 'Also wird Es unfelbar Got richten und dem / Satan steüren der sich in kleiner eingefleißter / gestalt großmütig gis getumelt. / Got shende und shmehe dich Satan / und gebe Gotfrid und Einigkeit vertrewliche redtlichkeit ohne aigennutzige lust und / begüren.'
3 Ibid., pp. 27–9: 'Nun Empfinde die Handt des Herrn / Welche auß Gerehtem Eiffer unnd Barmherzig / keit mich abermallen rühret ... / auch meine Alte wunden von newen mir auff zu reissen.'
4 StadtBA, Augsburger Ämterbesetzung, 1548–1806.
5 StadtAA, EWA 59, Miller Tagebuch, pp. 90–2. Cf. J. Kraus, *Das Militärwesen der Reichsstadt Augsburg, 1548 bis 1806* (Augsburg, 1980), pp. 139, 394.
6 StadtAA, EWA 59, Miller Tagebuch, p. 99.
7 Ibid.
8 Ibid., pp. 101–7; StadtBA, Augsburger Ämterbesetzung, 1548–1806.
9 R. P. Hsia, *Social Discipline in the Reformation: Central Europe, 1550–1750* (London, 1989); W. Reinhard, 'Zwang zur Konfessionalisierung? Prolegomena zu einer Theorie des konfessionellen Zeitalters', *Zeitschrift für Historische Forschung* 10 (1983), pp. 257–77; H. Schilling, 'Die "Zweite Reformation" als Kategorie der Geschichtswissenschaft' in idem (ed.), *Die reformierte Konfessionalisierung in Deutschland – Das Problem der 'Zweiten Reformation'* (Gutersloh, 1986), pp. 387–401; E. W. Zeeden, *Die Entstehung*

der Konfessionen: Grundlagen und Formen der Konfessionsbildung im Zeitlater der Glaubenskämpfe (Munich, 1965); idem, *Konfessionsbildung: Studien zur Reformaton, Gegenreformation und katholischen Reform* (Stuttgart, 1985).
10 Pierre Bourdieu referred to such daily practice as *habitus*, a 'durably installed generative principle of regulated improvisation'. The term describes well Matheus's private devotional practices that varied according to circumstance but maintained nonetheless a surprising degree of constancy. P. Bourdieu, *Outline of a Theory of Practice* (Cambridge, Eng., 1977), p. 16.
11 M. Heckel, 'Reichsrecht und "Zweite Reformation": Theologisch-juristische Probleme der reformierten Konfessionalisierung' in H. Schilling (ed.), *Die reformierte Konfessionalisierung in Deutschland – Das Probleme der 'Zweiten Reformation'* (Gutersloh, 1986), p. 15.
12 Hans-Christoph Rublack defined these shared norms as 'principles legitimizing social action' and included among them peace, unity and the common weal. H.-C. Rublack, 'Political and Social Norms in Urban Communities in the Holy Roman Empire' in K. von Greyerz (ed.), *Religion, Politics, and Social Protest: Three Studies on Early Modern Germany* (London, 1984), pp. 24–60.
13 Warmbrunn's term, 'biconfessional', though apt in the period after 1548, hardly captures the vibrant and varied 'confessional' life of Augsburg in the first decades of the Reformation. The same may very well be said of most south German cities in which the cause of religious reform fastened foot. Cf. P. Warmbrunn, *Zwei Konfessionen in einer Stadt: Das Zusammenleben von Katholiken und Protestanten in den paritätischen Reichsstädten Augsburg, Biberach, Ravenburg und Dinkelsbühl von 1548 bis 1648* (Weisbaden, 1983), passim.
14 Immenkötter, 'Kirche zwischen Reformation und Parität' in G. Gottlieb, et al. (eds), *Geschichte der Stadt Augsburg: 2000 Jahre von der Römerzeit bis zur Gegenwart* (Stuttgart, 1985), p. 400; cf. F. Roth, *Augsburger Reformationsgeschichte*, 4 vols (Munich, 1901–11), esp. Vol. II.
15 H. Immenkotter, 'Kirche zwischen Reformation und Parität,' p. 400; cf. J. Rasmussen, 'Bildersturm und Restauration' in *Welt im Umbruch: Augsburg zwischen Renaissance und Barock* (Augsburg, 1981), Vol. III, pp. 95–114.
16 So fierce was the resistance that the City Council was forced to expel the entire Protestant *ministerium* to secure compliance. P. Warmbrunn, *Zwei Konfessionen in einer Stadt*, p. 69.
17 Immenkötter, 'Kirche zwischen Reformation und Parität', p. 402.
18 P. Warmbrunn, *Zwei Konfessionen in einer Stadt*, p. 127.
19 B. Roeck, *Eine Stadt in Krieg und Frieden: Studien zur Geschichte der Reichsstadt Augsburg zwischen Kalenderstreit und Parität*, 2 vols (Göttingen, 1989), p. 124: 'Ergebnisse anderer Untersuchungen lassen den Schluß zu, daß es in der Tat vor allem äußeres Verhalten, "Lebenskreise" waren, um welche sich konfessionelles Bewußtsein kristallisierte und woraus auch ein konfessionsgebundenes Gruppenbewußtsein enstand.' Cf. R. van Dülmen, 'Religionsgeschichte in der historischen Forschung' in H. Berding (ed.), *Wege der neuen Sozial- und Wirtschaftsgeschichte* (Göttingen, 1980), pp. 36–59; E. François, *Die unsichtbare Grenze: Protestanten und Katholiken in Augsburg, 1648–1806* (Sigmaringen, 1991); M. Heckel, 'Autonomia und Pacis

Compositio: Der Augsburger Religionsfrieden in der Deutung der Gegenreformation', *Zeitschrift der Savigny-Stiftung für Rechtsgeschichte, Kanonistische Abteilung* 76 (1959): 141–248; H. Immenkötter, 'Kirche zwischen Reformation und Parität', pp. 391–412; P. T. Lang, 'Die Ausformung der Konfessionen im 16. und 17. Jahrhundert' in J. M. Valentin (ed.), *Gegenreformation und Literatur* (Amsterdam, 1979), pp. 12–19; L. Lenk, *Augsburger Bürgertum im Späthumanismus und Frühbarock* (Augsburg, 1969), esp. pp. 60–7; B. Moeller, *Imperial Cities and the Reformation* (Philadelphia, 1972), esp. pp. 41–115; E. Naujoks, 'Vorstufen der Parität in der Verfassungsgeschichte der schwäbischen Reichsstädte (1555–1648): Das Beispiel Augsburg' in J. Sydow (ed.), *Bürgerschaft und Kirche* (Sigmaringen, 1980), pp. 38–66; W. Reinhard, 'Konfession und Konfessionalisierung in Europa' in idem (ed.), *Bekenntnis und Geschichte: Die Confessio Augustana im historischen Zusammenhang* (Munich, 1980); idem, 'Zwang zur Konfessionalisierung: Prolegomena zu einer Theorie des konfessionellen Zeitalters', *Zeitschrift für historische Forschung* 10 (1983): 257–77; H. Schilling, 'Die Konfessionalisierung im Reich: Religiöser und und gesellschaftlicher Wandel in Deutschland zwischen 1555 und 1620', *Historische Zeitschrift* 246 (1988), pp. 1–45; Warmbrunn, *Zwei Konfessionen in einer Stadt*; E. W. Zeeden, *Die Entstehung der Konfessionen: Grundlagen und Formen der Konfessionbildung im Zeitalter der Glaubenskämpfe* (Munich, 1965); idem, 'Grundlagen und Wege der Konfessionsbildung in Deutschland im Zeitlater der Glaubenskämpfe', *Historischen Zeitschrift* 185 (1958), pp. 249–99.

20 H. Immenkötter, 'Kirche zwischen Reformation und Parität', pp. 403–5.
21 M. Schad, *Die Frauen des Hauses Fugger von der Lilie (15.–17. Jahrhundert)* (Tübingen, 1989), p. 54.
22 E. François, *Die unsichtbare Grenze*, pp. 46–7.
23 K. Muller (ed.), *Instrumenta Pacis Westphalicae. Die Westphälische Friedensverträge* (Bern, 1975), p. 26. Instrumenta pacis osnabrugense (IPO), Art. V, Section 1: 'In reliquis autem inter utriusque Religionis Electores, Principes, Status, omnes et singulos, sit aequalitas exacta mutuaque, quatenus formae reipublicae, constitutionibus Imperii et praesenti conventioni conformis est, ita ut, quod uni parti iustum est, alteri quoque sit iustum.'
24 Ibid., pp. 26–8. IPO, Art. V, Section 4: 'In specie autem quoad civitatem Augustam sint septem Senatores Consilii secretioris ex familiis patriciis delecti, ex his desumpti republicae Praesides duo, vulgo Stadtpfleger dicti, unus sit Catholicus, alter Augustanae Confessionis, ex reliquis quinque tres Catholicae Religioni et duo Augustanae Confessioni addicti. Senatores reliqui senatus, ut vocant, minoris, nec non Syndicii, Assessores Iudicii Urbani aliique Officiales omnes sint aequali numero utriusque Religionis'. Though relegated to minority position in the upper councils, Augsburg's Lutherans retained the right to claim one of the Catholic seats in specific instances, in which Council decisions were thought to be unfairly prejudiced.
25 Ibid., pp. 26–8. IPO, Art. V, Section 5: 'si uno anno duo officia (veluti quaestura et cura annonae vel aedelitii muneris) penes duos Catholicos et unum Augustanae Confessionis sint, eodem anno duo alia officia (veluti Praefectura rei tormentariae et collectarum) duobus ex Augustana Confessioni et uno Catholico commitantur; sequenti autem anno circa haec officia

duobus Catholicis, duo Augustanae Confessioni addicti et uno Catholico, unus Augustanae Confessionis surrogetur'.

26 Ibid., pp. 26–8. IPO, Art. V, Section 7: 'Templorum tamen et scholarum cuique parti suarum cura integra reservetur.'
27 P. Warmbrunn, *Zwei Konfessionen in einer Stadt*, p.181.
28 Ibid., p. 182.
29 L. Link, *Augsburger Bürgertum*, p. 79: 'Über ein Vierteljahr hatten die Kommissionen der beiden Exekutoren mit dem widerspenstigen Rat zu ringen, man ist mit ihnen umgesprungen schlimmer als mit lästigen Bittstellern.'
30 I. Bátori, *Die Reichsstadt Augsburg im 18. Jahrhundert*, p. 20.
31 P. Fassl, 'Wirtschaft, Handel, und Sozialstruktur', p. 470.
32 Historians of Augsburg have long noted the shift in distribution of wealth during the eighteenth century to the advantage of a Lutheran minority, a development that reversed the traditional social and ecomonic composition of the city. See: I. Bátori, 'Reichsstädtisches Regiment, Finanzen und bürgerliche Opposition', pp. 459–60; P. Fassl, *Konfession, Wirtschaft und Politik*, pp. 95–106; E. François, *Die unsichtbare Grenze*, pp. 73–110; J. Hartung, 'Die Augsburger Vermögenssteuer und die Entwicklung der Besitzverhältnisse im 16. Jahrhundert', *Schmollers Jahrbuch* 19 (1895), pp. 867–83; A. Mayr, *Die großen Augsburger Vermögen*, pp. 115–23.
33 E. François, *Die unsichtbare Grenze*, p. 45.
34 F. Junginger, *Geschichte der Reichsstadt Kaufbeuren im 17. und 18. Jahrhundert* (Neustadt a. d. Aisch, 1965), p. 160; P. Wallace, *Communities and Conflict in Early Modern Colmar: 1575–1730* (Atlantic Highlands, 1995), pp. 163–76.
35 E. W. Zeeden, *Die Entstehung der Konfessionen*, p. 181.
36 L. Lenk, *Augsburger Bürgertum*, p. 60: 'Die katholischen Erfolge bedrängten sie, und so schwankten ihre Gemüter in Furcht und Haß.'
37 Christian Friedrich Daniel Schubart as cited in D. Blaufuss, 'Das Verhältnis der Konfessionen in Augsburg 1555 bis 1648: Versuch eines Überblicks', *Jahrbuch des Vereins für Augsburger Bistumsgeschichte* 10 (1976), p. 49: 'Stadt der katholischen und protestantischen Schweineställe'.
38 F. Nikolai, *Beschreibung einer Reise durch Deutschland und die Schweiz im Jahre 1781* (Berlin / Stettin, 1786–87), Vol. 3, pp. 86–7: 'Einerseits bäckt man Toleranzpasteten, andererseits veranstaltet man Bälle, wo nur Katholiken oder nur Protestanten tanzen, oder (man veranstaltet) Verpachtungen von Äckern, wobei der Pächter erst zeigen muß, ob er glaubt, was die Kirche glaubt.'
39 B. Roeck, *Eine Stadt in Krieg und Frieden*, pp. 90–2.
40 E. François, *Die unsichtbare Grenze*, p. 12.
41 T. Nipperdey, *Religion im Umbruch: Deutschland, 1870–1918* (Munich, 1988), p. 155. Cited in E. François, *Die unsichtbare Grenze*, p. 11.
42 Cf. P. Fassl, *Konfession, Wirtschaft und Politik*, pp. 107–22; E. François, *Die unsichtbare Grenze*, pp. 143–243.
43 StadtAA, EWA 59, Miller Tagebuch, p. 1: 'Ach Herr Lehse mich bedenken das Jch sterben muss und / mein Leben Ein Zihl hat. und Jch davon / muss leben so leben wie dem Herrn Sterben so sterben wie dem Herrn / darumb wie lebeben [sic] oder sterben so sein wie des / Herrn. / Christlich leben macht Selig Seelig sterben und Ewige freud Ererben. / Ach Gott Hilft uns alle Dre Stukh Erwerben.'

44 Ibid., p. 12: 'Jm Nahmen Gottes Des Vatters Sohns und / Hailligen Gaistes denn 2 Aprill 1654 der Anfang / genommen. die hoch Gelobte Haillige Drey Faltigkeit / verleihe darzu glükh unnd Seegen und gleich wie Got / der Almechtige durch wunderbarliche weise mich wider aller / menshen vernunft geführt dz auch noh Ein blükh in die / Alte Millerishe Casata thon dorffen unnd dz mit guter furdank / Als Sei Er unsser fernerer Gnädiger Gott und Vatter / Jezt und Alezeit Ammen. Hoch Gebeten und Geprißen Amen.'
45 C. Koslofsky, 'Death and Ritual in Reformation Germany', Ph.D diss., University of Michigan, 1994, p. 23.
46 M. W. Flynn, *The European Demographic System, 1500–1800* (Baltimore, 1981), pp. 13–19. Cf. B. Rajkay, 'Bevölkerungsentwicklung in Augsburg, 1607–1650: Ein Vergleich der Pfarreien St. Anna und St. Moritz', M.A. thesis, University of Augsburg, 1984, pp. 69–71. Cf. R. Mols, *Introduction à la démographie historique des villes d'Europe du XIV au XVIII siècle* (Louvain, 1954), Vol. II, pp. 305–22; Vol. III, pp. 207–11.
47 Whereas scholars have paid much attention to death as a demographic force, they have but recently turned to its cultural and social implications. See: P. Aries, *L'homme devant la mort* (Paris, 1977); M. Vovelle, *Piété baroque et dechristianization en Provence au XVIIIe siècle: Les attitudes devant la mort d'aprés les clauses des testaments* (Paris, 1973); idem, *Mourir autrefois: Attitudes collectives devant la mort aux XVIIe et XVIIIe siècles* (Paris, 1974). Cf. D. Beaver, "Sown in dishonour, raised in glory': Death, Ritual and Social Organization in Northern Gloucestershire, 1590–1690', *Social History* 17 (1992), pp. 389–419; S. Cohn, *Death and Property in Siena, 1205–1800: Strategies for the Afterlife* (Baltimore, 1988); D. Cressy, 'Death and the Social Order: The Funerary Preferences of Elizabethan Gentlemen', *Continuity and Change* 5 (1989), pp. 99–119; C. Koslofsky, 'Death and Ritual in Reformation Germany'; L. Stone, *The Crisis of the Aristocracy, 1558–1641* (Oxford, 1965); S. Strocchia, *Death and Ritual in Renaissance Florence* (Baltimore, 1992).
48 For this discussion, I rely primarily on Koslofsky's useful analysis. See C. Koslofsky, 'Death and Ritual in Reformation Germany', pp. 27–55. Cf. P. Althaus, *The Theology of Martin Luther* (Philadelphia, 1966); L. P. Buck, 'The Reformation, Purgatory, and Perpetual Rents in the Revolt of 1525 at Frankfurt am Main' in P. Bebb and K. Sessions (eds), *Pietas et Societas: New Trends in Reformation Social History: Essay in Memory of Harold J. Grimm* (Kirksville, Mo., 1985); S. Ozment, *The Reformation in the Cities: The Appeal of Protestantism to Sixteenth-Century Germany and Switzerland* (New Haven, 1975).
49 R. Ombres, 'Latins and Greeks in Debate over Purgatory, 1230–1439', *Journal of Ecclesiastical History* 35 (1984), pp. 1–14.
50 J. Le Goff, *The Birth of Purgatory* (Chicago, 1984), esp. pp. 52–95, 154–76. Cf. C. Koslofsky, 'Death and Ritual in Reformation Germany', p. 30.
51 C. Koslofsky, 'Death and Ritual in Reformation Germany', pp. 47–53. Cf. J. Köstlin, *Luthers theologie in ihrer geschichtlichen Entwicklung und in ihren inneren Zusammenhange dargestellt* (Darmstadt, 1968), pp. 207–9, 373–6.
52 C. Koslofsky, 'Death and Ritual in Reformation Germany', p. 52.
53 StadtAA, EWA 59, Miller Tagebuch, p. 8: 'Got dem Almechtigen aber hat Es gefallen nach seinem Götlichen / wüllen dises Kintlein auß disem Jammerthal balt wegg / zuenemmen dann denn 7 Apprill abents zwishen 6

und 7 uhr / sanfft unnd Seelig wider Jnn dem Herrn entshlaffen. / denn 9 Apprill Jnn St Stephans Gots Aker begraben worden inn / des Zacharias Wilden begrabnuß. Got der Herr verleihe unns / seiner zeit auch allen Ein Seeliges Ende unnd neben Jme Eins / fröliche Auferstehung.'
54 Ibid., p. 26: 'entlich / sagt sie nun habe ich meine Herz außgelehrt unnd dankh / meinen lieben Got dz Er mir die Gnad verlihen / solhe zue volbringen. werde auh nun Jnn Gotes / Nahmen sannfft unnd Seelig dahinn sterben / Got beware mich. Unnd Du mein lieber Miller loß mir / dein Hand unnd bleib bei Mir. Die Herrn Doctores haben / Jhr noch ein Herztrünkhlein verehrt oder verordnet. Dz / hat sie getrunken unnd also damit sich auff die seiten / gelegt mein Arm zwishe ihren arm genommen Jre / Handen zue sammen Geshlossen unnd anfangen in die / Zün zue greifen doch Gesicht unnd Gehör auh guten / verstand behalten Aber die sprach manglet doh mit dem / mund unnd handen sovill anzeigen geton man nun / beten solle. Mich angesehen die augen gen Himmell / gewant unnd also inn dem Herrn Seelig entshlaffen / Sanfft unnd still. Got helft uns seiner Zeit auh hinach. / Ammen Ammen Ammen. Da Jst erfolgt sonstag / Abents umb 7 uhr ad diem 7 juni 1654.'
55 Ibid., pp. 87–8: 'Sanfft und Seelig under dem gebet unser / aller / Jhrer lieben angehörigen umbstehenden ... / Der wolle uns allen seiner zeit Seelig hinauf verhelffen / und uns Jnmitelst Jnn seinem Gnädigen shutz und shirm Erhalten.'
56 Ibid., p. 7: 'hats Got doch nit haben wolen / sondern wunderbarliche enderung darein gemacht'.
57 Ibid.: 'so sich alles gantz und gar willig erzeigt worauf Gottes / sonderbarre shickung abzuenemmen.'
58 Ibid., p. 8: 'Got dem Almechtigen aber hat Es gefallen nach seinem Götlichem wüllen dises Kintlein auß disem Jammerthal balt weg zuenemmen'. The use of terms such as 'aber' and 'Jammerthal' suggests a dubious reaction to inexplicable events and a pessimistic view of the world.
59 Ibid., pp. 27–9: 'Nun Empfinde die Handt des Herrn / Welche auß Gerehtem Eiffer unnd Barmherzig / keit mich abermallen rühret. / Jnn deme denn 25 7bris Anno 1654 der Liebe Got / nach seinem Gerechten willen unnd Heilligen Woll / gefallen mein Liebes Töchterlin Susannam mogen / freitags unb halb Sechs uhr auß disem zeitlichen leben / zue seinen Ewigen Frewden Sanfft unnd Stille / abgefordert, Das wir zwaar mit unserm grosen / shmerzen leiden unnd diß nach Gotes Willen / zue unserm Trost wüssen unnd behalten, dz nemlich / durch disen zeitlichen Hintrit nun mehr diß Seelige / Kint inn Ewiger frewd unnd Seeligkeit bei unserm / Erlößer unnd Hailandt Christo Jesu unnd seiner Herzlieben / Mueter Sich herlich befinden wirdt unnd dardurch / viller gefahr unndt Herzlaidt entrunen. Nun der Liebe Got / gebe dem Leib eine sannffte ruhe uns seiner Zeit samtlich / auch Einen Seeligen abshidt unnd neben allen Christ / Glaubigen ann jenem grosem Tag Eine Fröliche / Aufferstehung. Amen. / was angelangent denn gehabten zuestand des Seelig verstor / benen Töchterlins Jst selbiges wie vorngemelt denn / 6 Mai 1654 mitwuchs nachts umb 1/4 stund nach 9 uhr alhier / Durch meine Liebe Hausfraw nun mehr auch Seeligen Anna / Maria geborner Warmbergerin Jnn dise welt geborn / worden wie nun darauff denn 6 Juni wie vorn / gemelt durch denn unserm bedunkhen nach auh allzue /

früe Zeütigen hintrit ehrngemelter meiner Herzl[ieben] Haus / fraw Seeligen dises Susannalin Seelig neben Jhren / andern geshwisterten Jnnsonderheit Sie Zeitlich nit allein / Jhren natürlichen Mueter Milch müßen sonndrn auch / zue mueterloßen weisslin gemacht werden müeßen. / Alß hat doch der Liebe Got herrlich seinn Almacht und / vorsorg Erwüsen unnd inn der that bezeüget. Jnn / deme biß denn 21 7bris 1654 inn solher shöner ge / stalt unnd frisher gueter gesunthait erhalten dz / auch kein stundt wir deswegen etwas klagen könten biß da / malen fieng ein Catarra ann der setzt Jr zimmlich starkh / zue biß entlich denn 24 dis morgens umb 4 uhr dz vergiht / außgebrochen unnd etlich stund continuiert doh wider / abgeloßen unnd Zwar Zimmlich shwach gelegen biß 25 dis alß / dato morgens umb 2 uhr dz vergicht wider ershinen / unnd zwaar nimmer außgesezt biß der Geist außgefarn / beede Taag hat es niemalen geweinet mit den Händtlen / ein wenig gearbeit unnd allerseits gross Hütz gespürt / weßwegen dann auch ordenliche mitell gebraucht die / Herr Doctor Kneillin dise wenige Taag über verordnet / hate. nun Dem Lieben Got gat es nun allso gefallen / auch meine Alte wunden vonn newen mir auff zu reissen. Der selbige wolle meiner shonen unnd umb / seines Lieben Sohns Jesu Christi willen mir meine / Sünden verzeihen unnd vergeben nach seinem / Götlichen unnd Gnädigen willen mih verbinden / unnd wider Haillen.'

60 Ibid., p. 27: 'Nun der Liebe Got / gebe dem Leib eine sannffte ruhe uns seiner Zeit samtlich / auch Einen Seeligen absidt unnd neben allen Christ / Glaubigen ann jenem grosem Tag Eine Fröliche / Aufferstehung. Amen.'

61 Ibid., p. 85: 'Anno 1674 denn 31 Januari / hat der Liebe Got nach seinem Heilligen willen mir darinn / ein hartes abermalen erzeiget Jnn deme Er mir meine / Herzliebe Haußfraw von der seiten durch den zeitlichen / Dot entzogen.'

62 Ibid.: 'Ach Lieber Got wie hete Jch mit meinen / Kindern Jhre noch sowoll bedorfft sovil als wir / bedenken können. es hat aber deiner Götlichen weisheit / also gefallen und zwaar auch uns alle mit solcher / Gnad und Barmherzigkeit uns dabei angebliket / dz wir dir billich darum danken sollen und dz / nit underlassen wan wir bedenken dz aller unser / Zwekh und aigentliches Zill einig dahin gerichtet / Jst dz wir verlangen tragen Seelig zue Sterben / unnd dz Ende unsers Glaubens davon zue tragen / Ein Seeliges Ende vonn diser welt und einen seligen / Anfang der Ewigen Seeligkeit wornach alle Glaubige'.

63 Ibid., p. 86: 'mit diser meiner Herzliebe Haußfr. sel. habe Jch woll / Herz Jnniglich freuntlich und liebreich in der Forcht / Gotes gelebet vonn Anno 1654 biß 1674'.

64 Ibid.: 'Auser Jre mehrmelige / Leibes Krankheiten die shonn vor 14 Jahren ange-/fangen und fast nimmer mehr verlassen. Ach mein Got / wie meniche herzliche Wehklagen habe Jch vernomen mit / shmerzhafften gemüthe. O wie meniche notwendige / getrewe mitleidende freuntshafft habe ich beigetragen / und Got gebeten dz er uns wolle Gnädig sein. / Alle ordentliche mitel suchten wir dabei und hofften / durch Götliche Hülfe dz leben zue fristen.'

65 Ibid., p. 87: 'Aber / alles wolte nit nach unserm Wuntsch zue zeitlichen / besserung sich shiken sondern Got sterkte uns woll Jn / unser Hofnung durch mermelig Menigfeltig Erquik stunden / darbei wir verhofften es

wurde auch die zeitliche besserung / nit ausen bleiben damit wir also in Forcht und / Hofnung unser leben zuegebracht.'
66 Ibid., p. 87: 'Darum sagte ich dz der Liebe Got auch darin Barmherzig-/keit erwisen dz er neben dem gedult auch die Hofnung / verlihen und neben der Hofnung auch die Gnad dz dz shwere / Ansehen der obhanden gewesten Krankheit sich vor mehrerm / shmerzen geendiget.'
67 C. Koslofsky, 'Death and Ritual in Reformation Germany', p. 53.
68 Ibid., p. 54.
69 StadtAA, EWA 59, Miller Tagebuch, p. 15: 'Balt nach diser Geburt unnd Annoch inn der Kintbet / denn 3 Juni entwichenen Mitwuch nachts umb / 12 Uhren ruhte unns der Liebe Got nach seinem Väter / lichen Willen abermallen Hart Heim Jnn deme / Meine Liebe Hausfraw mit einem sohen Erbarmlih / Bauch Grimmen überfallen worden dz wir noh in selber / Stund Dr. Kneilin unnd fr. Daniel Östreicherin neben / meiner Gl. Mueter fr. S. Michael Miller hollen lassen / da wir dann samtlich vermeinet es seien shmerzen / vonn der Muter herrührent. Zue welchen man an orden / lichen mitelen nix ermanglen lassen. entlich in der nacht / ordnete Herr Dr. Kneilin ein Clistier so sie Zu sich ge / nommen welhes wol materia außgefürth aber die / shmerzen nit gemündert. Donnerstags früe ordnete / Er widerum eines welhes abermallen mitags / umb 10 uhren genommen worden so Zwaar vonn Jhr / kommen wenig und sovill als nix materia außgefürt / über dz die shmerzen nun vermehrt unnd so groser / Jammer darauff efolgt dz auch dem Jenigen so es nit / gesehen unmöglich Zu beshreiben'.
70 Ibid., p. 16: 'Zum Donnerstag / abents als keine besserung folgen wolte ordnete / Herr Dr. Kneilen einn Herz unnd Shmerz Trünklen / neben einer Salb denn Bauch so noh ershreklihe grimmen / erlite damit Zue shmiern. Beedes wurden selben / abents gebraucht unnd inn der nacht ließ die / Erbarmliche shmerzen zwaar nach aber grosse / Shwacheit erfolgte darauff dz sie vonn selbsten / auf kein Fuß Lupfen unnd sich weder zue einer / noh andern seiten hinlegen noch wenden könnte'.
71 Ibid., p. 17: 'Freitags mit tag der magen Sich anfangen erbrechen / unnd auff 2 mall woll bei Zwei maß gallisher materia / vonn Jr gestoßen darauff Sie Zwaar auch etwas besserung / befunden Zwaar gar nit lang dann neben dem dz sie Jrem / Herzen unnd Magen Jmmer zue geshrien unnd Got der Almechtigen / trewlich umb Hülff unnd Beistand Gebeten'.
72 Ibid., p. 18: 'Samstag vormitag / hat sie vernomen dz Herr M. Hopfer Jhr lieber Herr Gevater / wolte bei Jr einkheren darauff Sie sich sehr gefrewt / unnd auch ernstlich angeordnet dz mann alsbalt / denn Jenigen Gevater Pfennig so einn büchlein / Herrn Johan Arnts mit Shiltcrotengefaß unnd / mit silber souber angefast gewesen darauff den / Namen des lieben Todtlins Jüngsten Söhnlin Augustin / drauf gestochen ware. Zuvor hinauß shiken / solte so auch beshehen Herr Hopffer aber wüste nit / dz so gefärlih stunde unnd waren Jme damalen / auch sonsten geshäfft angefallen dz er nit kommen'. Regarding the economic relationship between Matheus and Matheus Hopfer the Younger, see the discussion in Chapter 3.
73 Ibid., pp. 19–20: 'unnd mit gaar Beherzeten Worten unndt / Gebärten Mich angesprochen dem nach Sie nun Jhre / Seele Got dem Almechtigen Abermallen bevollen / als seie es nun ann dem vonn mir auch freüntlich Abshid / zue nemmen solte mich darab nit entsezen dan es Jst Gotes Willen

fürnemlich erstens bedanket Sie sich aller / Trew unnd gut Taten mit villen umbstenden mit pit / Jhre liebe hinderlassne Kinderlin mit Zucht unnd Christlichem / Wandel Zue Auferziehen unnd mit gutem Exempel / vorzue gehen. Jnnsonderheit auch Jhre Liebe Alte Fraw / Fr Mueter Ernstlich anbevollen mit dem selbst ermessenen / Trost Sie wüß woll Jch werds nit verloßen unnd sovill / ann mir Kein Leidt verursachen. So dann bat Sie um / verzeihung woh Sie mich beleidigt hete. Jnndem übrig / wüste Sie anderst nit zue sagen als dz wir eben mit einader / Gelebt wie Sies hofte vor Got zue verantwurten / unnd es auh andern neben Christen zue gutem exempel / werde geleichtet haben. Darauff mit betrübten / meinem Gemüth unnd Herzen mih Jhrer seits frewdig / umbfangen unnd nach Herzlichem Jnbrünstigen / Kuß adio gesprochen darbei sagente nun mein Herz / Lieber shatz Jnn diser welt werden wir einander nit lang / mehr sehen Aber Jnn dem Ewigen Seeligen Leben / wollen unnd werden wir Einander wider finden'.
74 Ibid., p. 24: 'Alß nun / solhes meine Liebe Haußfraw Seel. ersehen wolt / Sie alßbalt denn Buben haben denn sie herzlih / geküsset bevollen solle Sich Gotseelig unnd / From Gehorsam gegenn mir unnd allen / seinen / obren erzeigen mit Herzbrechenden Worthen / denn selbigen unnd alle Jhre Kinder Got dem / Herrn bevollen.'
75 Ibid., p. 21: 'Disenn actum so Sie mit mir gepflogen hat eine / guete viertel stund gewehret alles mit groser / verwunderung Der umbstehenden. Darunder alte / leuthe die bei villen Sterbenden leüten vormals Sih / befunden solhes unverzagt unnd freüdiges gemuth / aber niemallen bei dem Absterben befunden das / eine solhe Personn die inn solher shwacheit gelegen / dergleichen Herzhafftigkeit unversehens erzeiget hete.'
76 C. Koslofsky, 'Death and Ritual in Reformation Germany', p. 297 and passim.
77 StadtAA, EWA 59, Miller Tagebuch, p. 26: 'Denn 11 Juni Jst die Leicht begangen worden / inn dem wagnerishen haus in heilliger creutz gasse / drein wir damallen gewohnet. die liecht / Predig geshehe durch Herrn Mag. Tomas Hopffer / beim heilligen creutz nahmitag die begrebnus in / St Stephan Gotes Akher inn der Zacharias Wildisher / begrabnuß. Alles beshehe inn volkreicher / mänge unnd der leicht tex war genommen.'
78 StadtAA, EWA 265, *Erneuerte Policey-, Zierd-, Kleider-, Hochzeit-, Kind-Tauf-, und Leich-Ordnung* (Augsburg 1683), Section 202.
79 StadtAA, EWA 59, Miller Tagebuch, pp. 29–30: 'Hieneben folgen die Leicht uncosten /

	fl.
Erstlich der Kintbet Kellerin so Jhr gewart	4.00
denn beeden megten…Jeder fl. 4	8.00
dem Teller so das Kind tragen	1.30
des Lieben Vatern Magt weils Jm Hauß / doch klage	1.30
für dz doten bährlein	0.45
Denn Cantores	3.00
Denn Beter	0.12
3 sakhell	0.30
gossenknecht	0.12
gemein amtgelt	0.12

das Amenn Leicht zusagen und Ein tuch / zu machen	2.30
dem Samuel mit trünkhgelt	1.12
fur ein zu mehre innblonion	1.00
Trinkgelt für die gelihene / Tuch vonn denn Hr. Hosennestel	0.12
Summa	24.45

80 C. Koslofsky, 'Death and Ritual in Reformation Germany', pp. 137–201. Cf. R. Lenz (ed.), *Leichenpredigten als Quelle historischer Wissenschaften*, 3 vols (Cologne, 1975; Marburg, 1979; 1984); R. Mohr, *Protestantische Theologie und Frömmigkeit im Angesicht des Todes während des Barockzeitalters* (Marburg, 1964); E. Winkler, *Die Leichenpredict im deutschen Luthertum bis Spener* (Munich, 1967).

81 StadtAA, EWA 59, Miller Tagebuch, pp. 41–6.

82 Ibid., p. 41: 'Der liebe Got aber wolte Zeitliches / gedeyen darzue nit geben sondern nach seinem Götlichen / Willen unnd des gueten Herrn Schorers Seel. offtmaligem / Eiferigem piten unnd flehen Jne auß disem Jammerthal / Zue seinem Ewigen Frewden Leben Nemmen und Abfordern.'

83 Ibid., p. 42: 'Deswegen / nah gethaner beicht unnd erlangter absolution auch des teüren / shazes theilhafftig worden da Er aber guete Zeit Zuvor unnd / auch hernach wenig unnd fast gaar nix geredet meinstens / allein geshinen als ob Er mit der Zungen nit recht fort / Könnte. mag aber woll sein dz Jme ein Paroxismus oder shläglin / angestoßen. Auß seinem erweißenden Aifer unnd über sich / hebung der Augen aber könnten wir woll spüren dz Er zue dem gebet grose Andacht inn dem Er solhes mit auf und Zue / thuen des mundes erwisen dz mann gleichsam die worth / spüren können dz mit eifer nach gesprochen unnd vonn / selbsten etliche gebet solher gestalt angefangen.'

84 Ibid., pp. 42–3: 'die gantz / Zeit über aber niemalen mit keinem under allen etwas des Absterbens halber geredt. noh vill weniger Abshid ge / nommen darab sich zwaar inn disem fall nit sonders / Zue verwundern weillen Er geraume Zeit vorher gegen / seiner L[ieben] Hausfraw Jnn sonderheit unnd auch dem / andern gesamten Kindern offtmals unnd guete Zeit Zuvor / vonn seinem Sterben gleichsamen Geprediget und gesungen / dz eines und anders wenns Jnn der Forcht des Herrn wird / nach denkhen genug Zue behalten ursach hat. Er wirdt / gleichsam gedacht haben was soll Jch ferners sagen wer / mir folgen will wird meine reden vorhin observirt / haben unnd sich aniezo deß errindern dis woll müese.'

85 See discussion in Chapter 3.

86 The printed funeral sermon survives. Cf. StadtBA, 4° Aug., 821-299. StadtAA, EWA 59, Miller Tagebuch, pp. 45–6: 'Sondern es könte auch kein Mensh annderst sagen als / dz Er ein Rechter Tapfferer Redtlicher unnd Auffrichtiger / biderman geweßen Jnn seinem wandel unnd handel mäniglih / guete sadisfaction geben witwen und weißen Jme wol / bevollen sein laßen unnd seinen Kindern mit guetem / Exempel solher gestalt vorgangen dz zue wüntshen were / andere mehr nachfolgen hete. Gotes Worth liebte Er / trefflich und sonderlich ware er Ein Aiferiger beter / wie Er dann Täglich seine gewise / Stunden zu beten / hate derinn Er seine Andacht sovill die menshliche shwacheit zu / last Excercirt unnd gewiß vonn Got dem Almechtigen / auch vill mit seinem angedehtigen gebet erhalten unnd gewonen. / was will Jch aber vill melden Lieben der du diß lessen wirdst. / Laß dirs allein dienen dz diser Herr Anthoni

214 Notes

Christoff Shorer / der Elter Seel gedächtnus Ein rehter Gotseliger bider / man gewesen. Denn Got lieb gehabt. Jme mit leiblih / unnd Geistlichem Seegen begegnet. Er hate zwaar / auh seine Creütz unnd shwere betrübnusen auff under / shidtliche weege. die gehören aber zue der liebe Christi.'

87 StadtAA, EWA 59, Miller Tagebuch, p. 77: 'Anno 1664 denn 10 Marzo ist mein Gel[iebter] Vater Herr / Michael Miller Jnn dem Herrn Jesu Christo Seelig / Entshloffen inn dem 60te Jaar seines Alters. / die leicht Predig ist Gehalten vom Herrn Fustennegger bei dem / H[eiligen] Creutz Jn der Newen Kürchen. Alwoh Er auch begraben worden / Jnn dem Chor vor dem Alter. / Leicht Text wahr / Aus dem Psalmen Davids / Beville dem Herrn deinen weeg und hoffe auff Jhn / Er wirdt wolmachen / seinen Ganzen Lebens Lauf habe Jch aufgesetzt / und dem Herrn Fusennegger eingehendiget dem Er / vonn wort zue worth also abgelesen. / davon hiebeigeheirt vonn mir / undershriben die warhoffte copia.'

88 From Luther's translation: 'Befehl dem HERRN deine wege / Und hoffe auff in / er wirds wol machen.' A more modern rendering occurs in *The New English Bible* (Oxford, 1971): 'Commit your life to the Lord; trust in him and he will act.'

89 StadtBA, 4° Aug. 821-215. B. Hopfer, *Traur-Gedicht auff den betrübten seeligen Abschied auß diesem Leben deß weiland ehrenvesten und Wohl-Fürnehmen Herren Michael Müllers Berühmten Handels-Herren in Aubsburg* (Augsburg, 1664).

90 Ibid.: 'Hier mag kein Schirm noch Schild absehren /
Noch wer er cleich von härtesten Stahl /
Und Diamandten überal /
So scharff-gewetzte Spieß abkehren.'

91 Ibid.: 'Jedoch der Ruhm erblasset nicht /
Allein der schwache Leib zerbricht.'

92 Ibid.: 'Von dem / was jhm am liebsten war /
Zureisen auff entlegne Strassen /
Dort / wo der kalte Nord regiert /
Damit inmahl erlangt würd /
Was lang von frommen Creutzes Hertzen /
Verlanget ward nicht ohne Schmertzen.'

The stanza refers to Michael's efforts to raise money on behalf of Holy Cross Church.

93 Ibid.: 'Und wer diß nicht gedultig trägt /
Der mag nicht / sonder falsches Gleissen /
Der Herren Christi Diener heissen.'

94 StadtBA, 2° Aug. 202-685. J. P. Scheffer, *Die früh- und wohl-vollbrachte Lebens-Schiffarth der weylande Wohl-Edlen/Hoch-Ehren und Tugend-Begabten Fr. Helena/geborner Schorerin Des Wohl-Edlen/Vesten/unnd Groß-Achtbaren Herrn Matthäus Millers Wohl-Vornehmen Handelß-Herren in Augsburg hertzgeliebtester Hauß-Frauen* (Strasbourg, 1674).

95 Ibid.: 'Alßo muß auch deß Menschen Leben /
Auff dieser Sünden-Meeres-Fluth /
Mehr mahl entanckert umbher schweben /
Durch vieler Trübsaals-Wellen Wuth /
Eh es am rechten Orth kan gründen /
Und die erwünschte Ruh-Statt finden.'

96 Ibid.: 'Alda der Schiffs-Herr Sie empfangen /
Als Seinen längst-vermählten Schatz /
Und Ihr nach allem Hertz-Verlangen /
Gegeben den bestimbten Platz /
Daß Sie jetzt süsse Engels-Freude /
Geneüßt / nach mittern Schiffarths-Leyde.'

97 Ibid.: 'Ihr aber nemt den Wittwer-Tittel /
Herr Miller / höchst betrübter Mann /
Weil hier Gott selbsten steht im Mittel /
Mit Ihm-gelassnem Willen an /
Und denckt / daß der die Farth geendet /
Der alles Unß zum besten wendet.'

98 StadtAA, EWA 59, Miller Tagebuch, p. 93. See also the discussion in Chapter 1.
99 StadtBA, S 40 Leichenpredigten 269–9.
100 StadtAA, EWA 59, Miller Tagebuch, pp. 85–9.
101 Ibid., p. 89: 'Dise meine Herzliebe Haußfraw Seel. Jst begraben bei / St. Anna Jnn dem Gotsäkerlin in Einem Begreb-/nuß die ich ekaufft vonn dem Gabriel Beg [sic] / hate zuegehört dem Maximilian Mair. Dessen / Wapen von Metal auf dem Stein gewesen / werde nun ein Newes darauf ordnen. / die Brf darüber sein ordentlich außgefertigt. / Haben mit Ankouffs fl. 27 noch uncosten costet / die begrebnuß aber gehöret mein Aigen. / sie Jst bei der eröfnung gantz New und nit einen / bein sonsten darin gefunden worden.

	fl.
der ankoff des grabs costete	27.00
dem stein mezel fuer dem grab / stein	40.00
dem selben zue legen	3.00
ein zue mauren	1.36
dem lumanit trinkgelt	1.30
dem Weienmeir die Brf. fertigen	1.30
[Summa]	73.36

102 StadtAA, EWA 614, Kauff-Brief über eine begräbnus in St. Anna Kirchen in Gotts-Ackerlen gegen Herrn Matthäo Miller allhier vom Gabriel Beegen, 14 February 1674.
103 C. Koslofsky, 'Death and Ritual in Reformation Germany', pp. 57–67. See also: P. Aries, *The Hour of Our Death* (Harmondsworth, 1983), pp. 29–92; S. Basset (ed.), *Death in Towns: Urban Responses to the Dying and the Dead,*

216 Notes

1000–1600 (London, 1992); H. Derwein, *Geschichte des Christlichen Friedhofs in Deutschland* (Frankfurt/M, 1931).
104 J. F. Rein, *Das gesamte augspurgische Evangelische Ministerium in Bildern und Schriften von den ersten Jahren der Reformation Lutheri bis auf Anno 1748* (Augsburg, 1749), p. 142: 'da er nun in seinem Amt allenthalben grossen grossen Eifer, absonderlich in Bestraffung der Widersprecher der Wahrheit bezeuget und viele Widerwärtigkeiten erduldet'. Riß was born on 26 April 1626, the son of a Lutheran pastor in Rothenburg ob der Tauber; he received his basic education in Rothenburg and at Augsburg's St Anna Collegium before graduating to the universities in Marburg and Strasbourg. In 1657, after seven years as a tutor (*ephorus*) to the sons of the Pfalzgraf of the Rheinland, Riß became Archdeacon, that is, first assistant pastor, of the evangelical Church of the Franciscans in Augsburg. Four years later, he moved to the Church of the Holy Cross, where he remained until 1684.
105 StadtAA, EWA 551, Tome II, Response by Georg Philip Riß, 16 May 1662: 'nach dem loblichen wolgegründeten Exempelm in der Kirchen Gottes, so an Christo dem Ertzbischoff unserer Seelen, dem lieben Propheten und Aposteln nach der überseeligen Reformation Zeit an allem getrewen Hürten und Lehrern…an den Predigern im Augsburg auch in der euseristen Betrangnus und Verfolgungs Zeit geleuchtet, umb der eusersten unumbgänglichen Noth willen, hat müssen ergriffen werden und dises auß dem einigen grund Hl. Göttlicher Schrifft auß Lieb der Warheit umb der Ehre Gottes und der Menschen Seeligkeit willen, welches ich gethan mit gebürendem ernst und eifer…dann ja die Papstish Lehrer alhier so shrifft- so mündtlich kein Fleiß sparen mit ihren Lugen den einfalttigen zweifelhaffte Gedanken zu machen ob nicht die Papstische Religion die rechte Religion sey'.
106 Ibid., p. 132. Cf. StadtAA, EWA 552, Tome I.
107 Ibid., p. 142.
108 StadtAA, EWA 551, Tome II.
109 Ibid.
110 One might translate it as 'The Mouse that Ate Out'.
111 StadtAA, EWA 551, Tome II, 22 April 1662.
112 StadtAA, EWA 551, Tome II, 20 August 1663. The funeral in question was that of Magdalena Elizabetha Gardin, the late wife of Nicolaus Wollwein. The text does not survive.
113 Ibid., UK, 20 August 1663.
114 Ibid., Fragestuckhe, 20 August 1663.
115 Ibid., Interrogatoria, 20 August 1663.
116 E. François, *Die unsichtbare Grenze*, passim.
117 B. Roeck, *Eine Stadt in Krieg und Frieden*, p. 119–21.

Conclusion

1 StadtAA, EWA 59, Miller Tagebuch, p. 7: 'Anno 1650 denn 25 Julli ann dem Tage Jacobi hat mir vor ehrngedahte / meine Liebe Hausehr Zum Andern Mall Einn Sohnlein gebohrn / inn dz Jammerthall / diser welt Morgens früh ein viertell / nach Zwey uhren welhes denn selben Tag nachmitag Jnn / der Evangelishen Pfarr Kürchen St. Anna nah der Abent /

Predig vom Herrn [ ] Getaufft worden unndt / bei derselbigen denn Nahmen Philip Jacob bekommen. / die Gevatern seinn gewesen Herr M. Philip Weber Pfarherr / unnd Senior bei St. Anna Herr Hanns Jacob Miller Älter / unnd Gabriel Hopffer vonn Nürmberg neben vorgemelter / Fr. Sara Hanns Jerg Rauhwölffin Alle selbst inn person.'
2 Ibid., p. 36: 'Jst ein gueter / fleißiger mann unnd vonn dem Herrn Veter Mag. Hopfer / mir regühmet worden.'
3 Ibid., p. 38.
4 Ibid., p. 39: 'A diem 28. 7ber habe Jch Jnn dem Nahmen Gotes denn Philip Jakob / neben dem Veter Michael inn die Cost Zue dem Herrn Rectori / nach Memmingen gethon Nahmens M. J. Conrad Hörman / Pfarherr zue Berg und Rector der Schuelen in Memmingen einem / Gaar Feinem und Gottseeliger Mann.'
5 Ibid., p. 40.
6 Ibid., pp. 97–8: 'Anno 1674. / Jnn dem monat [] hat mein Sohn Philip Jacob mir eröfnet / die Ehrliche zue Neigung zue des verstorbnen Hr. Hieronimo Mehrer / sel. Jungfr. Tochter Jungfr. Anna Maria Mehrerin. / Worauf Jme reiflich zue gemüth geführt was der Ehestand / Erfordere. Seine gute Jntent aber blibe fest gestelt / und wurde Jch demnach resolvierend mit der Jungfraw / Herrn Beiständ Herrn Oto Lauginger und Herrn Davidt / von Steten selbsten zue reden. Die deswegen Jhrer / Beistand Jhrer Meinung eingehellet und dergleichen / gegen affecto verspürend mir angedeutet / worauff denn Jn Gotes Namen Eine ordentliche / Werbung bei obgemelten Herrn Beistanden angestelt / erfolget den [] durch Herrn Baltas Miller Meinen / geehrten Herrn Shweher und Herrn Thomas Miller Meinen / gel. Bruder. die nun gewühriges Ja Worth erlanget / also dz der Hochzeitliche Ehren Tag auf dem [] / bestelt und die Copulation und Malzeit inn Herrn Oto / Laugingers Behaussung denn Ersten und Anderen Tag / nach grosszugigen oberkeitlichen vergünstigung Gotlob glüklich vol- /zogen worden.'
7 StadtAA, UK 9.12 / 278, Teilbrief, 17 February 1661.
8 His heirs were assessed fl. 27 kr. 38 in 1674. Of this sum, Anna Maria could claim no more than one-quarter. StadtAA, Steuerbücher 1674, p. 97c.
9. StadtAA, UK 9.17 / 283, Abkommenbrief, 18 January 1686.
10 StadtAA, EWA 59, Miller Tagebuch, p. 98.
11 Matheus did not share the opinion of modern social and cultural historians that the wedding celebration was a moment of cardinal social and cultural importance. See L. Roper, 'Going to Church and Street: Weddings in Reformation Augsburg', *Past and Present* 106 (1985): 62–101; M. Segalen, *Love and Power in the Peasant Family* (Oxford, 1983).
12 StadtAA, Steuerbuch 1674.
13 StadtAA, Steuerbuch, 1685. It is difficult to attribute the increase in property to any single cause. Philip Jakob's new wealth might have been the result of business success. It might also have come from his paternal inheritance.
14 StadtAA, Reichsstadt Akten 226, Stadtkanzlei, Transporte 1660–89, 10 November 1685. Cf. StaatsAA, Reichsstädte Literalien, Augsburg Nr. 562, Grundbuch, p. 308.
15 StadtAA, Repertorien 39, Augsburger Amterbesetzung, 1548–1806.

218 Notes

16 StadtAA, Reichsstadt Akten, 678, Oberpflegamt, Protokollbeilagen 1685–9, 6 March 1687. The guardians accused Philip Jakob of withholding his son's inheritance, which had been invested in the firm. In its financial arrangements as well as its violent disagreements, it resembles closely Matheus's dispute with the widow of his brother Daniel, Maria Stemmer.
17 L. B. Alberti, *The Family in Renaissance Florence*, p. 43. The passage occurs in Lorenzo's charge to his sons, including Leon Battista.
18 See, for example, H. Kamen, *The Iron Century: Social Change in Europe, 1550–1660* (New York, 1971), p. 195.
19 See M. Walker, *German Home Towns: Community, State, and General Estate: 1648–1871* (Ithaca, 1971), passim.
20 'Weillen dann nun Du aller Liebster Herr Jesu Christe Jnn / deinem heilligen worth unns wüssen lassen unnd beteurest / Warlich warlich Jch sage euch was Jhr denn Vater biten werdet / Jnn meinem Nahmen dz würdt er euch geben Johann am 16 / Also bitte Jch dich himmlisher Vater umb Deines Lieben Sohns / Jesu Christi willen du wollest disem unnd allen meinen / Lieben Kindern auch die Gnade Deines Heilligen Geistes Gnädiglih / verleihen der Jhnen die wahre Forcht Gotes anzünde welhe Jst / der weisheit anfang unnd die rechte Klugkeit wer darnoh Thut / des Lob bleibet Ewiglich. beseelige Sie auch mit deinen wahren / Erkantnuß behüete Sie vor aller Abgoterei unnd Falsher Lehre / laß Sie Jnn dem wahren Seeligmachenden Glauben und Jnn / aller Gotseeligkeit aufwaxen unnd darin biß am Ende ver / haren. Gib Jhnen Ein Glaubiges Gehorsames und Düemietiges / Herz auch die rechte weißheit unnd verstant dz Sie wachsen unnd zu / nemmen ann weisheit alter unnd Gnade bei Got und den menshen / Pflanze Jnn Jhr Herz die Liebe Deines Götlichen worths Das Sie / seyen andachtig Jnn Gebet unnd Gotes dienst Ehrerbietig / gegen die Diener des Worths unnd gegen Jederman aufrichtig / Jnn Hantlung Shamhafftig Jnn Gebärden Zuchtig in Siiten / warhafftig Jnn worthen Trew in werkhen Fleissig in geshäfften / Glükhselig inn verrichtung Jhres berufs unnd Amts / Verstendig in Sachen richtig inn Allen Dingen. Sanfftmütig / unnd freüntlich gegen Alle Menshen. / Behuete sie vor aller Ärgernuß diser Welt so voller argens Jst / dz sie nit verführet werden durch böse Gesellshafft las / Sie nit Jnn shlemmen unnd unzucht gerathen dz Sie Jhnen Jhr leben nit selbst verkürzen auch andere leüthe nit beleidigen / Seye ihr Schutz inn allerlei gefahr das Sie nit plötzlih umbkommen / laß mich Ja Herr nit unehr unnd shande sondern Frewde unnd Ehre / ann Jhnen erleben dz durch sie auh dein Reich vermehret unndt / die Zahl der Glaubigen Gross werde. dz Sie auh in deinem / Himmel umb deinen Tish hersitzen als die himmlishe Öhlzweige / unnd diech mit allen Außerwelthen Loben Ehren und Preisen / mögen. Durch Jesum Christum unserem Herrn Amen.' Ibid., pp. 36–7.
21 Cf. *The New English Bible with the Apocrypha* (New York, 1971).
22 StadtAA, EWA 59, Miller Tagebuch, p. 37.
23 J. H. G. von Justi, *Die Grundfeste zu der Macht und Glückseeligkeit der Staaten* (1761).

Index

absolutism, 58
account, merchant, vii, 15; *see also* ego documents; *ricordanze*
accountability, 76–7, 81–3, 101, 154
acumen, 101–2, 105–6, 153
affection, *see* emotion
Alberti, Leon Battista, 12–15, 43, 49–50, 52, 56, 57, 62, 83, 85–7, 97, 153, 155
Albrecht, Archduke of Austria, 25
Allegory of Commerce, 63, 64
Alms Lord (*Almosenherren*), 66
Alms Office (*Almosenamt*), 66, 184n. 91
Alsted, Johann, Heinrich, 89
Altenstetter, Daniel, 147
Ambtmann, Franz Christoph, 27
Amsterdam, 28, 101
Anna, St, Church of, 67, 71, 103–4, 136, 141, 142
Anna, St, Collegium, 150
Anna Raiser Foundation, 68, 69–70, 71, 116
apologia, 1, 7; *see also* ego document, memoir
Arigoni, Marc Antonius, 7
Aristotle, 14–15, 20, 85
Associate (*Beisitzer*), 65; *see also* Marriage Court
Augsburg, Bishop of, 53, 119; bureaucracy in, 53–6; charity in, 65–6, 67–9; coinage in, 188n. 4; confessional tension in 120–2, 143–6; crisis in 24, 93; death in, 125; Discipline Ordinance of, 63, 65; Guild Rising in, 54, 91; hierarchical society in, 91–3; *Hochstift*, 119; Interim, 119; multiple confessions in, 118; population in, 24, 25; recovery in, 94; Reformation Ordinance of, 118; Religious Peace of, 69, 117–18, 119, 120, 144, 147; social mobility in, 91–2; street addresses, 159n. 7; tax rates in 159n. 6; textile production in, 24, 27; topography of, 87; Vicar General of, 143; wealth in, 23, 91–4
Augustine, St, 15, 32
authority, charismatic, 53; patriarchal, 21, 53
autobiography, 15, 16–17, 31; *see also* ego document, memoir

bankruptcy, of Daniel Miller (brother), 100–2; *see also* Miller, Daniel (brother)
baptism, 20
Bátori, Ingrid, 55–6
Baumgartner, 92
Baur, 7
Baur, Hans Jakob, 75
Baur, Johannes, 39
Bavaria, 25, 54, 119, 145
Beck, 76
Beck, Matthias Friderich, 69
Beg, Gabriel, 141
Beza, Theodore, 50
Biel, Gabriel, 144
birth, 17, 22
Bocklerin, Regina (sister), 106
Bolzano, 70
bourgeois, definition of, 149; Matheus Miller as, 154
Bracciolini, Poggio, 49
Brahms, Johannes, 163n. 57
Bruni, Leonardo, 48–9
Bucer, Martin, 65
Building Master (*Baumeister*), 54, 55
Building Office (*Bauamt*), 56
bureaucracy, historical studies of, 57–60; Max Weber's theory of, 53, 54, 55, 56–7, 59
Burgau, 119
burgher, autonomous, Matheus as, 154
Burgomaster, 5, 48, 54, 55

220 Index

burial, 20; historical development of, 141
Bursar (*Austeiler*), 66
business, 42; of Gabriel Miller (uncle), 6, 7; of Hans Jakob Miller (uncle), 6, 7; of Matheus Miller, 27–8; of Michael Miller (father), 6, 7; of Philip Jakob Miller (son), 152

Cajetan, *see* Vio, Thomas de, Cardinal Cajetan
Calendar Conflict (*Kalendarstreit*), 69, 120
calico–printing, 27
Calvin, John, 50
Canisius, Peter, 120
capitalism, 58–9
career, 1
Carmelites, Discalced, 120
Caroline Constitution, 5, 65, 93, 119
catechism, 144
charity, 89; confessionalization in, 68–9
Charles V, Emperor, 5, 8, 92, 119
chronicle, 15; *see also* ego documents, memoir
church, Lutheran definition of, 50; state–controlled, 118
Cicero, 13, 48, 50, 52, 57, 76, 83, 85–7, 97, 114
civility, meaning of, 13; 163n. 48
clientage, 6
Coler, Johannes, 21, 46
Collector (*Einnehmer*), 54
Colmar, 122
Cologne, 5, 6
commemoration, 154; *see also* remembrance
Comenius, Johann Amos, 8
commune (*Zunft*), 54
Confessio Augustana, 117, 119, 142, 146, 155
confession, 2, 19, 116–48, 154–5; in Jürgen Habermas's theory, 59; impact on Augsburg's Lutheran community, 120–1; inadequacies of, 130, 136
confessionalism, 19; limits of, 129;

Matheus Miller's attitude toward, 124
confessionalization, 117–23; definitions of, 117; historical studies of, 122–4; meaning of, 147
continuity, 149, 151–2, 157
Council, Secret, 3, 5, 54, 65, 81, 119
Council, Small, 119
Couvreur, David, 28
credibility and creditworthiness, 6, 9, 83, 153–4; *see also* reputation
Crophius, Johannes, 39
crypt, 141–2
cuius regio, eius religio, 119
custodian (*Zechpfleger*), 70–81, 152; history of, 70–1; duties of, 73–4, 78

death, 9, 17, 22, 116–48, 154; as basis of solidarity, 133; Christian fortitude in, 135; descriptions of, 135; Lutheran theology of, 125, 139; of Matheus Miller, 157; of Thomas Miller (brother), 99; social functions of, 131
Deibold, Sigmund, 4
Dekker, Rudolf, 18
diary, vii, 15, 17, spiritual, 15, 16; *see also* ego document, memoir
dowry, 10, 33–4, 106, 151

economy, domestic, 12
education, 62; business, 4, 7–8; humanist, 1, 3, 50; of Philip Jakob Miller (son), 150, 155–6
Egger, Alexius, 39
ego documents, 18–19
Ehinger, Jakob, 78
Ehinger, Johannes, 113
Endorfer, Barbara, 3
Endorfer, Stephan, 3
Esaias, Pater, 80
Etzione, Amitai, 56–7
Eyb, Albrecht von, 32–3

Faber, Heinrich, 135, 136
Faing, Gilles da, 22

faith, 127, 128; ambivalence in, 124, 129, 140-1, 147-8; Lutheran theology of, 51-52
family, 14, 17, 42-3, 153; disputes in, 5, 8, 11; historical studies of, 29-31; interest and emotion in, 109-11; solidarity in, 12
fatalism, 140-1
Fleischbein, Johann Philip, 27, 28
Fleischbein, Nikolaus, 27, 28
Florence, 4, 8
Flowery Wedding Celebration, 38-42, 67, 139, 154; *see also* verse, occasional
Foucault, Michel, 29-30
Francesco, Lorentio, 4
Franciscans, 120
Francis I, King, 8
François, Etienne, 113, 123
Frankfurt am Main, 5,7, 28
Frederick Barbarossa, Emperor, 53
Freiburg, Berthold von, 32
friend, 12; Matheus as, 153
friendship, 2, 12, 85-115, 132, 154; calculation in, 87; utility in, 86
Fugger, 25, 119
Fugger, Hans, 24
Fugger, Ursula, 120
Füll, Jakob, 113
funeral, 129; ritual, 133-4; sacred and secular functions of, 133
Fustenegger, 137

Gallacino, Antonio, 4
Garreis, Anna Sabina, 69
Genoa, 28
Georg Regel Foundation, 152
Georg, St, Church of, 120
Gesellschaft der Mehrer, 43, 92
Gesellschaft von der Kaufleutestube, 92
Gevater-Pfennig, 131-2
gift, 84-5, 87, 96-103; as mark of solidarity, 97
gift-giving, 84-5, 87, 96-103
Glaser, Michael, 6
godparentage, 22, 111-14, 131-2; confessional tensions in, 113 definition of, 112; responsibilities of, 112; Matheus Miller's strategy of, 112-14
Goebelin, Johann Marcus, 69
Goldschmit, Priester, 75
Great Ravensburger Company, 161n. 24
Gregory XI, Pope, 144
Grot, Caspar, 78
Gulden, 188n. 4

Habermas, Jürgen, 58-60
Habisreitinger, Hans, 97
Habisreitinger, Hans Jakob, 151
Hamburg, 80
Hans Georg Österreicher Foundation, 116
Hartmann, Adam, 68
Heller, 185n. 4
Henry II, Duke of Rohan, 22-3
Hensius, Johann Ludwig, 39
Herrenstube, 43, 91
Hertner, Vincenz, 28
Herwart, 92
hierarchy, social, 2, 23, 42, 89, 93
Hobbes, Thomas, 105
Hofmaier, 92
Holder, Wilhelm, 144
Holy Cross, Church of, 70-81, 103-4, 117, 120, 142, 146, 152
Holy Cross, Priory of, 71
honor, 38, 107; meaning of, 113; in social relations, 90
Hopfer, Augustin, 131
Hopfer, Bartholomeus, 104, 136
Hopfer, Benedikt, 138
Hopfer, Gabriel, 112, 150
Hopfer, Matheus, the Elder (grandfather), 2, 104; wealth of, 3
Hopfer, Matheus, the Younger, 104-6, 131-2
Hopfer, Sibilla (mother), 2, 104
Hopfer, Thomas, 84, 103-4, 106, 133, 143
Hörmann, J. Conrad, 150
Hoser, Jakob, the Elder, 3
household, 20, 42, 86; as center of sociability, 97
Hübner, Marx, 65

222 Index

inheritance, 108–11, 151
interest, private, 153–4

James, St, Suburb, 88
Johann Georg Österreich Foundation, 69
Joseph I, Emperor, 39
Justi, Johann Heinrich Gottlob von, 156–7
justification, ethical, 111

Kaufbeuren, 122
Kaufleuteschaft, 43, 66, 134
Kaufleutestube, 34
Kaufleutezunft, 92
Keller, Friedrich, 39
Kempten, 10–11, 33–4, 107
kinship, 22
Kipper– und Wipperzeit, 2, 24–7; see also Augsburg, crisis in
Klosterbaur, Adam, 39
Kneilin, Dr, 130–1
Koch, Caspar, 10
Koslofsky, Craig, 133
Kreutzer, 188n. 4
Kriegsdorffer, Tobias, 150

Lady Suburg, 88
Lake Constance, 9
Lang, Zacharias, 152
Langenmantel, 92
Langenmantel, Heinrich, 70
Laub, 78
Laub, Georg, 112
Lauginger, Anton, 8
Lauginger, Otto, 67, 70, 150
law, sumptuary, 89, 94
Lech Quarter (*Lechviertel*), 87
Leipzig, 69, 101
Leutkirch, 9, 37
Leutpriesteraltar, 71
libri della famiglia, 17; see also ego documents, memoir
Libri della Famiglia, I, 12–15, 43, 49–50, 57, 85–7; see also Alberti, Leon Battista
Lidell, Philip, 28

The Life Voyage (*Lebens–Fahrt*), 139–40; see also verse, occasional
Lindau, 9
Lindeberg, Peter, 23
Livorno, 4
love see family, interest and emotion in
Lucca, 4
Luther, Martin, on office, 50–2
Lyon, 28

magistrate, 118
Mair, Christoff Georg, 109
Mair, Christoph Jörg, 72
Mair, Hans Christoph, 72–3, 76–7, 81, 96–7
Mair, Hans Georg, 72–7, 80–1
Mair, Maximilian, 141
Mantua, 7
Margaretha, St, Convent of, 68
market, influence on society, 90
marriage, 4, 10, 14, 17, 19, 22, 43, 153; attitudes toward, 42; calculation in, 42; emotion and interest in, 12, 22, 33, 36–8, 40, 42–5; of Matheus Miller, 9–11, 20–47; negotiations, 10; passion, 32–3; of Philip Jakob Miller (son), 150–2; requirements of, 32, 35; social mobility, 91, 95
Marriage Court, 59, 65, 116
Marx, Karl, 29
mastery, 155–7
Mees, Johann Paul, 69
Mehrer, Anna Barbara, 97
Mehrer, Anna Maria, 67, 97, 99, 150–1
Mehrer, Hieronymus, 150
Mehrer, Marx Christoph, 151
memoir, 1–2, 7, 11, 18–20, 60, 66, 101, 108, 157; confession in, 123–4, 146–7; contents of, 20; death in, 126, 133, 137–8, 140–1; demographic events in, 31–2; office in, 48; past in, 131; propriety in, 153–5; purpose of, 16, 30, 67, 83, 86, 111, 117, 140, 149, 155; remembrance in, 130; sociability in 96–111; structure

Index   223

memoir – *continued*
  of, 12, 17–18; voice in, 127;
  see also ego document
Memmingen, 10, 99, 150
Menius, Justus, 85
merchants, in hierarchical societies, 90
Merck, Johann Conrad, 1
militia, 48, 52, 82, 116; historical development of, 61–2
Miller, 43, 151
Miller, Anna Maria (daughter), 40
Miller, Anton Christoff (son), 40
Miller, Baltas (father-in-law), 36, 37, 43, 150
Miller, Daniel (brother), 26, 98, 99; bankruptcy of, 100–2
Miller, Gabriel (uncle), 2, 5, 81, 93; *see also* business, of Gabriel Miller (uncle)
Miller, Hans Jakob (uncle), 3, 5, 32, 81, 93, 112, 150; *see also* business, of Hans Jakob Miller (uncle)
Miller, Helena (daughter), 97
Miller, Johanna Katharina (wife), 26, 67, 139
Miller, Johanna Katharina (daughter), 26, 112
Miller, Matheus (son), 33, 72–3, 97, 104, 109, 120, 132
Miller, Michael (brother), 26, 37, 98
Miller, Michael (father), 2, 9, 11, 20; death of, 137–9; *see also* business, of Michael Miller (father)
Miller, Michael (son), 127
Miller, Philip Jakob (son), 20, 33, 67, 72–3, 97, 99, 109, 112, 132, 149–52, 155–6; *see also* business, of Philip Jakob Miller (son); marriage, of Philip Jakob Miller (son); office, of Philip Jakob Miller (son)
Miller, Sabina (sister-in-law), 113
Miller, Sibilla (daughter), 40, 66–7, 97, 104
Miller, Susanna (daughter), 128, 134
Miller, Thomas (brother), 26, 28, 98, 99, 150, 151
ministerium, 84, 102–3, 112

mobility, social, 42–3, 89–95, 111, 114–15, 149, 151, 154
morality, public, 83; *see also* virtue, civic
mourning, 40, 42
mutuality, 86

network, social, 2, 19, 86, 95–6
Nicodemism, 147
Nikolai, Friderich, 123
Nipperdey, Thomas, 123
notable, avocational, 56–7
Nuremberg, 5, 7, 8, 10, 27, 97, 112

observance, religious/ *see* worship
office, 12, 17, 19, 48–83, 86, 149; among bourgeoisie, 154; definition of, 55–6; of Philip Jakob Miller (son), 152; sale of, 91
office-holding, 48–83, 103; Lutheran theories of, 51–2; private interest in, 49–50; public service in, 48–50; reluctance toward, 62; *see also* interest, private; service
official, 2, 153
order, social, 89
Österreich, Johann Georg, 69
Österreicher, 25
Österreicher, Daniel, 130
Ottmar, St, Chapel of, 7

parity, 121–3
partisanship, 57
pater familias, 14, 19, 20; *see also* patriarch
paternalism, 6, 12, 47, 104, 154; sociability of, 97–8, 102–3
patriarch, 2, 22, 43, 136; Matheus Miller as, 153–4
patriarchy, 2, 6, 20–47, 111, 166n. 9, 171n. 67; authority in, 46; definition of, 45–6; flexibility of, 22, 45–7; historical studies of, 30–1; limits of, 45; practice of, 20–1, 46–7; theory of, 21
patriciate, 90, 94
patrimony, social, 87
patronage, 6, 57, 68, 95, 102–4, 111

Paul, St, 32, 33, 50, 52
Peace Festival, 74
Peer, Jeremias, 69
Peirler, Regina (sister), 26, 98
Pfründe, 67
pietism, 148
Pimmel, Sibilla, 151
Pisa, 4
Pistoia, 4
pleasure, in friendship, 85–7; see also friendship
prayer, 116–17, 124, 126–7, 155–6
Presser, Jakob, 18
propriety, 1, 40, 42, 48, 60, 83, 115, 117, 136, 153–7; meaning of, 13; in marriage, 38; in office, 80–1; in sociability, 101–2
providence, 17, 116, 128–9, 139–40
public sphere, 2, 48–83; see also office
Purgatory, 125
purification, 125

quietism, 148

Raiser, Anna, 68
Rat, 53; see also Council, Secret
Rauhwolff, Hans Jerg, 33, 72, 109–11, 150
Rauhwolff, Sara, 112, 150
Rauner, Narziß, 39, 40
Ravensburger, 92
reciprocity, 60, 86, 95, 100
Reformation, 63, 65, 118
Rehlinger, 25, 92, 119
Rehm, Hans Conrad, 70
Reischlin, 78
Rem, Lucas, 6, 8, 10, 92
remembrance, 136
rentes, 154
reputation, 5, 9, 152; see also credibility and creditworthiness; propriety
resignation, 139–40, 156
Restitution, Edict of, 71, 120–1
ricordanze, 16, 17; see also account, merchant; ego document, memoir
Riedinger, Martin, 28

Riß, Georg Philip, 39, 75, 76, 78, 80, 103, 142–7
Rodwesen, 81–2
Roeck, Bernd, 123, 147
Roschmann, Susanna, 120
Rotenhofer, Christoff, 27, 28

sacristan (*Meßmer*), 74
Salvador, St, College of, 120
salvation, Lutheran theology of, 125
satisfaction, Lutheran theology of, 125
Schaumeister, 55
Schlumff, 34
Schlumpff, Hans, 8–9
Schmalkalden, Articles of, 144
Schmezer, Georg, 78
Schoap, Zacharias, 7–8, 97
Schorer, 43, 151
Schorer, Anton Christoff, the Elder (father–in–law), 43, 104, 134–6
Schorer, Anton Christoff, the Younger (brother–in–law), 34, 35, 66, 97
Schorer, Christoff Jakob, 106
Schorer, Elisabeth (sister), 26
Schorer, Euphrosina Regina, 106
Schorer, Gabriel, 106
Schorer, Helena (wife), 26, 33, 41–2, 67, 104, 108, 127, 128, 135; death of, 139–42; marriage to Matheus Miller, 34–6
Schorer, Hieronymus, 141
Schorer, Jakob, 106
Schnurbein, Baltas, 5, 112
Schröken, Elias, 32
Secretary, City (*Stadtschreiber*), 54
Sedelmair, Georg, 78
Seelgeräte, 67
Seelhaus, 67
Seitz, Mang, 118
sermon, funeral, 134, 136, 138–9
Seneca, 13
service, 91, 95, 153
Siegler, 54
Siena, 4
sociability, 85–115; acumen, 111; interest and emotion in, 108; solidarity, 111, 114–15

society, civil, in Habermas's theory, 58–60; class, 90; hierarchical, 13 (*see also* hierarchy, social); patriarchal, 8 (*see also* patriarchy)
solidarity, 102–3, 105–7, 117
Sombart, Werner, 12
Sorokin, Pitirim, 90
Spangenberg, Cyriacus, 21, 33, 46
Spillberg, Johann, 76
St Gall, 8–9, 34, 137
Stadtbuch, 53
Stadtpfleger, 5, 48, 63, 65, 81, 119
Stadtrecht, 52
Stain, Melchior, 74
state, in Habermas's theory, 58–60
status, social, 22, 80, 87, 149, 151
Stemmer, Andreas, 102
Stemmer, Daniel, 102
Stemmer, Felicitas, 102
Stemmer, Georg, 102
Stemmer, Georg, the Elder, 100–1
Stemmer, Johann, 102
Stemmer, Maria, 100–2
Stemmer, Sibilla, 102
St Stephen's Cemetery, 126
Stetten, David von, 67, 105, 150
Steuden, 76
Stoic, 13, 85–7
Störr, Wolfgang, 97
stratification, social, 89; *see also* hierarchy, social; society, hierarchical
Sturmglocke, 56
Sulzer, Wolfgang, 70

Tagebuch, vii
Tax Master (*Steuermeister*), 54
Teller, 77
Tomasini, Innocentio, 4
Traur–Gedicht, 138–9; *see also* verse, occasional
trousseau, 34
Tubingen, 69

Ulm, 1, 8, 27
Ulrich, St, Church of, 120, 135
Upper City, 3, 87–8, 92
utility, in friendship, 85–7

Venice, 4, 27
venality, 57, 60
Verona, 4, 8
verse, occasional, 38, 138–40
Vienna, 11, 127
vindication, 1, 83, 154
Vio, Thomas de, Cardinal Cajetan, 145, 146
virtue, 13–14; bourgeois, 156–7; business, 52; civic, 76–7, 81, 83; in friendship, 85–7; office, 48, 52
vocation, 55
Vogel, Gabriel, 150

Wachter, Johann, 99
Wachter, Sabina, 99
Wankmüller, Johann, 70
Warmberger, 43, 151
Warmberger, Anna Maria (wife), 20, 26, 36, 72, 104, 126; death of, 130–4; marriage to Matheus Miller, 32–4
Warmberger, Hans Philip, 107–8
Warmberger, Johann, 32
Warmberger, Susanna, 108–11
wealth, attitude toward, 107; of Mair family, 186n. 120; of Gabriel Miller (uncle), 25; of Hans Jakob Miller (uncle), 25; of Matheus Miller, 28–9, 66, 149, 153; of Michael Miller (father), 2–3, 25; of Philip Jakob Miller (son), 152
Weber, Max, 46, 53, 90–1
Weber, Philip, 112, 149, 150
wedding, 1; of Philip Jakob Miller (son), 151–2
Wedding and Penalty Master (*Hochzeits– und Bußmeister*), 55
Weienmair, 109
Weinberg, Hermann, 31
Weiss, Christoph, 27
Welser, 6, 9, 10, 25, 92, 119
Welser, Hans, 118
Werner, Joseph, 76
Wertemann, 11
Wertenstein und Dallmaßingen, Georg Heinrich von und zu, 70
Westphalia, Treaty of, 71, 120, 121, 144, 147

Wideman, Tobias, 79
Wild, Susanna, 32
Wild, Zacharias, 133
Wilhelm, Matthias, 150
Wolff, Christian, 20
Wolff, Daniel, 4
Wolff, Georg, 4
Wollerein, Nicolas, 70
womanly freedom (*weibliche Freiheit*), 100
works, 82–3; Lutheran theology of, 51–2

worship, 117
Württemberg, 103, 106

youth, 8

Zeeden, Ernst Walter, 122
Zobel, 70
Zurich, 8